AI, Risk, Regulation, and Market Transformation in Intelligent Finance

Afef Rachid Amdouni
https://orcid.org/0000-0001-9625-300X
Taibah University, Saudi Arabia

IGI Global
Scientific Publishing
Publishing Tomorrow's Research Today

Vice President of Editorial Melissa Wagner
Director of Acquisitions Mikaela Felty
Director of Book Development Jocelynn Hessler
Production Manager Mike Brehm
Cover Design Jose Rosado

Published in the United States of America by
IGI Global Scientific Publishing
701 East Chocolate Avenue
Hershey, PA, 17033, USA
Tel: 717-533-8845 | Fax: 717-533-7115
Website: https://www.igi-global.com E-mail: cust@igi-global.com

Library of Congress Cataloging-in-Publication Data

(CIP Data Pending)
ISBN13: 979-8-2600-1603-9
Isbn13Softcover: 979-8-2600-1604-6
EISBN13: 979-8-2600-1605-3
British Cataloguing in Publication Data
A Cataloguing in Publication record for this book is available from the British Library.

Table of Contents

Detailed Table of Contents

Financial fraud poses a significant challenging to global economic stability. With increase in technological innovations and adoption of digital technologies there is a rise of digital transactions and so has been the case with the number of financial fraud schemes. This increase in the number and ways of financial fraud necessitates a need for robust detection and prevention mechanisms. The current book chapter explores the multifaceted approaches to combatting financial fraud. The chapter reviews several case studies and research findings that illustrate the successful application of these technologies. This chapter also address the future trend shaping the fraud detection and prevention techniques. Emerging technique like integration of behavioural biometrics and digital identity verification systems, big data analytics and deep learning-based fraud detection model have been discussed. The chapter concludes by emphasizing the need for ongoing collaboration among financial institutions, regulatory bodies, and technology providers.

The objective of this chapter is to evaluate the effectiveness of the M-score and F-score in detecting financial statement fraud in the Chinese market and to develop machine learning models tailored for detecting such fraudulent activities. The authors employ random sampling by industry to match fraudulent enterprises with non-fraudulent counterparts. Using this matched sample, they first test the effectiveness of the M-score and F-score in detecting financial fraud among Chinese listed companies. They then construct several machine learning models that incorporate the constituent variables of the F-score and M-score, along with an additional loss indicator. The

The integration of Artificial Intelligence (AI) into financial markets has transformed operational efficiency, risk assessment, and consumer engagement, while simultaneously exposing critical regulatory gaps. This paper conducts a comparative legal analysis of AI governance frameworks across the European Union, United States, Asia-Pacific, and India, highlighting divergent risk classifications, data governance models, and ethical oversight mechanisms. Using doctrinal and case study methodologies, the study evaluates India's hybrid regulatory approach spanning sector-specific guidelines, digital public infrastructure, and sandbox initiatives—and proposes a unified legal framework for AI in finance. Drawing lessons from insider trading regulation, the paper advocates for harmonized global standards that balance innovation with investor protection, algorithmic transparency, and market integrity.

Crowdfunding has garnered much attention from academics and practitioners as a practical approach to raising funds for projects or ventures. This research aims to understand the use of Artificial Intelligence (AI) algorithms in determining the use of Shariah-compliant Peer-to-Business (P2B) crowdfunding platforms. This study adopts Technology Acceptance Model and Unified Theory of Use of Technology to establish the conceptual model. Data is collected from 116 micro, small, and medium enterprises (MSMEs). Seven state-of-the-art AI algorithms, including Decision Tree (DT), Extra Tree (ET), K-Nearest Neighbors (KNN), Lo-gistic Regression (LR), Random Forest (RF), Support Vector Machine (SVM), and Extreme Gradient Boosting (XGBoost), are applied to evaluate the essential features of the Actual Use Behavior (AUB). The results indicate that RF, ET, and KNN are the top three methods in all AUBs. The findings suggest that incorporating AI in Shariah-compliant P2B

Preface

INTRODUCTION

The rapid integration of Artificial Intelligence (AI) into financial systems has extended far beyond improvements in predictive performance, fundamentally reshaping how financial markets are governed, regulated, and experienced by participants. While the first volume of this collection focuses on the methodological and application-oriented dimensions of AI in financial markets, the present volume shifts the analytical lens toward its institutional, regulatory, and systemic implications. As AI-driven systems become increasingly embedded within financial infrastructures, their evaluation can no longer be confined to accuracy or computational efficiency. Instead, greater emphasis must be placed on the conditions under which these systems operate, the risks they introduce, and the governance frameworks required to ensure their responsible and sustainable deployment. In this context, AI functions not merely as a technological tool, but as a structural force influencing market integrity, regulatory design, and financial stability. A central theme of this volume is the tension between innovation and control. While AI enhances financial systems through improved fraud detection, risk monitoring, and decision-making efficiency, it simultaneously introduces new forms of systemic vulnerability. These include algorithmic bias, model opacity, data dependency, and regulatory fragmentation—challenges that are particularly acute in environments characterized by institutional heterogeneity and evolving legal frameworks. This volume adopts an explicitly institutional perspective, positioning AI within the broader ecosystem of financial governance. It critically examines how regulatory structures, legal frameworks, and ethical considerations shape the deployment and impact of AI-driven systems. Rather than treating technological advancement as inherently beneficial, the contributions emphasize that the effectiveness of AI is contingent upon alignment with governance mechanisms, regulatory oversight, and socio-economic context. Moreover, the volume highlights the role of AI as a catalyst for structural transformation in financial systems. Beyond efficiency gains, AI influences market behavior, redefines regulatory boundaries, and contributes to financial inclusion. However, this transformative potential remains conditional and must be evaluated within the constraints of institutional capacity, policy coordination, and ethical accountability.

This volume contributes to the growing discussion on the governance, regulatory, and institutional implications of Artificial Intelligence in financial systems, with particular attention to how these dimensions shape the effectiveness and societal impact of AI-driven solutions.

Against this backdrop, the chapters in this volume collectively explore the intersection of AI with financial risk, regulation, governance, and market transformation. By integrating technical, economic, and policy perspectives, the volume provides a comprehensive and context-sensitive understanding of how AI is redefining the foundations of modern financial systems.

CHAPTER OVERVIEW

The structure of this volume reflects a conceptually integrated progression from risk-oriented applications of AI to broader regulatory, institutional, and societal implications.

Chapter 1: Combating Financial Crime Reviewing the role of AI and Machine Learning in Anomaly Detection and Fraud Prevention

This chapter examines the role of AI in detecting and preventing financial fraud within increasingly digitized financial systems. It reviews a range of advanced techniques, including deep learning, behavioral analytics, and anomaly detection frameworks, demonstrating their effectiveness in identifying complex fraud patterns. The chapter also addresses evolving fraud strategies and adversarial risks, emphasizing the need for adaptive and collaborative approaches involving financial institutions, regulators, and technology providers.

Chapter 2: Identifying financial statement frauds via machine learning - a comparative analysis based on Chinese listed companies

This chapter provides a comparative evaluation of traditional fraud detection models and machine learning approaches within the context of financial reporting.

Using empirical evidence from Chinese listed companies, it demonstrates the limitations of conventional scoring models and highlights the superior performance of machine learning techniques. The analysis emphasizes the trade-offs between false positives and false negatives, underscoring the importance of model selection and contextual adaptation.

Chapter 3: How Artificial Intelligence is Reshaping Business Transformation in Islamic Finance?

This chapter explores the transformative role of AI within Islamic finance, emphasizing its alignment with principles of transparency, ethical investment, and risk-sharing. Through case studies and qualitative analysis, it demonstrates how machine learning techniques enhance operational efficiency, fraud detection, and decision-making processes. The chapter also addresses the institutional and regulatory challenges associated with integrating AI into Shariah-compliant financial systems.

Chapter 4: Bias Mitigation and Algorithmic Fairness in AI-Driven Financial Decision Systems

This chapter critically examines the issue of algorithmic bias in financial decision-making systems. It analyzes different sources of bias, including data, model design, and feedback mechanisms, and evaluates a range of fairness metrics and mitigation strategies. Beyond technical considerations, the chapter highlights the ethical and regulatory dimensions of fairness, particularly in contexts characterized by data scarcity and socio-economic diversity.

Chapter 5: Towards a Unified Legal Framework for AI in Finance by Synthesizing Global Best Practices

This chapter addresses the regulatory fragmentation surrounding AI in finance by conducting a comparative analysis of legal frameworks across multiple jurisdictions. It identifies key inconsistencies in risk classification, data governance, and ethical oversight, and proposes a unified framework that balances innovation with investor protection and market integrity. The discussion contributes to ongoing debates on global regulatory harmonization.

Chapter 6: Artificial Intelligence-Enabled Computational Techniques in Determining the Use Behavior of Crowdfunding Platforms

This chapter applies AI techniques to analyze user behavior in crowdfunding platforms. It integrates behavioral models with machine learning algorithms to explain adoption patterns. The findings identify key determinants of user engagement and funding success. The study highlights the role of AI in improving financial inclusion. It also emphasizes the importance of behavioral and institutional factors.

Chapter 7: AI-Driven Volatility Prediction in GCC Financial Markets - A CNN-LSTM-Attention Approach

This chapter develops an advanced deep learning framework for volatility prediction in emerging financial markets. Focusing on the GCC region, it demonstrates the effectiveness of hybrid models in capturing complex temporal dependencies and improving predictive accuracy. The chapter also addresses challenges related to interpretability, data reliability, and practical implementation in emerging market contexts.

Chapter 8: Harnessing AI for Citizen Financial Literacy to Strengthen Oman's Stock Market

This chapter explores the role of AI in enhancing financial literacy and promoting broader market participation. Focusing on the case of Oman, it highlights how AI-driven tools can improve access to financial information and support informed investment decisions. The chapter also identifies structural barriers to financial inclusion and emphasizes the importance of integrating technological innovation with policy initiatives.

CONCLUSION

The contributions presented in this volume collectively demonstrate that the integration of Artificial Intelligence into financial systems is not merely a technological development, but a structural transformation with far-reaching implications for risk management, regulation, and market behavior. While AI offers significant potential in enhancing fraud detection, improving regulatory oversight, and supporting financial inclusion, its effectiveness remains inherently conditional upon institutional, regulatory, and socio-economic contexts.

A central insight emerging from this volume is that the challenges associated with AI in finance extend beyond technical limitations. Issues such as algorithmic bias, regulatory fragmentation, data governance, and institutional capacity are critical determinants of the sustainability and legitimacy of AI-driven financial systems. Addressing these challenges requires a shift from purely technical solutions toward integrated frameworks that combine technological innovation with governance, policy, and ethical considerations.

Moreover, the findings highlight the need for a more coordinated and interdisciplinary approach to AI deployment in finance. The increasing complexity of financial systems necessitates collaboration across academia, industry, and regulatory bodies to develop robust and adaptable frameworks capable of managing emerging risks while fostering innovation.

At the same time, the volume underscores the transformative potential of AI in reshaping financial systems, particularly in emerging markets. By enhancing transparency, improving access to information, and supporting financial literacy, AI can contribute to more inclusive and resilient financial ecosystems. However, realizing this potential requires addressing structural constraints related to data availability, institutional readiness, and regulatory alignment.

Ultimately, this volume demonstrates that the future of AI in finance will be defined not only by advances in technology, but by the ability to embed these technologies within coherent institutional, regulatory, and ethical frameworks that ensure their responsible and sustainable use.

Afef Rachid Amdouni
Taibah University, Saudi Arabia

Chapter 1
Combating Financial Crime:
Reviewing the Role of AI and Machine Learning in Anomaly Detection and Fraud Prevention

Sandhya Rai
http://orcid.org/0000-0001-6070-0277
Bennett University, India

Krishnendu Ghosh
http://orcid.org/0000-0002-7888-2950
Bennett University, India

Anand Kumar Rai
GL Bajaj Institute of Management and Research, India

ABSTRACT

Financial fraud poses a significant challenging to global economic stability. With increase in technological innovations and adoption of digital technologies there is a rise of digital transactions and so has been the case with the number of financial fraud schemes. This increase in the number and ways of financial fraud necessitates a need for robust detection and prevention mechanisms. The current book chapter explores the multifaceted approaches to combatting financial fraud. The chapter reviews several case studies and research findings that illustrate the successful application of these technologies. This chapter also address the future trend shaping the fraud detection and prevention techniques. Emerging technique like integration of behavioural biometrics and digital identity verification systems, big data analytics

DOI: 10.4018/979-8-2600-1603-9.ch001

and deep learning-based fraud detection model have been discussed. The chapter concludes by emphasizing the need for ongoing collaboration among financial institutions, regulatory bodies, and technology providers.

INTRODUCTION

Financial fraud and anomalies have become an increasingly concerning factor and a real challenge in the 21st century for individuals, corporations, and governments. Financial fraud involves misleading practices carried out with the intent of fortifying unlawful financial gain. It involves a extensive range of activities such as money laundering, credit card fraud, identity theft, insider trading, cyber-enabled scams, embezzlement, and fraudulent financial reporting. While fraud has existed for centuries, its nature, methods, scale, and global reach have expanded significantly in recent decades due to rapid technological advancement and the increasing digitization of financial systems.

Financial fraud and its growth are closely tied to the evolution of global finance, the Internet of Things, and digital connectivity. With the rising adoption of digital transactions, online banking, mobile payments, cryptocurrencies, and e-commerce platforms, opportunities for fraudulent activities have increased manyfold. According to the Association of Certified Fraud Examiners (ACFE, 2020), organizations across the globe have lost an estimated 5% of annual revenue to fraud, representing almost trillions of dollars in losses. The Federal Trade Commission (FTC, 2024) in the United States reported that in the year 2025, consumers lost almost $12.5 billion to financial fraud, which is a 38% increase from the previous year, mostly because of online scams and investment fraud. Similarly, the European Central Bank noted a steady rise in card-not-present fraud, particularly in e-commerce transactions. Multiple, factors including globalization. cross-border financial flow and digitization have contributed to this growth. Where globalization has opened the country boundary for all to operate across jurisdiction and made it easier for the fraudsters, technological innovation and advancement have created both prospects and vulnerabilities. With the growing and easy access of technologies like AI and deepfake; these are being misused to impersonate individuals and operate misleadingly on financial data. Fraudster are using these technologies to target inexperienced digital users.

Financial fraud is not only a crime but also a significant threat to the stability, credibility, and sustainability of the overall financial ecosystem. The ability to detect and prevent fraudulent activities at an early stage is therefore important for individuals, organizations, and regulators alike. Early detection can minimize the direct financial losses caused by fraudulent transactions and reduce the indirect costs associated with reputational damage, regulatory penalties, and improve the level of customers' trust. Financial fraud and anomalies, including money laundering and other illegitimate events, pose significant risks not only to individual institutions but also to economies and societies at large. This chapter is an attempt to unfold the role of AI and ML in combating financial irregularities, with a particular emphasis on fraud and anomaly detection and prevention. It reviews the evolution of fraud detection methods, highlights the strengths and challenges of AI-driven models, and examines real-world applications across banking, insurance, e-commerce, and capital markets

1. UNDERSTANDING ANOMALY DETECTION AND FRAUD PREVENTION

1.1 Definitions and Types of Anomalies

An anomaly can be defined as something that diverges from what is normal, expected, usual or standard. It is often defined as an unusual or irregular occurrence of data points that deviate from the expected patterns, events, or observations that do not fit with the general behaviour of data or a system. The literature suggests that there are mainly three types of anomality these includes point anomalies, contextual anomalies, and collective anomalies. Point anomalies, also known as individual data instances, are data points that deviate significantly from the rest of the dataset. These are singular observations that stand out due to their unique characteristics or values. These are the data points which do not align with a general data trend or pattern. An example of this could be an unusually large withdrawal from a bank account, which contrasts with the usual amount. Second type of anomalies, called contextual anomalies, are the anomalies that occur when a data instance is anomalous in a particular context but might be normal in another. For example, an unusually high stock trading volume during a calm market period would been indication of an anomalous behaviour, even though the same volume during a market crash may be normal. It is difficult to identify contextual anomalies as it requires an understanding of the context to accurately identify anomalies. Collective anomalies occur when a collection of related data points collectively acts anomalously, however, none of the individual data points might be considered anomalous on their own. A small but frequent fund transfer may be normal in a general context, by it could also indicate money laundering.

Table 1. Type of Anomalies

Type	Meaning	Financial Example
Point Anomalies	A single unusual event	Very large withdrawal from the account
Contextual Anomalies	Normal in one situation but Abnormal in another	High trading volume during market crash
Collective Anomalies	A group of activities that looks odd together	Many small funds transfer signalling fraud or money laundering

There is another approach to classify anomalies includes its categorization as accounting anomalies and behavioural anomalies. The accounting anomalies include inconsistencies or deviations in accounting records or practices, such as unexpected changes in financial statements or accruals. Whereas the behavioural anomalies arise due to the irrational behaviours of investors, such as herd behaviour, over-confidence, or anchoring. These behaviours can lead to market inefficiencies and mispricing of securities (Cervellati et al., 2024; Padmavathy, 2024). Identification of such irregularities is important as they can indicate errors, fraud, or other illegal activities such as identity theft, network intrusion, account takeover, and money laundering, risk, or any other significant issues that require further investigation. Addressing these anomalies is also essential for maintaining accurate financial reporting and compliance (Richardson et al., 2010). These events, if they go un-noticed, may result in undesired outcomes such as disruption in service and other breakdowns; thus, detecting anomalies and novel events is vital to the financial services industry. Anomaly detection, also known as outlier or novelty detection, refers to the process of identifying items, events, or observations that significantly differ from the expected norm within a dataset (Pang et al., 2021). Foorthuis had defined five dimensions, namely, data type, cardinality of relationship, anomaly level, data structure, and data distribution to help categorize anomalies into several broad groups and subtypes (Foorthuis, 2021).

In the financial sector, anomalies are often synonymous with fraud and indicate irregularities that deviate from expected financial behaviour; they vary from unusual transaction patterns to inconsistencies in financial statements. With the expansion and rapid adoption of modern technologies like the internet, social media, and hardware devices like smartphones and laptops, there has been an increase in the number of fraudulent activities (Kou, Lu, Sirwongwattana, & Huang, 2004). This has led to billions of dollars in business losses, and thus there is a need to identify fraud as soon as it happens, and undetected cases results in increasing cost over time (Association of Certified Fraud Examiners, 2020). Though there is no universally adopted definition of financial fraud, the most used definition is the one from the Association of Certified Fraud Examiners; it defines financial fraud as " any intentional or deliberate act to deprive another of property or money by guile, deception, or other unfair means" (ACFE 2004). By this definition, activities like credit card fraud, identity theft, securities fraud, mortgage fraud, money laundering, insurance fraud, and internet and cyber fraud are commonly included in financial fraud activities.

Credit Card Fraud: With the growing adoption of credit cards as a means of transaction, there is a growing trend in credit card fraud, which is expected to reach $43 billion by 2026 (Matt Rej, 2024). It is one of the most prevalent types of financial fraud, directly affecting both individuals and financial institutions, and is a significant concern for financial institutions worldwide due to its potential to cause substantial economic losses. This kind of fraud occurs when an individual unlawfully exploits another person's card information to carry out unauthorized purchases or obtain cash advances. Criminals often use stolen card details to make internet purchases or clone cards for physical transactions. Based on the mode of transaction and card uses, credit card fraud can be classified as application fraud and behavioural fraud, commonly known as offline and online fraud, respectively (Kou, Lu, Sirwongwattana, & Huang, 2004; Bolton & Hand, 2001). The other types of credit card fraud involves card theft, cloning, and identity theft. Application fraud occurs when someone else's personal information is provided to obtain a new card, while identity theft involves using another person's identity to access their credit card (Sailusha et al., 2020). Behavioural fraud consists of four types of actions, including card theft, use of stolen or lost cards, counterfeit cards or cloning, 'cardholder not present' fraud, and bankruptcy fraud. These fraudulent activities are enabled through techniques like phishing, data breaches, and skimming devices that capture credit card information (Sahin and Duman, 2011; Thennakoon et al., 2019).

Identity theft: The unlawful use of someone else's personal information without their consent., like bank account details, passwords, transaction PINs, and one-time passwords to commit fraud are part of the identity theft. For carrying out these kind of frauds unauthorized data are obtained through various means, including phishing emails, data breaches, skimming devices, or even dumpster diving. This information is used to open new lines of credit, make unauthorized purchases, or even commit crimes under the victim's name, causing significant hardship for the victim (Drew, 2020). At times, personal information of the individual is used to open new accounts, take out loans, or make unauthorized transactions. This causes significant personal and financial harm to victims (Choi and Lee, 2018). The individual feels at a loss not only in terms of financial but also emotional. Many times, they are dragged into legal entanglements, their credit score are affected, and they fail to get a loan (Ali et al., 2022).

Securities fraud: It involves misleading investors through false information in financial markets that leads to making buying or selling decision, usually leading to heavy financial losses. It also involves activities like insider trading, false financial reporting, and Ponzi schemes that mislead investors in stock and securities markets. In case of security fraud, usually false disclosures and manipulation of financial statements are common tactics used to attract investors and later trick them into the business (Reurink, 2018). There are also instances where individuals inflate property values or provide false information on loan documents for illicit gains; such cases fall under the mortgage fraud (Reurink, 2018). This type of fraud was notably rampant during the financial crisis of 2007-2009, where mortgage-backed securities and predatory lending practices led to widespread financial instability (Fligstein and Roehrkasse, 2016).

Corporate fraud and cyber fraud: Corporate fraud and cyber fraud are the other types commonly occurring financial fraud. Where corporate fraud includes misleading shareholders about company performance or embezzling company funds, cyber fraud includes phishing attacks, hacking, and online scams that exploit users through the internet (Podkolzina et al., 2021). Corporate fraud involves illegal or unethical conduct by companies or individuals within companies, intended for financial gain or to give a discriminatory advantage. Frauds like accounting fraud, insider trading, and misrepresentation of a company's financial status are included in corporate frauds. These frauds can severely damage trust and lead to investor losses and legal penalties (Gottschalk, 2010).

Money laundering: It is another type of financial fraud committed to convert illegal gains or illegally obtained money into seemingly lawful income. It is usually done through a complex arrangement of banking transfers or commercial transactions; majorly to support other criminal activities like terrorism (Han et al., 2020). The fraudster uses multifaceted sequence of banking transfer or commercial transactions; the aim is to hide the origins of illegally obtained money. This kind of process is usually followed by the criminal and the organization who wants to convert their illegal earnings legitimately. At times criminals may use methods like shell companies, trade manipulation, cash smuggling, or even cryptocurrencies to disguise unlawful earning. Anti-money laundering (AML) regulations and technologies are critical (Gottschalk, 2010) in identifying and preventing this type of fraud.

Insurance Fraud: When a person or organization deliberately deceives an insurance company to obtain money, benefits, or coverage they are not entitled to, such a kind of fraud is called insurance fraud. Aros et al., 2024 in their study have opined that insurance fraud occurs when incorrect claims are submitted in order to secure benefits or compensation that one is not legally entitled to Aros et al. (2024). This type of fraud is prevalent across various types of insurance, including health and automobile insurance, resulting in significant financial losses for both insurance companies and honest policyholders. There are various incidents where individuals or entities have been found faking accidents, injuries, thefts, or claims to receive unwarranted insurance pay-outs. It is not that only individual person are involved in such kind of fraud, at times groups or organizations may also be involved into it. Fictitious claims of damage, accidents, or theft are some common examples. Ali et al in their research claim that insurance fraud is the main reason for charging a higher premium and in this the honest policyholders suffer and also a significant loss is suffered by the insurance companies (Ali et al., 2022).

Investment fraud: Another type of financial fraud prevalent and observed is Investment fraud. This type of fraud is characterized by misleading practices that persuade investors to make decisions based on false or misleading information. Fraudulent schemes often result in notable financial losses, shaking investor trust, confidence, and disrupting the financial market's stability. The common ways in which investment fraud can appear in includes pyramid schemes, Ponzi schemes, and high-yield investment frauds. These schemes often promise remarkably high returns with minimal risk, attracting unsuspecting investors interested in quick profits. As per the study of Gottschalk (2010), Investment fraud encompasses illegal or unethical practices involving the solicitation of funds or the promotion of financial products that guarantee unusually high returns with minimal or no risk. Such schemes often exploit investor trust, particularly preying on individuals with limited financial literacy or investment expertise. A study examining investment fraud highlights that due to their larger socioeconomic status, victims are often embattled, making them attractive targets for fraudsters seeking significant financial gains (Deliema et al., 2019). The intricacy of financial transactions and products, impaired by technological innovations, has created new avenues for fraudulent activities where fraudulent practices can embellishment unnoticed until significant damage is done (Reurink, 2018).

1.2 Past Studies in the Financial Fraud Detection

A study of the Scopus database focusing on the domain of financial fraud, fraud detection, and related technological approaches led to the extraction of 144 articles and research papers spanning from 2004 to 2025, covering journal articles, conference papers, and other document types. During the literature review, it has been observed that over the last 2–3 years, research in Anomaly Detection and Fraud Prevention has gained momentum. Figure 1 illustrates a significant increase in the number of research works in this area, as per the Scopus database. The growing concerns for innovative financial fraud and anomalies need more and more attention. With the advent of advanced technology, AI and ML are continuously showing new avenues to timely predict and cope with financial fraud and anomalies.

Figure 1. Documents published by Year

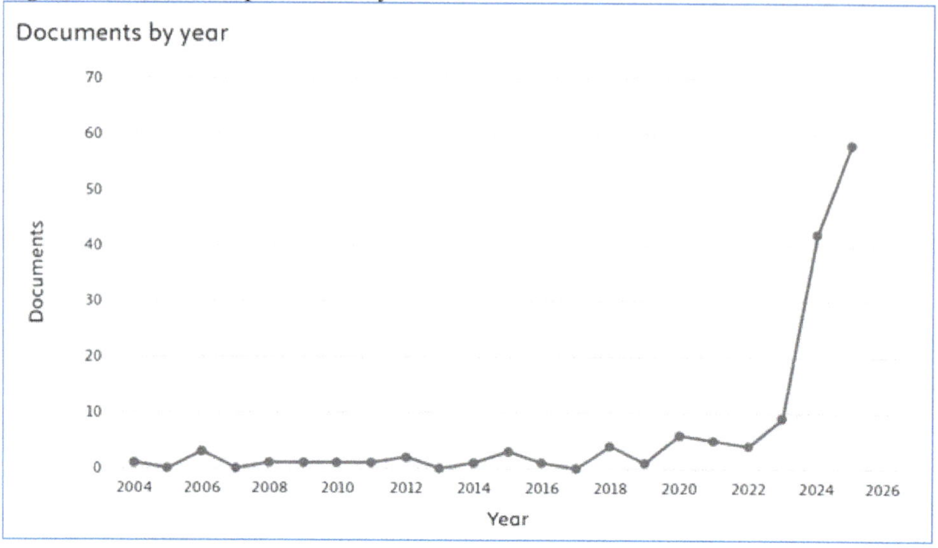

(Source: www.scopus.com)

While conducting the literature review, "anomaly AND detection AND fraud AND prevention" was used as a keyword, and 144 articles were shortlisted for further study. Out of these 144 articles, 143 articles are already published, and 1 article is under processing. The articles consist of Conference Paper (83), Article (38), Book Chapter (14), Conference Review (6), Book (2), and Review (1). The keywords which appeared more than 10 times are as follows: Anomaly Detection (80), Fraud Detection (62), Crime (57), Machine Learning (44), Fraud Prevention (39), Machine-learning (34), Learning Systems (23), Deep Learning (21), Network Security (16), Adversarial Machine Learning (13), Cyber Security (13), Finance (13), Learning Algorithms (13), Artificial Intelligence (12), Financial Fraud (12), Real-Time (12), Blockchain (11), Financial Security (11), Fraud (11), Unsupervised Learning (11), Data Analytics (10). The top author keywords include anomaly detection (116), fraud detection (89), crime (57), machine learning (53), and fraud prevention (48). Research reveals that anomaly detection, fraud detection, crime, and machine learning dominate the research landscape. The author keywords also emphasize technological approaches such as machine learning (34), deep learning (31), learning systems (23), financial security (18), and data analytics (17). This demonstrates a multi-disciplinary approach integrating finance, computer science, and security studies (Fig. 2).

Figure 2. Top Author Keywords (Top 15)

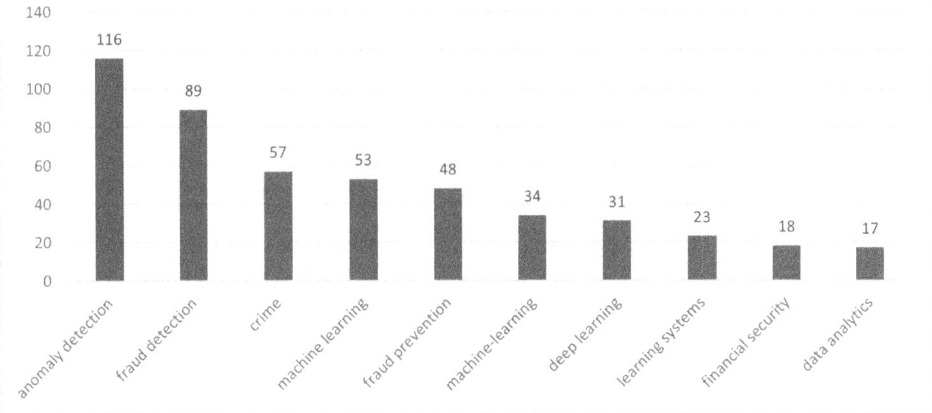

It is quite evident from the keywords of the existing studies that there is a significant role of AI, Deep Learning, and ML-based models in identifying fraudulent activities and preventing the same. India (62) researchers are leading, followed by the United States (23) and China (16) in research in this area.

A network visualization and bibliometric representation (Fig. 3) of the keywords used by these 144 studies. The bibliometric network visualization analysis of all keywords has been conducted with the help of the Bibliometrix software. In the diagram, the larger nodes like fraud detection, anomaly detection, machine learning, and cybersecurity indicate that these are the most frequently studied themes about financial fraud. The diagram also indicates the presence of one cluster around machine learning and anomaly detection, another involving blockchain and financial security, and a further cluster focusing on cybersecurity and risk assessment. This visualization suggests that the field is highly interdisciplinary, where technological innovations such as deep learning, adversarial learning, and blockchain are increasingly integrated into financial fraud prevention strategies. Overall, the network diagram itself is an indicative representation of the role of AI, ML, DL, and Blockchain in fraud and anomaly detection and the interconnected nature of research in financial fraud detection.

Figure 3. Network visualization of all keywords

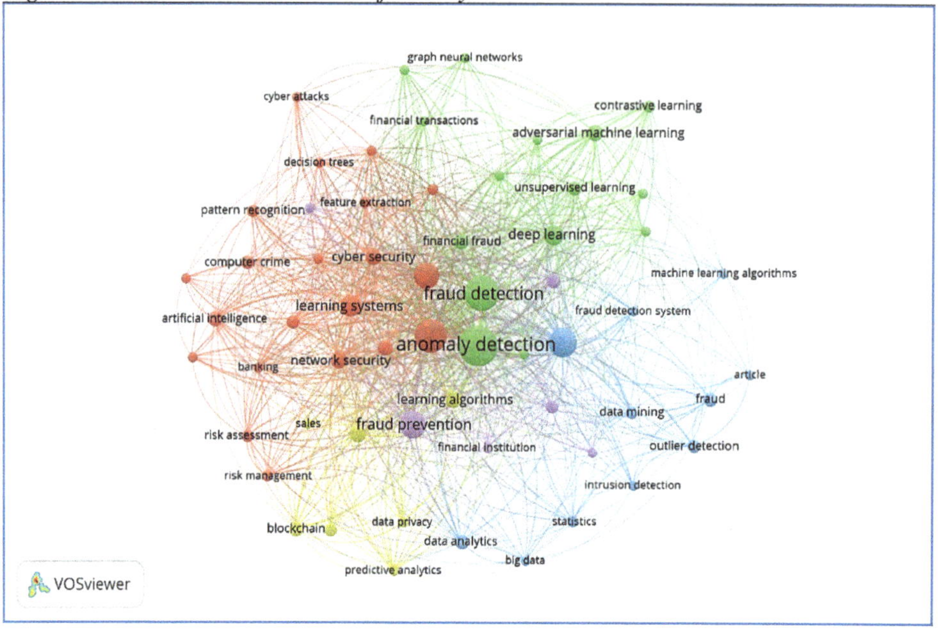

These research trends indicate a growing interest in the area and a need to develop solutions to handle the problems related to financial fraud detection. To understand how different methods can help in solving the problem, it is important to get a comprehensive understanding of the growth of various fraud detection methods.

2. EVOLUTION OF FRAUD DETECTION METHODS

The detection of financial fraud has undergone a significant transformation over the years, shifting from manual rule-based methods to sophisticated, AI-driven solutions. In the early stages, fraud detection relied heavily on human judgment, accounting reviews, and rule-based systems that flagged irregularities based on predefined criteria. Though these methods were effective to some extent, they have their own limitations w.r.t the ability to handle the huge volume of financial transactions and the complexity of such transactions. The implementation of technologies and the rise of e-commerce, digital banking, and electronic payment systems have made the task more problematic. These technologies also provided more opportunities to the fraudster, and a need was felt to look for stronger, more adaptive detection tools. This led to the introduction of data-driven methods such as anomaly detection, statistical modelling, and machine learning algorithms, which enabled automated identification of unusual patterns in massive datasets. The broad timeline of fraud detection methods are as follows(Table 2)

Table 2. Timeline of fraud detection methods

Year	Trend of Fraud Detection Models
1980 - 1990	Rule-based & Expert Systems
1990- 2000	Early AI & Neural Networks
2000-2010	ML Algorithms (Decision Trees, Regression, Clustering)
2010s-2015	Anomaly Detection & Real-time Monitoring
2015-2020	Unsupervised Learning & Blockchain Integration
2021-present	Deep Learning, Hybrid AI, Adversarial ML, Blockchain Forensics

With the advancement of technology and the advent of artificial intelligence, deep learning, and blockchain technologies, the real-time analysis of financial data became possible, and as a result, these methods became useful applications in financial fraud detection and prevention.

2.1 Traditional Fraud detection methods

Traditional financial fraud detection methods have formed the backbone of efforts to safeguard financial systems from deceptive practices. These methods have been used for decades, primarily before the rise of machine learning and advanced analytics and offer foundational insights into how fraud has been tackled historically. The primary traditional methods used in financial fraud detection include rule-based systems, statistical methods, manual reviews, transaction monitoring systems, identity verification, and authentication.

Rule-Based Systems: These are one of the oldest approaches to detecting fraud. These methods traditionally rely on predefined rules established through expert knowledge, focusing on transactions that deviate from normal patterns. Rule-based systems employ a set of "if-then" statements to identify anomalies or fraud based on transaction attributes. They categorize transactions as suspicious if they breach set limits or conditions. This kind of method is highly effective in environments where fraudulent behaviour fits easily identifiable patterns. As these methods are straightforward in their application, even a non-technical person can easily understand and use them. These methods are good for targeted monitoring for known fraud strategies. This transparency facilitates quick decision-making (Islam et al., 2024). Rule-based systems are generally fast, allowing them to work in real-time transaction environments where latency must be minimized (Miao, 2024). However, these systems face difficulty in scaling and adapting quickly to new fraud tactics because they depend on pre-defined, static rules. As sophisticated fraud techniques evolve, such static systems often prove inadequate and rules may become outdated, leading to inefficiencies and increased false negatives (Obeng et al., 2024). These methods also face challenges when the data is highly dynamic and has high dimensionality—a common feature of modern financial transactions. Also, rule-based systems might struggle to handle vast amounts of data effectively and are prone to generating false positives and negatives (Mohammad et al., 2024). They are also less effective when dealing with nuanced patterns that can't easily be defined (Miao, 2024).

Statistical and Analytical Methods: This method uses statistical techniques to identify anomalies in data. These include techniques like regression analysis and time-series analysis, and frequency analysis, which help identify anomalies in transaction patterns. These methods focus on transactions or behaviours that deviate significantly from the norm. for example, frequency analysis helps in observing unusual patterns in the number of transactions or events; scoring models assign risk scores based on the statistical probability of fraud, to name a few. The major advantage of this method is its ability to handle larger datasets than the manual method, and it is effective in identifying unusual patterns that may indicate fraudulent activity. These methods benefit from their mathematical robustness and have been used extensively to guide decisions in fraud detection. Yet, when it comes to dealing with large-scale, high-dimensional datasets typical in modern financial transactions, the methods are slow or less effective and hence need the help of technology. The evolving nature of fraud tactics also challenges the adaptability of these static methods (Sanad and Al-Sartawi, 2021).

Manual Reviews and Expert Analysis: Manual auditing and review involve human experts examining flagged transactions or accounts for suspicious activity. Before the digitization of financial records, manual reviews were essential for fraud detection. In this method, experts would meticulously examine transaction records to identify discrepancies or unusual activity. Even today, manual reviews and expert analysis remain crucial in verifying potential fraud flagged by automated systems. While manual scrutiny provides depth and context that automated systems cannot. The automated system is labour-intensive and time-consuming, a significant bottleneck in fraud detection processes (Miao, 2024). Many traditional systems combine these approaches to improve efficacy, using rules to flag transactions, statistical models to score them, and human analysts to review high-risk cases.

Transaction Monitoring Systems: Transaction monitoring involves detecting suspicious transactions through the real-time scrutiny of transactions. Traditional transaction monitoring systems typically use account history and transaction types to identify potential risks, offering alerts for high-risk transactions. With the increasing volume of transactions due to digital banking, these systems face challenges in scalability and accuracy, often dazed by the complexities and large volumes of data (Kurshan and Shen, 2020).

Identity Verification and Authentication: In financial services, identity verification and authentication are critical components of fraud prevention. Traditional methods include verifying personal information such as addresses, Social Security numbers, or other documents to validate an individual's identity. Another common method used is simple password-based authentication. Despite being foundational, these methods can fall short in the face of identity theft and advanced spoofing techniques, necessitating stronger, multi-factor authentication systems (Tang and Liu, 2024).

While traditional methods like rule-based systems, statistical analysis, and manual reviews provide a foundational framework for financial fraud detection, they face significant challenges in scalability, adaptability, and accuracy against sophisticated fraud strategies. However, these methods continue to serve as essential components within the broader strategy of preventing financial fraud, complementing advanced technological solutions (Noviandy et al., 2023).

2.2 New- Age Financial fraud detection Methods

With the rapid digitization of financial services, traditional fraud detection methods have become insufficient to handle new sophisticated and evolving fraud tactics. Modern or new-age financial fraud detection methods leverage advanced technologies such as artificial intelligence (AI), machine learning (ML), big data analytics, and real-time monitoring to detect and prevent fraudulent activities. The major new age technologies that help in detection and prevention of financial fraud includes Machine Learning-Based Detection, Artificial Intelligence and Deep Learning, Real-Time Monitoring and Predictive Analytics, Big Data Analytics, Biometrics and Behavioral Analytics.

Machine Learning-Based Detection: It is a modern method for financial fraud detection and prevention. It leverages the past data to make prediction about the future scenario. When used for detecting financial anomalies, the machine learning algorithms learn the patterns from historical transaction data and with their robust analytical capabilities, offer pattern recognition and features identification for detecting anomalies in financial data. The machine learning algorithm are majorly of two types, supervised machine learning models and unsupervised machine learning models. In supervised learning, the models are trained on the labelled data where transactions are pre-marked as fraudulent or legitimate and based on this the future transactions are predicted for their authenticity. Methods like Logistic regression, Random Forest, and XGBoost are example of supervised learning and are used for classifying new transactions. On the other hand, Unsupervised learning does not rely on labelled data, instead, it seeks to identify patterns and structures from the input data on its own. It focuses on detecting unusual patterns in unlabelled data i.e with the data where there is no pre-defined output or categories available. The goal of this kind of method is to identify hidden pattern, structures, groups, relations or cluster in the database. A few examples of unsupervised learning method in financial fraud detection includes K-means clustering and Isolation Forest, Principal Component Analysis (PCA) which are used to discover data structures and relationships (Solomatine et al., 2009) and are useful for identifying previously unknown fraud types. There is a third method which is a mix of supervised and unsupervised learning methods and is called semi-supervised learning methods. This method combines a small set of labelled data with a larger pool of unlabelled data to improve detection accuracy. This method leverage the strength of both the methods to improve the accuracy and efficiency of machine learning model. This method is very helpful while dealing with new and emerging fraud patterns, and reduces false positives, and efficiently handling large volumes of transaction data. Because of their ability to process large amounts of volatile data uncover subtle patterns indicative of fraudulent activity, these machine learning models have emerged as powerful tools for financial fraud detection. These models outperform traditional methods, particularly in real-time processing and w,r,t the accuracy of prediction. Algorithms such as Random Forest, Support Vector Machine (SVM), and Convolutional Neural Networks (CNNs) excel in identifying anomalies and classifying them as potential frauds. In their research Morán Dávila et al. (2023) found that Random Forests method indicates promising result with F1 scores exceeding 95%, indicating low variability in performance across different datasets (Morán Dávila et al., 2023). Thammareddi et al found that in modern banking, machine learning models provide enhanced capabilities for real-time transaction monitoring and pattern recognition which is crucial for detecting fraudulent activities even as they attempt to bypass traditional security measures (Thammareddi Et Al, L. (2023)). Supervised learning models is powerful tool when the goal is to predict outcomes based on past data with known results whereas unsupervised learning techniques are gaining traction for their ability to detect anomalies without the need for labelled training data. Unsupervised learning is gaining applications in the areas where the objective is to uncover hidden patterns that can provide insights without explicit labels or categories ((Kernel Methods in Computational Biology,, 2004); Solomatine et al., 2009). Unsupervised learning methods have found their applications in areas like Bitcoin fraud detection, where the dynamic nature of cryptographic transactions necessitates robust detection mechanisms capable of identifying fraudulent activity without relying on predefined labels (Monamo et al., 2016).

Artificial Intelligence and Deep Learning: AI and deep learning technologies are transforming the way the financial frauds is being detected and prevented. Deep learning based models leverages multi-layered neural networks to uncover complex, non-linear patterns in transactions, customer behaviour, and digital interactions. As a technology inspired by the human brain, these models learn to perform tasks by identifying patterns in vast amounts of data without explicit programming. Unlike traditional models, deep learning models can process high-dimensional data and automatically extract relevant features, reducing the need for manual feature engineering. As a result, they are improving the efficiency and rate of fraud detection by automating decision-making, learning from vast volumes of structured and unstructured financial data, and adapting to new fraud strategies (Mienye and Jere, 2024; Sizan et al., 2025). This approach offers high accuracy in detecting complex and subtle fraud patterns that traditional methods might miss. Also the ability of AI model to learn from new data enhances the financial institutions' ability to detect fraud in real-time (Vashishth et al., 2025). AI also helps in enhancing authentication methods. For example, biometric technologies powered by AI, such as facial recognition, fingerprint scanning, and voice recognition, offer a more secure and less vulnerable alternative to traditional passwords or PINs. These systems are harder to bypass and help ensure that only authorized users can access sensitive information Furthermore, AI can analyse the credibility of incoming communications. In email security systems, natural language processing (NLP), a branch of AI, can scan messages to detect phishing attempts by identifying deceptive language patterns or suspicious URLs, thereby preventing users from accidentally sharing personal information. AI-based cybersecurity tools also help in identifying malware and spyware threats before they cause harm. By continuously scanning files, apps, and system behaviour, AI systems can block malicious code or isolate compromised devices, thereby reducing the risk of unauthorized data collection. In deep learning neural network-based detection utilizes artificial neural networks to model complex patterns and interactions within transaction data, enabling the identification of sophisticated fraud schemes. Convolutional Neural Networks (CNNs) can be applied to structured data to detect intricate patterns, while Recurrent Neural Networks (RNNs) and Long Short-Term Memory (LSTM) networks are particularly effective for sequential data, such as tracking the progression of transaction histories over time. Though these models are very effective in tracking fraud, challenges like algorithmic bias, data privacy, and system vulnerabilities needs to be addressed to harness the full potential of AI and deep learning methods (Adhikari, 2024). Another challenge that these models' faces is scalability, especially for smaller institutions that may struggle with the resource demands of implementing advanced AI solutions (Adhikari, 2024). The way to address these challenges includes maintaining data quality, developing explainable AI models, and adhering to ethical AI use.

Real-Time Monitoring and Predictive Analytics: Real-time transaction monitoring employs AI algorithms to continuously track financial transactions and immediately flag any suspicious activity, enabling immediate correction activities. These technologies leverage machine learning and big data analytics to process vast quantities of transactional data, identify anomalies, and predict potentially fraudulent activities. Bello et al and Vashishth et al in their studies have found that techniques such as neural networks and anomaly detection are particularly effective, enabling the rapid detection of irregularities that indicate potential fraud (Bello et al., 2024; Vashishth et al., 2025). These models have also been found to significantly reduces the time it takes to detect fraud and, consequently, limits potential financial losses. By using machine learning algorithms, financial institutions can analyze transaction data in real-time, identifying patterns that deviate from normal activity. Techniques such as neural networks and anomaly detection are particularly effective, enabling the rapid detection of irregularities that indicate potential fraud (Bello et al., 2024; Vashishth et al., 2025). This capability significantly reduces the time it takes to detect fraud and, consequently, limits potential financial losses. Predictive analytics utilizes historical data and machine learning algorithms to predict future fraudulent activities, thereby enhancing fraud detection and risk management strategies. As financial transactions become increasingly digital, the ability to monitor and predict potential threats in real time is essential for maintaining financial security (Palakurti, 2023). The integration of real-time monitoring with predictive analytics allows financial institutions to act proactively against fraud, not only responding to incidents as they arise but also preventing them from occurring in the first place. This dual approach enhances the effectiveness of fraud detection systems and ensures higher levels of security and trust across financial services (Mohammad et al., 2024).

Big Data Analytics: Big Data Analytics plays a crucial role in modern financial fraud detection by enabling the processing and analysis of massive volumes of structured and unstructured financial data to identify suspicious patterns and anomalies. By leveraging technologies such as distributed computing, data mining, and predictive analytics, organizations can analyze transaction histories, customer behavior, social networks, and external datasets simultaneously. By processing large volumes of transactional data, financial institutions can identify anomalies that could indicate fraudulent behavior. The synergy between big data analytics and AI enhances the precision and scalability of fraud detection systems, ensuring they remain effective as transaction volumes increase and fraud tactics evolve (Palakurti, 2023).

Biometrics and Behavioral Analytics: Biometrics authentication involves identifying individuals based on their unique physiological and behavioral characteristics, such as fingerprints, facial recognition, and voice patterns. As these characteristics are inherently difficult to replicate they offer robust security solutions to verify identities and are increasingly adopted across various sectors, including financial services, to provide a high level of security and convenience compared to traditional systems like passwords or ID cards (Kataria et al., 2013). Behavioral analytics further complement these techniques by analysing patterns in user behaviour, such as typing speed, mouse movements, and transaction habits, to detect deviations that may signify fraud. The research by Palakurti indicate that behavioural insights, when integrated into machine learning models, significantly enhance predictive accuracy by capturing the subtle and complex nature of transaction fraud (Palakurti, 2023). This dual approach enhances security by making it significantly harder for fraudulent actors to impersonate legitimate users (Obeng et al., 2024). The integration of biometrics and behavioral analytics can leads to the creation of a multi-layered security approach, that offers a more comprehensive solution to financial fraud. By combining static biometric verification with dynamic behavioral analysis, financial institutions can detect anomalies in both identity verification and transaction behavior, reducing false positives and enhancing security (Stylios et al., 2016).

These new-age financial fraud detection methods harness the capabilities of machine learning, artificial intelligence, and big data and predictive analytics to offer unparalleled accuracy and adaptability. As these technologies continue to evolve, they promise to offer even more sophisticated defence against fraud, ensuring the integrity and trustworthiness of financial ecosystems (Zhang et al., 2009). They also allow financial institutions to maintain robust security measures and stay ahead of sophisticated fraudulent tactics. However, these techniques are not free from limitations; challenges such as data privacy, ethical considerations, and system vulnerabilities keep haunting them over time. And it is for this reason, it becomes more important that financial institutions, technology providers, and regulatory bodies join hands together and work for continuously improving the system (Odeyemi et al., 2024). The table below (Table 3) summarizes the difference between the traditional financial fraud detection method and modern methods.

Table 3. Summary of Traditional Financial fraud detection methods and New-Age Financial fraud detection methods

Aspect	Traditional Methods	Modern Methods
Approach	Rule-based, statistical, and manual review	AI/ML-driven, big data analytics, behavioural & biometric analysis
Techniques	Threshold rules, regression, manual audits, transaction monitoring, blacklists	Machine learning (supervised, unsupervised, semi-supervised), neural networks (CNN, RNN, LSTM), anomaly detection, real-time monitoring, big data analytics, behavioral biometrics, NLP
Data Used	Historical transaction data, predefined rules, known fraud lists	Large-scale structured and unstructured data, social networks, device data, sequential and behavioral data
Adaptability	Low – cannot detect new or evolving fraud patterns	High – learns and adapts to evolving fraud patterns

continued on following page

Table 3. Continued

Aspect	Traditional Methods	Modern Methods
Accuracy	Moderate – high false positives due to rigid rules	High – reduces false positives and improves detection of complex fraud
Speed	Often reactive, slow due to manual verification	Real-time or near real-time detection
Scalability	Limited – struggles with large volumes of transactions	Highly scalable – handles millions of transactions per second
Complexity	Simple to implement, transparent	Complex models, may be "black-box" and require advanced expertise
Resource Requirements	Low – mostly human resources and basic systems	High – requires computational power, AI models, and skilled personnel
Examples	Flagging transactions above threshold, KYC verification, manual audits, blacklist checking	Credit card anomaly detection using ML, real-time transaction monitoring, network analysis for fraud rings, behavioral biometrics, NLP for unstructured data
Strengths	Easy to implement, interpretable, effective for known fraud	Adaptive, proactive, highly accurate, detects sophisticated fraud patterns
Limitations	Reactive, cannot detect unknown fraud, high false positives	Requires high-quality data, privacy considerations, computationally intensive

3. FINANCIAL FRAUD DETECTION TODAY: EVIDENCE FROM RESEARCH AND PRACTICE

With the advancement of technology, the fraudulent schemes has also become more sophisticated making the detection and prevention more difficult. Traditional approaches based on manual oversight and static rules are often insufficient against modern, adaptive fraud techniques. The growing threat of fraud and anomalies in the digital age requires a proactive, multi-layered approach to prevention and detection. Organizations and individuals must prioritize robust security measures, continuous monitoring, and ongoing education to safeguard against these evolving threats. The advancement of technology facilitates the easy accessibility of information, even by unauthorized agents. The risks of fraud are evident across various sectors of the economy, including the Government Sector, Manufacturing Sector, Banking and Financial Services Sector, Healthcare Sector, Insurance Sector, Real Estate Sector, Retail and E-Commerce Sector, among others. All sectors are concerned about the increasing innovative trend of fraud.

In a recent article, Deloitte's Centre for Financial Services predicts that Gen AI could empower the nature and scope of fraud losses a compound annual growth rate of

32%, to reach US$40 billion in the United States by 2027, from US$12.3 billion in 2023, as mentioned in Fig. 4. (Lalchand, Srinivas, Maggiore, & Henderson, 2024).

Figure 4. Financial Losses due to Gen AI

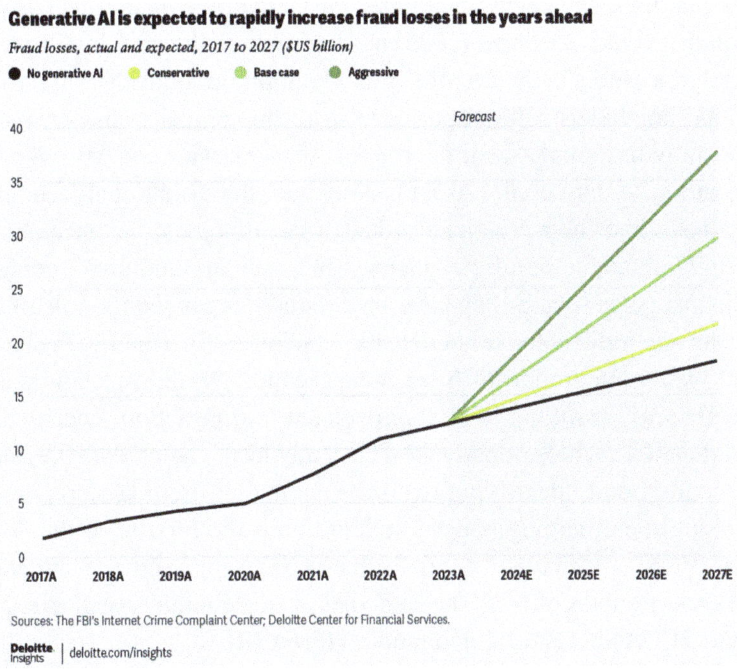

(Source: https://www.deloitte.com/us/en/insights/industry/financial-services/deepfake-banking-fraud-risk-on-the-rise.html)

Artificial Intelligence (AI) and Machine Learning (ML) have become crucial in anomaly detection and fraud prevention, particularly in the financial sector. These technologies offer advanced proficiencies to analyze huge datasets, identify patterns, and detect anomalies, revealing fraudulent activities. Traditional methods often fall short against sophisticated fraud schemes, demanding the integration of AI and ML to augment detection accuracy and efficiency. The application of these technologies spans various domains, including transaction monitoring, identity verification, and risk assessment, thereby safeguarding financial systems and ensuring economic stability.

Traditional methods have struggled to keep pace with the evolving strategies of fraudsters, demanding the adoption of AI-driven solutions. The integration of Artificial Intelligence (AI) in financial fraud detection embodies a substantial shift towards more efficient and accurate systems that address the complexities of modern financial fraud. This data-driven revolution in fraud detection not only augments security but also reduces false positives, thereby saving resources for financial institutions (Ismaeil, 2024). Rawal, R., Sachdeva, P., & Singhvi, A. S. (2025) have emphasized the inadequacy of the traditional methods of fraud detection and also talked about the role of advanced technology, especially the advanced algorithms of machine learning, which have facilitated the Generative AI to detect as well as to prevent banking fraud. Alsubaei (2025) has highlighted the growing importance of cybersecurity measures in the age of IoT and voluminous confidential information. Gupta (2023) emphasizes the importance of technological transformation in his study. The study has emphasized the role of AI techniques and ML algorithms in fraud prevention. Aslam et al. (2022) have opined that traditional fraud detection techniques have lost their practicality due to technological advancements. They have also highlighted the significant increase in financial fraud. In the context of the automobile insurance sector, they have successfully examined the role of different machine learning models for fraud detection. Whig & Sharma (2025) have stated the impact of the integration of blockchain technology and machine learning in the financial sector, resulting in an improvement in transaction security and combating fraudulent activities effectively. This study has examined a 99.9% accuracy rate of detecting fraud, identifying real-time anomalies, issuing alerts proactively, and addressing the emerging pattern of fraud with the mixing of the features of blockchain, such as immutability, real-time monitoring, and transparency, with predictive competencies of ML. The study has used techniques such as exploratory data analysis (EDA), XGBoost, and random forest (RF).

4. CASE STUDIES AND INDUSTRY APPLICATIONS

- Banking and financial services:

In India, the Department of Financial Services (DFS) has taken proactive initiatives to detect and prevent the mounting threat of digital financial fraud. The DFS has directed all the banks to espouse the advanced technology, such as AI & ML, to ensure a trustworthy financial system and to protect the common citizen from real-time mule account detection. A subsidiary of the RBI, named the Reserve Bank Innovation Hub (RBIH), has introduced MuleHunter.AI, an AI & ML model to enhance digital security by detecting deceitful activities and tracking suspicious accounts. (ANI, 2024).

To prevent credit card-related fraudulent activities, Mastercard has adopted generative AI-based predictive technology. This has helped Mastercard identify compromised cards at 300% faster speeds. With the help of a security solution named Cyber Secure, since 2020, Mastercard has successfully been able to alert the banks regarding any attempt to use the compromised cards. Even to provide a safe payment network, Mastercard has implemented a real-time anti-fraud decision solution named Decision Intelligence (DI) Pro, by using heat-sensing fraud patterns that can detect risky transactions within 50 milliseconds.

To improve efficiency and innovate within the financial industry, JPMorgan Chase, a US-based leading global financial services firm for transaction monitoring and document analysis, employs AI-powered systems, such as interbank payments on the Interbank Information Network (IIN) known as JPMorgan's COiN platform. An alternative to stablecoins for native cash settlement and payments operates on a permissioned blockchain platform, Quorum. Kinexys, proof-of-concept (PoC) on public blockchain, has issued a USD J.P. Morgan Deposit Token (JPMD). The organization has developed another in-house solution, named OmniAI, driven by AI/ML, to protect the confidential information.

A big name in Fintech, PayPal, has started reinventing itself in the field of digital commerce. AI-driven PayPal Commerce Platform ecosystem, powered by MCP (Model Context Protocol) frameworks, consists of API, Low code, Agentic, No code and Web hooks. PayPal has increased its real-time fraud detection by 10% with the help of AI.

To streamline its operations and customers' experience, global financial services provider American Express (Amex) has adopted Gen AI to achieve a competitive edge in this data-driven economy. With the help of big data, ML models, and predictive analysis, the company is identifying the fraud patterns and anomalies by analyzing large data. By applying NVIDIA's AI solutions, the company has successfully improved its accuracy in credit risk analysis, detecting fraud, and preventing the same. This real-time fraud detection, addressing emerging threats, has helped the company minimize financial losses and gain more and more customer trust. With the help of ML algorithms, Amex not only detects the suspicious transactions, also blocks the same immediately once detected. This strengthens the security, satisfaction, and loyalty of the customers.

- Insurance and healthcare

Insurance companies across the entire globe are facing increasing threats from various parties, including applicants, policyholders, agents, and organized criminal rings. The fraudulent activities which are common in the insurance sector are filing fake accidents or exaggerated claims, manipulating documents, fake death claims, the same claim to multiple insurance companies, selling counterfeit insurance policies, Misleading policy terms, delay in claim settlements, etc. To combat these increasing potential threats, the insurance companies have started taking advantage of advanced technology. Globally, the insurance companies are using ML, AI, Natural Language

Processing (NLP), predictive analytics, behavioural analytics, computer vision, etc., to analyze vast datasets and identify suspicious claim patterns in real-time.

With the help of sophisticated technology, an in-house solution, an in-house fraud-detection system, developed by Zurich Customer Active Management, or 'ZCAM,' helps the Zurich Insurance Group to solution to combat fraud across different insurance lines and manage rising costs. The Real-Time AI provides facilities such as suspicious anomalies, inconsistency in documents, behavioural patterns that lead to potential fraud, detection, and reduced fraudulent pay-outs. NLP helps to detect the fraudulent pattern of communication. Zurich's AI Image and Video Analysis. Faster processing of legitimate claims leads to higher customer satisfaction.

One of the world's largest insurance and financial services providers, Allianz Group, by leveraging AI-driven automation, machine learning, and predictive analytics, advances risk assessment, optimizes operational efficiency, and improves customer experience, by using AI Chatbots and Virtual Assistants and streamlining claims processing, detecting fraud with more accuracy, cutting settlement times drastically, and personalizing its insurance offerings.

Integration of AI has changed the entire landscape of the healthcare industry. In India, the National Health Authority (NHA) has engaged technology partners to develop and deploy anti-fraud measures using AI/ML and their techniques, such as Random Forest, Artificial Neural Networks (ANNs), Logistic Regression, Support Vector Machines (SVMs), etc, to detect and prevent healthcare insurance fraud.

5. CHALLENGES AND LIMITATIONS

On one side, the technological advancements have continuously helped the banking, insurance, and financial sectors in real-time fraud, anomaly detection, and prevention; on the other hand, the fraudsters are also adopting innovative, sophisticated avenues to conduct financial anomalies and fraud. The risk of cybersecurity has become a real concern for all stakeholders dealing with financial data and transactions. Due to malware and breaches of security, we have observed many times that data secrecy is at stake. The traditional methods are no longer effective in combating financial fraud and anomalies. A proactive strategy to early identification of suspicious activities needs highly effective tools. The challenges and limitations of the detection of fraud or anomalies with AI and ML are,

a) False positive and false negative: Due to a deficiency or mismatch of data, the system fails to identify data patterns, which can lead to failure of fraudulent transaction identification.

b) Quality of data: The Effectiveness of the fraud detection system depends on the high quality of data. Incomplete, erroneous, or obsolete data cannot produce a desired outcome.
c) Sophisticated fraud techniques: The technological advancements are continuously bringing in innovative patterns of fraud or anomalies. The fraudsters are also changing the modalities of the fraud and anomalies regularly.
d) Cost: Implementing advanced technology for the detection of fraud and anomalies and prevention is a very costly affair. Many companies may not be able to afford the same.
e) Scalability: Dealing with the sheer volume of financial information requires strong computational power and effective algorithms. The traditional systems are not enough. Sophisticated advanced technology and algorithms are the only way to deal with the same.
f) Technological advancements: Though the technological advancements have provided a lot of advanced techniques for real-time detection of fraud and anomalies, and prevention. At the same time, fraudsters are also reinventing the nature and mode of fraudulent activities. The continuous upgradation of the algorithm
g) Human expertise: The role of fraud analysts has become very crucial as they are the main architects behind the continuous upgradation of the complex and advanced algorithms. Handling artificial intelligence, machine learning algorithms, big data analytics, Blockchain tools, Natural language processing tools, and predictive modeling techniques requires huge expertise and skills.
h) Regulatory Compliance: to prevent fraudulent activities and to protect the customers, as well as the service providers, authorities, and regulatory bodies, several complex regulations. Cybersecurity has become a priority for many countries. Violation of regulatory measures can lead to severe consequences. RegTech or Regulatory Technology, has become crucial for the financial industry. RegTech is gaining paramount importance along with Fintech across the entire Globe.

CONCLUSION

Financial fraud detection has emerged as one of the most persistent challenges in today's increasingly digital financial ecosystem. The rapid growth of fraud, both in volume and sophistication highlights the vulnerabilities faced by businesses, financial institutions, governments, and individuals. Over time, fraud has taken many forms, ranging from identity theft, credit card fraud, insider trading, and money laundering to more modern cyber-enabled schemes such as phishing, account takeovers, and synthetic identity fraud. This evolution demonstrates that fraud is not static but continuously adapts to technological and regulatory changes. Traditionally, fraud detection relied on rule-based systems, statistical models, and manual reviews however these rule-based detection systems struggle to handle the **scale, speed, and complexity** of modern fraud. The emergence of new-age methods has transformed the field. Artificial Intelligence (AI), Machine Learning (ML), Deep Learning, Big Data Analytics, Behavioral Biometrics, and Real-Time Monitoring have enabled organizations to shift from reactive to proactive fraud detection. These approaches can process vast datasets, uncover hidden anomalies, and adapt to new fraud patterns in real time, offering a more dynamic, intelligent, and efficient solution. As fraudsters adopt more sophisticated techniques, organizations leveraging AI-driven detection systems will be better positioned to anticipate, detect, and mitigate fraudulent activities effectively.

In conclusion, the fight against financial fraud has evolved from basic, rule-based detection toward advanced AI-driven frameworks that ensure greater accuracy, adaptability, and resilience. As fraudsters continue to innovate, the effectiveness of fraud detection will depend on the ability of institutions to integrate advanced technologies with robust governance and risk management practices. Ultimately, the adoption of new-age methods not only strengthens fraud prevention but also safeguards customer trust, financial stability, and the credibility of institutions in the digital age.

REFERENCES

ACFE. 2004, Association of Certified Fraud Examiners. (2004). What Is Fraud? Retrieved Dec. 2, 2020, from https://www.acfe.com/fraud-101.aspx

ACFE. 2020. Association of Certified Fraud Examiners. (2020). Report to the Nations. Retrieved Dec. 5,2020, from https://acfepublic.s3-us-west-2.amazonaws.com/2020-Report-to-the

Adhikari, P.Jnr. (2024). Artificial Intelligence in fraud detection: Revolutionizing financial security. *International Journal of Science and Research Archive*, *13*(1), 1457–1472. DOI: 10.30574/ijsra.2024.13.1.1860

Ali, A., Elshafie, H., Eisa, T. A. E., Al-Dhaqm, A., Othman, S. H., Elhassan, T., Nasser, M., Saif, A., & Abd Razak, S. (2022). Financial Fraud Detection Based on Machine Learning: A Systematic Literature Review. *Applied Sciences (Basel, Switzerland)*, *12*(19), 9637. DOI: 10.3390/app12199637

Alsubaei, F. S. (2025). Smart deep learning model for enhanced IoT intrusion detection. *Scientific Reports*, *15*(1), 20577. DOI: 10.1038/s41598-025-06363-5 PMID: 40596059

ANI. (2024, Dec 8). Banks to use AI & machine learning to safeguard customers from financial frauds. The Economic Times. https://economictimes.indiatimes.com/tech/artificial-intelligence/banks-to-use-ai-machine-learning-to-safeguard-customers-from-financial-frauds/articleshow/116093347.cms?from=mdr

Aros Hernandez, L., Bustamante Molano, L. X., & Gutierrez-Portela, F.. (2024). Financial fraud detection through the application of machine learning techniques: A literature review. *Humanities & Social Sciences Communications*, *11*(1), 1130. DOI: 10.1057/s41599-024-03606-0

Aslam, F., Hunjra, A. I., Ftiti, Z., Louhichi, W., & Shams, T. (2022). Insurance fraud detection: Evidence from artificial intelligence and machine learning. *Research in International Business and Finance*, *62*, 101744. DOI: 10.1016/j.ribaf.2022.101744

Bello, H., Iyelolu, T., & Idemudia, C. (2024). Implementing machine learning algorithms to detect and prevent financial fraud in real-time. Computer Science &amp. *IT Research Journal*, *5*(7), 1539–1564. DOI: 10.51594/csitrj.v5i7.1274

Bolton, R. J., & Hand, D. J. (2001). Unsupervised profiling methods for fraud detection. Credit Scoring and Credit Control Conference VII. Edinburgh, UK.

Cervellati, E. M., Stella, G. P., & Angelini, N. (2024). *Behavioral finance and wealth management: Market anomalies, investors' behavior and the role offinancial advisors*. Virtus Interpress. DOI: 10.22495/bfwm

Choi, D., & Lee, K. (2018). An artificial intelligence approach to financial fraud detection under IoT environ-ment: A survey and implementation. *Security and Communication Networks*, *2018*(1), 5483472. Advance online publication. DOI: 10.1155/2018/5483472

Deliema, M., Shadel, D., & Pak, K. (2019). Profiling Victims of Investment Fraud: Mindsets and Risky Behaviors. *The Journal of Consumer Research*, *46*(5), 904–914. DOI: 10.1093/jcr/ucz020

Drew, J. M. (2020, April 22). A study of cybercrime victimisation and prevention: Exploring the use of online crime prevention behaviours and strategies. *Journal of Criminological Research, Policy and Practice*, *6*(1), 17–33. DOI: 10.1108/JCRPP-12-2019-0070

Fligstein, N., & Roehrkasse, A. F. (2016). The Causes of Fraud in the Financial Crisis of 2007 to 2009. *American Sociological Review*, *81*(4), 617–643. DOI: 10.1177/0003122416645594

Foorthuis, R. (2021). On the nature and types of anomalies: A review of deviations in data. *International Journal of Data Science and Analytics*, *12*(4), 297–331. DOI: 10.1007/s41060-021-00265-1 PMID: 34368422

FTC. 2024, Federal trade commission, retrieved on 15th september 2025 from https://www.ftc.gov/news-events/news/press-releases/2025/03/new-ftc-data-show-big-jump-reported-losses-fraud-125-billion-2024

Gottschalk, P. (2010). Categories of financial crime. *Journal of Financial Crime*, *17*(4), 441–458. DOI: 10.1108/13590791011082797

Gupta, P. (2023). Leveraging machine learning and artificial intelligence for fraud prevention. *SSRG International Journal of Computer Science and Engineering*, *10*(5), 47–52. DOI: 10.14445/23488387/IJCSE-V10I5P107

Han, J., Huang, Y., Liu, S., & Towey, K. (2020). Artificial intelligence for anti-money laundering: A review and extension. *Digital Finance*, *2*(3-4), 211–239. DOI: 10.1007/s42521-020-00023-1

Islam, S., Rezaul Karim, A. N. M., & Haque, M. M. (2024). A rule-based machine learning model for financial fraud detection. [IJECE]. *International Journal of Electrical and Computer Engineering*, *14*(1), 759. DOI: 10.11591/ijece.v14i1.pp759-771

Ismaeil, M. K. A. (2024). Harnessing AI for next-generation financial fraud detection: A data-driven revolution. *Journal of Ecohumanism, 3*(7), 811–821. DOI: 10.62754/joc.v3i7.4248

Kataria, A. N., Zaveri, T. H., Adhyaru, D. M., & Sharma, A. K. (2013). A survey of automated biometric authentication techniques. 1–6. DOI: 10.1109/NUiCONE.2013.6780190

Kernel Methods in Computational Biology. (2004). Massachusetts Institute Of Technology. DOI: 10.7551/mitpress/4057.001.0001

Kou, Y., Lu, C.-T., Sirwongwattana, S., & Huang, Y.-P. (2004). Survey of Fraud Detection

Kurshan, E., & Shen, H. (2020). Graph Computing for Financial Crime and Fraud Detection: Trends, Challenges and Outlook. *International Journal of Semantic Computing, 14*(04), 565–589. DOI: 10.1142/S1793351X20300022

Lalchand, S., Srinivas, V., Maggiore, B., & Henderson, J. (2024, May 29). Generative AI is expected to magnify the risk of deepfakes and other fraud in banking. Financial Services. https://www.deloitte.com/us/en/insights/industry/financial-services/deepfake-banking-fraud-risk-on-the-rise.html

Miao, Z. (2024). Financial Fraud Detection and Prevention. *Journal of Organizational and End User Computing, 36*(1), 1–27. DOI: 10.4018/JOEUC.354411

Mienye, I. D., & Jere, N. (2024). Deep Learning for Credit Card Fraud Detection: A Review of Algorithms, Challenges, and Solutions. *IEEE Access : Practical Innovations, Open Solutions, 12*, 96893–96910. DOI: 10.1109/ACCESS.2024.3426955

Mohammad, N., Khatoon, R., Sharmin, S., Imran, M. A. U., & Prabha, M. (2024). Combating banking fraud with it: integrating machine learning and data analytics. *The American Journal of Management and Economics Innovations, 6*(7), 39–56. DOI: 10.37547/tajmei/Volume06Issue07-04

Monamo, P., Marivate, V., & Twala, B. (2016). Unsupervised learning for robust Bitcoin fraud detection. 129–134. DOI: 10.1109/ISSA.2016.7802939

Morán Dávila, R. C., Castillo Sáenz, R. A., Vargas Murillo, A. R., García Huamantumba, E., Velarde Dávila, L., Pasquel Cajas, R. F., García Huamantumba, C. F., & Guanilo Paredes, C. E. (2023). Application of Machine Learning Models in Fraud Detection in Financial Transactions. *Data and Metadata, 2*, 109. DOI: 10.56294/dm2023109

Noviandy, T. R., Idroes, G. M., Maulana, A., Hardi, I., Ringga, E. S., & Idroes, R. (2023). Credit Card Fraud Detection for Contemporary Financial Management Using XGBoost-Driven Machine Learning and Data Augmentation Techniques. *Indatu Journal of Management and Accounting*, *1*(1), 29–35. DOI: 10.60084/ijma.v1i1.78

Obeng, S., Iyelolu, T., Akinsulire, A., & Idemudia, C. (2024). Utilizing machine learning algorithms to prevent financial fraud and ensure transaction security. *World Journal of Advanced Research and Reviews*, *23*(1), 1972–1980. DOI: 10.30574/wjarr.2024.23.1.2185

Odeyemi, O., Soyombo, O., Nwankwo, E., & Mhlongo, N. (2024). Reviewing the role of AI in fraud detection and prevention in financial services. *International Journal of Science and Research Archive*, *11*(1), 2101–2110. DOI: 10.30574/ijsra.2024.11.1.0279

Padmavathy, M. (2024). Behavioral Finance and Stock Market Anomalies: Exploring Psychological Factors Influencing Investment Decisions. Shanlax International Journal of Management, 11(iS1-Jan), 191–197. DOI: 10.34293/management.v11iiS1-Jan.7164

Palakurti, N.Naga Ramesh Palakurti. (2023). Emerging Trends in Financial Fraud Detection: Machine Learning and Big Data Analytics in Risk Management. International Journal of Advanced Research in Science. *Tongxin Jishu*, , 625–635. DOI: 10.48175/IJARSCT-13555D

Pang, G., Shen, C., Cao, L., & Hengel, A. V. D. (2021). Deep Learning for Anomaly Detection. *ACM Computing Surveys*, *54*(2), 1–38. DOI: 10.1145/3439950

Podkolzina, Irina & Belousov, Anatoliy & Uzdenova, Fatima & Romanko, Lyudmila & Chernikova, Olga. (2021). Forms of Financial Fraud and Ways to Minimize Risks. . DOI: 10.1007/978-3-030-69415-9_241

Rawal, R., Sachdeva, P., & Singhvi, A. S. (2025). The Significance of Generative AI in Enhancing Fraud Detection and Prevention Within the Banking Industry. Generative Artificial Intelligence in Finance: Large Language Models, Interfaces, and Industry Use Cases to Transform Accounting and Finance Processes, 159-173. DOI: 10.1002/9781394271078.ch9

Rej, M. (2024). Credit Card Fraud Statistics 2025, Retrieved Sept. 09, 2025 from https://merchantcostconsulting.com/lower-credit-card-processing-fees/credit-card-fraud-statistics/

Reurink, A. (2018). Financial fraud: a literature review. *Journal of Economic Surveys*, *32*(5), 1292–1325. DOI: 10.1111/joes.12294

Richardson, S. A., Wysocki, P. D., & Tuna, A. I. (2010). Accounting Anomalies and Fundamental Analysis: A Review of Recent Research Advances. SSRN Electronic Journal. DOI: 10.2139/ssrn.1762124

Sahin, Y., & Duman, E. (2011). Detecting credit card fraud by ANN and logistic regression. 315–319. DOI: 10.1109/INISTA.2011.5946108

Sailusha, R., Ramesh, R., Rao, G. R., & Gnaneswar, V. (2020). Credit Card Fraud Detection Using. *Machine Learning*, , 1264–1270. DOI: 10.1109/ICICCS48265.2020.9121114

Sanad, Z., & Al-Sartawi, A. (2021). *Financial Statements Fraud and Data Mining: A Review*. Springer., DOI: 10.1007/978-3-030-77246-8_38

Sizan, M. M. H., Akter, J., Islam, D. A., Ridoy, M. H., Sartaz, M. S., Roy, A., Tannier, N. R., Jobaer, M. A. A., & Chouksey, A. (2025). Advanced Machine Learning Approaches for Credit Card Fraud Detection in the USA: A Comprehensive Analysis. *Journal of Ecohumanism*, *4*(2). Advance online publication. DOI: 10.62754/joe.v4i2.6377

Chapter 2
Identifying Financial Statement Frauds via Machine Learning:
A Comparative Analysis Based on Chinese Listed Companies

Yue Chen
http://orcid.org/0009-0001-1171-7520
Business School, Durham University, UK

Guanming He
http://orcid.org/0000-0002-4879-6795
Business School, Durham University, UK

ABSTRACT

The objective of this chapter is to evaluate the effectiveness of the M-score and F-score in detecting financial statement fraud in the Chinese market and to develop machine learning models tailored for detecting such fraudulent activities. The authors employ random sampling by industry to match fraudulent enterprises with non-fraudulent counterparts. Using this matched sample, they first test the effectiveness of the M-score and F-score in detecting financial fraud among Chinese listed companies. They then construct several machine learning models that incorporate the constituent variables of the F-score and M-score, along with an additional loss indicator. The performance of these models in detecting financial fraud is comparatively assessed. The findings reveal that the M-score and F-score are largely ineffective in accurately identifying fraudulent firms in the Chinese market. In contrast, the machine learning models demonstrate satisfactory performance, with each model offering distinct advantages in reducing both false negatives and false positives.

DOI: 10.4018/979-8-2600-1603-9.ch002

INTRODUCTION

Financial statements disclosed by companies provide a direct reflection of their business and financial status. External users and markets assess a company's operational status through its financial statements, and use the disclosed financial data to analyze its business strategies and activities. As a result, the quality of financial statements plays a crucial role in ensuring the transparency of capital markets and the efficient allocation of capital resources. When companies prioritize presenting a positive financial image, they may face increased pressure into engaging in financial manipulation, elevating the risk of fraud. By manipulating financial data, such as concealing or inflating business activities and outcomes, the financial statements can diverge substantially from the company's actual business reality. Such financial reporting fraud undermines market transparency and erodes trust among investors in the stock market.

Detecting financial fraud is critical for two key reasons. First, financial fraud severely misleads investors, leading to inefficient resource allocation and obstructing capital from reaching companies with genuine growth potential. Fraudulent practices distort the true financial condition of enterprises, resulting in investment decisions based on false information (He, 2015). A notable example is the Kangmei Pharmaceutical fraud case, which shocked the market by fabricating bank deposits and sales income, causing significant harm to both investors and the public. Second, opaque or manipulated financial data erode the foundation of trust in business partnerships and misguide stakeholders, resulting in sub-optimal business decisions.

In this study, the authors posit that establishing robust financial monitoring mechanisms by integrating machine learning models for fraud detection may potentially enhance the identification and prevention of financial fraud, thereby protecting the interests of all business stakeholders. Existing models for identifying financial fraud, such as F-score and M-score, are popular due to their simplicity, enabling researchers and business stakeholders to easily derive these scores from publicly available financial statement data. However, these models largely rely on parameters that were estimated based on historical financial data from many years ago, making them less adaptable to current market dynamics, management strategies, and economic conditions. The F-score was developed in 2011 using data from 1982 to 2005, while the M-score was created in 1999 with data from 1982 to 1992. As such, these models fail to capture the complexities of fast-changing and unpredictable markets nowadays. Over years, shifts in economic conditions, evolving business practices, and the growing sophistication of financial fraud would likely render the models, based on outdated data, less reliable. Consequently, these models' persuasiveness and explanatory power are significantly diminished, limiting their ability to respond to the current market environment and emerging risks.

Moreover, both the F-score and M-score were originally developed based on U.S. market data, which presents a challenge when applying them to other markets. Substantial differences in cultural norms, institutional frameworks, economic conditions, and legal systems exist across countries and regions. For example, the legal systems, accounting standards, and business environments in China differ markedly from those in the United States, especially regarding legal threats and the costs associated with financial fraud. As a result, models built on U.S. data may be ineffective in other markets due to these disparities.

Based on the above discussion, the conventional models might lack the precision needed to accurately detect financial statement fraud within specific market conditions and time periods. Therefore, the authors propose the development of new models tailored to predict financial statement frauds within the context of the Chinese market. This chapter is structured into two main parts: The first part assesses the efficacy of F-score and M-score metrics by analyzing data drawn from the Chinese market across the years 2010-2019, a period characterized by comparatively stable economic circumstances. The second part focuses on constructing machine learning-based models to predict financial fraud during the same sample period. Four machine learning techniques — Random Forest, Gradient Boosting Decision Tree (GBDT), K-Nearest Neighbors (KNN) and Support Vector Machine (SVM) — are used to build fraud detection models based on data from Chinese listed companies. The results suggest that compared to the M-score and F-score models, machine learning models offer greater adaptability and predictive power by learning from large volumes of historical data, and significantly enhance the accuracy of financial fraud detection. The machine learning modeling provides external data users — including investors, auditors, and regulators — with advanced tools for fraud detection. It also contributes to the effective supervision of fraudulent enterprises, helping ensure the accuracy and transparency of their financial statements, and thereby promoting healthy development of the capital market. The implications of this study are extendable to other emerging markets worldwide, offering valuable insights and strategies to help these markets improve the quality of corporate reporting and reduce the occurrence of financial fraud.

This chapter makes several contributions to the existing literature. First, it evaluates the performance of both traditional financial fraud detection models (i.e., M-score and F-score models) and machine learning models within the Chinese market, offering a comparative analysis not yet done in the prior literature. This provides valuable insights into the applicability of different fraud detection models in this specific market. Second, by showing the limitations of M-score and F-score models in detecting corporate financial fraud in China, this chapter not only echoes the inferences of previous studies regarding these models (e.g., Lu and Zhao, 2020) but also underscores the importance of developing more effective models suited to local markets. Third, it applies and compares four distinct machine learning models, advancing understanding of the pros and cons of each approach. Notably, this study employs a balanced dataset approach, contrasting with the often-used imbalanced datasets in prior research. This approach offers a more accurate and fair assessment of model performance, particularly in evaluating false positive and false negative rates.

1. LITERATURE REVIEW

With the rapid development of global economy and the continuous expansion of financial markets, financial statement fraud has emerged as a pressing worldwide issue. This fraud not only jeopardizes the interests of investors but also undermines market integrity, fairness, and transparency (He et al., 2022). High-profile corporate scandals, such as Enron and WorldCom, have underscored the significance of this problem, sparking widespread attention and debate (Healy & Palepu, 2003; Rezaee, 2005). These events have prompted regulators and scholars to seek more effective methods for detecting fraud so as to ensure the credibility and transparency of financial reporting.

Traditional financial fraud detection models focus on analyzing financial statement data to assess the likelihood of corporate financial fraud. For example, Beneish's M-score (1999) and Dechow et al.'s F-score (2011) evaluate financial fraud risks by applying financial data and ratios to specific formulas. Yet, since financial markets grow substantially, the opportunities for managers and their companies to gain private benefits through fraudulent activities become increasingly tempting. As the tactics used in financial fraud become more sophisticated, the relevance of traditional detection models is being questioned. Moreover, their applicability across different markets is not universal. For instance, while the F-score model is effective in the U.S. market, its relevance to other regions might be limited (Ratmono et al., 2020).

To address the limitations of traditional fraud detection models, practitioners need to seek advanced technologies that enhance data analysis and system identification. Machine learning (ML) algorithms, in particular, have become increasingly popular in this regard (Zhang et al., 2025). Widely used machine learning techniques include support vector machines (SVM), random forests, and gradient boosting decision trees (GBDT), which have proven effective in analyzing and predicting the patterns and trends of financial data (Chen et al., 2022; Bao et al., 2020; Hajek & Henriques, 2017; Krupa and Minutti-Meza, 2022). Machine learning algorithms offer several advantages: they can process large volumes of raw financial data, automatically selecting the most relevant features for analysis, and uncovering hidden patterns that might not be apparent through traditional methods. This capability significantly improves the efficiency of fraud detection. Moreover, deep learning-based neural networks, which involve multi-layered data processing, are particularly adept at extracting complex features, further enhancing their ability to identify subtle or emerging fraud patterns (Gupta & Gill, 2012; Bao et al., 2020). These advancements make machine learning a promising approach to tackling financial fraud in an increasingly sophisticated market environment.

1.1 Introduction and Application of the M-score Model

The M-score model, developed by Beneish (1999), is a widely used tool for detecting financial fraud based on financial ratios and indicators. It utilizes eight variables such as the days sales in accounts receivable, gross margin, asset quality, to identify abnormal changes in financial ratios that may indicate manipulation of financial statements. Originally constructed using U.S. market data, the M-score has become a popular approach in U.S. for detecting financial fraud. Beneish (1999) confirms the model's relative accuracy through empirical analyses and highlights its value for investors and regulators in detecting fraudulent financial reporting.

Outside of U.S., numerous studies have explored the applicability of the M-score model in other markets. For example, Cecchini et al. (2010) apply the M-score model to the financial data of Italian listed firms and find that it could be effectively used in Italy, similar to its success in U.S. This suggests that the M-score model remains plausibly robust in European markets with economic conditions similar to those of the U.S. Further research has also examined the model's relevance in emerging markets, such as India. For example, Gupta and Gill (2012) apply the M-score to analyze financial reporting by Indian firms and find that in spite of differences in accounting systems and market conditions, the M-score was still capable of identifying financial fraud to a certain extent.

Although prior studies provide some evidence of the M-score model's applicability across different markets, they also highlight its limitations. For instance, Tarjo and Herawati (2015) show that, out of the 35 non-fraudulent companies, seven were incorrectly classified as fraudulent by the model. They also note that certain variables, such as the days sales in accounts receivable, asset quality, and leverage, have little or no impact on detecting financial fraud. Additionally, differences in financial reporting rules across industries can lead to misclassification, especially when data mining techniques are used (Tarjo & Herawati, 2015).

1.2 Introduction and Application of the F-score Model

The F-score model, developed by Dechow et al. (2011), is yet another fraud detection tool that uses financial ratios to identify potentially fraudulent financial statements. The model aggregates several financial ratios into a single composite score, including the accruals ratio, asset quality ratio, and sales growth ratio, among others. Dechow et al. (2011) find that the F-score model is particularly useful in distinguishing between firms involved in financial fraud and those that are not. Further research by Saleh et al. (2021) shows that the F-score model achieves an accuracy rate of 73.17% (76.22%) in identifying fraudulent (non-fraudulent) firms, making it more accurate than the M-score in detecting financial fraud.

The effectiveness of the F-score model in detecting financial fraud might be limited when applied to assess the risk of accounting fraud in non-U.S. countries, not least the developing ones. For example, Ratmono et al. (2020) study the manufacturing firms listed on the Indonesia Stock Exchange for the period 2014-2018, and find that the F-Score model identifies 284 out of 385 firms as having a high risk of financial statement fraud. They suggest that the model might over-identify fraud cases due to the Indonesia's distinct accounting standards, financial regulations as well as unique economic environments and capital markets, which undermine the F-score model's effectiveness compared to its application in the U.S. market.

1.3 Application of Machine Learning Models in Detection of Financial Statement Fraud

Four commonly used supervised learning algorithms for classification are support vector machine (SVM), random forest, K-nearest neighbors (KNN), and gradient boosting decision tree (GBDT). These four machine learning models are well-suited for detecting financial frauds. For one thing, they can handle large volumes of high dimensional data, facilitate feature learning, and enhance detection performance (Krupa and Minutti-Meza, 2022). For another, ensemble learning methods such as random forest and GBDT combine the outcomes of multiple base models to improve classifier accuracy (Chen et al., 2022). Given these strengths, the authors apply these four machine learning techniques to identify potential financial statement fraud among Chinese listed firms.

2. RESEARCH METHODOLOGIES

The authors seek to do an empirical analysis of the effectiveness of the M-score and F-score in the Chinese context and utilize machine learning algorithms to develop accounting fraud detection models for Chinese listed firms. The research models are elaborated on below.

2.1 Calculations of the M-score and F-score

The M-score model, proposed by Beneish in 1999, includes eight key indicators associated with the likelihood of earnings manipulation by a company, and is specified as follows:

$$M\text{-score}=-4.84+0.92\times DSRI+0.528\times GMI+0.404\times AQI+0.892\times SGI+0.115\times DEPI$$

$$-0.172\times SGAI-0.327\times LVGI+4.679\times TATA$$

Table 1. Definitions of M-score components

M-score	
DSRI	The current period's receivables-to-sales ratio / the previous period's receivables-to-sales ratio
GMI	The previous period's gross margin / the current period's gross margin
AQI	The current period's non-current assets ratio / the previous period's non-current assets ratio
SGI	The current period's sales / the previous period's sales
DEPI	The previous period's depreciation rate / the current period's depreciation rate, where depreciation rate = depreciation expense / fixed asset cost
SGAI	The current period's SG&A expenses-to-sales ratio / the previous period's SG&A expenses-to-sales ratio, where SG&A expenses = management expenses + sales expenses
LVGI	The current period's financial leverage ratio / the previous period's leverage ratio
TATA	Accruals-to-total assets ratio, where accruals = (Δ current assets - Δ cash) - (Δ current liabilities - Δ taxes payable) - depreciation expense

Note: Table 1 presents the formulas for the features used to calculate the M-score.

Table 1 presents the definitions of each financial ratio in the M-score model. The threshold for the M-score is set at -1.78, which distinguishes between firms likely to commit accounting fraud (i.e., those with an M-score above -1.78) and those that are not (i.e., firms with an M-score below -1.78).

The model of F-score, developed by Dechow et al. (2011), utilizes a different set of financial variables, such as changes in receivables, inventories, return on assets, and new share offering, to assess the likelihood of financial reporting fraud. The model is presented as follows.

$$F\text{-score} = -7.893 + 0.790 \times RSST\_ACC + 2.518 \times Ch\_rec + 1.191 \times Ch\_inv + 1.979 \times Soft\_assets + 0.171 \times Ch\_cs - 0.932 \times Ch\_roa + 1.092 \times Issue$$

Table 2. Definitions of F-score components

F-score	
RSST_ACC	Change in operating capital (ΔWC) + change in net non-cash operating assets (ΔNCO) + change in financial assets (ΔFIN) / the average total assets
Ch_rec	Change in accounts receivable / the average total assets
Ch_inv	Change in inventory / the average total assets
Soft_assets	(Change in total assets - PPE - cash and cash equivalent) / total assets
Ch_cs	(Sales revenue - change in accounts receivable) / sales revenue
Ch_roa	The current period's net profit / the current period's average total assets - the previous period's net profit / the previous period's average total assets
Issue	1 if equity or debt financing occurred, and 0 otherwise

Note: Table 2 presents the formulas for the features required to calculate the F-score.

The definition of each component of the F-score model is provided in Table 2. Dechow et al. (2011) establish multiple threshold points to differentiate between varying levels of fraud risk, with higher scores indicating a greater likelihood of accounting irregularities. Specifically, an F-score above 1 suggests an "above normal" risk of accounting fraud, while an F-score above 1.85 implies a "substantial" risk. For empirical analysis, the authors use an F-score greater than 1 as the primary criterion for identifying financial fraud, and an F-score greater than 1.85 as the secondary criterion.

2.1 Model Setup for Machine Learning

The authors employ four machine learning algorithms — Random Forest, GBDT, KNN, and SVM — in their modeling and analysis. They select all 15 features of M-score and F-score models, include an additional "loss indicator" feature, and fine-tune the parameters to enhance the model performance. They also compare the model outcomes by calculating key performance metrics including accuracy, false positive rate, and false negative rate to evaluate model effectiveness. To ensure an adequate number of features for the foregoing machine learning modeling, they calculate the variables for both the current year and the two preceding years. This approach enables the model to leverage temporal dynamics, capturing the evolution of financial indicators over time and expanding the feature pool.

3. EMPIRICAL ANALYSIS

3.1 Data Selection, Processing, and Analysis

Data required for the analysis, including the sample data of fraudulent firms uncovered by the China Securities Regulatory Commission (CSRC), the Shanghai Stock Exchange (SSE), and the Shenzhen Stock Exchange (SZSE), were sourced from the China Stock Market & Accounting Research (CSMAR) database. The sample period starts (ends) in 2010 (2019), the year after (before) the 2007-2009 global financial crisis (Covid-19 pandemic). The accounting irregularities examined include fabricated profits, inflated assets, false statements, and material omissions in financial statements. The authors utilize panel data, where fraud events in different years for the same fraudulent company are treated as separate cases. The dataset comprises 2,118 firm-year fraud cases, as detailed in Table 3, corresponding to 1,076 fraudulent listed companies.

Table 3. Violation Entities (partial)

Stock Code	Name	Punitive Authority	Violation Year	Violation Type
000038	*ST Datong	CSRC	2016;2017;2018	Fabricated Profits; False Statements
000519	Zhongbing Hongjian	SZSE	2015;2016;2017	Fabricated Profits
000523	Guangzhou Langqi	CSRC	2018;2019	Inflated Assets; Fabricated Profits; False Statements; Material Omissions
000636	Fenghua Gaoke	SZSE	2017	Fabricated Profits; False Statements
000662	Tianxia Delist	SZSE	2017;2018;2019	Fabricated Profits; False Statements

Note: Table 3 provides information on a selection of fraudulent companies. The first column lists the companies' stock codes. The 'Name' column shows their abbreviated names. The 'Punitive Authority' column indicates the regulatory body responsible for imposing penalties, which includes the China Securities Regulatory Commission (CSRC) and the Shenzhen Stock Exchange (SZSE). The 'Violation Year' column displays the year in which the fraudulent activity occurred. The 'Violation Type' column describes the specific type of fraud committed by each company. Additionally, *ST indicates "Special Treatment." This label is used to indicate that companies are under financial distress or have reported losses for consecutive years, signaling a potential risk of delisting.

3.2 Data Manipulation and Consolidation

The authors process the original data through the following steps. For the violation sample data, they use the stock code as the primary key to consolidate the data, resulting in a single row representing all the violation years for each company.

For the financial statement data, they begin by selecting the annual reports of the sample firms. Using the stock code and fiscal year as identifiers, they concatenate the financial data through Python programming, organizing all financial statement items for each company and fiscal year into a single row. Next, they filter the necessary variables for the M-score and F-score, retaining only the relevant data. They then add the corresponding financial data from the preceding years in new columns within the filtered dataset, as shown in Table 4. The machine learning models are constructed based on features derived from the current year and the previous two years to predict fraudulent activities for the current year.1

Table 4. Processed Financial Statement Data (Partial Display of Rows and Columns)

Stock Code	Name	Industry	Reporting Date	Total Assets$_t$ (CNY)	Total Assets$_{t-1}$ (CNY)	Total Assets$_{t-2}$ (CNY)	Total Assets$_{t-3}$ (CNY)	Total Assets$_{t-4}$ (CNY)
000002	Vanke A	RE	2019/12/31	1730000000000.00	1530000000000.00	1170000000000.00	831000000000.00	611000000000.00
000002	Vanke A	RE	2018/12/31	1530000000000.00	1170000000000.00	831000000000.00	611000000000.00	508000000000.00
000002	Vanke A	RE	2017/12/31	1170000000000.00	831000000000.00	611000000000.00	508000000000.00	479000000000.00
000002	Vanke A	RE	2016/12/31	831000000000.00	611000000000.00	508000000000.00	479000000000.00	379000000000.00
000002	Vanke A	RE	2015/12/31	611000000000.00	508000000000.00	479000000000.00	379000000000.00	296000000000.00
000002	Vanke A	RE	2014/12/31	508000000000.00	479000000000.00	379000000000.00	296000000000.00	216000000000.00
000002	Vanke A	RE	2013/12/31	479000000000.00	379000000000.00	296000000000.00	216000000000.00	138000000000.00
000002	Vanke A	RE	2012/12/31	379000000000.00	296000000000.00	216000000000.00	138000000000.00	119000000000.00
000002	Vanke A	RE	2011/12/31	296000000000.00	216000000000.00	138000000000.00	119000000000.00	100000000000.00
000002	Vanke A	RE	2010/12/31	216000000000.00	138000000000.00	119000000000.00	100000000000.00	48507917571.00
000004	Guonong Keji	PM	2019/12/31	1494490266.00	351177470.20	268844295.60	223716293.00	398673507.10
000004	Guonong Keji	PM	2018/12/31	351177470.20	268844295.60	223716293.00	398673507.10	338282581.10
000004	Guonong Keji	PM	2017/12/31	268844295.60	223716293.00	398673507.10	338282581.10	242152079.60
000004	Guonong Keji	PM	2016/12/31	223716293.00	398673507.10	338282581.10	242152079.60	192913568.90
000004	Guonong Keji	PM	2015/12/31	398673507.10	338282581.10	242152079.60	192913568.90	196307219.50
000004	Guonong Keji	PM	2014/12/31	338282581.10	242152079.60	192913568.90	196307219.50	184219435.70

continued on following page

Table 4. Continued

Stock Code	Name	Industry	Reporting Date	Total Assets$_t$ (CNY)	Total Assets$_{t-1}$ (CNY)	Total Assets$_{t-2}$ (CNY)	Total Assets$_{t-3}$ (CNY)	Total Assets$_{t-4}$ (CNY)
000004	Guonong Keji	PM	2013/12/31	242152079.60	192913568.90	196307219.50	184219435.70	230512058.70
000004	Guonong Keji	PM	2012/12/31	192913568.90	196307219.50	184219435.70	230512058.70	167810585.20
000004	Guonong Keji	PM	2011/12/31	196307219.50	184219435.70	230512058.70	167810585.20	169822594.00
000004	ST Guonong	PM	2010/12/31	184219435.70	230512058.70	167810585.20	169822594.00	204304637.70
000005	Shiji Xingyuan	EPEM	2019/12/31	3031840976.00	3121423379.00	2912099984.00	2527235374.00	2194008790.00

Note: Table 4 presents the processed financial statement data for selected companies. The first column lists the companies' stock codes. The “Name” column provides their abbreviated names. The “Industry” column designates the sector in which each company operates, using abbreviations such as RE for Real Estate, PM for Pharmaceutical Manufacturing, and EPEM for Ecological Protection and Environmental Management. The “Reporting Date” column specifies the date of the financial data, followed by columns that detail “Total Assets” for the reported year, as well as for the previous one, two, three, and four years, extracted from a broader financial dataset.

3.3 Utilizing Stratified Random Sampling by Industry to Extract Modeling Datasets

After removing observations with missing values in variables required for the M-score and F-score, the final dataset includes 615 cases of financial frauds and 6,557 instances of non-financial frauds, resulting in a ratio of 1:10.7. This represents a highly imbalanced sample. Therefore, the authors employ the method of random sampling (Bao et al., 2020). For all 615 fraud cases, they develop a Python program to generate a control group through stratified sampling by industry.2 The sampling criteria require that the selected non-fraudulent firms should have exhibited no fraudulent activity throughout the sample period from 2010 to 2019, and that the selected non-fraudulent data come from the same industry and financial year as the instances of fraud. These criteria ensure horizontal comparability between fraudulent and non-fraudulent firms, thereby enhancing the model's predictive performance. The objective of the sampling is to achieve a 1:1 balance in the ratio of fraudulent and non-fraudulent instances within each industry for the same year. However, due to the strict sampling criteria, some industries do not have a sufficient number of samples to meet the requirements. Consequently, a total of 614 non-fraudulent instances were extracted from the dataset.

The authors calculate the M-score and F-score, with the formulas for each listed in Table 1 and Table 2, respectively. To effectively enhance model performance, they add the variable indicating whether a company is experiencing a loss in a year, because such a company is prone to commit financial fraud. In addition to calculating the financial indicators for the current year to compute the M-score and F-score, they also calculate the corresponding indicators for the previous one and two years for the machine learning modeling. A statistical analysis of the financial indicators is performed on the selected 615 fraudulent instances and 614 non-fraudulent instances, as shown in Table 5.

Table 5. Statistical Analysis of Features Used for Modeling

Feature	Mean_ Fraud	Mean_Non_ Fraud	Median_ Fraud	Median_Non_ Fraud	Variance_ Fraud	Variance_Non_ Fraud
Receivables Turnover Index$_t$	4.215216645	1.691374785	1.043823628	1.050836566	2176.646039	61.91999825
Gross Margin Index$_t$	0.793416692	0.896696118	0.984646922	0.992471639	83.60178418	7.012965164
Asset Quality Index$_t$	2.798516652	1.180700909	1.046174829	1.017881351	730.1974089	0.679459274
Sales Growth Index$_t$	1.517970581	1.332067354	1.02035718	1.086576854	23.09424162	18.12021909
Depreciation Rate Index$_t$	1.356814529	1.048507646	0.958798827	0.969455246	18.774775	0.308869023
Selling, General & Administrative Expenses Index$_t$	1.316438391	1.075218972	1.039559246	1.032836649	4.019285909	0.126290182
Financial Leverage Index$_t$	1.071354236	1.038123243	1.012655797	0.994722961	0.205106014	0.201995384
Total Accruals to Total Assets Ratio$_t$	- 0.011321409	-0.005233702	-0.033927796	-0.012623897	0.058991754	0.021199795
Accrued Receivables$_t$	0.076945846	0.067837151	0.029227254	0.040553891	0.16480476	0.031782971
Receivables Change Rate$_t$	0.017603948	0.017842078	0.004296062	0.005522967	0.005401384	0.002074942
Inventory Change Rate$_t$	0.01134314	0.01606429	0.002036714	0.00491135	0.012727685	0.004086787
Soft Assets Ratio$_t$	0.587737774	0.54673254	0.592333484	0.550973788	0.043024675	0.035595182
Cash Sales Ratio$_t$	0.975065347	0.972717241	0.99090157	0.990096755	0.03022741	0.009502886
ROA Growth Rate$_t$	0.040649834	-0.00273098	-0.003366167	-0.002272749	0.971578763	0.004817573
Whether Refinanced$_t$	0.331707317	0.399022801	0	0	0.222038611	0.240194802
Receivables Turnover Index$_{t_1}$	4.698820127	1.696365095	1.08525305	1.03748732	2268.911314	67.92651246
Gross Margin Index$_{t_1}$	1.138229844	1.116999989	0.992140174	0.993017629	7.64856584	29.3451681
Asset Quality Index$_{t_1}$	2.426796383	1.218062782	1.031893293	1.014916566	701.7064435	1.052072156
Sales Growth Index$_{t_1}$	1.543613781	2.116130633	1.059693399	1.112714136	24.61562048	363.9861355

continued on following page

Table 5. Continued

Feature	Mean_ Fraud	Mean_Non_ Fraud	Median_ Fraud	Median_Non_ Fraud	Variance_ Fraud	Variance_Non_ Fraud
Depreciation Rate Index$_{t_1}$	1.049444058	1.184062188	0.969065055	0.971706822	0.344418607	5.0579465
Selling, General & Administrative Expenses Index$_{t_1}$	1.116148859	1.051248249	1.035089977	1.021580685	0.466815132	0.087724231
Financial Leverage Index$_{t_1}$	1.130378251	1.105822152	1.023355029	1.0147079	0.784085086	1.819162461
Total Accruals to Total Assets Ratio$_{t_1}$	0.003924837	-0.014684851	-0.020186136	-0.016205778	0.208791472	0.010179475
Accrued Receivables$_{t_1}$	0.000268602	0.0554528	0.028173507	0.041278016	1.77591405	0.01400569
Receivables Change Rate$_{t_1}$	0.015875104	0.018656514	0.005013213	0.007421286	0.005732525	0.001791667
Inventory Change Rate$_{t_1}$	0.020722194	0.019594816	0.003679462	0.006770234	0.013322485	0.00690428
Soft Assets Ratio$_{t_1}$	0.571849615	0.532835125	0.561889048	0.538138152	0.042035519	0.03446954
Cash Sales Ratio$_{t_1}$	0.997261036	0.974840593	0.989247954	0.987473978	0.092207863	0.006054769
ROA Growth Rate$_{t_1}$	- 0.049996332	-0.001034616	-0.004208839	-0.000451311	0.938394035	0.003335765
Whether Refinanced$_{t_1}$	0.323577236	0.345276873	0	0	0.219231482	0.226429532
Receivables Turnover Index$_{t_2}$	9.030628782	1.682886893	1.047576263	1.028554212	33701.0578	50.79197818
Gross Margin Index$_{t_2}$	1.055211956	0.960089709	1.012187332	1.006852987	6.141047179	5.389746144
Asset Quality Index$_{t_2}$	2.374796481	1.743856973	1.013416003	1.013042645	472.288924	113.3856653
Sales Growth Index$_{t_2}$	2.527656316	1.824544676	1.087705703	1.124351416	286.6618747	206.3727717
Depreciation Rate Index$_{t_2}$	1.092886032	1.134122515	0.975791764	0.973770004	0.841520935	3.821793222
Selling, General & Administrative Expenses Index$_{t_2}$	1.092429855	1.128635709	1.022900864	1.031037898	0.291538313	4.170005434
Financial Leverage Index$_{t_2}$	1.141730775	1.083815802	1.026350746	1.020094659	0.756007424	0.140854998

continued on following page

Table 5. Continued

Feature	Mean_ Fraud	Mean_Non_ Fraud	Median_ Fraud	Median_Non_ Fraud	Variance_ Fraud	Variance_Non_ Fraud
Total Accruals to Total Assets Ratio$_{t_2}$	- 0.016330811	-0.012971781	-0.015664028	-0.015268813	0.078919916	0.009591498
Accrued Receivables$_{t_2}$	0.047041381	0.055181658	0.026298594	0.047651547	0.05537813	0.015546986
Receivables Change Rate$_{t_2}$	0.014508457	0.017251405	0.004623619	0.00674958	0.003015183	0.002058322
Inventory Change Rate$_{t_2}$	0.020882877	0.021441529	0.008640557	0.009571335	0.00967671	0.005456848
Soft Assets Ratio$_{t_2}$	0.55337035	0.521059139	0.541986121	0.515351133	0.038341003	0.03612371
Cash Sales Ratio$_{t_2}$	0.985896957	0.976840592	0.989615274	0.989264798	0.014308435	0.009239894
ROA Growth Rate$_{t_2}$	0.323577236	0.315960912	0	0	0.219231482	0.216482191
Whether Refinanced$_{t_2}$	-0.000162	0.0016838	-0.0017931	-0.0012176	0.02137532	0.030576408
Whether Loss Incurred$_t$	0.575609756	0.796416938	1	1	0.24468102	0.162401496
Whether Loss Incurred$_{t_1}$	0.603252033	0.825732899	1	1	0.239728821	0.144132823
Whether Loss Incurred$_{t_2}$	0.660162602	0.809446254	1	1	0.224713329	0.154494636

Note: Table 5 presents the statistics of 48 features used for modeling, including Mean_Fraud, Mean_Non_Fraud, Median_Fraud, Median_Non_Fraud, Variance_Fraud, and Variance_Non_Fraud.

According to the M-score model: $M = -4.84 + 0.92 \times DSRI + 0.528 \times GMI + 0.404 \times AQI + 0.892 \times SGI + 0.115 \times DEPI - 0.172 \times SGAI - 0.327 \times LVGI + 4.679 \times TATA$, fraudulent companies should have higher (lower) average values for the receivables turnover, gross margin, asset quality, operating revenue, depreciation, and total accruals to total assets ratio (the sales and administrative expenses and financial leverage) than non-fraudulent companies. However, Table 5 reveals opposite results for the indices such as gross margin index, total accruals to total assets ratio, sales and administrative expenses, and financial leverage. Likewise, based on the F-score model: $F = -7.893 + 0.79 \times RSST\_ACC + 2.518 \times CH\_EC + 1.191 \times CH\_INV + 1.979 \times SOFT\_AS + 0.171 \times CH\_CS - 0.932 \times CH\_ROA + 1.029 \times ISSUE$, fraudulent companies should have higher averages for accrued receivables, changes in receivables, inventory changes, the proportion of soft assets, the cash-to-sales rate, and the incidence of re-financing, but a lower average ROA growth rate, compared to non-fraudulent companies. On the contrary, the authors find opposite mean results for the inventory change rate, incidence of refinance, and ROA growth rate. They also find some median results (e.g., those for accrued receivables and inventory change rate) inconsistent with the F-score modeling. Collectively, these results suggest that applying M-score and F-score models might not produce effective outcomes in the Chinese market.

3.4 Performance of the M-score and F-score Models in the Chinese Market

According to the models of M-score and F-score, a company's financial statement would have a high likelihood of accounting fraud for a fiscal period if the M-score is above -1.78 or the F-score exceeds 1. Figure 1 and Figure 2 depict the scatter plot distributions of the M-scores and F-scores, respectively. The graphs reveal that both the M-scores and F-scores fail to effectively differentiate between fraudulent and non-fraudulent samples in the Chinese market. The distributions of M-scores for both fraudulent and non-fraudulent samples largely overlap, with a relatively small proportion of observations falling below the -1.78 threshold. This contradicts the expectation that fraudulent companies would predominantly have scores above this value while non-fraudulent companies would cluster below it. For the F-score, no sample observation has a value exceeding 1.85, as indicated by the orange line in Figure 2. Even if the scoring threshold is lowered to 1, the predictive capability of the F-score remains insignificant. In fact, with the exception of a single observation with an F-score above 1, all other observations have an F-score of 1 or lower, making them indistinguishable, as shown by the blue line in Figure 2, in terms of the likelihood of committing an accounting fraud.

Figure 1. M-Score Analysis Overview

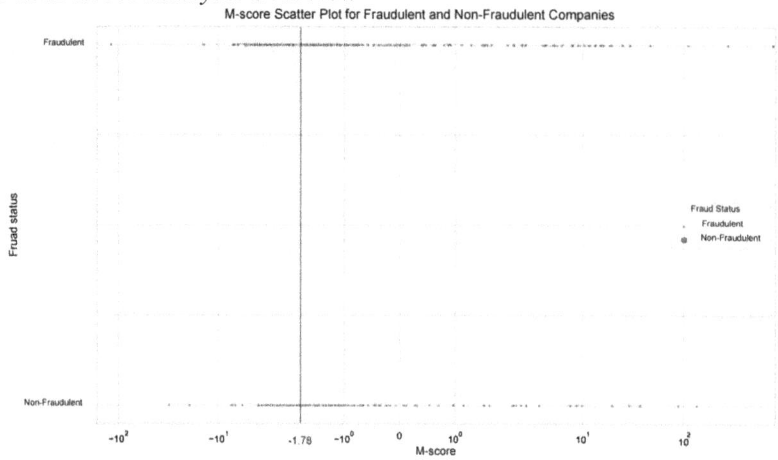

Note: *In the graph, the green dots represent the distribution of M-score values for financially fraudulent cases, while the red dots represent the distribution of M-score values for non-fraudulent cases. The blue line represents a benchmark: M-score = -1.78.*

Figure 2. F-Score Analysis Overview

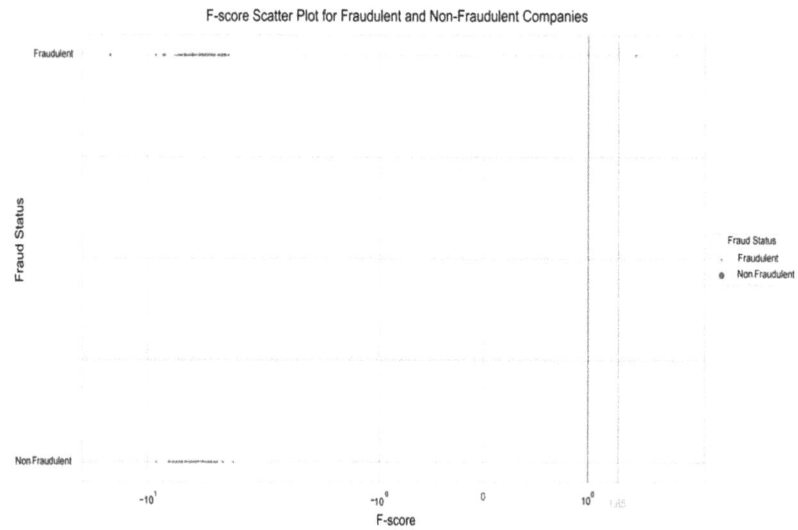

Note: *The green dots in the graph represent the distribution of F-scores for financially fraudulent cases, while the red dots indicate the distribution of F-scores for non-fraudulent cases. The blue line is a benchmark where F-score equals 1, and the orange line is another benchmark where F-score equals 1.85.*

Table 6 shows the statistical analysis of the results. The accuracy of detecting financial fraud using the M-score and F-score models is fairly low. The M-score model achieves an accuracy rate of only 53.1%, with a false positive rate of 23.5% and a high false negative rate of 70.4%. The F-score model has an accuracy of 50.0%, with a false positive rate of 0% and a false negative rate of 99.9%. Here, accuracy refers to the proportion of correct predictions out of the total dataset; the false positive rate indicates the proportion of non-fraudulent data incorrectly classified as fraud; and the false negative rate represents the proportion of fraudulent misclassified as non-fraud. Both models show unsatisfactory predictive performance, characterized by low accuracy and high misclassification rates. Notably, the F-score's near-zero false positive rate stems from classifying almost all samples as non-fraud. The relatively low accuracy further highlights the model's substantial limitations particularly in the Chinese market.

Table 6. Predictive Performance of the M-score and F-score Models

Model	Accuracy Rate (%)	False Positive Rate (%)	False Negative Rate (%)
M-score	53.1	23.5	70.4
F-score	50.0	0.0	99.9

Note: Table 6 summarizes the predictive performance of the M-score and F-score models, including accuracy rate, false positive rate, and false negative rate.

In summary, both the M-score and F-score models perform unsatisfactorily in detecting financial fraud within the samples, suggesting that these models are not directly applicable to the Chinese market. This underscores the need for adaptations or the creation of new models tailored to the unique financial reporting environment in China.

3.5 Machine Learning-Based Model for Detecting Financial Fraud in the Chinese Market

Since financial fraud detection pertains to a binary classification problem, this study opts for four widely-used classification models — Random Forest, GBDT, KNN, and SVM models — to develop and compare their predictive performance. The foregoing 48 financial indicators covering three years serve as features for the machine learning models. A portion of the data used in the machine learning is shown in Table 7.

Table 7. Input Indicators for Machine Learning Modelling A

Stock Code	Stock Abbreviation	Industry	Date of Statistics	Engaged in Fraud	Receivables Turnover $Index_t$	Gross Margin $Index_t$	Asset Quality $Index_t$	Sales Growth $Index_t$	Depreciation Rate $Index_t$	SG&A Expenses $Index_t$	Financial Leverage $Index_t$	Total Accruals to Total Assets $Ratio_t$
300008	Shanghai Jiahao	PTSI	2013-12-31 00:00:00	1	0.315054644	1.021254224	0.947415323	0.888943985	0.980529093	1.308312144	0.952619447	-0.125520436
300008	Shanghai Jiahao	PTSI	2014-12-31 00:00:00	1	1.434946924	1.800406087	3.668516924	3.57337272	1.043918975	0.345073304	2.27780142	0.02501299
300008	Shanghai Jiahao	PTSI	2015-12-31 00:00:00	1	1.391575793	1.231027637	0.786990875	1.413589274	0.826834659	0.716937543	1.239742567	0.034097885
002398	Jianyan Group	PTSI	2013-12-31 00:00:00	0	1.039027852	1.042757122	0.92780348	1.354547542	0.826148994	1.09705215	1.236260545	0.090051493
002469	Sanwei Engineering	PTSI	2013-12-31 00:00:00	0	0.86102247	0.855835095	0.885845555	1.289436483	0.853150015	1.359331877	0.889453866	0.031408011
002469	Sanwei Engineering	PTSI	2014-12-31 00:00:00	0	1.954127802	1.068948582	0.829257626	1.313529826	0.937015013	0.728978949	1.542499061	0.273120249
600184	Photoelectric Shares	PTSI	2014-12-31 00:00:00	1	1.006883814	0.951919781	0.866225671	1.053436036	0.929098019	1.027456973	1.165463972	-0.135224983
002021	Zhongjie Resources	PTSI	2015-12-31 00:00:00	1	0.853073797	1.984187561	2.505318822	0.64722081	0.897284003	1.417343262	0.596426449	0.250889494
000528	Liugong	PTSI	2014-12-31 00:00:00	1	1.521933763	0.941962278	0.869332377	0.817931006	0.814392522	1.246853341	0.969965288	0.018445259
000528	Liugong	PTSI	2015-12-31 00:00:00	1	1.4045607	0.859305451	1.162980845	0.646609639	1.221318334	1.334203546	1.00851903	-0.094718021

Note: Table 7 provides essential information for a subset of the sampled companies, along with the values of the 48 variables utilized in model construction. The first four columns—Stock Code, Stock Abbreviation, Industry, and Date of Statistics—offer fundamental background details for each company. In the Industry column, "PTSI" refers to the Professional Technical Services Industry. The "Engaged in Fraud" column is a binary indicator, with a value of 1 signifying involvement in fraudulent activity and 0 indicating no fraud. The subsequent columns in Panel A present the values of 8 selected variables, while the remaining panels present the rest.

Table 8. Input Indicators for Machine Learning Modelling B

Stock Code	Stock Abbreviation	Industry	Date of Statistics	Engaged in Fraud	Accrued Receivables$_t$	Receivables Change Rate$_t$	Inventory Change Rate$_t$	Soft Assets Ratio$_t$	Cash Sales Ratio$_t$	ROA Growth Rate$_t$	Refinanced$_t$	Receivables Turnover Index$_{t-1}$
300008	Shanghai Jiahao	PTSI	2013-12-31 00:00:00	1	-0.085376984	-0.11271398	0.024514049	0.264767469	1.307897353	-0.016442567	1	3.419856996
300008	Shanghai Jiahao	PTSI	2014-12-31 00:00:00	1	0.442523	0.11944628	0.263696963	0.687710245	0.861645651	0.031065318	1	0.315054644
300008	Shanghai Jiahao	PTSI	2015-12-31 00:00:00	1	0.086532856	0.093178191	0.112485583	0.753129472	0.882411473	-0.008266617	1	1.434946924
002398	Jianyan Group	PTSI	2013-12-31 00:00:00	0	0.183626662	0.130274122	0.003841506	0.677426094	0.842071609	-0.005827916	0	1.392910155
002469	Sanwei Engineering	PTSI	2013-12-31 00:00:00	0	0.041369685	0.024334857	0.031109609	0.382636644	0.953402786	0.022104928	1	0.85555218
002469	Sanwei Engineering	PTSI	2014-12-31 00:00:00	0	0.315521687	0.315264846	-0.014493577	0.687912836	0.440197651	0.004023175	0	0.86102247
600184	Photoelectric Shares	PTSI	2014-12-31 00:00:00	1	0.045897987	0.010573461	0.043109342	0.596585172	0.984303332	0.083484786	0	0.871876429
002021	Zhongjie Resources	PTSI	2015-12-31 00:00:00	1	0.118172431	-0.049018651	-0.052971617	0.518323	1.193086049	-0.159339267	0	0.945851695
000528	Liugong	PTSI	2014-12-31 00:00:00	1	0.022431563	0.031749993	-0.025998876	0.668977387	0.933711355	-0.005836481	0	1.294769846
000528	Liugong	PTSI	2015-12-31 00:00:00	1	-0.02603554	-0.015464718	-0.041648275	0.652078394	1.047847978	-0.007979579	0	1.521933763

Note: Panel B provides essential information for a subset of the sampled companies, along with the values of the 48 variables utilized in model construction. The first four columns—Stock Code, Stock Abbreviation, Industry, and Date of Statistics—offer fundamental background details for each company. In the Industry column, "PTSI" refers to the Professional Technical Services Industry. The "Engaged in Fraud" column is a binary indicator, with a value of 1 signifying involvement in fraudulent activity and 0 indicating no fraud. The subsequent columns in Panel B present the values of 8 selected variables, while the remaining panels present the rest.

Table 9. Input Indicators for Machine Learning Modelling C

Stock Code	Stock Abbreviation	Industry	Date of Statistics	Engaged in Fraud	Gross Margin Index$_{t-1}$	Asset Quality Index$_{t-1}$	Sales Growth Index$_{t-1}$	Depreciation Rate Index$_{t-1}$	SG&A Expenses Index$_{t-1}$	Financial Leverage Index$_{t-1}$	Total Accruals to Total Assets Ratio$_{t-1}$	Accrued Receivables $_{-1}$
300008	Shanghai Jiahao	PTSI	2013-12-31 00:00:00	1	1.19213539	1.37170937	0.804141336	0.97521693	1.803599852	0.923049511	0.058152961	0.120470466
300008	Shanghai Jiahao	PTSI	2014-12-31 00:00:00	1	1.021254224	0.947415323	0.888943985	0.980529093	1.308312144	0.952619447	-0.125520436	-0.085376984
300008	Shanghai Jiahao	PTSI	2015-12-31 00:00:00	1	1.800406087	3.668516924	3.57337272	1.043918975	0.345073304	2.27780142	0.02501299	0.442523
002398	Jianyan Group	PTSI	2013-12-31 00:00:00	0	0.895429191	1.486283903	1.32776135	1.107719912	1.081763834	1.373424738	0.075034258	0.171391742
002469	Sanwei Engineering	PTSI	2013-12-31 00:00:00	0	1.180435042	7.001992828	1.763355447	0.679165369	1.027042288	0.972667601	0.10076006	0.168334248
002469	Sanwei Engineering	PTSI	2014-12-31 00:00:00	0	0.855835095	0.885845555	1.289436483	0.853150015	1.359331877	0.889453866	0.031408011	0.041369685
600184	Photoelectric Shares	PTSI	2014-12-31 00:00:00	1	1.312445166	1.26841546	0.923616891	1.042845552	0.825839933	0.856633249	-0.067203408	-0.089474961
002021	Zhongjie Resources	PTSI	2015-12-31 00:00:00	1	1.097793101	0.632500063	0.881114385	0.840111639	1.119462553	0.93653086	0.004552929	-0.004807063
000528	Liugong	PTSI	2014-12-31 00:00:00	1	0.804061115	0.917409732	0.996438616	0.987213457	1.079721837	0.98685589	-0.02274583	-0.031883316
000528	Liugong	PTSI	2015-12-31 00:00:00	1	0.941962278	0.869332377	0.817931006	0.814392522	1.246853341	0.969965288	0.018445259	0.022431563

Note: Panel C provides essential information for a subset of the sampled companies, along with the values of the 48 variables utilized in model construction. The first four columns—Stock Code, Stock Abbreviation, Industry, and Date of Statistics—offer fundamental background details for each company. In the Industry column, "PTSI" refers to the Professional Technical Services Industry. The "Engaged in Fraud" column is a binary indicator, with a value of 1 signifying involvement in fraudulent activity and 0 indicating no fraud. The subsequent columns in Panel C present the values of 8 selected variables, while the remaining panels present the rest.

Table 10. Input Indicators for Machine Learning Modelling D

Stock Code	Stock Abbreviation	Industry	Date of Statistics	Engaged in Fraud	Receivables Change Rate$_{t-1}$	Inventory Change Rate$_{t-1}$	Soft Assets Ratio$_{t-1}$	Cash Sales Ratio$_{t-1}$	ROA Growth Rate$_{t-1}$	Refinanced $_{-1}$	Receivables Turnover Index$_{t-2}$	Gross Margin Index$_{t-2}$
300008	Shanghai Jiahao	PTSI	2013-12-31 00:00:00	1	0.097517927	0.017616461	0.373849353	0.758065756	-0.093027385	0	1.530937157	1.192215357
300008	Shanghai Jiahao	PTSI	2014-12-31 00:00:00	1	-0.11271398	0.024514049	0.264767469	1.307897353	-0.016442567	1	3.419856996	1.19213539
300008	Shanghai Jiahao	PTSI	2015-12-31 00:00:00	1	0.11944628	0.263696963	0.687710245	0.861645651	0.031065318	1	0.315054644	1.021254224
002398	Jianyan Group	PTSI	2013-12-31 00:00:00	0	0.182670268	0.010721526	0.564886512	0.758834136	0.017539771	0	0.843795276	0.793161413
002469	Sanwei Engineering	PTSI	2013-12-31 00:00:00	0	0.084600785	0.004822259	0.385681795	0.816231301	0.014169545	1	1.269421003	1.087138202
002469	Sanwei Engineering	PTSI	2014-12-31 00:00:00	0	0.024334857	0.031109609	0.382636644	0.953402786	0.022104928	1	0.85555218	1.180435042
600184	Photoelectric Shares	PTSI	2014-12-31 00:00:00	1	-0.041651006	-0.050786007	0.554281923	1.065883887	-0.055567391	0	0.883421241	0.820166719
002021	Zhongjie Resources	PTSI	2015-12-31 00:00:00	1	-0.016971749	-0.01767597	0.562862669	1.0557775	-0.012542937	0	0.928205953	1.005084528
000528	Liugong	PTSI	2014-12-31 00:00:00	1	0.028003787	-0.024099631	0.65375995	0.950195163	0.002524559	0	1.350176958	1.144492853
000528	Liugong	PTSI	2015-12-31 00:00:00	1	0.031749993	-0.025998876	0.668977387	0.933711355	-0.005836481	0	1.294769846	0.804061115

Note: Panel D showcases essential details for a select group of sampled companies along with the values of the 48 variables employed in building the model. The initial four columns—Stock Code, Stock Abbreviation, Industry, and Date of Statistics—offer foundational data for each company. Notably, within the "Industry" column, 'PTSI' represents the Professional Technical Services Industry. The 'Engaged in Fraud' column serves as a binary indicator, where a value of 1 indicates that the company has been involved in fraudulent activities, whereas a value of 0 signifies no such involvement. The remaining columns in Panel D present the 8 chosen variables' values, while the remaining panels present the rest.

Table 11. Input Indicators for Machine Learning Modelling E

Stock Code	Stock Abbreviation	Industry	Date of Statistics	Engaged in Fraud	Asset Quality Index$_{t-2}$	Sales Growth Index$_{t-2}$	Depreciation Rate Index$_{t-2}$	SG&A Expenses Index$_{t-2}$	Financial Leverage Index$_{t-2}$	Total Accruals to Total Assets Ratio$_{t-2}$	Accrued Receivables$_{-2}$	Receivables Change Rate$_{t-2}$
300008	Shanghai Jiahao	PTSI	2013-12-31 00:00:00	1	4.199357326	1.633730269	0.827101774	1.014642423	1.344604844	0.098781202	0.242613755	0.035698842
300008	Shanghai Jiahao	PTSI	2014-12-31 00:00:00	1	1.37170937	0.804141336	0.97521693	1.803599852	0.923049511	0.058152961	0.120470466	0.097517927
300008	Shanghai Jiahao	PTSI	2015-12-31 00:00:00	1	0.947415323	0.888943985	0.980529093	1.308312144	0.952619447	-0.125520436	-0.085376984	-0.11271398
002398	Jianyan Group	PTSI	2013-12-31 00:00:00	0	0.922413003	1.657782649	0.851806614	1.037235573	0.978425462	0.089511504	0.144826797	0.074702076
002469	Sanwei Engineering	PTSI	2013-12-31 00:00:00	0	1.147015152	1.443869949	2.162630586	1.047824909	1.524055367	-0.006015434	0.112932153	0.086623569
002469	Sanwei Engineering	PTSI	2014-12-31 00:00:00	0	7.001992828	1.763355447	0.679165369	1.027042288	0.972667601	0.10076006	0.168334248	0.084600785
600184	Photoelectric Shares	PTSI	2014-12-31 00:00:00	1	1.041061856	0.962000161	0.958753127	1.147648228	0.985899283	-0.086309027	-0.048602308	-0.035401014
002021	Zhongjie Resources	PTSI	2015-12-31 00:00:00	1	0.845171564	1.305671887	1.085316009	0.931722301	1.054940549	-0.026811611	-0.019735062	0.021132061
000528	Liugong	PTSI	2014-12-31 00:00:00	1	1.034151665	0.706425142	0.992800782	1.363097485	0.986344935	0.002905685	-0.020573343	-0.004616016
000528	Liugong	PTSI	2015-12-31 00:00:00	1	0.917409732	0.996438616	0.987213457	1.079721837	0.98685589	-0.02274583	-0.031883316	0.028003787

Note: Panel E features key information for a subset of sampled companies, including the values of the 48 variables utilized in developing the model. The initial four columns—Stock Code, Stock Abbreviation, Industry, and Date of Statistics—offer foundational details for each company. 'PTSI' within the "Industry" column denotes the Professional Technical Services Industry. The 'Engaged in Fraud' column functions as a binary indicator, with a value of 1 indicating the presence of fraudulent activity and a value of 0 indicating no such activity. Subsequent columns in Panel E present the values of 8 chosen variables, while the remaining panels present the rest.

Table 12. Input Indicators for Machine Learning Modelling F

Stock Code	Stock Abbreviation	Industry	Date of Statistics	Engaged in Fraud	Inventory Change Rate$_{t-2}$	Soft Assets Ratio$_{t-2}$	Cash Sales Ratio$_{t-2}$	Refinanced$_{t-2}$	Incurred a Loss$_t$	Incurred a Loss$_{t-1}$	Incurred a Loss$_{t-2}$
300008	Shanghai Jiahao	PTSI	2013-12-31 00:00:00	1	0.065413378	0.266565607	0.933278979	0	1	1	1
300008	Shanghai Jiahao	PTSI	2014-12-31 00:00:00	1	0.017616461	0.373849353	0.758065756	0	1	1	1
300008	Shanghai Jiahao	PTSI	2015-12-31 00:00:00	1	0.024514049	0.264767469	1.307897353	1	1	1	1
002398	Jianyan Group	PTSI	2013-12-31 00:00:00	0	0.007255979	0.426105506	0.892522115	0	1	1	1
002469	Sanwei Engineering	PTSI	2013-12-31 00:00:00	0	-0.01627212	0.246255569	0.710501214	0	1	1	1
002469	Sanwei Engineering	PTSI	2014-12-31 00:00:00	0	0.004822259	0.385681795	0.816231301	1	1	1	1
600184	Photoelectric Shares	PTSI	2014-12-31 00:00:00	1	0.006173273	0.573655135	1.055212631	0	1	0	0
002021	Zhongjie Resources	PTSI	2015-12-31 00:00:00	1	0.041322479	0.594409514	0.948412493	0	0	1	1
000528	Liugong	PTSI	2014-12-31 00:00:00	1	-0.017627254	0.68915895	1.00828479	1	1	1	1
000528	Liugong	PTSI	2015-12-31 00:00:00	1	-0.024099631	0.65375995	0.950195163	0	0	1	1

Note: Panel F summarizes foundational details for a selected group of sampled companies, inclusive of the values for the 48 variables employed in constructing the model. The initial four columns—Stock Code, Stock Abbreviation, Industry, and Date of Statistics—offer essential background information for each company. 'PTSI' within the "Industry" column represents the Professional Technical Services Industry. The 'Engaged in Fraud' column serves as a binary indicator, with a value of 1 indicating that the company has been involved in fraudulent activities and a value of 0 indicating no such involvement. The following columns within Panel F present the values of 8 chosen variables.

All features are standardized to ensure uniform scaling across the dataset, which enhances model training efficiency, improves performance, and increases generalizability across various machine learning models. The Random Forest, GBDT, KNN, and SVM models address these issues by selecting highly important and relevant features. In particular, the Random Forest and GBDT models employ the "Select-From-Model" algorithm to assess feature importance and select the most significant features; the KNN model utilizes recursive feature elimination; and the SVM model applies the "Select-K-Best" algorithm based on statistical tests. Experimental validation reveals that the Random Forest and GBDT models achieve optimal performance with 12 selected features, while the KNN and SVM models perform the best with 15 features. The selected features for each model are detailed in Table 8.

Table 13. Feature Selection for Different Machine Learning Models

Model	Selected Features
Random Forest	Asset Quality Index$_t$, Sales Growth Index$_t$, SG&A Expenses Index$_t$, Total Accruals to Total Assets Ratio$_t$, Asset Quality Index$_{t-1}$, Sales Growth Index$_{t-1}$, SG&A Expenses Index$_{t-1}$, Receivables Change Rate$_{t-1}$, Soft Assets Ratio$_{t-1}$, Cash-to-Sales Ratio$_{t-1}$, ROA Growth Rate$_{t-1}$, Depreciation Rate$_{t-2}$.
Gradient Boosting Decision Tree (GBDT)	Asset Quality Index$_t$, Sales Growth Index$_t$, Depreciation Rate Index$_t$, SG&A Expenses Index$_t$, Total Accruals to Total Assets Ratio$_t$, Soft Assets Ratio$_t$, Accounts Receivable Sales Index$_{t-1}$, Asset Quality Index$_{t-1}$, Sales Growth Index$_{t-1}$, Depreciation Rate Index$_{t-1}$, SG&A Expenses Index$_{t-1}$, Financial Leverage Index$_{t-1}$.
K-Nearest Neighbors (KNN)	Asset Quality Index$_t$, Sales Growth Index$_t$, Depreciation Rate Index$_t$, SG&A Expenses Index$_t$, Total Accruals to Total Assets Ratio$_t$, Inventory Turnover Rate$_t$, Soft Assets Ratio$_t$, Cash-to-Sales Ratio$_t$, ROA Growth Rate$_t$, Asset Quality Index$_{t-1}$, Sales Growth Index$_{t-1}$, SG&A Expenses Index$_{t-1}$, Total Accruals to Total Assets Ratio$_{t-1}$, RSST Accrued Items$_{t-1}$, Soft Assets Ratio$_{t-1}$
Support Vector Machine (SVM)	Depreciation Rate Index$_t$, SG&A Expenses Index$_t$, Financial Leverage Index$_t$, Soft Assets Ratio$_t$, Refinancing Status$_t$, Accounts Receivable Sales Index$_{t-1}$, Soft Assets Ratio$_{t-1}$, SG&A Expenses Index$_{t-2}$, Financial Leverage Index$_{t-2}$, Accounts Receivable Turnover Rate$_{t-2}$, Soft Assets Ratio$_{t-2}$, Cash-to-Sales Ratio$_{t-2}$, Loss Indicator$_t$, Loss Indicator$_{t-1}$, Loss Indicator$_{t-2}$

Note: Table 8 outlines the selected features that were incorporated into the machine learning models, including Random Forest, Gradient Boosting Decision Tree (GBDT), K-Nearest Neighbors (KNN), and Support Vector Machine (SVM). The feature sets for each model were selected to optimize their respective performance contributions and are ranked in descending order of their correlation importance within each model.

Using the holdout method, a standard practice in machine learning (e.g., Raschka, 2018; Yadav & Shukla, 2016; Wyrobek, 2020), the dataset was randomly split into an 8:2 ratio for training and testing. The training set was utilized to train the models, while the test set was employed to assess the predictive performance of the trained models. Using the selected feature sets, modeling for Random Forest, GBDT, KNN, and SVM was built on the training set. Finally, parameter tuning was performed using grid search with cross-validation to determine the optimal model parameters, completing the modeling process.

The test sets were fed into the four trained models, and a statistical analysis was conducted to compute accuracy, false negative rates, and false positive rates. The experiments were independently repeated ten times, and the results are presented in Table 9.

Table 14. Results of Machine Learning Model Experiments

Accuracy				
	RandomForest	**GradientBoosting**	**KNN**	**SVM**
1	62.20%	67.07%	61.38%	62.20%
2	61.38%	67.07%	60.98%	63.41%
3	65.04%	62.20%	64.23%	67.07%
4	67.48%	64.63%	65.45%	67.48%
5	59.35%	66.67%	62.60%	64.23%
6	66.67%	68.70%	59.35%	65.45%
7	61.79%	65.04%	58.54%	61.38%
8	68.29%	64.23%	64.23%	60.98%
9	66.67%	65.04%	59.76%	59.76%
10	71.95%	64.23%	60.98%	60.57%
Mean	65.08%	65.49%	61.75%	63.25%
Maximum	71.95%	68.70%	65.45%	67.48%
Variance	0.001339981	0.000318766	0.000480697	0.00067487
False Negative Rate: The proportion of fraudulent samples which are incorrectly classified as non-fraudulent samples.				
	RandomForest	**GradientBoosting**	**KNN**	**SVM**
1	40.00%	37.82%	51.22%	55.74%
2	31.19%	41.22%	51.75%	43.36%
3	40.35%	36.67%	41.41%	48.41%
4	35.04%	43.08%	46.22%	42.86%
5	43.70%	32.11%	53.39%	47.41%
6	33.60%	34.15%	50.39%	45.38%
7	36.00%	36.36%	49.58%	49.17%
8	31.62%	36.36%	50.41%	48.09%

continued on following page

Table 14. Continued

Accuracy				
9	35.59%	36.72%	50.40%	50.82%
10	23.97%	41.22%	44.00%	56.93%
Mean	35.11%	37.57%	48.88%	48.82%
Minimum	23.97%	32.11%	41.41%	42.86%
Variance	0.00280102	0.00103035	0.00128253	0.001976284
Average true Negative Rate	64.89%	62.43%	51.12%	51.18%
Maximum true Negative Rate	76.03%	67.89%	58.59%	57.14%
False Positive Rate: The proportion of non-fraudulent samples which are incorrectly classified as fraudulent samples.				
	RandomForest	**GradientBoosting**	**KNN**	**SVM**
1	35.54%	28.35%	26.02%	20.16%
2	44.53%	23.48%	28.03%	30.83%
3	30.30%	38.89%	29.66%	16.67%
4	29.36%	26.72%	23.62%	21.67%
5	37.80%	34.31%	22.66%	25.38%
6	33.06%	28.46%	29.91%	22.41%
7	40.50%	33.60%	33.86%	28.57%
8	31.78%	35.09%	21.60%	28.70%
9	31.25%	33.05%	29.75%	29.84%
10	32.00%	29.57%	33.88%	17.43%
Mean	34.61%	31.15%	27.90%	24.17%
Maximum	29.36%	23.48%	21.60%	16.67%
Variance	0.002186059	0.001910519	0.001709568	0.002449119
Average true Positive Rate	65.39%	68.85%	72.10%	75.83%
Maximum true Positive Rate	70.64%	76.52%	78.40%	83.33%

Note: Table 14 presents the performance metrics of four machine learning models, highlighting key indicators such as accuracy and error rates. To mitigate the impact of random variability on the results, each model was executed ten times, resulting in a total of 40 experimental iterations across all models. For each iteration, the authors calculated the accuracy, false negative rate, and false positive rate. Subsequently, statistical analyses were conducted on the results from the four models, including the computation of mean, maximum value, variance, average true negative rate, maximum true negative rate, average true positive rate, and maximum true positive rate.

It is evident that the machine learning models performed well in the Chinese market. The Gradient Boosting Decision Tree model and the Random Forest model achieved the highest accuracy, with average rates of 65.08% and 65.49%, respectively, across ten trials. The KNN and SVM models showed slightly lower accuracy, at 61.75% and 63.25%, respectively. However, the KNN and SVM models excelled in terms of true positive rates, averaging 72.10% and 75.83%, respectively. In individual trials, the Random Forest model reached the highest single accuracy rate of 72%, while the SVM model achieved the highest true positive rate of 83.3%. Regarding model stability, the GBDT model had the lowest variance in accuracy, indicating the greatest stability, while the KNN and SVM models exhibited slightly less stability, and the Random Forest model showed the most variability. In terms of false negative rates, the Random Forest model performed the best, followed by the Gradient Boosting model, while the KNN and SVM models exhibited relatively higher false negative rates. The variance in false positive rates among the four models was similar, showing comparable stability.

3.6 Summary of findings

The prediction results of the M-score and F-score models were previously presented using scatter plots in Figures 1 and 2, with accompanying statistical analyses presented in Table 6. The M-score model achieves an accuracy of only 53.1%, with a false positive rate of 23.5%. However, the false negative rate is as high as 70.4%. The F-score model has an accuracy rate of only 50.0%, with a false positive rate of 0% and a false negative rate of 99.9%. The scatter plots and analysis of the M-score results reveal that the M-score predictions are largely inaccurate, barely outperforming random guessing. While the false positive rate remains low, suggesting a minimal misclassification of non-fraudulent companies as fraud, the false negative rate is alarmingly high at 70.4%, underscoring the model's relatively weak performance in detecting fraudulent companies. On the other hand, the F-score model's 50.0% accuracy is largely the result of classifying over 99.9% of the data as non-fraud. Despite the modeling dataset being selected in a 1:1 ratio of fraudulent to non-fraudulent samples, the F-score model's 50.0% accuracy is not a true indicator of its effectiveness. The 99.9% false negative rate highlights that the F-score model is almost ineffective, failing to accurately identify financial fraud in the samples. The low performance of the M-score and F-score models confirms the concerns that the authors had before they start the analysis.

Among the four machine learning models, the Gradient Boosting Decision Tree (GBDT) model performs the best in terms of both accuracy and stability. It achieves the highest average accuracy rate and exhibits the lowest variance in accuracy, false positive rate, and false negative rate. Its 65.49% accuracy rate is comparable to that of well-known fraud prediction models in the U.S. market (Dechow et al., 2011). While the Random Forest model has an average accuracy rate lower than the GBDT model by half a percentage point, it achieves the highest single accuracy rate among all the models, with an instance in the test where the prediction accuracy exceeded 70%. However, its large variance in both accuracy and false positive rates indicates less predictive stability, implying a greater risk of inconsistent performance and occasional low-accuracy prediction.

When considering false positive rates alone, the KNN and SVM models perform better. However, their low false positive rates come at the expense of high false negative rates, indicating a pronounced bias towards labeling fraudulent cases as non-fraud. Unlike the F-score model, which misclassifies nearly all fraudulent cases as non-fraud, the KNN and SVM models still correctly identify about half of the fraud samples, showing their substantial fraud detection capability. From another perspective, if a sample is identified as fraudulent by either the KNN or SVM model, it is more likely to be truly fraudulent compared to those identified by the GBDT or Random Forest models.

In summary, all four machine learning models perform relatively well in the financial fraud detection, effectively overcoming the limitations of the M-score and F-score models in the Chinese market. In practice, it is advised not to rely on a single model. By contrasting the more accurate GBDT and Random Forest models with the KNN and SVM models that have lower false positive rates, practitioners can secure a more robust and effective approach to fraud detection.

CONCLUSION

As data analytics advance and the market environment evolves, detecting financial fraud remains a critical and challenging area of research. This chapter aims to evaluate the effectiveness of traditional models (M-score and F-score) and machine learning models in detecting financial statement fraud in the Chinese market. The results have important implications for practitioners.

First, the authors show that the traditional fraud detection models are ineffective in the Chinese market, highlighting the need for models to be tailored to specific markets. This finding carries considerable implications for regulatory authorities, investors, and auditors, emphasizing the need for caution when applying the conventional models. For instance, investment institutions evaluating Chinese firms should adjust their risk assessment models according to the local context to better identify risks of financial fraud. To improve proactive oversight, securities regulators could implement a rolling monitoring system that leverages the machine learning models, trained on the chapter's selected features, to identify potential fraud at an early stage. Each quarter, listed firms would be assigned a risk score; those surpassing a critical threshold would enter a two-tiered supervisory process: (i) an automated alert requiring auditors to provide targeted documentation (e.g., account receivables, inventory) and (ii) prioritized on-site inspections of the highest-risk firms. Such a framework would enable regulators to allocate oversight resources more efficiently, strengthen market integrity, and maintain the balance between technological automation and professional judgment.

Second, the machine learning models proposed in this study offer more accurate tools for detecting financial fraud in the Chinese market. In specific, the GBDT and Random Forest models demonstrate high prediction accuracy, making them valuable for financial analysts and auditors. Additionally, the KNN and SVM models excel in minimizing false positives, presenting new opportunities for practical applications. For instance, during annual audits, audit firms can employ these high-accuracy models to conduct an initial assessment of client companies' financial data, identify potential fraud risks, and improve the efficiency of audit resource allocation.

Finally, this study highlights the potential benefits of integrating multiple models in real world applications. For instance, high-accuracy models like GBDT or Random Forest could be combined with models that have a low false-positive rate, such as KNN or SVM. Comparing results across different models allows for more informed decision-making, thereby improving the effectiveness and precision of fraud detection. In practice, audit firms could embed ensemble and SVM models into client acceptance and engagement planning. Prospective clients flagged as high risk would undergo enhanced due diligence, while ongoing audits could leverage a dual-model approach: low false-positive models (SVM, KNN) to minimize unnecessary procedures, and high-recall models (GBDT, Random Forest) to direct substantive testing toward areas most susceptible to misstatement or fraud. Such a combined approach would not only improve fraud detection but also support smarter allocation of audit resources.

While this study has yielded meaningful results and implications, it also has several limitations that suggest directions for future research. First, while the authors compare four machine learning models, developing other algorithms or ensemble methods may also offer favorable performance in fraud detection. Future studies could explore additional machine learning techniques to further enhance detection accuracy. Second, this chapter focuses on financial data as the M-score and F-score models do, so as to facilitate a relatively clean comparison of these conventional models with the machine learning modeling. Yet, incorporating non-financial factors, such as corporate governance structures and management behavior, could provide a more comprehensive approach to identifying fraudulent activities. Third, this chapter does not fully account for the impact of varying economic conditions on model performance. For instance, the COVID-19 pandemic has had a profound impact on the global economy, potentially influencing the models' predictive capabilities. Future research could assess the effectiveness of the models across different economic periods to evaluate their stability and adaptability. Lastly, since this study is based on the Chinese market, replicating the analysis for other emerging markets would be valuable. A cross-market comparison would help assess the generalizability of the models and the influence of diverse market conditions on fraud detection.

REFERENCES

Bao, Y., Ke, B., Li, B., Yu, Y. J., & Zhang, J. (2020). Detecting accounting fraud in publicly traded U.S. firms using a machine learning approach. *Journal of Accounting Research, 58*(1), 199–235. DOI: 10.1111/1475-679X.12292

Beneish, M. D. (1999). The detection of earnings manipulation. *Financial Analysts Journal, 55*(5), 24–36. DOI: 10.2469/faj.v55.n5.2296

Cecchini, M., Aytug, H., Koehler, G. J., & Pathak, P. (2010). Detecting management fraud in public companies. *Management Science, 56*(7), 1146–1160. DOI: 10.1287/mnsc.1100.1174

Chen, X., Cho, Y. H., Dou, Y., & Lev, B. (2022). Predicting future earnings changes using machine learning and detailed financial data. *Journal of Accounting Research, 60*(2), 467–515. DOI: 10.1111/1475-679X.12429

Dechow, P. M., Ge, W., Larson, C. R., & Sloan, R. G. (2011). Predicting material accounting misstatements. *Contemporary Accounting Research, 28*(1), 17–82. DOI: 10.1111/j.1911-3846.2010.01041.x

Gupta, R., & Singh Gill, N. (2012). A data mining framework for prevention and detection of financial statement fraud. *International Journal of Computer Applications, 50*(8), 7–14. DOI: 10.5120/7789-0889

Hajek, P., & Henriques, R. (2017). Mining corporate annual reports for intelligent detection of financial statement fraud – A comparative study of machine learning methods. *Knowledge-Based Systems, 128*, 139–152. DOI: 10.1016/j.knosys.2017.05.001

He, G. (2015). The effect of CEO inside debt holdings on financial reporting quality. *Review of Accounting Studies, 20*(1), 501–536. DOI: 10.1007/s11142-014-9305-8

He, G., Li, Z., & Shen, D. (2022). The role of earnings management in equity valuation. In Lee, C., & Lee, A. (Eds.), *Encyclopedia of Finance* (pp. 2061–2094). Springer Nature. DOI: 10.1007/978-3-030-91231-4_90

Krupa, J., & Minutti-Meza, M. (2022). Regression and machine learning methods to predict discrete outcomes in accounting research. *Journal of Financial Reporting, 7*(2), 131–178. DOI: 10.2308/JFR-2021-010

Palepu, K., & Healy, P. M. (2003). The Fall of Enron. *The Journal of Economic Perspectives, 17*(2), 3–26. DOI: 10.1257/089533003765888403

Raschka, S. (2018). Model evaluation, model selection, and algorithm selection in machine learning. *arXiv preprint*, available at: https://arxiv.org/abs/1811.12808 (accessed 19 December 2024).

Ratmono, D., Darsono, D., & Cahyonowati, N. (2020). Financial Statement Fraud Detection with Beneish M-Score and Dechow F-Score Model: An Empirical Analysis of Fraud Pentagon Theory in Indonesia. *International Journal of Financial Research*, *11*(6), 154. DOI: 10.5430/ijfr.v11n6p154

Rezaee, Z. (2005). Causes, consequences, and deterence of financial statement fraud. *Critical Perspectives on Accounting*, *16*(3), 277–298. DOI: 10.1016/S1045-2354(03)00072-8

Saleh, M. M. A., Aladwan, M., Alsinglawi, O., & Almari, M. O. S. (2021). Predicting Fraudulent Financial Statements Using Fraud Detection Models. *Academy of Strategic Management Journal*, *20*(3), 1–2.

Tarjo, , & Herawati, N.Tarjo and Herawati. (2015). Application of Beneish M-score models and data mining to detect financial fraud. *Procedia: Social and Behavioral Sciences*, *211*, 924–930. DOI: 10.1016/j.sbspro.2015.11.122

Wyrobek, J. (2020). Application of machine learning models and artificial intelligence to analyze annual financial statements to identify companies with unfair corporate culture. *Procedia Computer Science*, *176*, 3037–3046. DOI: 10.1016/j.procs.2020.09.335

Yadav, S., & Shukla, S. (2016). Analysis of k-fold cross-validation over hold-out validation on colossal datasets for quality classification. *2016 IEEE 6th International Conference on Advanced Computing (IACC)*, 78-83.

Zhang, C. A., Jiang, L., Cho, S., & Vasarhelyi, M. A. (2025). Predicting material misstatements using machine learning. *The Accounting Review*, *100*(6), 225–262. DOI: 10.2308/TAR-2024-0035

ENDNOTES

1 The authors select features from the previous one and two years for their machine learning modeling to optimize both data quality and model performance. Using features from three or more years ago would lead to substantial sample loss, rendering machine learning model training inefficient. Additionally, as shown in Table 8, features from the two years preceding a fraud incident exhibit low correlation significance and provide limited value to the model. Features from

even further back are unlikely to be utilized effectively. Existing studies (e.g., Hajek & Henriques, 2017) show that data from the year of a fraud incident possesses significant predictive value, reinforcing the notion that data from earlier years has limited practical utility.

2 The authors do the random sampling, based on Shenwan's secondary industry classification in China, to ensure a balanced and representative sample distribution across industries. The Shenwan Industry Classification is a sectorial categorization methodology widely used in the Chinese securities market (Li, 2022). Stratified sampling based on this industry classification not only adheres to the industry classification rules in the Chinese market, but also ensures sufficient granularity for stratification.

Chapter 3
How Artificial Intelligence Is Reshaping Business Transformation in Islamic Finance

Early Ridho Kismawadi
http://orcid.org/0000-0002-9420-5212
IAIN Langsa, Indonesia

Swati Gupta
Canterbury Institute of Management, Australia

Mohammad Irfan
http://orcid.org/0000-0002-4956-1170
Chandigarh University, India

ABSTRACT

This paper explores how AI is reshaping business transformation in Islamic finance, emphasizing its role in enhancing transparency, improving risk-sharing mechanisms, and promoting ethical investments. Through the integration of AI, particularly machine learning algorithms such as NGBoost, Islamic financial institutions are optimizing financing assessments, detecting fraud, and personalizing customer services. AI's ability to process vast amounts of data enables Islamic finance to overcome traditional limitations in scalability, efficiency, and market resilience. The paper presents qualitative research, including case studies of Islamic financial institutions that have adopted AI. The study provides valuable insights for policy-makers, financial institutions, and technology developers aiming to drive sustainable and ethical growth in the Islamic finance industry.

DOI: 10.4018/979-8-2600-1603-9.ch003

1. INTRODUCTION

Islamic finance has long been a key element in promoting ethical and stable financial practices. With basic principles such as the prohibition of usury (interest), risk sharing, and an emphasis on social justice, Islamic finance consistently offers an alternative to the conventional financial system that is vulnerable to speculative risks and unethical practices. Previous research has shown that Islamic finance is more resilient to financial crises compared to traditional financial systems. However, despite its success in promoting ethical financial practices, Islamic finance faces challenges in terms of technological innovation, scalability, and reaching a wider audience, including non-Muslims. As the digital landscape evolves, new opportunities arise for Islamic finance to integrate advanced technologies, such as artificial intelligence (AI), to drive business transformation and improve operational efficiency.

While there is a growing interest in the digital transformation of Islamic finance, especially in the adoption of technologies such as blockchain and AI, the intersection between these technologies and the basic principles of Islamic finance remains unexplored. There is still a lack of comprehensive research addressing how AI can be leveraged to enhance the core values of Islamic finance, such as ethical investment, transparency, and risk sharing, while contributing to the modernization and scalability of Islamic financial services.

This paper provides a unique perspective by examining the intersection between AI and Islamic finance, with a focus on how AI can transform business transformation within the Islamic finance sector. While the potential of AI in conventional finance has been extensively explored, the application of AI in Islamic finance, especially in aligning technological advances with sharia-compliant practices, has not been sufficiently studied. This paper aims to fill this gap by exploring how AI can improve the efficiency, transparency, and ethical basis of Islamic finance.

The logic behind this paper lies in the growing convergence between technology and finance, where AI plays a crucial role in business transformation. AI's ability to analyze big data sets, predict market trends, and optimize financial decisions is in line with the core values of Islamic finance, which aims to promote fairness, transparency, and ethical practices. By integrating AI, Islamic finance can not only modernize its operations but also increase its resilience to market volatility, ultimately offering a more efficient and affordable alternative compared to the conventional financial system.

This paper aims to answer the following question: How can artificial intelligence be leveraged to drive business transformation in Islamic finance while maintaining its ethical principles? Specifically, this paper explores the potential of AI to increase transparency, optimize financial risk sharing, and increase customer engagement, while still complying with sharia law.

The study uses a qualitative approach, combining case studies from Islamic financial institutions that have integrated AI in their operations with a review of the existing literature on the application of AI in financial services. Primary data was collected through interviews with experts in the field of Islamic finance and AI technology, providing a deeper understanding of the challenges and opportunities in combining these two domains. Secondary data is collected from reports, academic journals, and industry analysis.

The study found that AI has begun to be applied in Islamic finance for tasks such as financing assessment, fraud detection, and customer service automation. AI shows potential in improving the principles of transparency and fairness, key elements of Islamic finance, by enabling a more efficient and accountable decision-making process. The integration of AI in Islamic finance has the potential to increase financial inclusion, reduce operational costs, and improve the customer experience, while remaining in line with ethical principles.

Additional findings suggest that AI can play an important role in improving the governance structure of Islamic financial institutions. AI-based tools such as machine learning algorithms can help ensure that investments are compliant with sharia law by automating the screening of assets for ethical and legal considerations. This level of automation can improve the efficiency and accuracy of sharia compliance, which in turn increases investor confidence and institutional accountability.

This paper contributes to the growing knowledge of the digital transformation of Islamic finance by providing a comprehensive analysis of the role of AI in transforming business practices in the sector. This paper offers valuable insights for policymakers, financial institutions, and technologists interested in the potential of AI to drive sustainable and ethical growth in the Islamic finance industry. The paper is structured as follows: Part 2 reviews the literature on Islamic finance and AI, highlighting key developments and challenges in both areas. Part 3 describes the research methodology and data collection process. Part 4 presents key findings, while Part 5 discusses the implications of AI integration in Islamic finance. Finally, Section 6 concludes this paper with recommendations for future research and practice in this area.

2. LITERATURE REVIEW

2.1. Use of Ngboost (Natural Gradient Boosting) for Predictive Analysis

Artificial Intelligence (AI) has become an important catalyst in banking sector innovation, especially in predictive analytics used to improve decision-making.

AI, through various applications and solutions, serves to improve operational efficiency, data security, and the overall customer experience. This can be seen from the ease provided to customers in accessing services, faster processing of financial transactions, and increased accuracy in fraud detection, which are top priorities for financial institutions. The use of AI in machine learning, including algorithms such as NGBoost, provides advantages in financing risk assessment and default prediction. Research by Mor et al. demonstrates the effectiveness of AI algorithms in detecting risks in the banking sector, where NGBoost helps distinguish between legitimate and risky transactions, thereby helping banks maintain their financial health (Mor et al., 2022). Additionally, the integration of AI in banking systems can provide managers with better information about customer behavior, improve user experience and increase customer loyalty.

AI also facilitates the development of more in-depth predictive analytics tools, providing accurate insights into customer behavior. By leveraging machine learning algorithms, banks can identify patterns in previously undetected data, giving them an edge in designing products that suit customer needs. This concept includes the development of robo-advisors that assist clients in investment planning, risk analysis, and portfolio management. In the context of security, AI technology plays a role in improving the protection system against fraudulent activities. Timely fraud detection becomes crucial when transactions occur in real-time. AI algorithms are capable of processing a large number of transactions quickly, labeling suspicious transactions based on historical behavior and analysis of transaction patterns. This helps reduce financial losses and increase customer trust in financial institutions. Furthermore, AI can improve the customer experience by providing more personalized services through an intelligent customer relationship management (CRM) system. AI can help predict customer needs and provide relevant solutions based on previous interactions, thereby strengthening customer engagement with the banking system.

Ngboost is a boosting algorithm used to provide non-negative probabilities, allowing the model to measure predictions more accurately in contexts that require confidence estimates such as financing risk assessments and loan default predictions. NGBoost (Natural Gradient Boosting) has been recognized as an effective method in building predictive models that generate non-negative probabilities, which is particularly useful in the context of credibility estimation, especially in the banking sector for financing risk assessment and loan default prediction. This method is a more accurate approach in dealing with the uncertainty inherent in financial decision-making. NGBoost not only acknowledges instability in data, but also seeks to leverage it to generate more reliable information for financial institutions (Dichev et al., 2025). In the banking sector, financing risk assessment is a crucial aspect that affects the financial sustainability of institutions. The use of methods such as NGBoost can improve accuracy in predicting the likelihood of customer default.

NGBoost optimizes probability estimation models by reducing the risk of inaccurate predictions, a capability that has proven to be invaluable in complex financing data analysis (Dichev et al., 2025).

NGBoost's contribution to banking innovation is also evident in its ability to handle unbalanced datasets, a common challenge in financing assessments. These algorithms carefully allocate attention to underrepresented data groups, helping financial institutions to pay attention to customers with higher risk profiles. Khemakhem et al. emphasize that this approach has a significant impact on the development of models that are more equitable and responsive to the needs of end-users (Khemakhem et al., 2018). In the context of the use of AI and machine learning techniques, NGBoost contributes to creating transparency and accountability in risk assessment systems. The implementation of this algorithm in the management of the bank's customer portfolio can improve operational efficiency and effectiveness (Al-Araj et al., 2022). With more transparent modeling, stakeholders can identify the reasons behind certain decisions, thereby strengthening consumer trust in financial institutions.

Figure 1. Ngboost's Impact on Financial Institutions

In the context of financial institutions, the ability to make accurate predictions regarding risk and asset management is essential for effective decision-making. Ngboost (Natural Gradient Boosting), a natural gradient-based reinforcement method, offers significant potential in improving the accuracy of predictive models in the financial sector. Ngboost combines the boosting technique with a natural gradient learning approach, which allows the system to optimize predictions by considering the probabilistic distribution of the data, rather than just mean values or deterministic estimates. This approach is particularly useful in credit risk prediction, portfolio management, and cash flow forecasting, where the uncertainty and complexity of the relationships between variables are very high. For example, in credit risk analysis, Ngboost can provide the probability of success or failure of the borrower based on the various factors involved, allowing financial institutions to make more informed decisions when it comes to granting credit.

One of the main advantages of Ngboost is its ability to overcome uncertainty in data. In the financial world, uncertainty is inevitable, whether it's related to market fluctuations, monetary policy, or even consumer behavior that can't be predicted with certainty. Ngboost is designed to provide probabilistic distribution estimates, not just point numbers, that allow financial institutions to handle and account for these uncertainties in decision-making. This is especially important in the context of investment risk management and cash flow projections, where more realistic estimates based on probabilistic distributions are more beneficial than single predictions that can be highly biased.

Ngboost also offers flexibility in handling the non-linear relationships often encountered in financial data. Many factors in economics and financial markets, such as market trends, monetary policy, or consumer responses to price changes, have non-linear and complex relationships. Ngboost, with its ability to handle non-linear relationships through boosting, allows for more accurate and reliable modelling than techniques that can only handle simple linear relationships. This makes Ngboost particularly suitable for use in analyses that involve a variety of economic and financial factors interacting with each other in complex ways.

Additionally, Ngboost can handle large data efficiently, allowing financial institutions to analyse large amounts of transaction datasets. In a world that is increasingly reliant on big data, the ability to analyse and extract insights from customer transaction data, market movements, or macroeconomic data has become critical. Ngboost can be used to analyse various economic variables that affect investment risk or customer behaviour, providing more precise and data-rich predictions, ultimately improving the quality of decisions made by financial institutions.

One of the challenges often faced by traditional predictive models is overfitting, where the model is over-tuned to the trained data and is unable to generalize well on new data. Ngboost addresses this problem with a more adaptive approach to data distribution, allowing the model to further generalize to data that is not yet visible. This means that models built with Ngboost have a better capacity to deliver reliable results when applied to more varied real-world data, reducing the likelihood of prediction errors in unforeseen scenarios.

In credit risk analysis, Ngboost offers a great benefit by providing a probability of success or failure of the loan, which allows financial institutions to be more precise in assessing creditworthiness. This is very important in estimating the potential risks faced by financial institutions in providing credit to customers. With probabilistic distribution estimation, financial institutions can better manage their loan portfolios, reducing the risk of losses due to defaulted loans.

The implementation of Ngboost is also highly relevant in cash flow forecasting, which involves projecting uncertainties related to future income and expenses. By considering probabilistic distributions in cash flow predictions, Ngboost provides more realistic forecasts and allows financial institutions to conduct long-term financial planning with greater confidence. This helps them in planning more effective fund and investment management strategies, as well as reducing uncertainty that can affect long-term financial decisions.

Portfolio management can be improved by using Ngboost to analyse risk and return on investment. By taking probabilistic distributions into account, these models can provide a more comprehensive picture of the potential returns and risks associated with the various assets in the portfolio. This allows financial institutions to make more informed investment decisions, optimize asset allocation, and minimize risks that investors may face.

2.2. More Accurate Financing Assessment

AI, particularly through machine learning techniques, has helped banks in improving the accuracy of financing assessments. By utilizing algorithms such as neural networks and support vector machines, banks can analyze big data to determine the feasibility of customer financing more effectively (Khemakhem et al., 2018). This is especially important given the potential losses resulting from lending to high-risk borrowers. Khemakhem et al. (2018) mentioned that the application of AI in financing risk assessment not only provides better outcomes but also increases financial inclusion for individuals who were previously underserved by financial institutions (Khemakhem et al., 2018).

Figure 2. Application of AI in Islamic Finance

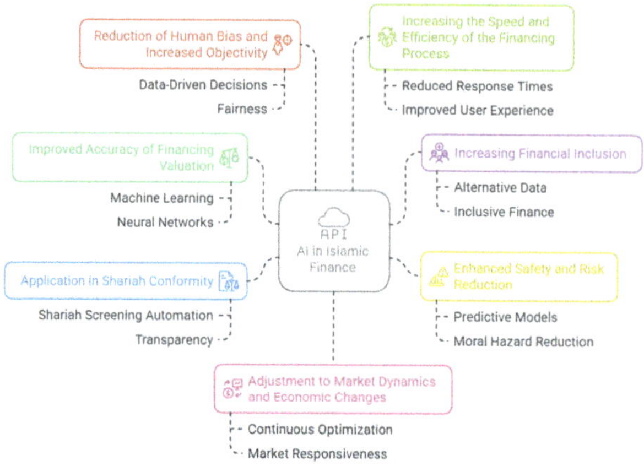

The application of Artificial Intelligence (AI) in financing assessment in the Islamic financial sector presents many benefits, ranging from increasing the accuracy of valuation to accelerating the entire financing process. One of the most important aspects is the improvement of the accuracy of financing valuations. Using Machine Learning (ML) techniques and Neural Networks, AI can process large amounts of data that include credit history, transaction data, demographic information, and even external data such as market trends or global economic conditions. This technology allows Islamic banks to build more sophisticated and accurate scoring models compared to traditional methods that rely solely on credit scores or financial statements. AI can also learn historical patterns to identify borrowers who tend to make payments on time or who are at high risk. For example, with the use of support vector machines (SVMs), borrowers can be classified into low, medium, or high-risk categories, allowing banks to make faster and more efficient financing decisions.

AI also plays a role in increasing financial inclusion, an important principle in Islamic finance. This technology provides an opportunity for individuals previously underserved by the traditional banking system, such as those with no credit history or access to banking services, to obtain financing. By using alternative data, such as transaction behaviour or mobile service usage, AI allows banks to assess the eligibility of borrowers who were previously deemed unworthy. This is in line with the goal of Islamic finance to provide equitable access to financing to underserved communities.

In terms of security and risk reduction, the application of AI is very beneficial in identifying risks early. With predictive models, AI can map possible payment failures based on historical data, making the financial system more proactive in dealing with financial issues. AI can help reduce moral hazard and adverse selection by considering holistic factors in the assessment, such as personal financial management patterns and future liquidity conditions. This allows financial institutions to make more informational and secure decisions.

AI also plays an important role in ensuring sharia compliance in financing. With the automation of sharia screening, Islamic banks can ensure that investments and financing provided are in accordance with sharia principles, such as the prohibition of riba (interest) and speculation (gharar). This automated process reduces human error and increases efficiency in maintaining sharia compliance, which in turn increases investor and customer trust. This implementation also increases transparency, one of the core principles in Islamic finance.

Furthermore, AI reduces human bias in financing assessments. In the conventional system, credit ratings are often influenced by subjective factors or personal biases. With AI, decisions are made based on objective data and pre-defined parameters, ensuring that financing is fairer and not affected by prejudice. This is especially important in Islamic finance, where fairness and transparency are the main principles.

Not only in terms of accuracy and fairness, AI also speeds up the entire financing process. AI can process data faster than manual evaluations, which allows financial institutions to make decisions faster. With reduced response times, customers can receive financing faster, improve user experience and operational efficiency.

AI can adapt to market dynamics and rapid economic changes. Machine learning algorithms can update and adjust valuation models based on the latest data and market conditions, allowing banks to better manage financing risks in volatile market conditions. The ability to continuously optimize processes based on learning from data ensures that financial institutions remain responsive to the ever-changing global marketplace.

2.3. More Effective Fraud Detection

Fraud in the banking sector can harm both banks and customers. AI contributes to fraud detection by analysing transaction patterns and identifying suspicious activity in real time (Mytnyk et al., 2023). The applied machine learning model can be programmed to learn from previous data, improving its ability to detect more astute fraud that may not be detectable by conventional methods. Research by Mytnyk et al. highlights that the utilization of AI in the recognition of fraudulent bank transactions can significantly improve the accuracy of fraud detection (Mytnyk et al., 2023).

Figure 3. AI in Banking Fraud Detection

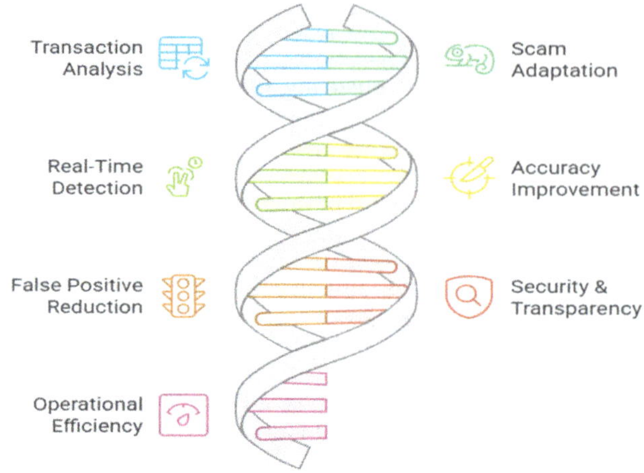

The application of Artificial Intelligence (AI) in fraud detection has significantly transformed the banking sector by providing advanced tools to identify suspicious activity. One of the key features of AI is its ability to analyse transaction patterns using algorithms such as machine learning (ML) and deep learning. These algorithms can process large amounts of transaction data in real-time, allowing for faster and more accurate detection of suspicious activity compared to traditional methods that rely on static rules and manual checks. AI systems learn from historical data and continue to refine its ability to identify patterns of behaviour that indicate fraud. In contrast to conventional systems that may flag transactions based on predetermined criteria, AI can uncover more complex and subtle anomalies that are most likely undetectable using legacy techniques. This real-time analysis enables faster response times to fraudulent activity, reduces potential financial losses, and improves security for banks and customers.

Another significant advantage of AI in fraud detection is its ability to adapt to new types of fraud. Traditional fraud detection systems often struggle to keep up with the rapid development of fraudulent schemes. However, AI machine learning models are designed to continuously evolve and improve themselves based on new data. The system can learn from previous fraud incidents and recognize new fraud patterns or tactics that were previously unknown. This adaptability ensures that AI remains effective even as fraud tactics become increasingly sophisticated, allowing the system to stay ahead of the curve and detect fraud that traditional systems might miss. As fraud schemes develop, AI adaptability is becoming critical to ensuring the long-term success of fraud detection systems.

AI's ability to detect fraud in real-time is another crucial feature. Real-time detection is essential to minimize the impact of fraudulent transactions, as it allows banks to intervene before fraud reaches a significant scale. This capability reduces the time delay between the occurrence of suspicious activity and the response of fraud detection systems, which is often a limitation of manual surveillance or rule-based systems. In comparison, AI can assess thousands of transactions per second, identifying and flagging anomalies almost instantly. This speed of detection is critical to prevent financial losses, and prompt intervention is essential to minimize risks to banks and their customers. This ability to act quickly is a breakthrough in reducing the consequences of fraud, making it a fundamental improvement compared to traditional methods.

In terms of accuracy, research by Mytnyk et al. (2023) emphasizes that AI can improve the precision of fraud detection, especially for more complicated or hidden cases that are difficult to detect with traditional methods. Traditional systems often fail to detect complex scams because they rely on simple algorithms or fixed rules. AI, on the other hand, uses advanced pattern recognition and anomaly detection to identify subtle discrepancies in transaction data that may not trigger attention in conventional systems. By continuously refining its algorithms based on past data, AI can detect patterns that were previously unknown or too complex to be discovered by traditional methods. This improves the accuracy of fraud detection, especially for cases where fraudulent behaviour is hidden or disguised in legitimate transaction volumes.

One of the significant benefits of AI in fraud detection is its ability to reduce false positives. In traditional fraud detection systems, false alarms often occur, where legitimate transactions are falsely considered suspicious. This leads to unnecessary delays and disruptions for customers, as well as increased investigation costs for banks. AI-based systems, however, are more precise in identifying real cases of fraud while reducing the incidence of false positives. By learning from the data and improving its accuracy over time, AI systems can make more reliable decisions, ensuring that only truly suspicious activity is flagged. This not only improves operational efficiency but also improves the customer experience by reducing unnecessary checks on legitimate transactions.

AI also contributes to the security and transparency of banking transactions. By improving the accuracy of fraud detection, banks can ensure that their financial operations are more secure, reducing the likelihood of undetected fraudulent activity. This has led to increased customer confidence in the bank's ability to protect their assets. Additionally, for institutions operating on Islamic financial principles, AI's role in ensuring transparency and fairness is critical. Islamic finance emphasizes ethical practices and transparency, and AI enhances this by providing a more robust and accountable fraud detection framework. By minimizing the risk of fraud and ensuring that all transactions are legitimate, AI helps maintain the integrity of

Islamic financial institutions and supports its commitment to fair and transparent financial practices.

Lastly, AI significantly improves operational efficiency within financial institutions. By automating the fraud detection process and reducing reliance on manual checks, banks can save time and resources previously used to verify and investigate suspicious transactions. AI's ability to automatically flag and investigate suspicious activity ensures that the entire fraud detection process is more streamlined and cost-effective. It also frees up human resources to focus on more complex tasks that require human intervention, further improving the overall efficiency of the bank's operations. Additionally, by reducing the potential for financial losses due to fraud, AI helps prevent significant economic damage, making bank operations more profitable and sustainable in the long run.

The integration of AI in fraud detection systems is a major advance compared to traditional methods. Its ability to analyse large amounts of transaction data in real-time, adapt to new fraud techniques, improve accuracy, reduce false positives, and improve operational efficiency makes it an invaluable tool for modern banking security. As fraud evolves, AI will play a crucial role in helping financial institutions protect their assets and those of their customers, ensuring security, transparency, and trust in the financial system. For institutions that adhere to ethical practices and transparency, such as those in the Islamic finance sector, AI offers a means to improve operational integrity and customer trust, which is in line with the core values of fairness and transparency in financial transactions.

2.4. Personalization of Financial Services Offerings

By applying AI to customer data analysis, banks can provide more personalized services tailored to individual needs. This includes developing relevant products and offering services that suit customer preferences based on analysis of their behaviour. Research shows that personalization can increase customer loyalty and strengthen the relationship between banks and customers (Jannah et al., 2024).

Figure 4. Personalization of financial services

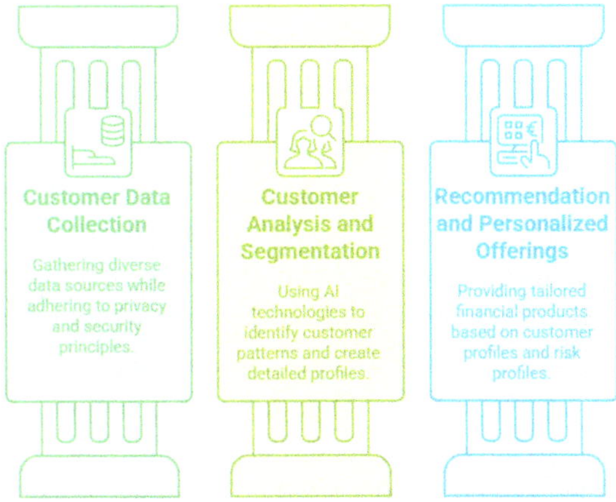

Personalization of financial services means the provision of products and services that are specifically designed to be tailored to each customer's unique preferences, needs, behaviours, and characteristics. This concept marks a significant shift from a traditional generic approach to a more customer-focused model individually, thanks to the support of cutting-edge technologies, particularly Artificial Intelligence (AI).

2.4.1. Customer Data Collection

The application of AI-based personalization in the banking sector is carried out through three main interrelated processes. The first stage is Customer Data Collection, where AI leverages various data sources, both structured and unstructured, to gather in-depth information about each customer. Structured data includes neatly organized information such as financial transaction history, credit score, demographic data (age, income, education, occupation), account balances, investment portfolios, and payment records. Meanwhile, unstructured data includes information that is more free in form but no less valuable, such as customer behaviour when doing online activities, patterns of use of digital banking applications, interactions on social media, customer feedback, and recorded communication with customer service. Because this data is sensitive, banks must collect it by upholding the principles of privacy protection and data security (Kismawadi, 2024), in line with Islamic law regarding privacy protection and Islamic business ethics, including the principles of transparency, clear consent, and protection from abuse.

2.4.2. Customer Analysis and Segmentation

The second stage is Customer Analysis and Segmentation, where various AI technologies such as Machine Learning (ML), Deep Learning, and Natural Language Processing (NLP) are used to accurately identify customer patterns, preferences, habits, and tendencies. Machine Learning algorithms systematically analyse data to find patterns of customer behaviour, such as saving habits, spending patterns, or investment preferences. Deep Learning, as an advanced branch of Machine Learning, enables the processing of complex data by detecting deep relationships between variables, including sentiment analysis from customer feedback or conversations on social media. Meanwhile, NLP helps AI understand text data, capture the meaning of conversations, and extract valuable insights from customer communications. As a result, banks are able to build highly detailed customer profiles, then group them into specific segments based on similarities in behaviour, life stage, risk profile, transaction style, or other characteristics. For example, a segment could be a young customer with a digital lifestyle, a conservative investor, or a group of customers who need long-term financial planning.

2.4.3. Recommendation and Personalized Offerings

The third stage is Recommendation and Personalized Offerings. At this stage, AI translates the results of analysis and segmentation into service recommendations that are predictive—predicting future financial needs—and prescriptive—providing concrete suggestions that best suit the customer's situation. For example, AI can automatically recommend sharia investment products such as sukuk or sharia mutual funds to customers with low to medium risk profiles. For customers who need financing, AI can recommend a mudharabah (profit-sharing) or murabahah (profit margin) based sharia financing product that best suits their financial capabilities and ethical preferences.

AI-based personalization is not only able to increase customer satisfaction, engagement, and loyalty, but also strengthen customer trust in banks. In the context of Islamic finance, this also ensures that the services provided remain in line with sharia principles such as justice, transparency, honesty, and protection of customer interests. Through this approach, Islamic banks can provide a more relevant, competitive, and sustainable financial services experience in the era of digital transformation.

Figure 5. Benefits of AI in Personalization of Financial Services

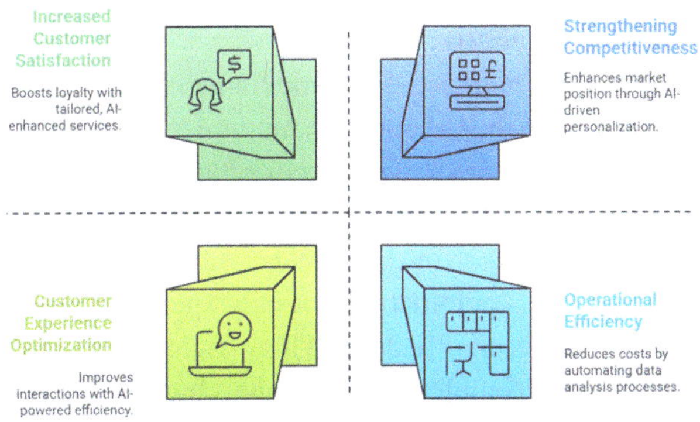

Personalization of financial service offerings brings various strategic benefits that have an impact on customer satisfaction, operational efficiency, and the competitiveness of financial institutions. First, increasing customer satisfaction and loyalty is one of the most tangible impacts of personalized services. By using AI, banks are able to understand the specific preferences, behaviours, and needs of each customer in depth. Services that are more relevant, on target, and in accordance with individual conditions make customers feel valued and cared for, not just considered as a number in the portfolio. In the context of Islamic finance, this is very important because the relationship between Islamic financial institutions and customers is not only based on business contracts, but must also be built on the principles of trust (amanah), mutual respect, and justice. The higher customer satisfaction, the greater the chance of building sustainable long-term loyalty.

Second, another significant benefit is the optimization of customer experience. With AI-based personalization, interactions between banks and customers become more effective, responsive, and efficient. For example, an automated recommendation system integrated with a sharia chatbot allows customers to get halal investment product suggestions such as sukuk or sharia mutual funds in real-time without having to visit a branch office or wait for a queue of conventional services. AI is able to learn about customers' common questions, provide quick answers, and help navigate various product options that suit their sharia preferences. All of this supports the creation of a service experience that is comfortable, fast, transparent, and in accordance with the principle of benefit (maslahah) in Islam, which is to provide the greatest benefits for customers.

Third, the application of AI in service personalization also plays an important role in strengthening the competitiveness of Islamic financial institutions in an increasingly competitive market. In the digital era, the young generation as the largest market segment now demands banking services that are fast-paced, accessible, and relevant to their lifestyles. Banks or Islamic financial institutions that are able to leverage AI to offer services tailored to individual needs will have a significant competitive advantage over institutions that still use a generic approach. It also supports the digital transformation agenda in the Islamic financial ecosystem, while proving that sharia principles can go hand in hand with modern technological advancements.

Fourth, from an internal perspective, AI contributes greatly to the operational efficiency of banks. Customer data analysis that was once time-consuming, labour-intensive, and at risk of human error can now be automated by AI systems with a higher level of accuracy. This automation not only speeds up work processes, but also reduces operational costs significantly. This efficiency is in line with the principle of taysir in Islam, which emphasizes the importance of providing convenience and simplifying the process, without neglecting compliance with sharia provisions. Thus, Islamic banks can provide high-quality services but still be efficient in terms of resources.

These four benefits are interconnected and support the achievement of the strategic goals of Islamic financial institutions: improving customer welfare and satisfaction, strengthening trust-based relationships, building a competitive advantage in the digital market, while maintaining business efficiency and sustainability. This is clear evidence that the application of advanced technologies such as AI, when designed with sharia values in mind, can be a very effective instrument to strengthen the Islamic financial ecosystem in the era of global digital transformation.

3. ARTIFICIAL INTELLIGENCE IN FORECASTING

AI enables the use of predictive analytics that can predict market trends and customer behaviour. This assists banks in making data-driven strategic decisions and gives them a competitive advantage in financial planning and risk mitigation (How et al., 2020). Ngboost, for example, is an algorithm that can improve financing risk analysis and decision-making based on more accurate probabilities (Khemakhem et al., 2018).

In an era where markets move very dynamically and complexly, the ability to predict the direction of stock prices, commodities, exchange rates, and overall market trends is a decisive factor in smart investment decision-making. Traditional methods such as technical or fundamental analysis have limitations in that they are usually only capable of processing a limited amount of historical data and are often unable to identify complex non-linear patterns. This is where AI, through Machine Learning (ML) and Deep Learning technologies, offers a competitive advantage (Dahiya et al., 2024; Goel et al., 2023; Meenakshi & Jayakani, 2025).

AI can process huge volumes of data, including structured data such as financial statements, historical prices, transaction volumes, as well as unstructured data such as market news, social media sentiment, and macroeconomic policy publications. With this approach, AI models can recognize hidden patterns, relationships between invisible variables, and early indicators that affect price fluctuations in the capital market. Deep learning, through its artificial neural networks, is highly effective in detecting highly complex patterns of multi-layered data, resulting in more adaptive and accurate predictions than traditional approaches.

The advantage of AI lies in its ability to self-learn. AI models can automatically update their prediction algorithms based on the latest data coming in at all times, so that it is able to adapt to rapidly changing market conditions. For example, if there is geopolitical turmoil, a sudden release of economic data, or investor sentiment changes drastically, an AI system can quickly capture those dynamics and upgrade predictions without having to manually reset.

In practice, investors or portfolio managers utilize the output of these predictions to formulate more appropriate investment strategies, reduce the risk of losses, and capture market opportunities more precisely. In the Islamic finance sector, AI-based forecasting can also be applied to monitor and predict the movements of Islamic investment instruments such as sukuk, sharia stocks, or sharia mutual funds, while adhering to sharia principles such as avoiding excessive speculation (*maysir*) and misleading information (*gharar*). Forecasting with AI is not just a technological innovation, but has become an important instrument to support smarter, faster, and real-time data-driven decision-making. This strengthens investor confidence, improves market efficiency, and supports the realization of a financial market ecosystem — including the Islamic capital market — that is more transparent, adaptive, and sustainable in the digital era.

Figure 6. Forecasting with AI

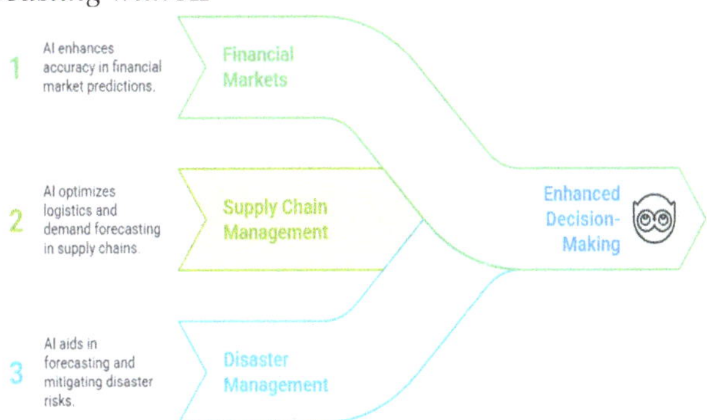

Supply Chain Management (SCM) is one of the important elements in the operational sustainability of many industrial sectors, ranging from manufacturing, retail, logistics, to Islamic finance that have a real sector financing portfolio such as trade and distribution of goods. In practice, supply chain challenges are often related to demand uncertainty, supply fluctuations, logistics delays, and the risk of disruptions that can trigger cost inefficiencies and lost market opportunities (Olasiuk et al., 2023). This is where the role of Artificial Intelligence (AI) becomes very significant because AI is able to optimize supply chain operations through improved accuracy of end-to-end planning, monitoring, and process control.

With real-time data analytics capabilities, AI can process a wide variety of large data—from market demand trends, logistics traffic conditions, weather, customer consumption trends, to changes in global trade policies. This technology predicts product demand more accurately through demand forecasting based on Machine Learning, so that companies can adjust production levels or purchase raw materials more efficiently. On the inventory management side, AI also helps minimize excess or understock by devising storage patterns that are adaptive to market changes. In terms of logistics, AI is able to identify the most optimal delivery routes, accurately estimate travel times, and detect potential risks of delivery delays due to bad weather or other emergency conditions.

From a risk management perspective, AI supports early detection of potential supply chain disruptions, such as raw material supply crises, drastic changes in logistics prices, or disruption to supplier partners. With these predictive insights, supply chain managers can prepare mitigation plans faster, switch distribution lines, or find alternative suppliers before risk develops into a major problem.

In the context of the financial industry, especially Islamic banking, which often finances real sector activities through schemes such as *murabahah* (buying and selling), *salam* (order financing), or *istisna'* (manufacturing financing), AI in supply chain management supports the smooth flow of financing by minimizing the risk of delays, wasted costs, and losses to customers' businesses. This indirectly supports the principles of *maslahah* (benefit) and *amanah* (trust) between Islamic banks, business partners, and their customers. The application of AI in Supply Chain Management not only supports operational cost efficiency, but also creates a supply chain that is more adaptive, resilient, and responsive to risks, supports better decision-making, and maintains the trust of stakeholders across the business ecosystem.

Disaster Management is a crucial field that increasingly utilizes the predictive capabilities of Artificial Intelligence (AI) to anticipate, respond, and mitigate risks arising from natural disasters and other emergency conditions (Ishrat et al., 2025). By leveraging historical and real-time data—such as weather patterns, geological data, satellite data, and IoT sensors in the field—AI can process information at scale to detect patterns that precede disasters, such as earthquakes, floods, tropical storms, wildfires, or landslides. Through Machine Learning technology, AI is able to create predictive models that continuously learn from the latest data so that potential risks can be anticipated earlier with a much better level of accuracy than traditional methods.

The advantage of AI lies in the speed of analysis and the ability to provide early warning to authorities, the public, and business people. Thus, evacuation, asset rescue, infrastructure protection, or supply chain adjustments can be carried out in a more planned manner to minimize the impact of physical, financial, and human safety losses. In the context of industries, including the financial sector, AI capabilities in disaster management support business continuity plan planning and risk management so that business operations can continue to run even in the face of emergencies.

For the financial industry—especially Islamic banks or finance institutions that heavily fund real sectors such as agriculture, logistics, or property—AI in disaster management also supports a more comprehensive portfolio risk evaluation. For example, banks can monitor potential flood risks in *mudharabah* or *istisna'* financing project areas, and anticipate their impact through financing restructuring or mitigation plans. This is in line with the principles of prudence (*tahthir*), justice (*'adl*), and protection of benefits (*maslahah*) for customers affected by disasters. The application of AI in Disaster Management not only impacts human safety and business continuity, but also contributes to creating a more resilient, adaptive, and aligned financial and business ecosystem with human values and social responsibility.

4. AI IN RISK MANAGEMENT

4.1. Financial Risk Management

Financial Risk Management is one of the most critical functions in the financial industry, including conventional banking and Islamic finance. Risks in the financial world include various aspects, ranging from financing risk, market risk, operational risk, to fraud risk (Bansal et al., 2024; Faisal et al., 2025; Katamaneni et al., 2024; Khan et al., 2025). In traditional practice, risk identification, assessment, and mitigation are often done manually with conventional statistical approaches, which tend to take a long time, rely solely on historical data, and are less adaptive to rapidly changing market conditions. The Artificial Intelligence (AI) technological revolution has significantly changed this paradigm (Kismawadi et al., 2023). With advanced analytics capabilities, AI delivers models that can improve accuracy in the identification, assessment, and mitigation of financial risks. First, in the aspect of risk identification, AI can analyse large and diverse amounts of data—both structured data such as financial statements, loan history, and unstructured data such as digital transaction activities, customer behaviour, or communication patterns on social media. Through Machine Learning (ML) and Deep Learning, AI can detect anomalous patterns that may be missed by manual approaches. For example, AI systems can automatically monitor suspicious transactions to detect potential fraud in real-time.

Second, in risk assessment, AI helps improve the accuracy of customer credit risk evaluation. Traditional credit scoring models generally rely only on fixed variables such as income, employment, or credit history. On the other hand, AI models are able to enrich assessments by considering non-traditional variables, such as digital payment behaviour, routine spending patterns, and customer interactions on online platforms. Thus, default risk can be predicted more accurately, even for prospective customers who do not have a long credit history (*thin file customers*). Third, AI is also revolutionizing market risk management and portfolio optimization. With predictive analysis capabilities, AI can model market volatility more dynamically. This model is able to process global market data in real-time, estimate asset price movements, analyse correlations between financial instruments, and provide recommendations for portfolio adjustments to minimize the risk of loss. AI can even simulate *stress testing* to assess the resilience of the portfolio to extreme market scenarios, such as exchange rate fluctuations, fluctuations in commodity prices, or changes in monetary policy.

One of the main advantages of AI is the ability to provide insights in real-time. Traditional approaches often rely on risk reports generated periodically (Kismawadi et al., 2023), e.g. weekly or monthly. AI, with its powerful computing architecture, allows financial institutions to monitor risk profiles directly and respond to potential threats quickly. This provides a competitive advantage because mitigation decisions can be made in a timely manner, before the risk develops into a larger loss.

In the context of Islamic finance, the application of AI to risk management also needs to consider sharia principles, such as fairness (*'adl*), prudence (*tahthir*), and clarity of transactions (*gharar*). For example, AI models for Islamic financing risk evaluation can help minimize *asymmetric information* between Islamic banks and customers, as well as ensure that every financing decision is made based on objective and transparent risk assessments.

AI is not just a technological tool, but a strategic instrument to build a financial risk management system that is more resilient, predictive, adaptive, and aligned with modern market dynamics. AI's advantages in detecting hidden patterns, providing real-time data-driven predictions, and rapidly adjusting risk mitigation strategies make it an essential element in the digital transformation of financial risk management, both in the conventional sector and in the Islamic finance ecosystem.

Figure 7. Risk Management with AI

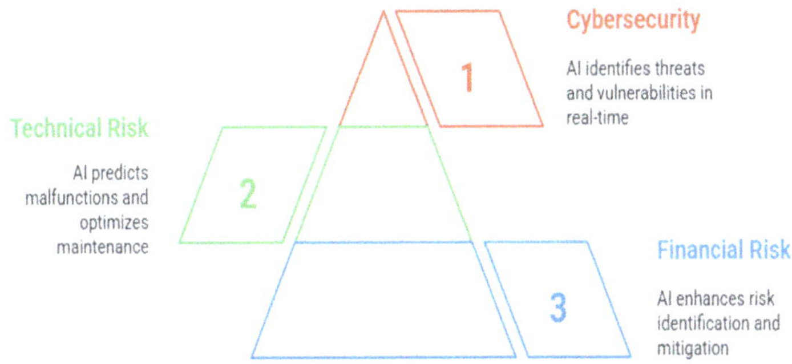

4.2. Technical Risk Management

Technical Risk Management is basically the management of risks related to technical and operational aspects, such as the reliability of systems, equipment, or supporting infrastructure (Shkodinsky et al., 2024). In technology-intensive industries such as manufacturing and energy, AI has proven to be effective in helping detect anomalies early, predict potential equipment breakdowns, and optimize maintenance schedules to minimize operational disruptions. This proactive approach has a direct impact on cost efficiency, operational sustainability, and faster decision-making based on real-time data. Interestingly, the principles and approaches of Technical Risk Management are also very relevant for the financial industry, although the context is different. In the financial sector, *technical risk* is not only related to physical machines, but more to the reliability of information technology infrastructure (IT systems), digital transaction networks, core banking systems, cloud infrastructure, and digital banking applications. Technical risks in the financial sector include server downtime that causes online banking services to be inaccessible, data security system vulnerabilities that open up opportunities for hacking (cyber-attacks), or real-time transaction system failures that can harm customers and bank reputations.

This is where AI plays a strategic role. With real-time monitoring capabilities connected to thousands of operational data points, AI is able to detect technical anomalies in IT systems, such as abnormal traffic spikes, suspicious access patterns, or potential bugs that could cause system crashes. AI also supports the concept of predictive maintenance in banking IT infrastructure. For example, AI can predict when servers will experience overload or when hardware needs to be replaced, so that corrective actions can be taken before major outages occur.

In the context of Islamic finance, the implementation of AI-supported Technical Risk Management is increasingly important because every technical disruption in sharia digital banking services can have a direct impact on customer trust (amanah) and service quality that should be transparent, efficient, and in accordance with sharia principles (maslahah). System failures can trigger financial losses, transaction delays, or even violations of the principle of openness (*gharar*). Therefore, Islamic financial institutions must ensure that their systems are always reliable, secure, and monitored on an ongoing basis.

The AI-based Technical Risk Management approach supports the financial industry in maintaining the reliability of digital infrastructure, improving data and transaction security, and ensuring seamless 24/7 service continuity. This not only reduces the potential for operational and reputational losses, but also serves as proof that digital transformation in the financial sector, especially Islamic finance, is carried out with the principles of prudence and high trust, in line with sharia values.

4.3. AI and Cybersecurity

Cybersecurity is one of the crucial aspects in the modern financial industry ecosystem that relies heavily on digital infrastructure. Cyber threats such as malware attacks, data hacking, phishing, ransomware, and customer identity theft can cause significant financial losses and damage the reputation of financial institutions. In this context, the application of Artificial Intelligence (AI) brings a significant leap in system security efforts because AI has the ability to detect potential threats and vulnerabilities in real-time, which traditional approaches do not have (Ishrat et al., 2025). By leveraging technologies such as Machine Learning and behavioural analytics, AI systems can continuously monitor network activity, recognize normal access patterns, and then detect anomalies or suspicious activity that have the potential to become cyberattacks. For example, AI is able to identify unauthorized login attempts from unnatural locations, detect brute force attacks, and analyse data traffic to anticipate sensitive information leaks. The advantage of AI lies in its speed in providing early warning signals and recommendations for mitigation actions, so that security responses can be made immediately before threats develop into serious incidents. In the financial industry, this is vital because the digital banking system operates 24/7 and serves millions of transactions that must be guaranteed security.

For Islamic financial institutions, the protection of customer data is not only a regulatory obligation but also closely related to the principles of amanah and hifdz al-sirr (maintaining confidentiality) in Islam. Data leakage or misuse of customers' personal information is contrary to Islamic business ethics and can undermine the *trust* that is the basis of the long-term relationship between banks and customers. Therefore, the application of AI in cybersecurity supports Islamic financial institutions to ensure that data and transaction security is always maintained, digital services continue to run smoothly without the disruption of cyberattacks, and all activities continue to comply with the principles of justice and transparency in accordance with sharia. Thus, AI not only serves as a protective technology, but also as an essential element in realizing a reliable, secure, and integrity digital financial ecosystem.

5. CONCLUSION

The application of Artificial Intelligence (AI) in the Islamic financial sector has a significant impact in improving the efficiency, transparency, and operational accountability of Islamic financial institutions. With AI's ability to analyse large amounts of data and predict market trends, financial institutions can conduct more precise financing assessments, faster fraud detection, and personalize services for customers. This not only speeds up business processes, but also ensures that sharia principles are maintained, such as fairness, transparency, and prudence in risk management. AI also supports the modernization of Islamic financial institutions' operations, reduces costs, and improves the customer experience, strengthening their competitiveness in an increasingly competitive global market.

The application of Artificial Intelligence (AI) in Islamic finance has various important implications for various related parties. For Islamic financial institutions, the adoption of AI can improve operational efficiency and precision in decision-making, particularly in financing assessment and risk management. This technology also enables financial institutions to provide more personalized services, increase transparency, and strengthen accountability in accordance with Sharia principles. On the other hand, AI also plays a role in expanding financial inclusion by providing wider access for individuals who were previously underserved by the conventional banking system. For regulators and policymakers, the adoption of AI demands the creation of a regulatory framework that can support the adoption of this technology without compromising Sharia principles. They must ensure that AI technology is used in a manner that complies with Sharia law, while maintaining integrity and ethics in financial transactions. On the customer side, customers will benefit from faster, more efficient, and more convenient services, while strengthening trust in Islamic financial institutions.

Based on the findings in this study, there are several recommendations that can be applied to increase the effectiveness of AI adoption in Islamic finance. First, Islamic financial institutions need to continue to invest in the development of AI technologies that are compliant with Sharia principles, such as through the development of algorithms that can automate investment screening and financing in accordance with Sharia law. This will improve operational efficiency and ensure that the principles of justice, transparency, and Sharia compliance are maintained. Second, it is important for regulators to establish clear and comprehensive guidelines regarding the application of AI in Islamic finance. These guidelines should include the protection of customers' personal data, system integrity, and compliance with Sharia principles. Regulators also need to develop a framework to oversee and monitor the use of AI in this sector to avoid potential abuse. Third, Islamic financial institutions should increase collaboration with technology developers and academics to ensure that the AI technology implemented is truly in line with market needs and supports the sustainability of the Islamic finance industry. Education and training for workers in the Islamic finance sector related to AI technology need to be strengthened, to ensure better understanding and application of the technology in the future.

Further research can expand this study by examining more deeply the practical challenges faced by Islamic financial institutions in implementing AI, especially in terms of compliance with Sharia standards. Further studies can explore the long-term impact of the use of AI on financial inclusion, particularly in improving financial access for marginalized segments of society.

Further research can also explore the potential of integrating AI with other technologies, such as blockchain and big data, to improve efficiency and security in Islamic financial transactions. Further testing of more advanced AI algorithms and their relevance and compliance with Sharia law could also be an interesting topic to investigate. More in-depth research is needed on the ethical aspects of the application of AI in Islamic finance, focusing on how this technology can improve social and economic welfare without causing inequality or harming certain parties. This research can provide broader insights into how technology can play a role in achieving equitable economic and social goals within the framework of Sharia.

REFERENCES

Al-Araj, R., Haddad, H., Shehadeh, M., Hasan, E., & Nawaiseh, M. (2022). The effect of artificial intelligence on service quality and customer satisfaction in Jordanian banking sector. *WSEAS Transactions on Business and Economics, 19*, 1929–1947. DOI: 10.37394/23207.2022.19.173

Bansal, U., Bharatwal, S., Bagiyam, D. S., & Kismawadi, E. R. (2024). Fraud detection in the era of AI: Harnessing technology for a safer digital economy. In *AI-driven decentralized finance and the future of finance* (pp. 143–164).

Dahiya, V. K., Dahiya, R., Dev, R., Sharma, A., Sharma, A., Kiran, P. B. N., Yadav, P. S., & Yadav, S. (2024). Exploring the role of artificial intelligence in predictive analytics for financial markets. In *Proceedings of the 2024 International Conference on Computing, Sciences and Communications (ICCSC 2024)*. DOI: 10.1109/ICCSC62048.2024.10830442

Dichev, A., Zarkova, S., & Angelov, P. (2025). Machine learning as a tool for assessment and management of fraud risk in banking transactions. *Journal of Risk and Financial Management, 18*(3), 130. DOI: 10.3390/jrfm18030130

Faisal, S. M., Khan, W., & Ishrat, M. (2025). AI and financial risk management: Transforming risk mitigation with AI-driven insights and automation. In *Artificial intelligence for financial risk management and analysis* (pp. 281–305).

Goel, M., Tomar, P. K., Vinjamuri, L. P., Reddy, G. S., Al-Taee, M., & Alazzam, M. B. (2023). Using AI for predictive analytics in financial management. In *Proceedings of the 2023 3rd International Conference on Advance Computing and Innovative Technologies in Engineering (ICACITE 2023)* (pp. 963–967). DOI: 10.1109/ICACITE57410.2023.10182711

How, M., Cheah, S., Khor, A., & Chan, Y. (2020). Artificial intelligence-enhanced predictive insights for advancing financial inclusion: A human-centric AI-thinking approach. *Big Data and Cognitive Computing, 4*(2), 8. DOI: 10.3390/bdcc4020008

Ishrat, M., Khan, W., & Faisal, S. M. (2025). AI and risk forecasting: Leveraging AI for environmental, social, and governance compliance. In *Artificial intelligence for financial risk management and analysis* (pp. 307–334).

Jannah, N., Bahri, M. I., Kismawadi, E. R., & Handriana, T. (2024). The effect of green brand image and green satisfaction on green brand equity mediated green trust outpatient's. *Quality - Access to Success, 25*(198), 381–390. DOI: 10.47750/QAS/25.198.40

Katamaneni, M., Agrawal, P., Veera, S., Sahoo, A. K., Sidhu, K. S., & Hasan, M. F. (2024). AI-based risk management in financial services. In *Proceedings of the 2024 2nd International Conference on Computational and Characterization Techniques in Engineering and Sciences (IC3TES 2024).*

Khan, W., Ishrat, M., & Faisal, S. M. (2025). AI-powered risk assessment: Innovations, challenges, and future prospects. In *Artificial intelligence for financial risk management and analysis* (pp. 59–91).

Khemakhem, S., Said, F., & Boujelbène, Y. (2018). Credit risk assessment for unbalanced datasets based on data mining, artificial neural network and support vector machines. *Journal of Modelling in Management, 13*(4), 932–951. DOI: 10.1108/JM2-01-2017-0002

Kismawadi, E. R. (2024). Sustainable Islamic financial inclusion: The ethical challenges of generative AI in product and service development. In *Exploring the ethical implications of generative AI* (pp. 237–258).

Kismawadi, E. R., Irfan, M., Al Muddatstsir, U. D., & Abdulkarim, F. M. (2023). Fintech innovations: Risk mitigation strategies in Islamic finance. In *Fintech applications in Islamic finance: AI, machine learning, and blockchain techniques* (pp. 35–58).

Meenakshi, A., & Jayakani, S. (2025). Exploring the impact of artificial intelligence on financial risk prediction and management. In *AIP Conference Proceedings* (Vol. 3306). DOI: 10.1063/5.0276529

Mor, S., Aneja, R., Madan, S., & Gupta, S. (2022). Artificial intelligence and loan default: The case of commercial banks in India. *Strategic Change, 31*(6), 571–580. DOI: 10.1002/jsc.2529

Mytnyk, B., Tkachyk, O., Shakhovska, N., Fedushko, S., & Syerov, Y. (2023). Application of artificial intelligence for fraudulent banking operations recognition. *Big Data and Cognitive Computing, 7*(2), 93. DOI: 10.3390/bdcc7020093

Olasiuk, H., Kumar, S., Singh, S., Nagpal, G., & Ganushchak, T. (2023). Exploring the thematic clusters of artificial intelligence applications in supply chains using topic modelling and text mining: A machine learning insight. In *Proceedings of the 4th IEEE International Conference on Smart Technologies in Computing, Electrical and Electronics (ICSTCEE 2023).* DOI: 10.1109/ICSTCEE60504.2023.10584847

Ridho Kismawadi, E., Irfan, M., & Shah, S. M. A. R. (2023). Revolutionizing Islamic finance: Artificial intelligence's role in the future of industry. In *The impact of AI innovation on financial sectors in the era of industry 5.0* (pp. 184–207).

Shkodinsky, S., Syrovatskaya, V., & Khokhoeva, Z. (2024). The role of artificial intelligence in forecasting and managing technical risks. *Reliability: Theory and Applications, 19*(Special Issue 6), 210–216. DOI: 10.24412/1932-2321-2024-681-210-216

Chapter 4
Bias Mitigation and Algorithmic Fairness in AI-Driven Financial Decision Systems

Taiwo Shotunde
http://orcid.org/0009-0003-2189-4314
University of Oxford, UK

ABSTRACT

Technological advances in AI bring efficiency to financial systems but also amplify algorithmic bias. This chapter examines data, model, and feedback loop biases, illustrated through cases of predatory lending and discriminatory insurance. It explores fairness metrics such as demographic parity, equalised odds, and individual fairness, alongside mitigation strategies in pre-processing, in-processing, and post-processing. Beyond technical fixes, the chapter stresses ethical governance, regulatory frameworks like the EU AI Act, and Ethics-by-Design approaches. Special attention is given to the Global South and Gulf Cooperation Council, where data scarcity and cultural constraints complicate fairness, yet also foster innovative, context-sensitive solutions. The chapter concludes that algorithmic fairness is central to socially responsible finance, requiring both technical precision and ethical oversight to sustain trust and inclusion in evolving financial markets.

1. INTRODUCTION

There has been a long-standing desire in financial markets to achieve a perfect and instantaneous efficient system. Human errors, biases, and exhaustion must all

DOI: 10.4018/979-8-2600-1603-9.ch004

be mitigated to achieve this efficiency. Advancements in technology today have partially achieved this goal. Artificial Intelligence can now implement algorithmic trading that executes transactions in a fraction of a second, and has credit scoring machine learning models that can evaluate someone's creditworthiness in a handful of seconds. Significant risks accompany the imminent globalisation and systematisation of finance through AI. This risk involves systemic collapse and individual harms, such as an automated application denial. Picture a young entrepreneur living in Dubai. Automatically, an application for a business loan is denied. She has this as an outcome because the system relies on outdated data, underneath which new market entrants lack credit histories. Another hypothetical example is about a businesswoman who resides in Riyadh. Her driving record, as well as the insurance record, is irrelevant to the conversation. In this case, the primary focus of attention is the exorbitant fee for the insurance premium, which is unjustifiably high and substantially disproportionate to the cost a man would be required to pay. This is all due to the driving behaviour assessed by the algorithm with the 'gender bias.' Sadly, these examples are not random but show the state of finances in algorithmic form.

Automated AIs base their predictions on the amount of capital, insurance, or investment created from millions of data points, and the AIs have been programmed to analyse. Even with all this data, AIs are programmed with an underlying bias which inhibits them from remaining neutral. These systems learn from patterns in historical data; in doing so, they risk encoding the biases and inequalities we have worked so hard to overcome (Barocas & Selbst, 2016). A central challenge is balancing the profit-oriented efficiency of algorithmic finance with the principle of fairness. The consequences of failing to bridge this gap are consequential. On the one hand, the undignified experiences of individuals subjected to unfair rejections are bad enough. Conversely, the risk of systemic inequality compounded by AI is far worse. This type of social discrimination erodes the public trust in financial institutions, and, along with the emerging EU AI Act, incentivises heavy scrutiny and regulation. It also disproportionately affects large segments of the population, undermining financial inclusion goals on a global level (Zetzsche et al., 2020).

This chapter's focus is to prove that algorithmic bias, in this context, is a risk that is far more consequential than a mere technical glitch. It undermines the stability and legitimacy of the financial ecosystem. Reducing this risk requires a complex, intertwined solution. The challenge of bias detection and mitigation involves various sophisticated technological frameworks. However, these frameworks remain abstract without a pervasive bias, an ethical governance framework and contextual sensitivity, especially in the developing world. To start traversing this rugged terrain, the chapter will first break the bias in artificial intelligence in finance. Then it will equip the readers with a new set of fairness instruments, explaining the available techniques and approaches to discrimination predictive analytics. Finally, it will outline a framework for mitigating bias through ethical policy, operational governance, and regional context, establishing a foundation for equitable financial innovation.

2. LITERATURE REVIEW

2.1. The Foundations of Fairness in Financial AI

The continuing attempt to comprehend and lessen the impact of algorithmic bias is no longer the focus of new studies. It is developing much faster than the pace of new interdisciplinary studies. This emerging framework provides financial entities with practical and conceptual insights to address these issues. Conversations about covering the resource start with the controversial yet widely accepted fact that algorithms are impartial. The analytic contributions of Barocas and Selbst (2016) show with nuance how the architecture of big-data analytic systems can result in 'disparate impact.' They contend that a modicum of bias can, and often is, integrated at each stage in the machine learning workflow in the data value chain - historical biases are coupled with data assemblies and target variables that may encode proxy discrimination. That is especially true in finance, where innumerable models are trained using data spanning centuries of historical records of lending, hiring, and policing. For instance, zip code logic can and will serve as a proxy for race, effectively digitising the practice of redlining and disallowing entire communities equitable access to financial resources. Friedler et al. (2019) prescribe the problem under allocative harm (the denial of a resource to someone) and representational harm (the imbalanced stereotyping of a group), which gives the much-needed vocabulary for understanding the kinds of harms biased financial AI can cause.

A second strand of literature began formulating fairness as a measurable construct to counter these harms. This scholarship supplies the vital instruments to translate ethical apprehensions into a palpable result. Hardt et al. (2016) on "equality of opportunity" in supervised learning is often credited with an epoch-defining contribution when proposing that a classifier should equally make errors on different protected groups (e.g., loan defaults should be equally predicted for men and women). This principle, known as equalised odds, is more constrained than older approximations such as demographic parity, which insists on a minimum approval rate that often results in a fairness-accuracy trade-off in lending to lower-risk, more discriminatory demographics. Earlier, Dwork et al. (2012) proposed an "individual fairness" notion, claiming that cases ought to be treated alike, with the accompanying logic of risk-based pricing. This is often the target of criticism due to a glaring absence of embodiment. The presence of these competing and, more often than not, nonoverlapping definitions (Kleinberg et al., 2016) gives a more poignant message: fairness is not, in any sense, technical.

Selecting a metric involves a contextual decision with the inherent potential for bias, the balancing act that any financial institution must perform while keeping context in mind. At the same time, a significant debate has begun on using these technologies in finance from an ethical standpoint. Legal, economic, and philosophical scholars have voiced concerns over the possible threats to autonomy, justice, and transparency. In the work of Butt (2024), the opaque accountability and due process of opaque 'black box' models are discussed in detail. An algorithm denying a loan raises 'the right to an explanation', a hazy and complex balancing of the fundamental rules of consumer protection law (Goodman & Flaxman, 2017). In addition, ethical issues must be considered on a broader scale than the individual. Multiple institutions may use similar biased models to withhold credit from whole productive industries/communities systematically. This stifles growth and adds to the financial system's newly created, concentrated risks.

Still, international regulators and standard-setters have continued to pay attention to the potential for systemic risk, with some noting the emergence of a "fourth pillar" in the body of literature. In reports prepared by the Bank for International Settlements (BIS) and the Financial Stability Board (FSB), it is suggested that the procyclicality and herding behaviour phenomena might be positively reinforced and intensified through the use of "black box" homogeneous AI models. In the use case proposed by the Basel Committee on Banking Supervision (BCBS) (2024), it is implied that strong and defensible governance of the models is needed, partly because the operational risk that stems from model bias, and thus enduring discrimination, is high. Authors and institutions have been expanding on the works of the said think-tank, with the Alan Turing Institute (2023) arguing that there exists a component of prudent risk management, the absence of which algorithmic discrimination still carries undue and unrecognised reputational damage, legal, and public trust penalties, and thus, risks that compromise the stability of the firm.

Despite the available literature, the gap which persists needs to be addressed. The central focus remains within Western economies regarding the theories, metrics, and case studies. These economies have long perfected the digitisation of finance and the development of regulatory frameworks and have long had access to them. All the emerging markets, especially the Gulf Cooperation Council (GCC) region, face these issues. Such regions possess unique distance conditions, including financial ecosystems that are less digitally advanced and evolving at a high rate, unique structures such as a high-growth population and social frameworks, and cultural idiosyncrasies laden with the principles of Islamic finance that refrain from usury and promote PLS financing. All the foundational works on bias have yet to be tested in these conditions. What payment systems' "doctrine of fairness" in a credit scoring model needs to be evaluated, especially in the GCC, which has a sizeable expatriate population and a fluid workforce. In the context of developing countries, what are the parameters that proxy fairness, and how do they relate to local understandings of the protected class? All the aforementioned aspects. The existing explained toolkit is relevant. However, the toolkit appears to be mainly suited to Western economies. The next challenge for practitioners is adapting these tools for the distinct context of emerging markets, where algorithmic fairness is the hardest and the most needed, uncharted and complicated territories.

3. UNDERSTANDING BIAS IN FINANCIAL AI

For effective algorithmic bias mitigation, its complexity needs to be accepted. As we will explain, Bias is not a single issue but a multifaceted problem that manifests at various stages of financial AI systems, each with its own mechanics and consequences. Realising this typology is the first step for any institution earnest about building equitable technology.

3.1. Categories of Biases

Data Bias: Bias most often seeps in through the data itself. Historical data, while rich in predictive potential, often contains ingrained societal inequalities. Historical data is a snapshot of the past, including the persistent social inequalities and discriminatory practices of the past (Nuti, 2019). A model predicting decades of loan applicants from a bank steeped in redlining—describing the systemic disregard of services to the dominant minority neighbourhoods—will learn to associate specific zip codes with a higher risk. This is historical bias (Mehrabi et al., 2021). A model, even without sensitive attributes such as race and gender, hunts for proxies such as postal address, occupation, and browsing history describing the protected attribute. For instance, some findings from Bartlett et al. (2022) show that even without the variable gender, a model still deduced and discriminated lending outcomes through factors related to a borrower's field of study. A second data-related problem is the underrepresentation of relevant attributes in the data problem, which is also Representational Bias.

This is especially pertinent in developing economies, where "unbanked" populations are, by definition, absent in traditional credit databases. The problem of data bias is particularly pronounced in regions with vast populations unserved by formal financial institutions. In Kenya, the broad adoption of mobile money services, such as M-Pesa, has enabled lenders to use transactional records as a primary alternative data source for credit scoring. While this innovation continues to improve the financial inclusion of many to some extent, there is a systemic risk of excluding a significant portion of the most disadvantaged constituents of society. People who do not engage with digital technologies, predominantly as a result of poverty, age or geographic remoteness, become invisible or algorithmically erased. This represents a new kind of "representational harm" (Friedler etal, 2019), whereby the instruments designed to promote inclusion facilitate the stratification of society along the lines of technology use, and denial of credit to those who need it most and who reside on the margins of the financial ecosystem.

These models would be built solely on existing customers' data, meaning new market segments would be omitted entirely, along with their creditworthiness, resulting in financial marginalisation.

Model Bias: From a different perspective, data is not the only place where bias can arise. Bias can also stem from the very framework of the model and decisions made by the model's builders. In this context, model or algorithmic bias results from how a problem is mathematically framed (Kordzadeh & Ghasemaghaei, 2022). Selecting an outcome variable, which the model is built to predict, is an inherently subjective process. Suppose a bank's only focus on defining a 'good' loan is the one that 'earns' money, they may also 'learn' not to lend to small developing businesses or to people with stable but low incomes, because the margins offered are low. This kind of bank model encapsulates the obsessive pursuit of profits above everything else, ultimately fostering bias against a particular class. In addition, the chosen model's architecture is also essential. Deep neural networks are notoriously known for their fantastic 'success' in achieving accuracy, but also have a high 'failure' in transparency, making it difficult to check for discriminatory pathways (Taherdoost, 2023). Other, more straightforward and interpretable models may be easier to determine fairness, but predictively, they may lose accuracy. This exemplifies that tension in the field.

Feedback Loops Bias: The feedback loop is undoubtedly the most damaging type of bias. When a biased model is implemented, it starts generating data supporting the model's biases (Kallus & Zhou, 2018). Imagine a case where an investment bank's hiring algorithm, because of historical bias, tunes down applicants from non-target universities. If this algorithm starts rejecting candidates, company employees are likely to continue coming from a minimal set of schools. The hire data is then utilised to retrain the model, which makes that model more biased and exclusionary. In lending, the case where a model denies loans to residents of a specific neighbourhood, because that model will 'predict' that those residents, denied the ability to build a credit history, will lead to future denials of credit, becomes true, because those residents spatially cannot escape from the algorithm's definition of credit history. The algorithm creates a self-fulfilling prophecy, systematically denying residents of specific neighbourhoods access to credit and preventing them from building the financial history needed to reverse the algorithm's prediction (O'Neil, 2017).

3.2. Case Studies of Systemic Harm

The 2019 Apple Card case released by Goldman Sachs shows gender bias in algorithms. Even if the root cause was never discovered, there remained an opacity. Customers, like Steve Wozniak. Complained that shared accounts with access to superior credit histories were not awarded to women with accounts (Roush, 2024). Geared towards the investigated response, the societal outcry warranted a response. Numerous discussions were held, and it was agreed that the principle of the system was broken. No matter which view was taken, it was a blow to confidence in the fiscal authorities and, with chilly blasé-point algorithms, the trust with which they were approached (Wamsley, 2024).

Integrating AI technology into India's system of Aadhaar illustrates the paradox involving technology implementation in emerging economies. These systems, meant to improve service delivery and reduce fraud, also paradoxically increase the exclusion of marginalised communities. Algorithmic authentication and eligibility determination will likely fail for manual labourers possessing low-quality biometric data or individuals with little digital presence (Mann & Sahni, 2022). This phenomenon exemplifies representational harm, in which the system's design invisibilizes the most vulnerable. The same can be said for the GCC. FinTech lenders using alternative data for credit scoring are likely to replicate, often unknowingly, the societal contours of the data. For example, telecom data may serve as proxies for the nationality, which, in the case of the low-income migrant workers, can reinforce biases emerging from their citizens' differing usage patterns, thereby perpetuating, under the guise of technology, socio-economic disparities (Alfadhel, 2017).

In insurance, the discriminatory use of postal codes in insurance equity pricing is a classic case of proxy discrimination. Postal codes, according to insurance underwriters, are a legitimate element of risk density assessment (crime rate, accident rate, etc.). Still, many urban areas they tend to use are proxies for race and class. Angwin et al. (2017) in ProPublica, noted that in minority neighbourhoods, motorists, on average, pay insurance premiums that are hundreds of dollars more than in white neighbourhoods, even when the accident risk is the same. The algorithm, designed solely to optimise risk correlation, can set a "tax" on specific zip codes, disproportionately penalising individuals, irrespective of their driving patterns, to the systemic inequalities in their "driving" conditions.

3.3. The Ripple Effect

The consequences of these cases reach much further than those who experience them firsthand. These consequences continue to jeopardise the integrity of the financial ecosystem. On the macro level, the systematic denial of credit to potentially opportunity businesses and creditworthy people in certain areas blocks the economic growth and the innovation, and it locks in poverty while putting a cap on the total assets the economy can productively utilise. This is not a social issue; it is a capital inefficiency that diminishes the economy's effectiveness.

In the case of the financial institutions, the jeopardy is just as harsh. Biased algorithms carry a real reputational risk, which, in the case of other such matters, results in a consumer backlash which causes the company to lose a great brand. Biased algorithms also possess a real risk. Under the new stringent laws, such as the EU AI Act, which identifies specific AI risk as high, delineates the protected rights, and requires impact evaluations in these domains, the fine for not adhering to the obligations can reach as high as 6% of the global market revenue. In addition, the risk the model portends is even greater. Umeaduma (2024) cites that models with biased, self-reinforcing feedback loops lose their ability to enhance their accuracy with the changing world norms, resulting in great catastrophic risk mispricing and financial loss. Ultimately, the pervasive application of biased AI undermines the deep trust that constitutes the pillar of the entire economic landscape. If patrons feel that the system is designed to work against them, their trust and participation in the institutions shall be withdrawn, posing a real legitimacy crisis. This is a greater cost than a single fine from the regulation. Understanding these multifaceted forms of bias is a critical business and ethical imperative in the age of algorithms.

4. FAIRNESS METRICS AND EVALUATION FRAMEWORKS

Having categorised the types of bias, financial institutions can now implement a structured framework for addressing them. Vague goals of "being fair" are insufficient to counter the measurable reality of algorithmic discrimination. This requires a rigorous approach based on calculable parameters: a set of calculable parameters and analytic constructs that can convert the ethical tenet of fairness to a quantifiable outcome, subject to legal disclosure, and auditable. This toolkit facilitates transition from aspirational to operational, offering newly available means of detection and diagnosis for discriminatory patterns, and discriminatory practices might be inferred to lie in the institution's AI systems.

4.1. The Metrics of Justice

The notion of fairness has spurred many competing mathematical frameworks. Each captures a distinct dimension of what it means to be "fair." Selecting one is not a technical matter. It is a matter of weighing competing business values. One of the simplest is demographic parity, also known as statistical parity. It posits that a decision, such as loan approval, has to be granted at the same rate irrespective of different protected classes, such as men and women (Mougan et al. 2023). Suppose that a bank operates at two branches. The branches are located in different neighbourhoods that have different demographic compositions. Under demographic parity, the approval rate for loans from each branch is supposed to be the same. This is the central example. This is how social justice is applied, as shown by the example of lending. Demographic parity has a serious flaw. It does not consider what the populations in each group are supposed to meet. (Loukas & Chung, 2023). The only way to meet demographic parity for one group is to approve an uncreditworthy applicant, while for the other group, the only way to meet the set target is to reject a creditworthy applicant. This is why the principle of risk-based pricing is violated. It is the only principle in lending that is for the equal treatment of the different loan applicants. The principle of equitable lending is ignored. It balances outcome with risk.

Like Demographic Parity, algorithmic fairness metrics pose a GCC-specific paradoxical moral issue. Licensing metrics, which stipulate hiring ratios within specified demographic groups, run counter to nationalisation policies, such as Saudi Arabia's Nitaqat, or the UAE Emiratisation, which emphasise the preferential employment of citizens over a substantial migrant workforce for socio-economic objectives. Such a hiring algorithm would be criticised as 'unacceptable' as it would counter compliant policies and be politically central to the dominion. This poses a significant paradox: to what extent can an algorithm be defined as 'fair' should it reside at the foundation of a constructed definition of 'global' fairness, or should it be pegged to 'real' and legally actionable societal goals within that State? This conflict illustrates the fundamental problem that fairness, as a concept, does not have an absolute definition and, instead, is a social construct (Kleinberg et al., 2018). As a result, such principles of fairness should be reconsidered within the appropriate political and geographical contexts.

The Equalised Odds concept is a much more complex acknowledgement of Hardt et al. This says a classifier could be biased and still be equally wrong. In particular, the true positive and the false favourable rates must be equal or nearly equal to each other in each considered demographic. From a banking perspective, this implies that the model should be equally proficient in predicting a borrower's creditworthiness and default, irrespective of the borrower's race and gender. It allows an algorithm to discriminate between groups of people based on the difference in default rates, provided that a discriminatory entity is not being applied to the algorithm's output. It concerns undue discrimination exercised while using the algorithm, not the discrimination that might arise from its production.

One of the approaches described in the paper by Dwork et al (2012) is Individual Fairness, which both philosophers and computer scientists support. This principle claims that "an individual is as good as the outcome." This is a more individual outcome as opposed to a group outcome. A fair loan algorithm would give two applicants vastly more offers than their competitors, regardless of their demographic background, as long as they have the same income, credit history, and debt-to-income ratio. How does one come up with a definition of "similarity" akin to declaring a winner in a competition? This is the challenge that is being posed. It is incredibly domain-relevant knowledge to determine the factors that are fair to consider when deciding to lend money to automate the process.

4.2. Accuracy vs. Fairness

A critical yet unavoidable tension exists: In many cases, there is a tension between optimising for predictive accuracy and optimising for fairness. This is not a problem, but a characteristic of the mathematics of model-building, as Kleinberg et al. (2018) demonstrate. A model aims to identify the most accurate patterns within the data to reduce as much error as possible. In the presence of historical data with underlying biases, as in the case of underestimating women in entrepreneurship, an accurate model will memorise that pattern and continue to reinforce it. With a high degree of accuracy, it will predict the lower approval rates as a response to biased data.

When applying these metrics, forcing the model to be fair usually involves unequal accuracy to the historical training data. The organisation has to tell the algorithm to suppress specific correlations that, although powerful, are unfair, even if its predictions become somewhat less "perfect" in some statistical sense. There is no need to come up with an answer to a technical question. Instead, the issue will be resolved as a business and ethical trade-off. What is the expense of a percentage point of accuracy compared to the cost of having discriminatory outcomes, paying regulatory fines, and harming your reputation? Asking this question shows that the organisation's sustainability rests on pursuing fairness to the economy's bottom line. A " fair " model, but alleged to be less "accurate", is far more beneficial to the organisation than a perfectly accurate but discriminatory model.

4.3. Model Audit

Understanding metrics and trade-offs is pointless without a means to implement them. This is where model audit comes in—the rigorous and expanding financial AI health check. Auditing moves fairness from an abstracted idea to a clinical evaluative practice. One of the most illuminating techniques is subgroup analysis. It is the application of estimating the amount of model predictive error and splitting the metric across some protected characteristics (for instance, race, sex and the relative postal code (address) to estimate false favourable rates (Chung et al., 2024). Alarming gaps indicate probable discrimination. An example of discrimination is an audit of a payment fraud interception procedure. In this case, the audit might show more false positives for transactions from certain countries.

Counterfactual analysis is also an important tool. This asks: What would the model's output be if only one protected attribute differed? An auditor might take the case of a rejected female borrower and construct a counterfactual where every attribute is the same except the gender attribute is changed to male. If the model says 'approved', it is a strong sign of gender bias. There are more practical tools, besides the AIF360, which assist model testing pre- and post-deployment.

An audit is not ever a one-time activity. In this case, it is a case of the need for sustained attention. Biases can change, new ones emerge, and decay as the world adjusts. The need for regular fairness auditing to be incorporated in the same way as post-risk management stress-testing on the financial AI development is most pronounced. Financial institutions cannot simply aspire to fairness; they must measure, verify, and defend their fairness outcomes.

5. TECHNICAL METHODS FOR BIAS MITIGATION

Having defined the disease of algorithmic bias and the criteria for its detection, "the focus now shifts to the available techniques for algorithmic bias mitigation. While powerful, these techniques are not universal solutions; each has philosophical assumptions, practical constraints, and potential unintended consequences. A critical analysis reveals that the choice of mitigation strategy is not only technical but also ethical in its nuances, requiring an understanding of the financial context in which such a strategy would be deployed.

5.1. Pre-Processing

The very beginning of the attack is at the root of the issue: The Data. Weighing involves assigning each case within a dataset different amounts of importance (Ren et al. 2018). For instance, loan applications from a neglected yet trustworthy demographic would be assigned greater importance to address the historical bias. This ensures that the model shifts focus to these applications during the training phase of the model. Resampling takes on a more aggressive strategy, and thus can be described as either over-sampling the minority group (manufacturing duplicates of existing data points) or under-sampling the majority group to establish a more even distribution of the dataset (Yousefimehr et al. 2025). However, these approaches possess rather serious shortcomings. Over-sampling can result in overfitting, where a model learns to recognise patterns, but instead memorises the replicated examples, thus diminishing its overall effectiveness on actual data (Mujahid et al. 2024). On the other hand, under-sampling ignores potentially valuable data, which wastes information and can result in increased accuracy (Sadaiyandi et al., 2023). Having access to sophisticated techniques like SMOTE for synthetic data generation, underrepresented groups can now be allocated entirely new, yet plausible data points (Mukherjee & Khushi, 2021). A significant risk is that synthetic data may fail to capture the complexity of real-world social dynamics, thereby masking rather than eliminating underlying biases. In this case, the synthetic data can remain redundant, as Žliobaitė (2017) states, "...mask rather than eliminate the underlying social issues encoded in the data." It changes the dataset symptoms without actually solving the problem of bias in the first place.

5.2. In-Processing

Understanding the challenging nature of data cleaning, intuitive processes attempt to 'embed' fairness during the algorithm's refinement training (Scaria et al., 2024). One way to achieve this transformation is by reformulating a model's objective function with fairness interventions. Fairness-constrained optimisation defines a fairness metric—equalised odds—as a constraint the model must attend to while minimising its prediction error (Xinying Chen & Hooker, 2023). The model is constrained to a solution deemed accurate by the elements of fairness. Adversarial debiasing contrives a more nuanced, technically sophisticated model (Hong et al., 2021). Two neural networks engage in a game-theoretic Relation: a primary network predicting accurately a creditable outcome (credit risk) and an adversarial network responsible for predicting the protected variable (race) from the primary's predictions. In this case, the primary network is trained to maximise predictive accuracy and 'fool' the adversary by 'under-predicting,' learning to streamline the prediction funnel along the channel that optimises accuracy and fairness while minimising the discernible sensitive attribute. The strength of in-processing is its directness; it integrates fairness around the model's architecture. The primary concern remains a paradox between the closeness of these techniques to the core model and the sheer computational difficulty. These techniques will typically necessitate custom-built techniques and considerable depth concerning the subject, making these techniques less popular than the benign pre- or post-processing techniques. Such techniques require a fundamental re-engineering of the model for the sake of fairness, which is powerful, but comes at a significant cost.

5.3. Post-Processing

The last category of actions taken pertains to addressing the consequences of actions already taken. In the case of model post-processing, there is an assumption of model bias, but the technique works on the premise of adjusting a model's outputs after making predictions (Tanaka & Shimoda, 2023). Most financial service providers find this technique the easiest to implement because it avoids the costly problem of retraining an entire model from scratch. The most widespread method of post-processing corrections is limited calibration. In contrast to using a single threshold score to decide on loan approval, customised thresholds are designed for each cohort sub-group so that the false positive rate is minimised for each one. A modified decision rule that exemplifies this technique is a situation in which a target population, a subgroup that has historically been marginalised, is assigned a lower decision rule threshold for approval to a loan because the model has systematically underestimated their creditworthiness. This technique is the most popular in achieving model statistical parity, but it seems also to be the most controversial. It has been argued that affirmative action should amount to equally weighted affirmative action in an automated form. It can be affirmatively stated that it is a business model that claims to tackle the problem of historical discrimination. Still, criticism is that it conditions low standards for specific cohorts and higher standards for others, which can also be reverse discrimination. This is also problematic because it relies on the decision maker's access to sensitive, classified information. Blunt as it might be, post-processing is effective; it allocates a level of fairness to the output, but does nothing to mitigate the bias within the model, resulting in a muddy model that constantly needs adjustment and rectification.

5.4. Tools of the Trade

The good news is that these techniques no longer have to be constructed from the ground up. There is a collection of open source resources that almost arms the protagonist. AIF360 from IBM is a detailed expansion toolkit that offers a marked their-mod framework for measuring, analysing, bias reporting and mitigation on an extensible bias in the entire reporting and decision-making pipeline (Bellamy et al, 2019). It offers implementations for all the method techniques discussed above. Another formidable library is Microsoft Fairlearn, which focuses on the framework of the evaluation and mitigating the unfairness of the machine learning models (Dudik et al, 2020). These toolkits broaden the availability of bias mitigation. It enables institutions' financing to incorporate these biases in the standard MLOps workflow. The tools, however, do not replace the necessity of thoughtful strategy formulation. These tools serve as an ensemble; their value is unlocked when data scientists, ethicists, and business leaders combine the right tool to use, when to use, and the rationale behind that decision. Unchecked use of a mitigation strategy from a toolkit without discerning the underlying assumptions will lead to new problems of a different kind.

In conclusion, the methods of eliminating bias while preserving fairness within the technical systems of the institution continue to grow. Each technique represents a departure from the others: pre-processing techniques aim to correct biased historical data, in-processing builds fairness directly into the model, and post-processing adjusts the model's outputs to correct unfairness. Perhaps the most salient point to any financial institution is that there is no best technical solution. In this case, it is essentially a function of the context: the kind of model used, the accompanying regulatory regime, the goal of the business, and the particular definition of fairness applicable in the case. Technical mitigation is essential; however, it only works optimally when there is oversight, wisdom and a sincere devotion to the ethical values the technical mitigation serves.

6. ETHICAL GOVERNANCE AND OPERATIONALISING FAIR AI

While technical methods for mitigating bias are potent tools, without strong governance, technical solutions are temporary fixes within the broader challenge of mitigating bias. The model may be set and verified as technically fair, but is subject to misuse. An audit performed once can be sidelined and set aside. A project intended to be executed for a desirable social or economic goal may be appeased or scuttled to meet the commercial demand. In the absence of strong governance, technical solutions become tactical in the strategic battle against bias. To succeed, institutions must develop ethical infrastructures that embed fairness into governance, ensuring interoperability with organisational culture and legal requirements.

6.1. Regulatory Frameworks as Guardrails

A key change driver is the rapid evolution of framework regulations, with the European Union AI Act as the foremost example— it is the first comprehensive approach to artificial intelligence legislation anywhere in the world that utilises a risk-based approach. The implications for financial AI are significant. The Act classifies AI systems employed in credit scoring and the recruitment process as high risk, thus triggering a stringent set of mandatory requirements. These requirements include, but are not limited to, impact assessments of fundamental rights, advanced frameworks of data governance, extensive data governance documentation, human oversight, and extreme transparency obligations regarding data to the users (European

Parliament, 2025). In particular, the Act requires oversight and control of bias as a legal obligation instead of a best practice approach. The fines for noncompliance with the Act are set at €35 million, or 7% of the global turnover, a legal requirement for maintaining bias oversight.

Instead of framing this within the context of a regulatory burden, these organisations see the Act as a framework for responsible and innovative practices. The legal requirements in the EU AI Act serve as a checklist that is externally set for responsible and ethical innovation. It also eliminates the risk of ethical slippage, often justified as a competitive edge. The EU Act is a global benchmark for compliance for international financial organisations, even in regions outside Europe. In the area, regulatory action is still in its early stages but progressing rapidly. The UAE Council for Artificial Intelligence (2018) and the Saudi Data and Artificial Intelligence Authority (SDAIA) (Memish et al., 2021) are formulating national strategies for artificial intelligence which focus on ethical considerations and trust. Though more insubstantive than the curtailing EU model, these strategies indicate a regional 'end goal'. This 'end goal' is increasingly relevant for banks and fintechs operating in the region. Developing governance practices compatible with emerging regional expectations and global standards, such as the EU AI Act, positioned as proactive public policy, is a strong argument for an emerging competitive advantage that enhances international reputation for trust and ease of business. This kind of unrivalled approach to risk is increasingly in demand by investors and partners.

6.2. Ethics-by-Design

Auditing a model for bias only after it is built is inefficient and costly, similar to inspecting a completed building for foundational design flaws. The expense of the changes needed is most often a compromise. The answer is Ethics-by-Design - the inclusion of ethical frameworks into every tier of the entire lifecycle of the AI system, from scoping the problem to deployment and monitoring (Brey & Dainow, 2024).

The change is monumental and reflects the following:

- **At Scoping:** A multidisciplinary team composed of legal, compliance, and ethics professionals considers whether an AI is necessary and for what purpose, instead of framing the problem as whether it can be done.
- **At Data Collection:** Before a single line of code is written, teams systematically analyse the historical and representational prejudices in the potential data sources.
- **At Development:** Fairness and accuracy metrics are selected and tested during training of the model, rather than as an afterthought.

- **At Deployment:** Thorough plans for human oversight, mechanisms for appeal, and ongoing oversight are all incorporated in the launch checklist as an integral part of the system.

Ethics-by-Design redefines downstream validation and lifts fairness as a design constraint. It accepts the reality that, in most cases, design failures are the most prominent. This is the stance of the IEEE, which Aligned Ethically argues that the core ambitions of design should include human wellbeing and equity, not treated as optional considerations (Chatila et al, 2018).

6.3. The Human Firewall

Ultimately, the governance of these rules and principles lacks corporal realities to scrutinise and enforce them. Governance is "governed" by bodies constructed. This requires erecting a "human firewall," a multi-level internal construct devoted to ethical scrutiny.

The primary layer comprises designated functions. Appointing a Chief Ethics Officer or a Head of AI Ethics signals a serious institutional commitment. This person is responsible for policy development, implementation, and the primary ethics oversight on AI systems.

The secondary layer comprises interdisciplinary task forces. An AI Ethics Board, a 'cross-section' of the internal risk-legal-compliance-product-data science clusters and offered externals in ethics-sociology-consumer advocacy, provides oversight and critical challenge. This board is tasked to examine and evaluate select AI constructs and processes during critical milestones to provide the necessary intelligent scrutiny on the steps and offer 'better thinking' on the intended and unintended, the possible and the impossible.

The third layer, you might argue in terms of practicality, would be documentation. It also represents the final 'output' of AI governance. Works such as Model Cards and Datasheets for Datasets foster transparency and enable responsibility (Mitchell et al. 2019, Gebru et al. 2021). Model Cards, for example, outline how developed AI models can be documented. It requires the model to be divided into a few performance characteristic segments covering, at a minimum, use case intentions, limitations, detailed fairness evaluations across some sub-populations, and performance metrics. This pushes the developers towards a systematic and comprehensive explanation of the shortcomings of a model and helps the other stakeholders, be it a loan approver or supervisor, understand the model's functionalities and mesh their workflows accordingly. This ensures there are records of how decisions were made, and there are steps to ensure accountability of the model developers. This also serves to increase the model creators' accountability.

In summary, the weapons are the technical solutions. The rest of the systems are the ethical governance, which organises and regulates the use of these weapons and aligns the use of these systems to address the ethical issues. These systems are within the organisation. The protagonist of this case considers the completion of moral and structural governance to be the most decisive factor in ensuring that the fight against bias is won today. For the future, the fight is embedded against the coming challenges of tomorrow.

7. FAIRNESS IN EMERGING MARKETS AND THE GCC CONTEXT

For financial institutions committed to algorithmic fairness, the challenge grows in complexity when operating in emerging markets, especially the region comprising the Gulf Cooperation Council (GCC) member states. Standard fairness approaches developed for data-rich, formally organised Western jurisdictions are often insufficient in these contexts. The application of fairness here is no longer a straightforward problem. It requires a bold rethinking of the problem, an appreciation of complex structural issues, social practices, and an overhaul of classical problem-solving frameworks. The forms of bias in these regions are often more subtle and complex, and the consequence of inaction is the exacerbation of digital exclusion.

7.1. The Data Desert and the Informal Mosaic

The most pressing issue is a phenomenon known as data scarcity. The GCC nations are more prosperous than the developed markets, yet when it comes to traditional credit assessment, GCC nations remain 'data deserts' (Aljawareen 2017). Many of the population, even young professionals, expatriates and women entering the formal workforce for the first time, are near or 'no credit' customers. Unfortunately, the credit history 'no-file' customers possess is less than ideal since it lacks standard emission records, employment records, utility payments, and other records that these FICO credit scoring models consider. Another aggravating issue is informal economies, convoluted family businesses, and other non-digitally formatted analytics that are borderline impossible to structure and classify for algorithmic parsing. From the onset, any model based on formal sector data is systematically blind to the realities of these economically marginalised verticals.

Moreover, the basic demographic attributes used in fairness auditing in the West may not be acceptable or may even be unlawful. In the case of many nations within the Gulf Cooperation Council, the explicit use of data involving race, religion, or tribe is either culturally delicate or forbidden in law (Alfadhel, 2017). Although intended to eliminate discrimination, these laws create extreme obstacles to the ever–present problem of bias mitigation. How can an institution perform an audit without being able to measure tribal or racial parameters or attributes directly? This results in an over–reliance on proxy attributes, resulting in an inefficient methodology where detection and bias mitigation become an indirect and inferential process. The demographic realities of the region, wherein there is a disproportionate ratio of expatriates to citizens, further complicate matters in the absence of an adequate framework for fairness. There are many discriminating non–citizens, and national policies are aimed at encouraging the economic participation of citizens.

7.2. The Proxy Problem

In an environment that lacks data and a plethora of protected attribute restrictions, the proxy problem emerges as the primary conduit of algorithmic discrimination, assuming distinctively localised manifestations. The proxy discrimination problem in our context takes a geographically specific form. Many readily available features in alternative credit scoring systems are discriminatory in a covert manner.

To illustrate this, a model could account for postal codes as a feature. In a GCC city, a zip code may not reflect affluence, but rather the ethnic/national composition of the migrant labour class (e.g., a zone primarily accommodating South Asian construction workers vs one accommodating Western executives). An algorithm would assume the former zip code is "higher risk", thus applying a digital form of the kafala (sponsorship) system-based discrimination. Other data sources, such as mobile phone information, widely used for alternative scoring, are just as problematic. The make of the phone, the intervals of the top-up payments, the payment patterns, and the social network can be indicators of one's nationality, social standing, or even religion. A pattern of frequent, small top-ups could signal a precarious cash flow typical of low-paid migrant workers. Thus, discrimination will be exercised compared to users with post-paid contracts. Just the same, the employer's name can serve as a form of discrimination. An algorithm can be programmed to assume employees of small local contracting firms are at higher risk than employees of large, state-owned enterprises. Thus, creating a new form of digital class system. What is most disconcerting about these proxies is their apparent neutrality. They seem to make model predictions more accurate, yet in truth, they amplify and automate the clearly biased social constructs of the area.

7.3. A Case for Contextual Innovation

Regardless of these obstacles, the challenges of this frontier also provide unparalleled chances for disruption and innovative new solutions to out-of-date systems.

One does not abandon using algorithms; instead, one must add contextual intelligence. Consider a fictional case study of the 'NBD Bank' in the UAE. Confronted with the no-file problem, NBD intends to develop a more inclusive credit score.

Rather than relying on questionable proxies, its data scientists work in participatory design with community leaders and sociologists. They construct culturally relevant and less discriminatory alternative data sets. These may include:

- **Rental Payment History:** Digitisation, accompanied by extracting information and insights from the process, conducted through the Bayut and Property Finder platforms.
- **Education and Certification Records:** Working with partner organisations to use completed education and active professional credentialing indicators of ambition and professional stability.
- **Telco Payment History:** Using aggregated, anonymised post-paid mobile account data, with user opt-in consent to data collection.
- **Charitable Donations (Zakat):** For the residents, and with due regard to privacy, the record of formal digital philanthropic donations may, under certain circumstances, indicate some degree of social integration, as well as financial stability.

What is being proposed is not merely a technological apparatus but an amalgamation of social and technological features. Its fairness is audited using novel approaches that attempt to estimate biases without breaching privacy safeguards, possibly via tailor-made strategic alliances with academics, vetted under special ethical approvals. This "GCC Score" would make different kinds of mistakes than a Western model, but it would be more just— it would grant credit to people previously denied access to credit, and thus, would foster real financial inclusion. This example shows that the fairness test in emerging economies is not about mathematical precision. It is about whether the algorithmic system is intended to comprehend and service the distinctive social and economic context of the country in which it operates. For this protagonist, success in this dimension is the ultimate proof that their fairness is not an intention to comply with but part of a genuinely novel and sustainable business psychology.

8. THE FUTURE CHALLENGE: GENERATIVE AI

The ability to generate artificial human-like text using large language models and generative AI tools highlights yet another shift in the fairness field in algorithmic finance. In contrast to conventional models that make predictions, generative systems create and generate novel content in prose, computer code, and synthetic datasets. This content creation poses new fairness challenges that go well beyond the traditional scope of discrimination. The essence of the problem is in how these "stochastic parrots" (uninformed and unfiltered replicas of the text for the entirety of the internet) generate, remix and recombine patterns and ideas from gigantic corpuses of training data full of biases and inequalities (Bender et al., 2021). The ability to create and generate text of remarkable coherence and dispassionate arguments deepens existing challenges and introduces new challenges of discrimination that are harder to identify and address.

To begin with, GenAI has a greater ability to create biases that are qualitatively different from previous ones. Bias becomes a vital battleground in language; a language and dialect served to an LLM-powered customer service chatbot may yield different levels of helpfulness, politeness, or persuadability, and, as a result, degrade service to weaker and impoverished non-native speakers and speakers of regional dialects. Moreover, it can also feature offensive content or content with damaging stereotypes, thereby damaging the reputation due to association. However, Bias in reasoning is more subtle and poses far greater challenges. For example, a generative model tasked with reasoning a credit denial may instead conjure a text that sounds plausible and legally vetted for all intents and purposes, masquerading as a discriminatory reasoning with an intricate web of plausible deniability. This "reasoned" bias is more dangerous than simply receiving a poor score, as it cloaks discrimination in bias traditionally associated with fairness, and thus avoids the traditional auditing where statistics are the primary outputs (Raji et al., 2022). Lastly, the equity content bias is a financial text bias that commands significant attention regarding the potential disruption it can bring to market integrity. GenAI that has been tasked with preparing analyst reports, market overviews, and investment news can exacerbate the impact of underlying narratives and reinforce existing cognitive biases about the credit risk afforded to entire sectors or developing countries due to the erroneous economic conclusions ingrained in the training datasets.

Thus, GenAI serves as an amplification mechanism. Due to the unprecedented scale and scope of its training data, it can encode and operationalise social biases at speeds and volumes never possible. A situated prejudice within the frameworks of an obscure online conversation can be assimilated, abstracted, and utilised across billions of consumer engagements, transforming an isolated bias into a systemic one. This amplification may perpetuate and automate patterns of inequality and discrimination seen in history, masked as advanced technology.

Proposed changes are drastic enough that elements used in traditional auditing will need drastic adjustments. As foundations, frameworks to reduce predictive discrimination and governance over error rates are inadequate. New and novel auditing tools that can examine a generative system's novel and unbounded outputs and structures will need to be invented. Considerable resources will need to be invested in developing prompt-injection probes, a framework to assess fairness in evaluating form generative and other new metrics to assess latent biases in a model obscured by mercurial systems. The focus changes from "What bias, if any, was exhibited in the reasoning of this decision?" to "What worldviews and biases are embedded in this model's entire generative capacity?" Interdisciplinary work combining the forensic detail of technical auditing with the wondering and deep qualitative scrutiny of the social sciences will be needed if justice and equity are designed and engineered into Generative Finance.

9. CONCLUSION

This chapter has analysed algorithmic bias in finance, proposed methods for its mitigation, and argued for a revised design philosophy centred on protection. The first phase was to categorise the manifestations of bias and how it becomes embedded in systems through the incidence of legacy data, model fallacies, and self-reinforcing feedback loops and the very real impacts of such systems – discriminatory lending practices, predatory insurance, and exclusion. In response, we outlined a framework of quantifiable fairness metrics and auditing practices to measure and ensure fairness. This leads us to a most critical set of technical interventions, ranging from pre-processing data to post–processing the outputs of a model, each of which had unique and philosophically balanced tradeoffs. However, technical solutions alone cannot resolve fairness issues. Lasting fairness requires an ethical governance structure: evolving rules, a proactive Ethics-by-Design approach, oversight from an Ethics Board, and robust model documentation such as Model Cards. These technical, ethical, and operational components have become the new norm for ethical and responsible innovation design.

The core message of this exploration remains clear, and algorithmic fairness is not a peripheral compliance issue or a charitable afterthought. It is an essential, core component of future financial systems. It is a primary source of stability, a safeguard against reputational and legal exposure, and the foundation for fostering enduring trust with a diverse clientele, an industry built on accurate risk measurement. The inability to assess and address the systemic risk of bias constitutes a grave neglect of fiduciary responsibility and ethical expectation. It is possible to have an intelligent and efficient financial system that is also equitably just. This analysis argues that, in the long run, an economic system cannot be one without the other.

Despite this, the frameworks and techniques listed here are the starting points of a far longer and more involved discussion. Even now, these systems are the first generation of tools designed for a world characterised by predictive models and analytical AIs. With the advent of generative AI and large language models (LLMs), the world is entering a new epoch which will change the challenge and make it more complex. Such models will not simply assess creditworthiness; they will also write news of analyst reports that shift the market, execute trades based on finely-grained contextual interpretations of news, and communicate with users through hyper-personalised chatbots. The biases they will acquire from the unfiltered, vast internet will be more intricate and contextualised—and far more potent than the statistical correlations we are grappling with now. A denial won't characterise the generative model's bias, but rather a beautifully formulated, persuasive explanation for the biased outcome. Every financial institution must now face the more relevant challenge of auditing its AI for fairness, rather than assuming whether it will do it. The next advancement of AI will test the commitment to fairness, introducing biases that are more complex and difficult to identify.

REFERENCES

Alfadhel, K. A. (2017). The GCC human rights declaration: An instrumentation of cultural relativism. *arab law quarterly, 31*(1), 89-98.

Aljawareen, A. F. (2017). Innovation in the GCC countries: An economic analysis. *Journal of Economics*, *5*(4), 51–62.

Angwin, J., Larson, J., Kirchner, L., & Mattu, S. (2017, April 5). Minority Neighborhoods Pay Higher Car Insurance Premiums Than White Areas With the Same Risk. *ProPublica*. Retrieved from www.propublica.org/article/minority-neighborhoods-higher-car-insurance-premiums-white-areas-same-risk. Accessed September 5, 2025.

Barocas, S., & Selbst, A. D. (2016). Big data's disparate impact. *California Law Review*, *104*, 671.

Bartlett, R., Morse, A., Stanton, R., & Wallace, N. (2022). Consumer-lending discrimination in the FinTech Era. *Journal of Financial Economics*, *143*(1), 30–56. DOI: 10.1016/j.jfineco.2021.05.047

Basel Committee on Banking Supervision. (2024). *Core Principles for Effective Banking Supervision*. Retrieved from https://www.bis.org/bcbs/publ/d573.pdf. Accessed September 1, 2025.

Bellamy, R. K., Dey, K., Hind, M., Hoffman, S. C., Houde, S., Kannan, K., Lohia, P., Martino, J., Mehta, S., Mojsilović, A., Nagar, S., Ramamurthy, K. N., Richards, J., Saha, D., Sattigeri, P., Singh, M., Varshney, K. R., & Zhang, Y. (2019). AI Fairness 360: An extensible toolkit for detecting and mitigating algorithmic bias. *IBM Journal of Research and Development*, *63*(4/5), 4–1. DOI: 10.1147/JRD.2019.2942287

Brey, P., & Dainow, B. (2024). Ethics by design for artificial intelligence. *AI and Ethics*, *4*(4), 1265–1277. DOI: 10.1007/s43681-023-00330-4

Butt, J. S. (2024). From bureaucracy to black box: Revolutionizing natural justice and due process in administrative law. *Acta Universitatis Danubius. Administratio*, *16*(1), 7–47.

Chatila, R., Firth-Butterfield, K., & Havens, J. C. (2018). Ethically aligned design: A vision for prioritizing human well-being with autonomous and intelligent systems version 2.

Chung, T. K., Gueldner, P. H., Aloziem, O. U., Liang, N. L., & Vorp, D. A. (2024). An artificial intelligence based abdominal aortic aneurysm prognosis classifier to predict patient outcomes. *Scientific Reports*, *14*(1), 3390. DOI: 10.1038/s41598-024-53459-5 PMID: 38336915

Dudík, M., Chen, W., Barocas, S., Inchiosa, M., Lewins, N., Oprescu, M., Qiao, J., Sameki, M., Schlener, M., Tuo, J., & Wallach, H. (2020). Assessing and mitigating unfairness in credit models with the fairlearn toolkit. *White paper. URL:* https:// tinyurl. com/2x37jece

Dwork, C., Hardt, M., Pitassi, T., Reingold, O., & Zemel, R. (2012, January). Fairness through awareness. In *Proceedings of the 3rd innovations in theoretical computer science conference* (pp. 214-226). DOI: 10.1145/2090236.2090255

European Parliament. (2025 Feb. 19). "EU AI Act: First Regulation on Artificial Intelligence." *European Parliament*. Retrieved from www.europarl.europa.eu/topics/en/article/20230601STO93804/eu-ai-act-first-regulation-on-artificial-intelligence

Friedler, S. A., Scheidegger, C., Venkatasubramanian, S., Choudhary, S., Hamilton, E. P., & Roth, D. (2019, January). A comparative study of fairness-enhancing interventions in machine learning. In *Proceedings of the conference on fairness, accountability, and transparency* (pp. 329-338). DOI: 10.1145/3287560.3287589

Gebru, T., Morgenstern, J., Vecchione, B., Vaughan, J. W., Wallach, H., Iii, H. D., & Crawford, K. (2021). Datasheets for datasets. *Communications of the ACM*, *64*(12), 86–92. DOI: 10.1145/3458723

Goodman, B., & Flaxman, S. (2017). European Union regulations on algorithmic decision-making and a "right to explanation". *AI Magazine*, *38*(3), 50–57. DOI: 10.1609/aimag.v38i3.2741

Hardt, M., Price, E., & Srebro, N. (2016). Equality of opportunity in supervised learning. *Advances in Neural Information Processing Systems*, ●●●, 29.

Hong, J., Zhu, Z., Yu, S., Wang, Z., Dodge, H. H., & Zhou, J. (2021, August). Federated adversarial debiasing for fair and transferable representations. In *Proceedings of the 27th ACM SIGKDD Conference on Knowledge Discovery & Data Mining* (pp. 617-627). DOI: 10.1145/3447548.3467281

Kallus, N., & Zhou, A. (2018, July). Residual unfairness in fair machine learning from prejudiced data. In *International Conference on Machine Learning* (pp. 2439-2448). PMLR.

Kleinberg, J., Ludwig, J., Mullainathan, S., & Rambachan, A. (2018, May). Algorithmic fairness. In *Aea papers and proceedings* (Vol. 108, pp. 22-27). 2014 Broadway, Suite 305, Nashville, TN 37203: American Economic Association. DOI: 10.1257/pandp.20181018

Kleinberg, J., Mullainathan, S., & Raghavan, M. (2016). Inherent trade-offs in the fair determination of risk scores. *arXiv preprint arXiv:1609.05807.*

Kordzadeh, N., & Ghasemaghaei, M. (2022). Algorithmic bias: Review, synthesis, and future research directions. *European Journal of Information Systems, 31*(3), 388–409. DOI: 10.1080/0960085X.2021.1927212

Loukas, O., & Chung, H. R. (2023). Demographic parity: Mitigating biases in real-world data. *arXiv preprint arXiv:2309.17347.*

Mehrabi, N., Morstatter, F., Saxena, N., Lerman, K., & Galstyan, A. (2021). A survey on bias and fairness in machine learning. *ACM Computing Surveys, 54*(6), 1–35. DOI: 10.1145/3457607

Memish, Z. A., Altuwaijri, M. M., Almoeen, A. H., & Enani, S. M. (2021). The Saudi Data & Artificial Intelligence Authority (SDAIA) vision: Leading the kingdom's journey toward global leadership. *Journal of Epidemiology and Global Health, 11*(2), 140–142. DOI: 10.2991/jegh.k.210405.001 PMID: 33876596

Mitchell, M., Wu, S., Zaldivar, A., Barnes, P., Vasserman, L., Hutchinson, B., Spitzer, E., Raji, I. D., & Gebru, T. (2019, January). Model cards for model reporting. In *Proceedings of the conference on fairness, accountability, and transparency* (pp. 220-229). DOI: 10.1145/3287560.3287596

Mougan, C., State, L., Ferrara, A., Ruggieri, S., & Staab, S. (2023). Beyond demographic parity: Redefining equal treatment. *arXiv preprint arXiv:2303.08040.*

Mujahid, M., Kına, E. R. O. L., Rustam, F., Villar, M. G., Alvarado, E. S., De La Torre Diez, I., & Ashraf, I. (2024). Data oversampling and imbalanced datasets: An investigation of performance for machine learning and feature engineering. *Journal of Big Data, 11*(1), 87. DOI: 10.1186/s40537-024-00943-4

Mukherjee, M., & Khushi, M. (2021). SMOTE-ENC: A novel SMOTE-based method to generate synthetic data for nominal and continuous features. *Applied System Innovation, 4*(1), 18. DOI: 10.3390/asi4010018

Nuti, A. (2019). *Injustice and the reproduction of history: Structural inequalities, gender and redress*. Cambridge University Press. DOI: 10.1017/9781108325592

O'neil, C. (2017). *Weapons of math destruction: How big data increases inequality and threatens democracy*. Crown.

Ren, M., Zeng, W., Yang, B., & Urtasun, R. (2018, July). Learning to reweight examples for robust deep learning. In *International conference on machine learning* (pp. 4334-4343). PMLR.

Roush, T. (2024, Oct. 23). *Apple and Goldman Sachs Fined over $89 Million for Misleading Apple Card Customers. Forbes.* Retrieved from www.forbes.com/sites/tylerroush/2024/10/23/apple-and-goldman-sachs-fined-over-89-million-for-misleading-apple-card-customers/. Accessed August 22, 2025.

Sadaiyandi, J., Arumugam, P., Sangaiah, A. K., & Zhang, C. (2023). Stratified sampling-based deep learning approach to increase prediction accuracy of unbalanced dataset. *Electronics (Basel)*, *12*(21), 4423. DOI: 10.3390/electronics12214423

Scaria, A. G., Subramanian, V., George, N. K., & Sengupta, N. (2024, October). Algorithms and recidivism: A multi-disciplinary systematic review. In *Proceedings of the AAAI/ACM Conference on AI, Ethics, and Society* (Vol. 7, pp. 1292-1305). DOI: 10.1609/aies.v7i1.31724

Taherdoost, H. (2023). Deep learning and neural networks: Decision-making implications. *Symmetry*, *15*(9), 1723. DOI: 10.3390/sym15091723

Tanaka, T., & Shimoda, M. (2023). Pre-and post-processing techniques for reinforcement-learning-based routing and spectrum assignment in elastic optical networks. *Journal of Optical Communications and Networking*, *15*(12), 1019–1029. DOI: 10.1364/JOCN.503599

The Alan Turing Institute. (2023). Data Protection, AI, and Fairness. Retrieved from www.turing.ac.uk/data-protection-ai-and-fairness. Accessed September 1, 2025.

Umeaduma, C. M. G. (2024). Behavioral biases influencing individual investment decisions within volatile financial markets and economic cycles. *Int J Eng Technol Res Manag*, *8*(03), 191.

Wamsley, L. (2024, Oct. 23). *Apple and Goldman Sachs Ordered to Pay $89 Million over Apple Card Failures. NPR.* Retrieved from www.npr.org/2024/10/23/g-s1-29566/apple-goldman-sachs-fine-apple-card-cfpb. Accessed August 28, 2025

Xinying Chen, V., & Hooker, J. N. (2023). A guide to formulating fairness in an optimization model. *Annals of Operations Research*, *326*(1), 581–619. DOI: 10.1007/s10479-023-05264-y PMID: 37361073

Yousefimehr, B., Ghatee, M., Seifi, M. A., Fazli, J., Tavakoli, S., Rafei, Z., Ghaffari, S., Nikahd, A., Gandomani, M. R., Orouji, A., & Kashani, R. M. (2025). Data Balancing Strategies: A Survey of Resampling and Augmentation Methods. *arXiv preprint arXiv:2505.13518.*

Zetzsche, D. A., Arner, D. W., & Buckley, R. P. (2020). Decentralized finance. *Journal of Financial Regulation*, *6*(2), 172–203. DOI: 10.1093/jfr/fjaa010

Žliobaitė, I. (2017). Measuring discrimination in algorithmic decision making. *Data Mining and Knowledge Discovery*, *31*(4), 1060–1089. DOI: 10.1007/s10618-017-0506-1

Chapter 5
Towards a Unified Legal Framework for AI in Finance by Synthesizing Global Best Practices

Shashank Solanki
http://orcid.org/0009-0002-5923-0516
Christ University, India

Sheetal Singh
http://orcid.org/0000-0002-7266-8910
Christ University, India

ABSTRACT

The integration of Artificial Intelligence (AI) into financial markets has transformed operational efficiency, risk assessment, and consumer engagement, while simultaneously exposing critical regulatory gaps. This paper conducts a comparative legal analysis of AI governance frameworks across the European Union, United States, Asia-Pacific, and India, highlighting divergent risk classifications, data governance models, and ethical oversight mechanisms. Using doctrinal and case study methodologies, the study evaluates India's hybrid regulatory approach spanning sector-specific guidelines, digital public infrastructure, and sandbox initiatives—and proposes a unified legal framework for AI in finance. Drawing lessons from insider trading regulation, the paper advocates for harmonized global standards that balance innovation with investor protection, algorithmic transparency, and market integrity.

DOI: 10.4018/979-8-2600-1603-9.ch005

1. INTRODUCTION

1.1 Background

The introduction of Artificial Intelligence (AI) in the financial markets has been one of the most game-changing trends in the field of finance in modern times. Algorithms of machine learning, predictive analysis, robo-advisory systems, automated credit scoring, and fraud detection systems have greatly improved the accuracy, efficiency and inclusiveness of financial services. For instance, algorithmic trading is a form of trading that involves the use of trading models based on AI which absorb humongous amounts of data and make trades in milliseconds to provide financial institutions with an edge, and which also created new regulatory hurdles. Similarly, AI-based tools for credit scoring and risk that can facilitate faster decision-making have raised serious issues around algorithmic bias, and privacy and fairness in financial decision making, etc., While there are obvious operational advantages of using AI in finance, current regulatory frameworks have struggled to keep up with the pace of changing technology. Most legal systems are still grounded on traditional regulatory instruments that were not designed keeping in mind the specific risks of AI, leaving large governance gaps. The delay of technological innovation and regulatory evolution creates loopholes in the system and uncontrolled data use and automated decision-making in financial markets (Chen, Wu, and Zhao, 2023).

In India, the financial industry has been actively adopting AI in different sectors - digital payments, automated lending, insurance underwriting and fraud detection. Initiatives such as Unified Payments Interface (UPI) and Account Aggregator framework are some of the instances of increased dependence of India on the digital public infrastructure to enable AI-propelled financial services. Regulatory Sandbox mechanisms, for example, the one undertaken by both RBI (Reserve Bank of India) and SEBI (Securities and Exchange Board of India) are an evolved step towards balancing innovation and regulation (Pardhey & Yuni, 2023). However, by such efforts, the country of India still does not have a comprehensive and harmonized legal regime which reconciles innovating Artificial Intelligence (AI) and associated principles of accountability, fairness and data protection under Digital Personal Data Protection (DPDP) Act, 2023. The need for a coherent regulatory ecosystem is therefore of the utmost importance (Çela, Vajjhala, & Aslani, 2025).

1.2 Problem Statement

The speed with which AI has spread into the financial sector has revealed the shortcomings of the existing frameworks with respect to regulation; on a national and international level. The European Union, for example, has implemented a centralised risk-based EU Artificial Intelligence Act (2024), the US is still adopting a scattered sector-specific approach; while the Asia and Pacific regional is adopting a hybrid regulatory and sandbox approach. India's framework is still sector-dependent and does not have standardised norms around algorithmic transparency, ethical accountability and classification of risks across sectors.

This patchwork regulatory environment creates a number of legal and ethical challenges. First, AI decision-making is a “black-box” which impairs transparency and accountability. Second, algorithmic bias has the potential to result in financial impacts that are discriminatory against vulnerable groups. Third, cross-border data flows and requirements for localization make it difficult for the multinational financial institutions to comply. These issues in turn call for the convergence of technology governance, ethics and regulatory consistency (Bernardy & Spiwack, 2021; see also the evolution of the law on insider trading in the past - a situation where, in the absent of coherent framework, there were gaps in enforcement and opportunities for market manipulation). Similarly fragmented AI regulations are opening up opportunities of systemic risk as well as regulatory arbitrage. As is the case with insider trading harmonization, principles of transparency, consistent compliance and international cooperation are indispensable for ensuring market integrity (Drame-Maigne et al., 2021). Thus, the regulation of AI in the financial space will need to be informed not only by the local legal realities in India, and the global best practices.

1.3 Objectives of the Study

This research aims to fill the regulatory and policy gaps in relation to AI in financial markets by means of the following objectives:

1. Comparative Study of Global Regulatory Frameworks: Compare AI regulatory regimes of European Union, United States, Asia-Pacific and India - to analyse the difference in risk classification, disclosure, enforcement and ethical oversight.
2. Evaluation of India's Sector-Specific AI Regulation: Analyse India's sectoral initiatives, such as RBI and SEBI sandbox, digital public infrastructural institutional mechanism such as India AI Safety Institute (proposed) to place India in the perspective of international trends on AI governance.
3. Proposal for a Harmonised Legal Framework for AI in Finance: Develop a harmonised legal framework based on comparative best practices that supports investor protection and the innovation-friendly compliance through: consistency in categorising risk, data governance and ethical responsibility

1.4 Research Methodology

This study uses the doctrinal and the comparative approach to legal research which is common among quality legal research.

1. Doctrinal Analysis: Critical analysis of the statues, regulations, guidelines and case laws that govern the usage of AI in financial markets (Ibrahim et al., 2024). The analysis takes into consideration cross-sector Indian regulatory materials issued by the RBI, the SEBI and the IRDAI and international instruments such as the EU AI Act (to be issued in 2024), the GDPR and the principles issued by the Organisation for Economic Cooperation and Development (OECD).
2. Comparative Study: Comparative analysis of regulatory models of the EU, the US, Asia-Pacific and India with the goal to identify and best practices, legal gaps and areas for harmonization of e.g. risk class, integrity oversight, compliance interoperability (Minkkinen, Zimmer, & Mäntymaki, 2022).
3. Case Study Analysis: Use of Indian Fintech companies under the regulatory sandbox frameworks to analyse the practical problems of AI governance, regulatory compliance and viability of the proposed unified frameworks (Shalaby, 2024).
4. Synthesis and Recommendations: It is important to synthesize the doctrinal and comparative results to make recommendations to the regulators, policymakers and financial institutions with view to ensure the deployment of responsible AI, consistent compliance and preservance of the integrity of the market (Robles & Mallinson, 2025).

2. CONCEPTUAL FRAMEWORK

2.1 Definition and Scope of AI in Finance

Financial artificial intelligence (AI) - Innovation and application of artificial intelligence and machine learning to the financial services market, including machine learning, predictive analytics, and algorithmic trading, robo-advisory systems, and so on. The technologies will enable the financial institutions to process complex information and make more decisions as well as be more efficient in their operations. Probs 10: The machine learning models are programmed to make decisions (grounded on previous and present data), identify patterns, and implement dynamic changes to be made in both trading and lending models (Regulatory Compliance and AI, 2024).The predictive analytics is employed to predict the market, credit risk, fraud detection, algorithmic trading to trade at a high speed, low latency and to trade at the highest efficiency. Robo-advisors refer to automated services that include customized recommendations on investments offered by the computer to help retail investors gain access to the services of wealth management, which is automation based on AI.

India has implemented AI in digital lending, insurance claims detection, fraud prevention and onboarding customers. We already have the outcome of automated underwriting algorithms making eligibility and creditworthiness decisions on loans in milliseconds; natural language processing and image recognition are being used to accelerate the claims processing of insurers. In addition to it, FinTech companies also use AI-based chatbots and virtual assistants with multilingual support and emotional analysis and products recommendations (Vettriselvan et al., 2025).

Takeaway: Artificial intelligence (AI) is changing how decisions are made and the service delivery in the financial industry, but it is also being adopted at a rapid pace without a legal structure that will make the technology fair, accountable and transparent.

2.2 Legal and Ethical Challenges

There is a complex ethical and legal issue in the application of AI in finance, where the deep-learning models and neural networks are used in an obscure way.

(a) The Black-Box Problem and Algorithmic Bias

Since the 1980s, it has been known that algorithmic bias is a concern in computing, and with black box algorithms; yet, it is an issue that has no relation to the algorithms. However, most of the developed AI models are, in practice, black boxes whereby the AI model takes its predictions (e.g. credit scoring, market forecasting, etc.) without having to explain them. This ambiguity can take the form of algorithmic discrimination where biased training material has provided an unreasonable response to a group of people based on their demographic (Chen et al., 2024). This has been initiated being proposed by numerous regulators around the globe (European Banking Authority (EBA, 2024) and Reserve Bank of India (RBI, 2023) by providing a central role in explaining why AI-based system of decisions works.

Recommendation: The regulators should ensure that they make model interpretability and independent auditing compulsory in order to minimise bias and maximise the fairness of AI-based finance.

(b) Data Privacy and the DPDP Act, 2023

The AI models utilized in the Indian finance are trained on large datasets and this brings out the question of privacy which is controlled by (DPDP) Digital Personal Data Protection Act, 2023. The accounting organizations must ensure that the legal justification (legality, consent, and storage limitation) is dealt with regarding the very process of data processing. The cross border finance transactions have instead been complicated with the increased demands of localisation. As an example, multinational banks that use AI as credit scoring tools should ensure the DPDP requirements are in line with GDPR requirements when it comes to transferring data (De Almeida, Santos and Farias, 2021). The purpose restriction and the algorithmic transparency have been pointed out by the MeitY guidelines of offering AI-enabled decision systems by the year 2024.

Recommendation: DPDP Act in India can be updated in accordance with the global standards on data exchange as one of the largest aspects of responsible AI usage in the cross-border finance.

(c) Cybersecurity and Cross-Border Data Risks

The AI financial systems are associated with interconnected systems that are easily hackable and their information can be altered. The data breaches across borders are far worse as the popularity of the cloud-based financial infrastructures has skyrocketed. According to the BIS cyber resilience report 2024, the high value targets (mentioned earlier, algorithmic trading and robo-advisory systems) are still being attacked systematically via coordinated cyber-attacks. Cybersecurity implications required in different countries: The introduction of CERT-In guidelines in India, NIS2 Directive in the EU has created much confusion to the fintech companies that operate at the global level.

Recommendation: It is necessary to have the international standards of cybersecurity and immediate reporting of threats to rely on AI-based financial ecosystems.

(d) Risks of Manipulation in High-Frequency and Algorithmic Trading

AI-based high-frequency trading (HFT): The schemes make thousands of orders a nanosecond, in microseconds, so it can cause an imbalance in the market and may lead to a rise of volatility in the market. Lastly, the outcome of these algorithms can include flash crashes or permit ill intentions that can be difficult to identify using the standard surveillance systems. The world regulators already start acting, the SEC Market Structure Reforms 2023 in the U.S. include surveillance systems based on AI, and SEBI algorithmic trading circular (to be introduced in 2024) include real-time audits.

Recommendation: The control of HFT must be algorithmic, reportable and auditable, and the control must be executed in a manner that promotes openness in the disclosure standards of information..

2.3 Lessons From Insider Trading Regulation

The history of the insider trading regulation provides useful parallels to the AI regulation of the financial industry.

(a) Fragmented Standards and Enforcement Gaps

The Standard: The Standards are Discontinuous. The Enforcement Gaps: The Enforcement Disjoint.

Previously, the different jurisdictions have had some inconsistencies that have made loopholes in insider trading and loci of arbitrage. Another aspect in the same theme is that the issue of AI governance on the international level is fractured in the sense that the high-risk application and compliance standards have various definitions and it can lead to the inability to monitor international financial firms (Kayani and Hasan, 2024).

Takeaway: AI regulatory fragmentation may be helped through the application of certain homogenous standards of interpretation that are used in the backdrop of insider trading..

(b) Analogy to AI Governance

Similarly, since the asymmetry in flow of information between the developers and the investors/regulators was brought about by insider trading, opaque AI systems can create an information flow asymmetry. Proprietors of the proprietary algorithms are able to withhold risk parameters that will bring about distortion and damages to market investors. Artificially intelligent financial markets can recreate that artificially constructed opaque market which is the rationale behind the insider-trading laws so far as no criterion of consistent disclosure exists.

Takeaway: Fairness of Information and a level playing field: Disclosure of AI Model requirement must depend on the regime of insider-trading.

(c) Significance of Harmonization

This literary piece shows that there should be harmonisation and criminalisation of insider trading jurisprudence on principles. The global financial regulators are currently utilizing the information sharing platforms to create uniformity. Having such a history, it is time to provide the AI regulation in the financial industry with the elements of transparency, fairness, responsibility, and inter-agency coordination (Singh, Kaunert, and Kaushik, 2024).

Takeaway: One such way of ensuring that the establishment of innovation is realized without undermining market integrity is harmonization of the field of AI in finance as a starting point of harmonizing the regulation of insider trading.

3. COMPARATIVE ANALYSIS OF LAW AND ARTIFICIAL INTELLIGENCE (AI) IN FINANCIAL SECTOR

The framework to govern artificial intelligence (AI) in the financial sector continues to vary from jurisdiction to jurisdiction, in line with the proportion of innovation, risk tolerance, consumer protection and ethical governance. Financial markets now use AI systems heavily - from algorithmic trading to predictive credit scoring, to robo-advisory services, fraud detection and automation of customer services (Vukovic, Dekpo-Adza, & Matovic, 2025). While these applications bring efficiencies, as well as access to the markets, they also bring risks, such as algorithmic discrimination, lack of transparency into decision-making, vulnerability to cybersecurity risk and potential manipulation of the market. It is thus important to conduct a comparative legal analysis in order to establish the differences in regulations and best practices for a harmonized international approach to AI in finance.

3.1 European Union

The European Union (EU) has introduced an approach to the governance of AI based on risk through a centralized model of artificial intelligence governance with the Artificial Intelligence Act (AI Act) which was formally adopted in 2024. The Act appraises the AI systems under the risk that is posed (unacceptable, high, limited, minimal) under the circumstances of the risk of serious violations of fundamental rights, consumer protection and financial stability. High-risk systems e.g, algorithmic credit scoring, automated trading systems, robo-advisory tools are subject to strict requirements such as technical documentation, data quality controls, human oversight, audit trails and post-market monitoring (Ridzuan et al., 2024)

In addition to the AI Act, the General Data Protection Regulation (GDPR) still requires the necessity of explicit consent to be obtained for the use of data, as well as the guarantee of the right to explanation for an automated decision (Singh, 2022). The AI Act 2024 and GDPR 2016/679 are a joint regime which is focussed on accountability and transparency of algorithmic decision making. The EU's holistic approach - based on the European Commission's guidelines for its implementation by 2025 and the recommendations of the European Securities and Markets Authority (ESMA) - enforces the EU as a global standard setter in AI governance within the financial sector that combines responsibility and market stability.

Transition

While the EU is a centralized ex ante approach, the United States is a sector specific and decentralized approach which is an example of how regulation philosophy impacts innovation and enforcement.

3.2 United States

Artificial intelligence (AI) regulation in finance is still sectoral and agency driven in the US. Oversight is scattered between a number of different regulators: algorithmic and high-frequency trading is regulated by the Securities and Exchange Commission (SEC), use of AI in derivatives by the Commodities Futures Trading Commission (CFTC) and use of AI in consumer credit and lending by the Consumer Financial Protection Bureau (CFPB).

Recent developments have been toward more co-ordination. In 2023-2024, the White House Executive Order on Safe, Secure and Trustworthy AI (2023) and SEC AI Risk Management Bulletin (2024) promoted the adoption of common governance principles throughout financial agencies. Arrangements for enforcement are now taking the form of a combination of compliance audits, administrative actions and court adjudication in order to ensure that AI instruments are deployed in an ethical manner (Camilleri, 2023).This decentralized but dynamic structure provides innovation but at the same time create a fragmentation. The development of inter-agency working groups and AI ethics advisory boards is a slight step in the right direction for more inter-operable supervisory mechanisms, which can find a balance between the incentives for innovation and the need for safeguards for systemic risk.

Transition

In contrast to the centralization of the EU and the fragmented model of the US, jurisdictions of the Asia-Pacific region have a hybrid regime - a combination of prescriptive regulation and experimentation and innovation-friendly.

3.3 Asia-Pacific

The Asia-Pacific region possesses a range of governance structures for AI: from state-centric command systems in China to sandbox-based innovation regimes in Singapore, and is diverse in the ways that it develops and prioritizes culture.

3.3.1 China

China has an extremely centralised and prescriptive regulatory regime. The Provisions on the Administration of Algorithmic Recommendation Services, 2022 as amended by the Cyberspace Administration of China (CAC) Guidelines 2023, is that financial institutions should be required to disclose the algorithmic design, the source of data and training processes. AI that is used in assessment of credit, fraud detection and automatic trading are under algorithmic audits, cybersecurity inspection and fairness testing (Freeda et al., 2024). Following this, Fintech Development Plan for 2024 of the People's Bank of China reiterates oversight and highlights the importance of avoiding algorithmic discrimination - suggesting that China would prefer to carry on with state-led transparency and risk mitigation in AI finance.

3.3.2 South Korea

South Korea is inspired by the EU and has incorporated explainability and accountability principles in financial AI. Under the exposure to the Artificial Intelligence Framework Act (2023), and Financial Services Commission AI Ethics Guidelines (2024), high-risk applications (e.g., credit scoring, robo-advisory) need to be documented with the algorithm, have a human-in-the-loop validation, and be audited on compliance periodically (Kayani & Hasan, 2024). The Korean model is conscious cosmopolitanization without neglecting locally emphasized consumer protection concerns.

3.3.3 Singapore

Singapore is one example of the balanced model of sandbox driven innovation, and responsible innovation. The Monetary Authority of Singapore (MAS) was expanded its Artificial Intelligence Governance Framework (2023 Edition), Veritas Initiative 2.0 (2024) which contains the principles of Fairness, Ethics, Accountability and Transparency (FEAT). These frameworks allow financial institutions to employ AI models under regulated environments and then introduce them on a large scale (Pereira, 2020). MAS's approach is to assure faith in the marketplace through experimentation coupled with consumer protection, and is now being imitated by other emerging economie.

Transition

Whilst jurisdictions do vary in the Asia-Pacific region, India's regulatory ecosystem is unique in the combination of sectoral regulation and digital public infrastructure and sandbox experimentation - a pragmatic hybrid model.

3.4 India

As per a report published by NITI Aayog, India's regulatory framework for AI in finance is a combination of sectoral regulation, a digital public infrastructure, and experimentation through sandboxes (Sharma, Beniwal, & Garg, 2022).

3.4.1 Regulators

The financial industry is supervised by different institutions namely:

- Reserve Bank of India (RBI): Regulates AI-based lending, fraud detection and risk assessment.
- Securities and Exchange Board of India (SEBI): Regulates algorithm trading as well as robo-advisory trading platforms.
- Insurance Regulatory and Development Authority of India (IRDAI): Governance in the use of AI for underwriting and risk modelling.

Furthermore, recent updates include RBI's Framework for FinTech Sandbox (2024) and also SEBI Circular on AI/ML Systems in Trading (2023), which proposes to adhere to standardized testing procedures and audit capabilities to make adherence to ethics possible.

3.4.2 Regulatory Sandboxes

RBI, SEBI and IRDAI in their sandboxes provide for a controlled AI innovation with a real-time regulatory supervision (Giumelli and Onderco, 2021). AI-based credit-risk models and anti-fraud analytics applications were part of RBI's 2023-2024 sandbox cohort; an example of India's ability to experiment responsibly around risk.

3.4.3 Digital Public Infrastructure

India's Digital Public Infrastructure (DPI): the Digital Public Infrastructure is a part of India Stack, which is also known as Unified Payments Interface (UPI) and Account Aggregator Framework, that provides secured data sharing rails to power AI applications. UPI will be growing in 2024 And the adoption of Open Credit Enablement Network (OCEN) will make financial ecosystems even more interoperable and transparent in AI-driven finance.

3.4.4 Data Governance

The Digital Personal Data Protection (DPDP) Act 2023 provides a comprehensive data protection system, focusing on the consent of the user, accountability of algorithms and legal cross-border transfers (Kashefi, Kashefi, & Mirsaraei, 2024). The notified rules of 2024 under the Act describes obligations of Data Fiduciaries in relation to AI based profiling and automated decision making which will bring India on par with the GDPR level of safeguards.

3.4.5 Emerging Institutions and Policy Initiatives

India has institutionalized AI regulation, which is the proposed IndiaAI Mission (2024) and the IndiaAI Safety Institute that will be responsible for model safety, fairness and audit. Integrating the NITI Aayog's AI for financial inclusion update (2024) which stresses on responsible use of AI in the access to credit and risk management and strengthening the ethical innovation behind financial governance.

3.4.6 Analytical Perspective

India's approach to regulation is based on hybrid approach of regulation, digital infrastructure and sandbox testing which is meant for innovation with consumer protection and market integrity (Cepec & Grajzl, 2021). The Indian experience serves as a model which is replicable for the emerging economies which are seeking to reconcile local realities with global AI norms.

Table 1. Comparative Analysis of Global AI Regulatory Frameworks in Finance (Emphasis on India)

Jurisdiction	Regulatory Model / Key Legislation	Supervisory Authority	Risk-Classification Approach	Key Compliance Requirements (Finance-Relevant)	Recent Updates (2023 – 2025)
European Union	*Artificial Intelligence Act (2024)* and *GDPR (2016/679)* – centralized, risk-based framework	European Commission; ESMA; EBA	Four tiers – Unacceptable / High / Limited / Minimal risk	Mandatory technical documentation, human-oversight provisions, data-quality audits, and post-market monitoring	2024 AI Act adopted; ESMA guidelines on AI use in trading (2025)
United States	Decentralized, sector-specific statutes; no single AI law – governed by agency guidance	SEC; CFTC; CFPB; Federal Reserve	Functional risk categorization based on activity (securities, derivatives, consumer finance)	Disclosure of AI model use, cyber-resilience controls, case-specific enforcement	White House Executive Order on AI (2023); SEC AI Risk Management Bulletin (2024)
China	Centralized command-and-control model – *Algorithmic Recommendation Provisions (2022)* and CAC Guidelines (2023)	Cyberspace Administration of China (CAC); People's Bank of China	State-defined risk tiers with mandatory algorithm audits	Algorithm filing and audit reports, data localization, bias testing	2023 CAC Guidelines tightened AI audit rules; PBOC Fintech Development Plan (2024)
South Korea	EU-inspired risk-based regulation – *AI Framework Act (2023)*	Financial Services Commission (FSC)	High/Medium/Low risk categories with mandatory audits for high-risk finance	Algorithm documentation, explainability reports, ethics audits	FSC AI Ethics Guidelines (2024) implemented
Singapore	Sandbox-based innovation model – MAS FEAT Principles & AI Governance Framework (2023)	Monetary Authority of Singapore (MAS)	Contextual risk evaluation within sandbox testing	Participation in sandbox, impact assessments, audit logs, explainability disclosures	Veritas Initiative 2.0 (2024) expanded AI risk testing and transparency requirements
India	Hybrid model – sector-specific regulators (RBI, SEBI, IRDAI) + DPDP Act (2023) + sandbox frameworks	RBI; SEBI; IRDAI; MeitY	Emerging risk-tiered classification under sandbox framework	Algorithm audit trails, consent under DPDP 2023, sandbox reporting	RBI FinTech Sandbox Framework (2024); SEBI AI/ML Circular (2023); IndiaAI Mission (2024)

Table 1 presents a comparative snapshot of AI regulatory approaches across major jurisdictions. It highlights three dominant models—centralized risk-based systems (EU and China), decentralized sectoral frameworks (United States), and hybrid or sandbox-driven approaches (Singapore and India). Each regime varies in

enforcement style, risk classification, and oversight mechanisms, reflecting different balances between innovation and consumer protection. The table underscores the growing global convergence toward transparency, algorithmic accountability, and human oversight, which are becoming universal pillars of AI governance in financial markets.

4. INDIAN CASE STUDY

Artificial Intelligence (AI) is being applied in India, and it is transforming the traditional financial activities through simplifying the processes, affordability, and availability of financial services. Nonetheless, the use of the technology has resulted in regulatory and legal challenges in the context of market integrity, investor protection and algorithmic accountability (De Carvalho 2022). This part can be used in the hypothetical case SEBI v. Zerodha and an actual world regulatory program (RBI fintech Sandbox) to introduce the evolving nature of AI in India.

4.1 Hypothetical Case: SEBI v. Zerodha – AI-Driven Algorithmic Trading

4.1.1 Context

The hypothetical case of Zerodha and SEBI provides a clue of compliance and governance concerns, which can occur with the application of AI in trading platforms of retail use. It has one of the largest brokerage companies in India (Zerodha) that employs AI algorithms to execute orders automatically and provide predictive advice on investment. Although such systems have led to enhanced trading efficiency, there has been increased concerns with regard to transparency, fairness and systemic risk management. In comparison to the traditional algorithms, the AI models are trained dynamically, that in most cases results in a black-box decision making mechanism, where even the operators cannot adequately explain the outcomes (Cheng and Gong, 2024). This obscurity poses a possible challenge of market manipulation, shareholder dis-favor and non-observance of SEBI regulatory standards.

4.1.2 Key Legal Issues

1. **Lack of Transparency/Algorithmic Trading**

SEBI rules require, that brokerage platforms must have extensive audit trails and documentation of how the algorithmic decision-making process works out. This would be unless it is done in an open manner and the principle of fair trading could be defied and the market confidence lost.

2. **Investor Protection and Market Integrity**

The Security and Exchange Board of India Act 1992 and SEBI (Prohibition of Fraudulent and Unfair Trade Practices) Regulations 2003 apply to the AI based trading activities. Misbehavior in the form of biased or skewed results of AI that translate into distorted market results can result in civil and/or administrative fines (Kayani and Hasan, 2024).

3. **SEBI Guidelines and Insider Trading Provision are mandatory**

Even though SEBI has not yet enacted any particular regulation about AI, it has issued advisories in favor of the ethical application of algorithm trading systems. The insider trading prevention, reduction of information asymmetries and reduction of algorithmic risks have a focus within these advisories. This case brings out the issue of incompatibility between new emerging practices of AI and the existing securities law regime in India.

4.1.3 Enforcement and Regulatory Mechanisms

SEBI, in such an instance, will have an interest in a gradual investigation and posing the following questions:

- Zerodha AI model logic and architecture technical audit;
- Audit trails and internal control procedures to confirm that there are sufficient internal controls, grievance procedures
- Leveraging Excessive Market Potential / Unfair Advantage.

The enforcement measure might be fines and requiring the pre-trade algorithms auditing to either halting the AI operation (at least temporarily) and issuing new instructions by the concerned regulators. The foregoing measures reveal that the risk-based strategy of SEBI on AI in financial markets has been changing over time (Sharma, Beniwal, and Garg, 2022).

4.1.4 Lessons for Harmonization and Risk-Based Classification

The SEBI v. The Zerodha case illuminates the necessity of the risk approach to the classification of AI in India, with references to the character of the AI applications (high-risk applications, which are trading algorithms and low-risk advisory tools). Additionally, this insists on same transparency conditions, algorithmic audits and redressal of bias (based on the international standards of the EU AI Act and the Organisation for Economic Cooperation and Development (OECD AI Principles). Altogether, the argument of unscrupulous adaptive regulation to protect innovation by investor and market protection is posed in the case.

4.2 Customer Data Practice: Customer Data Work Case RBI FinTech Sandbox Pilot

4.2.1 Overview and Regulatory Context

The Reserve Bank of India (RBI) has been exceptionally active to pilot financial solutions on the basis of AI in the shape of Regulatory Sandbox initiative. Being regulated, the sandbox provides fintech companies with the chance to test machine-learning software - in predictive credit scoring, fraud detection and automatic verification of customers - without worry of the regulators scrutinizing their activities. It can be described as a controlled environment that represents an innovation ecosystem with a very low systemic risk (Vettriselvan et al., 2025).In recent Cohort (2023-2024), AI-based micro-loan underwriting and real-time fraud monitoring and ESG-based investment scoring were the pilots featured in RBI FinTech Department Annual Report (2024) and Regulatory Sandbox Cohort Announcement (2023).

4.2.2 Applications and Benefits

1. **Financial Inclusion** – AI-based credit scoring enables access to formal financing - by enabling individuals who cannot get access to formal credit history and who can use alternative data to secure employment.
2. **Operational Efficiency** – The manual credit assessment and fraud detection procedures are reduced and this increases the processing speed and leads to increased stability of the financial system.
3. **Innovation and Market Development** – Sandbox participation will be a field where one can experiment in a secure way that will not only lead to innovation and competition of products but also do so with the jurisdiction of the authorities.

4.2.3 Risks and Challenges

1. **Algorithmic Bias** – ML Models make use of the past information, which may cause bias such that some individuals will not get credit or get access to investments among others.

2. **Data Privacy and Security** – The processing of the sensitive personal and financial data involves a strict compliance with the Digital Personal Data Protection Act, 2023, the RBI circulars and privacy compliance in the corresponding industries.
3. **Systemic and Operational Risk** – unmonitored systems of AI may lead to unforeseen vulnerabilities that result in the rise of contagion risks in related markets.

4.2.4 Regulatory Response and Oversight

The sandbox framework of RBI has some safeguards that entail:

- frequent reporting of performance and results of the AI model
- compulsory disclosure of algorithm parameters;
- bias detection and mitigation procedures
- Post pilot assessment in order to meet the requirements on risk management.

These mechanisms are indicative of the attitude of RBI to supervised innovation - i.e. encouraging innovation prudentially.

4.2.5 Implications for Indian AI Governance

India test-and-regulate - the sandbox - is a means to enable innovation to occur within predetermined goals of risk. It has significant implications to national AI policy making that highlights on the establishment of a balanced model of AI regulation that is proportional, ethical and that safeguards investors. Application of the sandbox learning in international standards such as the OECD AI Principles and EU AI Act will assist India in transitioning to harmonized and sectoral AI Governance frameworks (Minkkinen, Zimmer and Mantymaki, 2022).

5. CHALLENGES IN HARMONIZED AI REGULATION

Artificial intelligence (AI) has already invaded the financial market with all its might and would lead to a paradigm shift in algorithm trading, credit rating, fraud detection and risk management. Nevertheless, the spread of AI technologies throughout the planet posed a number of regulatory and legal issues, particularly those of coordination of governance regimes across jurisdictions. The combination of transnational financial markets and the lack of transparency of the algorithm has resulted in an uneven and broken regulatory space. Moreover, various ethical guidelines, various supervisory abilities and various forms of risk occur in various jurisdictions that makes harmonisation a difficult undertaking (Robles and Mallinson, 2025). In this section of the paper, the author critically evaluates the five most significant issues concerning how to establish a consistent legal framework on AI in the financial sector on cross-border.

5.1 Divergent Risk Classification Models

In fact, they find the absence of harmonisation on the categorisation on risk-based of AI systems across the globe as one of the challenges that banks are facing. The degree of regulatory monitoring and compliance rules of financial institutions is the amount of risk classification. One of the better examples of this is the EU Artificial Intelligence Act (2024), which has a risk-based framework to classify AI applications as being high-risk (banned) or low-risk, with more stringent documentation and audit requirements being in place on the former just as with credit scoring or automated trading (De Carvalho, 2022).Nonetheless, even regulators such as the Securities and Exchange Commission (SEC) and the Consumer Financial Protection Bureau (CFPB) publish guidance without a standardized taxonomy - the model that the United States continues to use in a sectorial model. The adoption in the Asia-Pacific region is varied - although China was the first to adopt the use of algorithmic audits of high-risk financial models with its Race-to-the-Top in 2023 and its Regulation on Deep Synthesis Algorithms, South Korea has adapted the categorical model and uses it in its 2024 AI Ethics Guidelines. India RBI, SEBI and IRDAI have sectoral regulators who are applying the sandbox testing and risk assessment that they have had.

Real life example: The authorities of the European supervisory authorities have described the AI-based credit scoring models as high risk in 2024 and this has made the banks such as ING and Deutsche Bank to consider the algorithmic impact assessment before implementing such models. This classification posed cross-border compliance risk on the U.S.-based fintechs who are offering the same products in Europe. It is the difference, which is involved in the problem of multinational financial organizations and the asymmetry of the compliance and the problem of different regime to different regime of classification resulting in different levels of oversight.

5.2 Cross-Border Data Transfer Restrictions

The AI governance of the finance sector is based on convenient access to vast volumes of financial, personal or behavioural information. It is however very hard to train models and detect cross-border fraud because of the variousdata transfer regulations. Digital Personal Data Protection Act, 2023 (DPDPA) Digital Personal

Data Protection Act, 2023 (DPDPA) regulates the transfer of sensitive personal information as regards to localisation and contractual protection. International transfers that fall under the local or general contractual terms apply to an EU General Data Protection Regulation (GDPR) Article 44 -50 (Freeda et al., 2024).

Practical analogy A case in point is the European Union (EU) and United States (US) launched the Data Privacy Framework in the year 2024 that removed the concept of adequacy and introduced the concept of limited adequacy of US providers but not India, such that Indian fintechs cooperating with European banks would be required to establish regional data silos. This copying renders the model inefficient and the cost of operation is great. In a recent research, performed by the Organisation Economic Co-operation and Development (OECD, 2024) about the AI technologies adoption, the non-homogeneity of DTPs can slay interoperability of AI models by 20 per cent of the global population. Nonetheless, a compromise between these opposing models remains necessary through multilateral acceptance of the mechanisms of adequacy (Chen, Wu, and Zhao, 2023).

5.3 Algorithmic Transparency and Explainability

AI systems are normally black-boxes and hence the regulation responsibilities are challenging. The step of transparency and explainability in empowering regulators, financial institution and consumers to knowledge the pathways of the decisions is very crucial. A human oversight system and post market monitoring system are required to be established under the EU AI Act (2024) in high risk AI systems. Although the disclosure principles (and not necessary explainability principles) exist in the U.S. SEC and FTC, the Indian sectoral regulators (RBI, SEBI) have imposed audit trails and bias-mitigating mechanisms - which aims at purging discrimination on the ground of factors (such as caste, gender or socio-economic status).

Real world example: in fact, in UK in 2023, an AI-based lending platform was investigated by the UK Financial Conduct Authority (FCA) because of the lack of transparency in their decision making, and they were required to publish model explainability reports - a practice accepted in EU and OECD guidelines on algorithmic accountability (Bernardy and Spiwack 2021). This has, in turn, implied that the various jurisdictions have divergent transparency requirements, so that regulatory uncertainty and international consensus on the norms on algorithmic auditability and accountability are introduced.

5.4 Ethical Concerns

Accountability: This can be established by the ethical governance to make responsible AI adoption founded in financial terms, which fosters equity, accountability, and inclusiveness. The lack of regulation of the AI systems implies that the bias of the system may be reproduced further and the marginalized groups may be even more deprived of the access to finances. The fact that the fairness-review, human oversight, and compulsory impact assessment of systems with high risk were touched upon in the structure of the AI Principles published by the Organisation for Economic Cooperation and Development (OECD) (2024) and the artificial intelligence (AI) Act in the European Union (2024). The ethical regulation in India is taking the shape of RBI, SEBI, IRDAI regulations and the proposed Institute of AI Safety, India (IndiaAI Safety Institute) will assist in the development of the ethical norms (Cepec & Grajzl, 2021).

Real world case: In 2024, RBI dismissed an AI-based micro-credit model because of the possibility of gender bias during training data, highlighting the need to ethically regulate financial products. But on the one hand it is possible to note that with the absence of ethically consistent standards on a global basis what may be ethical in one jurisdiction may lead to non-compliance with other ethical standards in other jurisdictions that pose cross-border compliance risks and reputational risk to financial institutions.

Figure 1. Challenges in Global AI Regulation

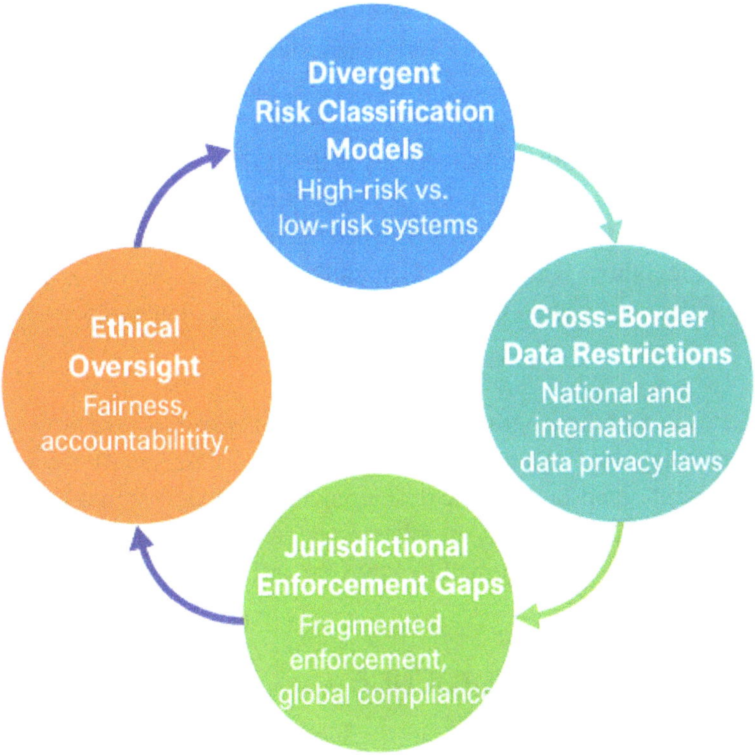

As Figure 1 shows, there are interrelated challenges to the development of a coherent system of international governance of artificial intelligence (AI), at least as it relates to financial markets. A circular flow diagram format is used to describe these four key regulatory issues, where each of the four nodes represents each of the four regulatory issues.

- **Divergent Risk Classification Models (Blue):** AI systems are classified as low or high risk based on a wide variety of jurisdictions which is perceived to result in varied regulatory threshold and compliance burden. This variation limits the ability to implement cross border and mitigation strategies.
- **Cross-Border Data Restrictions:** Teal (Cross-Border data restrictions) are those restrictions which are introduced by national and regional data privacy laws (or in the case of sector-specific restrictions, the algorithmic training may be restricted). Some examples of this are the GDPR, the Indian DPDP

Act and some restrictions at the level of the government sector. The limits constrain the scalability and interoperability of the built AI systems.

- **Jurisdictional Enforcement Gaps (Green):** Inconsistent laws and enforcement with regards to accountability and fragmented oversight due to jurisdictional gaps. This contradiction undermines the efforts of international compliance and opens the space for regulatory relays.
- **Ethical Oversight (Orange):** As it comes to the ethical oversight of AI, this domain seems to be a relatively unlevel playing field in terms of the capacities of organizations to undertake AI, between those who are ethical, accountable, and fair, and those who are not. Generally, the ethical principles are not absolute but ideal and should only be used to practical extent in the business world.

The loop-like design of the diagram provides an amazing insight into how such difficulties are not isolated but rather form a cycle and are, therefore, inter-connected. The latter all represent an obstacle to the development of a coherent international AI regulatory framework, particularly in relation to the financial services sector, where it is common to have algorithmic black-boxing and systemic risk.

6. POSSIBILITIES OF CONVERGENCE

The rate of adoption of artificial intelligence (AI) in financial markets has led to a lack of uniformity with firms operating across jurisdictions operating in different regulatory jurisdictions, thus giving rise to cross-border compliance, investor-protecting and operational challenges. Although various regulatory models are being adopted in countries, such as the centralized AI Act in the European Union, the industry-based approach in the United States, and emerging hybrid models (e.g. India), there is an urgent need to develop convergence mechanisms to balance AI governance without stifling innovation. The convergence of AI regulation can lead to an increase in legal certainty, enhanced financial integrity on a global scale, consumer rights, and ethical application of AI technologies.This section delineates four key possible operationalisation avenues for the notion of convergence: mutual recognition agreements, cross-border regulatory sandboxes, global ethical frameworks for AI and structured public-private partnerships (Ibrahim et al., 2024).

6.1 Mutual Recognition Agreements of AI Standards

Mutual Recognition Agreements (MRAs) are the instruments employed by jurisdictions to acknowledge the equivalence of each other's standards for meeting the requirements and certification of AI. Within the financial industry, MRAs can have an important role in reducing the incidence of repetitive audits, minimizing the cost of cross-border compliance of multi-national financial institutions, and also assisting in the smooth deployment of artificial intelligence enabled services across markets (Pereira, 2020).

Such agreements are founded on the principle of regulatory equivalence which implies that the jurisdiction takes into consideration similar standards of risk management, transparency and ethical control. For example, as part of the EU (European Union) and United States (US) FinTech Memorandum of Understanding (MoU) on cybersecurity and anti-money laundering supervision, a precedent on mutual recognition has been set. As is the case with AI governance, MRAs could be used to achieve cross-recognition of algorithmic audit reports, AI risk classifications, and bias-mitigation certifications. Such mechanisms would minimize regulatory fragmentation, increase investor confidence and provide more legal certainty to the cross-border introduction of AI-driven products by financial firms. Furthermore, MRAs facilitate the alignment of standards - risk assessment standards, transparency requirements and audit standards - and therefore enable a shared regulatory framework for AI in finance (De Almeida, Santos, & Farias, 2021).

6.2 Cross-Border Regulatory Sandboxes

Regulatory sandboxes: These are platforms that allow fintech companies and financial institutions to develop and test out the AI-powered innovations under regulated conditions and regulatory oversight. Cross-border sandboxes take the idea a step further by allowing for experimentation across a number of jurisdictions.

For example, India and Singapore have the India-Singapore FinTech Bridge which includes alignment of sandbox regulations between RBI and MAS, sharing of supervisory experience and exchange of information on AI-based financial products. Such collaborations help to support interoperability and allow regulators to recognize common principles related to the compliance aspects of model validation, privacy of data and risk management. By standardising testing protocols and reporting frameworks, cross-border sandboxes ease the confusion of innovators and pave the way for collaborative certification systems for AI. They also contribute to the strengthening of international supervision through the provision of ecosystems of collective learning, which integrates technical know-how and regulatory supervision.

6.3 Embracing Global AI Ethics Frameworks

Finance industry AI must adhere to universally agreed ethical values. The OECD AI Guidelines and the G20 AI Guidelines offer internationally agreed-upon standards of AI development for AI transparency, accountability, fairness, privacy and human supervision (Kour & Schutte, 2025).

In order to implement the following principles, regulators and financial institutions can take the following steps:

1. AI Impact Assessments: All high-risk AI systems (algorithmic trading or credit-scoring models) have to go through the evaluation and assessment process; therefore, this process should be ex-ante, which specifically looks at the risks posed by the AI system both from an ethical and financial perspective.
2. Model-Card Documentation - Model card documents should be standardized, include all the important information, such as data sources, training process, performance metrics, fairness measurements, etc. Documentation should be granular enough to be auditable.
3. Continuous Ethical Audits and Human Oversight - Institutions must have human oversight and periodic third party audit of deployed models.
4. Compliance with National Laws - Embedding the principles of the organisation of economic co-operation (OECD) and the group of twenty (G20) into national laws (ICB, RBI, SEBI and IRDAI) - Embedding the notion of ethics into binding what is law.

By establishing these principles in national regulations, and making them mandatory rather than voluntary, ethical AI governance is established. Universalised approaches can help to drive interoperability across jurisdictions, reduce opportunities for regulatory arbitrage, and establish investor confidence in AI-enabled financial systems. Lastly, the adherence to ethical standards promotes the integrity and inclusivity of the global financial markets.

6.4 Public–Private Partnership

"We need to have a formal public-private partnership (PPP) model to facilitate the transition of AI governance principles into practice." These partnerships enable the regulators to keep up with evolving technological and ethical issues and the industry stakeholders to effectively put into practice the compliance expectations.

Co-regulatory mechanisms, advisory committees, joint working groups, or sandbox advisory boards are some of the different mechanisms of public-private collaboration that could be considered. In India, both RBI and SEBI sandbox initiatives have been actively engaging industry stakeholders in the testing of transparency measures and reduction of bias. At the global level, multi-lateral working groups hosted by international organizations such as the OECD and the Bank for International Settlements (BIS) are established to get regulators, AI experts, and financial institutions to work together to develop policy responses to the issues.Legally, these alliances enable the conversion of guidelines into enforceable standards, which is the perfect combination of innovation and responsibility. Additionally, they provide an opportunity for continuous optimization of AI policies, changing the standards as technology develops and ensuring that governance models are flexible to emerging threats. Iterative Collaboration: PPPs facilitate a dynamic and flexible regulatory framework for AI in international financial markets.

6.5 Synthesis of Convergence Mechanisms

Together, these pathways of convergence - mutual recognition agreements, cross-border sandboxes, global frameworks of ethics and public-private partnerships - form a multidimensional map for aligning AI governance across jurisdictions. Although each of the mechanisms deals with distinct problems of regulation and operation, each is part of a single system of international cooperation.

For India, such an approach would bring national innovation plans in line with international practices, build regulatory legitimacy and facilitate the responsible implementation of AI in the finance sector. Such mechanisms are likely to help reduce systemic risks, boost investor confidence and encourage international consistency of the legal framework surrounding AI in financial markets (Giumelli & Onderco, 2021) by providing legal interoperability, ethical conformity and harmonized governance.

Table 2. Opportunities for Regulatory Convergence in AI Governance (Including India)

Mechanism	Description	Benefits	Example Jurisdictions
Mutual Recognition	Recognition of foreign AI audits & certifications	Reduced compliance burden	EU-US, India-Singapore
Cross-border Sandbox	Joint regulatory test environment	Encourages innovation	India-Singapore fintech sandbox
Global Ethics Standards	OECD/G20 AI principles	Responsible AI adoption	EU, US, OECD members

Table 2 contains the list of potential areas of emerging regulatory convergence in the governance of AI with special relevance to India in the international context. Reciprocity of foreign AI auditing and certification can potentially alleviate compliance burden and ease cross border dealings. Other rising sandboxes are cross-border, e.g., India-Singapore fintech bridge which allows the parties to use an AI innovation and test it cross-border under a common control environment of regulatory authorities. Meanwhile, such international ethics regulations as those of the Organization for Economic Cooperation and Development and G20 are the

shared moral framework for a responsible development of AI. Cumulatively, the above mechanisms will lead to harmonisation and de-fragmentation, as well as trust in AI systems between jurisdictions.

Figure 2. Proposed Unified AI Regulatory Framework for Finance

Figure 2 illustrates a five pillar framework that encompasses the pillars of artificial intelligence (AI) of legal and regulatory framework in financial systems. At the centre of each pillar lies an important aspect of governance, which aims to establish the international good practice at global level, and balancing sectoral risks and ethical needs.

7. PROPOSED COMMON LEGAL SYSTEM: A FIVE-PILLAR UNIFIED FRAMEWORK FOR AI IN FINANCE

Artificial Intelligence (AI) is quickly becoming part of financial markets and there is a need for a comprehensive regulatory framework to allow innovation while ensuring investor protection and market stability. Inspired by the global regulatory frameworks and the emerging financial-AI dynamics in India, this section proposes a 5-pillar convergent legal architecture to attain responsible AI oversight (Kashefi, Kashefi & Mirsaraei, 2024). Taken together, these pillars address the areas of formalised risk management, standardised compliance, ethical responsibility, formalised collaboration between stakeholders and internationalisation. The framework outlined provides a useful guide for policymakers and financial institutions on how to responsibly embrace AI while mitigating the risks on a systemic, consumer and market level while at the same time driving growth through innovation

7.1 Pillar 1: Risk-Based Classification of AI

AI governance in the financial industry is based on risk-based classification. Under this approach, AI systems are categorized on the basis of its potential implications on consumers, the functionality of markets and monetary stability. More robust regulatory controls, ongoing audits and impact assessment of AI systems to ensure that they are at least auditable and traceable, and also undergo regular audits to detect impact on different stakeholders and outcomes. Moderate supervision is applied to medium risk applications such as robo-advisory platforms and very little regulation is applicable to low risk applications such as internal analytics applications.

Implementation Measures

For this pillar, the EU AI Act (2021) could be the source for adopting a national AI-risk taxonomy, as it mandates the obligation for continuous auditing of performance and mandatory registration of high-risk systems for RBI and SEBI's sandbox regimes. This will ensure transparency, proportionality and regulatory flexibility with regard to the financial ecosystem of India.

7.2 Pillar 2: Interoperable Compliance and Data Governance

This pillar is dedicated to harmonization of AI compliance mechanisms between the regulatory and jurisdictional space. Given that fintech is predominantly international as is data processing, so should data governance. Regulatory fragmentation must be avoided by aligning Digital Personal Data Protection (DPDP) Act, 2023 with sectoral regulations of RBI, SEBI and IRDAI (Ridzuan et al., 2024).

Implementation Measures

Compliance templates, data consent frameworks and bi-lateral data exchange agreements that would respect the principles of the OECD and GDPR would be produced. Regulatory sandboxes have the potential to facilitate the testing of harmonized reporting and compliance systems to ensure interoperability, all in line with privacy requirements.

7.3 Pillar 3: Ethical Supervisory Oversight

Ethical governance: AI can drive financial decision-making in an unethical way if it is not governed ethically. Explainability mechanisms and audit trails to trace the logic behind the algorithms are needed to be able to detect bias and unfairness by regulators (Shalaby, 2024).

Implementation Measures

Financial institutions must have real-time audit logs, perform fairness testing to uncover bias and submit themselves to third-party verification audits. Also, each regulator (RBI, SEBI, IRDAI, etc) should establish "AI Ethics Cell" to report on the ethical compliance and a review should be done on complaints by consumers and pattern of the complaints to prevent discrimination outcomes.

7.4 Pillar 4: Structured Public-Private Collaboration

His pillar is concerned with creating partnerships with the private sector and establishing public-private partnerships that can contribute to the sustainability of the health systems.AI governance is a joint effort between the private innovators and public sector (Vukovic, Dekpo-Adza, & Matovic, 2025).

Implementation Measures

AI compliance standards should be developed in advisory panels that consist of regulators, fintech companies, academia and industry associations. Further, creating an AI Finance Forum India can help in knowledge sharing, building capabilities and creating open source compliance tools. The evidence-based dynamic regulatory adjustment through feedback loops should be institutionalized in a sandbox.

7.5 Pillar 5: Multilateral Cooperation in Global Regulatory Platforms

Many of the functions of AI in finance are transnational, so it is important to have multilateral convergence. India's active participation in institutions such as IMF, BIS and the OECD would strengthen its voice in the development of global norms for AI governance (Kour & Schutte, 2025a)

Implementation Measures

India needs to pursue MRAs in AI-risk assessment with its neighbours, align domestic standards with BIS and OECD transparency standards and also participate in international pilots such as the India-Singapore fintech partnership to experiment with multi-jurisdictional AI audit regimes.The proposed five pillar integrated framework provides a great framework of responsible AI governance in the financial markets. The framework will also facilitate innovation and financial stability, by bringing together risk-based regulation, interoperable compliance standards, ethical governance, collaborative governance and cross-border regulatory convergence. This unifying regulatory framework positions India as a leader in establishing global standards for the ethical and secure deployment of AI-powered financial systems.

Table 3. Mapping of Pillars to Key Laws and Institutions

Pillar	Core Objective	Relevant Laws / Guidelines	Primary Institutions
1 Risk-Based Classification	Tier AI systems by financial risk	EU AI Act (2021); RBI & SEBI AI-risk frameworks	RBI, SEBI, MEITY
2 Interoperable Compliance & Data Governance	Harmonize data and compliance standards	DPDP Act 2023; GDPR; OECD AI Principles	RBI, SEBI, IRDAI, OECD
3 Ethical Supervisory Resources	Ensure transparency and fairness	EU AI Act; RBI Digital Lending Guidelines (2022)	RBI, SEBI, Ethics Cells
4 Public-Private Collaboration	Institutionalize co-regulation & knowledge-sharing	RBI/SEBI Sandbox Frameworks; FinTech Charters	RBI, SEBI, Industry Bodies
5 Multilateral Cooperation	Achieve cross-border regulatory alignment	OECD Guidelines; BIS AI Reports; IMF FinTech Notes	IMF, BIS, OECD, RBI, SEBI

8. CONCLUSION

This paper provides a comparative analysis of regulatory regimes governing the use of Artificial Intelligence (AI) in financial markets with a particular emphasis on the emerging regulatory framework in India. The results indicate a large amount of heterogeneity among jurisdictions in their approach to AI governance. The European Union (EU) has come up with a risk-based approach to its AI Act, where the main emphasis is the transparency, auditability and consumer protection of AI systems. The regulatory environment in the United States is decentralized and agency specific (such as the Security and Exchange Commission (SEC) and the Consumer Financial Protection Bureau (CFPB)). The fragmented regulatory structure has been a result of this structure, which allows for innovation. In the Asia-Pacific region, the picture is mixed with China having introduced mandatory ex-ante algorithm audits, while South Korea has adopted EU inspired risk classification systems (Pardhey & Yuni, 2023).

Amidst all this diversity, India's model with its sector-specific programs like regulatory sandboxes, digital public infrastructures, the soon-to-be IndiaAI Safety Institute, and the Digital Personal Data Protection (DPDP) Act 2023, is a pragmatic balance between innovation and oversight. This dual approach is a manifestation of the policy objective of India to promote technological development, while protecting the integrity of the markets and the interests of the consumers.The necessity of a common international regulatory framework to balance innovation and ethical responsibility and investor protection emerges from this comparative analysis. Fragmentation of standards and physical barriers to the cross-border sharing of data continue to hamper harmonized compliance as well as even-handed enforcement. Insider trading laws have taught us lessons that AI-enabled financial ecosystems are likely to face similar jurisdictional gaps, information asymmetries and enforcement issues, thus necessitating coordinated international mechanisms to address them (Camilleri, 2023). In particular, building transparent, accountable and trustworthy AI-enabled financial services will depend on the development of harmonised global standards that reduce compliance burden for multi-national institutions while building a higher degree of confidence, fairness and accountability in AI-based finance.

8.1 Recommendations

A. Regulators

To do justice to the proper guarantee of proper governance, the regulators should indeed change their practice on both the short, medium and long-term perspectives: in the short-term (0-1 year), national and supranational regulators should issue risk-based guidelines specific to the application of AI to financial markets. Regulatory sandboxes offered by RBI, SEBI and IRDAI must be expanded and interconnected in cross-border innovation programs, where innovation would be developed in a controlled environment (Drame-Maignc et al., 2021).

Over the medium term (1-3 years), regulators should have standardised reporting templates, introduce a mandatory ethical review mechanism and common audit requirements to increase transparency and comparability.In the longer term (3+ years), domestic frameworks should align with those of international organisations such as the OECD, BIS and IMF in order to ensure interoperable supervision and minimise regulatory arbitrage across jurisdictions.

B. Financial Institutions (Banks, FinTechs, and Insurance Firms)

In the short term, institutions should implement internal AI compliance regimes to ensure that institutions meet the national and international commitments.In the medium term, there are key measures that the firms need to implement in order to institutionalise bias mitigation controls, ensure algorithmic transparency, and ensure proper audit trails for accountability.In the long-term, they must implement continuous monitoring systems and also improve cross-jurisdictional cooperation to forecast new risks and changing regulatory requirements (Pardhey & Yuni, 2023).

C. International Cooperation

Peer to peer learning remains an important way to achieve coherent AI governance. Over the short term, nations should step up cooperation with Global standard setters, such as the Organisation for Economic Cooperation and Development (OECD), Bureau of International Settlement (BIS) and Fund Monetary International (IMF), for knowledge sharing and joint capacity building and harmonization of definitions (Drame-Maigne et al., 2021); Over the medium term, work on mutual recognition of AI audit certifications, cross-border regulatory sandboxes and interoperability pilots.Over time, the development of universal ethical standards and processes of cooperation will foster common regulatory expectations and result in investor faith, traditional and new markets alike will be guided by consistent standards of equity and accountability.

8.2 Limitations and Future Research

While the study takes into account the policy and legal developments until mid-2025, it is mostly based on doctrinal and comparative research rather than on empirical analysis. Future studies should take actual enforcement effects, institutional measures of performance and stakeholders' perceptions into account in order to assess the impact of harmonized AI-finance frameworks on market efficiency and ethical compliance, as well as on innovation dynamics.

8.3 Closing Reflection

In conclusion, while the transformative potential of AI in the financial markets is clear, it should be balanced with an appropriate regulatory framework in terms of legal stability as well as ethical considerations. India's sectoral approach coupled with a permissive approach to innovation offers a sustainable framework for governance of AI that can be perched upon at global levels (Pardhey & Yuni, 2023). An internationally coherent legal system that is risk sensitive and ethical will ensure the safety of investors, the integrity of markets, and a technologically advanced world in the age of intelligent finance that is guided by ethics.

REFERENCES

Bernardy, J., & Spiwack, A. (2021). Artefact for _Evaluating linear functions to symmetric monoidal categories_ [Dataset]. In *Artifact Digital Object Group*. DOI: 10.1145/3462282

Camilleri, M. A. (2023). Artificial intelligence governance: Ethical considerations and implications for social responsibility. *Expert Systems: International Journal of Knowledge Engineering and Neural Networks*, *41*(7), e13406. Advance online publication. DOI: 10.1111/exsy.13406

Çela, E., Vajjhala, N. R., & Aslani, B. (2025). Artificial intelligence in legal systems. In *Chapman and Hall/CRC eBooks*. DOI: 10.1201/9781003541899

Cepec, J., & Grajzl, P. (2021). Creditors, Plan Confirmations, and Bankruptcy Reorganizations: Lessons from Slovenia. *European Business Organization Law Review*, *22*(3), 559–589. DOI: 10.1007/s40804-021-00221-3

Chen, B., Wu, Z., & Zhao, R. (2023). From fiction to fact: The growing role of generative AI in business and finance. *Journal of Chinese Economic and Business Studies*, *21*(4), 471–496. DOI: 10.1080/14765284.2023.2245279

Chen, Z. Z., Ma, J., Zhang, X., Hao, N., Yan, A., Nourbakhsh, A., Yang, X., McAuley, J., Petzold, L., & Wang, W. Y. (2024, May 2). *A survey on large language models for critical societal domains: finance, healthcare, and law*. arXiv.org. https://arxiv.org/abs/2405.01769

Cheng, L., & Gong, X. (2024). *Appraising regulatory Framework towards Artificial General Intelligence (AGI) under Digital Humanism*. Deleted Journal., DOI: 10.1515/ijdlg-2024-0015

De Almeida, P. G. R., Santos, C. D. D., & Farias, J. S. (2021). Artificial Intelligence Regulation: A framework for governance. *Ethics and Information Technology*, *23*(3), 505–525. DOI: 10.1007/s10676-021-09593-z

De Carvalho, P. S. (2022). Retaining Influence in Post-Brexit International Financial Regulation: Lessons from the UK's FinTech Framework. *Journal of Financial Regulation*, *8*(1), 104–131. DOI: 10.1093/jfr/fjac004

Dramé-Maigné, S., Laurent, M., Castillo, L., & Ganem, H. (2021). Centralized, Distributed, and Everything in between. *ACM Computing Surveys*, *54*(7), 1–34. DOI: 10.1145/3465170

Freeda, A. R., Anju, A., Kanthavel, R., Dhaya, R., & Vijay, F. (2024). Integrating AI-Driven technologies into service marketing. In *Advances in marketing, customer relationship management, and e-services book series* (pp. 375–394). DOI: 10.4018/979-8-3693-7122-0.ch018

Giumelli, F., & Onderco, M. (2021). States, firms, and security: How private actors implement sanctions, lessons learned from the Netherlands. *European Journal of International Security*, *6*(2), 190–209. DOI: 10.1017/eis.2020.21

Ibrahim, A., Almasria, N. A., Alhatabat, Z. A., Ershaid, D. J. A., & Aldboush, H. H. (2024). Transforming financial services with artificial intelligence and machine learning. In *Advances in finance, accounting, and economics book series* (pp. 129–148). DOI: 10.4018/979-8-3693-8507-4.ch008

Kashefi, P., Kashefi, Y., & Mirsaraei, A. G. (2024). *Shaping the future of AI: balancing innovation and ethics in global regulation*. Uniform Law Review., DOI: 10.1093/ulr/unae040

Kayani, U., & Hasan, F. (2024). Unveiling Cryptocurrency impact on financial markets and traditional banking Systems: Lessons for sustainable blockchain and interdisciplinary Collaborations. *Journal of Risk and Financial Management*, *17*(2), 58. DOI: 10.3390/jrfm17020058

Kour, M., & Schutte, D. P. (2025a). Artificial intelligence and accounting. In *Routledge eBooks*. DOI: 10.4324/9781003571643

Minkkinen, M., Zimmer, M. P., & Mäntymäki, M. (2022). Co-Shaping an ecosystem for responsible AI: Five types of expectation work in response to a technological frame. *Information Systems Frontiers*, *25*(1), 103–121. DOI: 10.1007/s10796-022-10269-2

Pardhey, N., & Yuni, D. N. (2023). Legal efficiency of Secure Transactions Framework in India. In *Advances in finance, accounting, and economics book series* (pp. 171–182). DOI: 10.4018/979-8-3693-1038-0.ch011

Pereira, C. M. (2020). Unregulated Algorithmic trading: Testing the boundaries of the European Union Algorithmic Trading regime. *Journal of Financial Regulation*, *6*(2), 270–305. DOI: 10.1093/jfr/fjaa008

Ridzuan, N. N., Masri, M., Anshari, M., Fitriyani, N. L., & Syafrudin, M. (2024). AI in the Financial Sector: The Line between Innovation, Regulation and Ethical Responsibility. *Information (Basel)*, *15*(8), 432. DOI: 10.3390/info15080432

Robles, P., & Mallinson, D. J. (2025). Advancing AI governance with a unified theoretical framework: A systematic review. *Perspectives on Public Management and Governance*, *8*(4), 213–227. Advance online publication. DOI: 10.1093/ppmgov/gvaf013

Shalaby, A. (2024). Digital Sustainable Growth Model (DSGM): achieving synergy between economy and technology to mitigate AGI risks and address global debt challenges. *Journal of Economy and Technology*. DOI: 10.1016/j.ject.2024.08.003

Sharma, N., Beniwal, S., & Garg, P. (2022). ANT Colony based Optimization model for QOS-Based task scheduling in cloud computing environment. SSRN *Electronic Journal*. DOI: 10.2139/ssrn.4237751

Singh, B., Kaunert, C., & Kaushik, T. K. (2024). Unscrambling financial fraud with AI and machine learning in E-Commerce transactions. In *Advances in finance, accounting, and economics book series* (pp. 253–271). DOI: 10.4018/979-8-3693-4382-1.ch013

Singh, V. K. (2022). Regulatory and legal framework for promoting green digital Finance. In *Economics, law, and institutions in Asia Pacific* (pp. 3–27). DOI: 10.1007/978-981-19-2662-4_1

Vettriselvan, R., Velmurugan, P. R., Regins, J. C., Maheswari, S. U., & Joyce, R. (2025). Best practices, ethical challenges, and regulatory frameworks for AI integration in banking. In *Advances in computational intelligence and robotics book series* (pp. 377–410). https://doi.org/DOI: 10.4018/979-8-3693-9356-7.ch015

Vuković, D. B., Dekpo-Adza, S., & Matović, S. (2025). AI integration in financial services: A systematic review of trends and regulatory challenges. *Humanities & Social Sciences Communications*, *12*(1), 562. Advance online publication. DOI: 10.1057/s41599-025-04850-8

Chapter 6

Artificial Intelligence-Enabled Computational Techniques in Determining the Use Behavior of Crowdfunding Platforms

Niusha Shafiabady
Australian Catholic University, North Sydney, Australia

Muntadher A. Ali
National Academy of Professional Studies, Australia

Robert M. X. Wu
University of Technology Sydney, Australia

Siva Muthaly
Western Sydney University, Australia

Prabhu Sivabalan
University Technology Sydney, Australia

Wajeeha Ali
Asia Pacific University, Malaysia

Fareed Ud Din
http://orcid.org/0000-0001-6122-2043
University of New England, Australia

James Vakilian
Charles Darwin University, Australia

ABSTRACT

Crowdfunding has garnered much attention from academics and practitioners as a practical approach to raising funds for projects or ventures. This research aims to understand the use of Artificial Intelligence (AI) algorithms in determining the use

DOI: 10.4018/979-8-2600-1603-9.ch006

of Shariah-compliant Peer-to-Business (P2B) crowdfunding platforms. This study adopts Technology Acceptance Model and Unified Theory of Use of Technology to establish the conceptual model. Data is collected from 116 micro, small, and medium enterprises (MSMEs). Seven state-of-the-art AI algorithms, including Decision Tree (DT), Extra Tree (ET), K-Nearest Neighbors (KNN), Lo-gistic Regression (LR), Random Forest (RF), Support Vector Machine (SVM), and Extreme Gradient Boosting (XGBoost), are applied to evaluate the essential features of the Actual Use Behavior (AUB). The results indicate that RF, ET, and KNN are the top three methods in all AUBs. The findings suggest that incorporating AI in Shariah-compliant P2B crowdfunding enhances financial inclusivity by enabling more efficient resource allocation and supporting the growth of MSMEs

1. INTRODUCTION

As a practical approach to raising funds for projects or ventures, crowdfunding has garnered much attention from academics and practitioners (Rejeb et al., 2023), as it can contribute to the financing of sustainable businesses (Cumming et al., 2024). However, recent research highlights that crowdfunding is more successful in cultural and creative industries in countries where financial resources allocated to cultural and creative activities are high (Cicchiello et al., 2022). By deploying disruptive technologies, Financial Technology (FinTech) has made tectonic shifts in the dynamic finance industry. FinTech bridges the credit gap created by the traditional banking channel (Stefanelli et al., 2022). The use of emerging digital technologies for crowdfunding in Fintech platforms, such as artificial intelligence (AI), can help increase financial inclusion, reduce reliance on traditional banking systems, and promote the development of innovative and sustainable fintech solutions (Rejeb et al., 2023; Sharma et al., 2023). FinTech firms may increase borrowers' creditworthiness through big data analytics and algorithms Sharma et al., 2023). As one of the pioneering countries in applying regulations for FinTech, Bahrain pioneers the use of Shariah-compliant Peer-to-Business (P2B) crowdfunding platforms in the Middle East. These platforms provide Islamic financing solutions for small and medium enterprises (SMEs). Given SMEs usually lag behind in getting the limelight of resources (Din & Anwer, 2013), there are protocols that provide benefits to SMEs including technological advancements (Ud Din et al., 2019).

In many Islamic economies, MSMEs face persistent financing gaps due to limited collateral, strict banking procedures, and varying regulatory standards. Studies in Malaysia and Bahrain indicate that low digital literacy and limited awareness of fintech opportunities further constrain participation in online crowdfunding ecosystems (Javanmardi et al., 2024; Central Bank of Bahrain, 2017). In the Islamic financial ecosystem, MSMEs constitute the backbone of socio-economic development but face persistent barriers to accessing capital. According to the Islamic Development Bank (2024) (Najib et al., 2025) over 70% of MSMEs in OIC member states remain either unbanked or underbanked. The slow adoption of digital finance stems not only from regulatory fragmentation (Wu et al., 2024), but also from limited awareness of digital tools, low financial literacy, and weak technological infrastructure (Abidin et al., 2025). Shariah-compliant crowdfunding offers a viable alternative financing path aligned with ethical and equitable principles. Ethical use of AI plays a transformative role in this space by enhancing credit assessment accuracy, optimizing campaign visibility, and ensuring trustworthiness in platform operations (Adamu, 2024). Addressing these structural constraints is essential to realizing the potential of Shariah-compliant crowdfunding as an inclusive financing mechanism (Najib et al., 2025).

Despite these advances, there remains a significant research gap regarding the role of AI in the context of crowdfunding platforms in the Middle East. Specifically, the extent to which AI algorithms can assist FinTech managers in understanding user behavior on Shariah-compliant crowdfunding platforms remains underexplored. Addressing this gap is crucial for maximizing the potential of these platforms by refining their capacity to meet the financial and developmental needs of MSMEs.

In recent years, a growing body of global scholarship has investigated the role of artificial intelligence within FinTech ecosystems, reflecting how machine learning and data analytics transform user decision processes, credit assessment, and financial inclusion. Recent literature demonstrates that ensemble models such as XGBoost and CatBoost outperform traditional regression techniques in predicting campaign success and investor sentiment in crowdfunding markets (Park et al., 2024). Similarly, deep-learning sentiment analysis is also used to forecast donation behavior, highlighting how explainable AI enhances investor trust in peer-to-peer lending environments (Jhaveri et al., 2019).

Within Islamic finance, researchers have begun contextualizing these advances around Shariah principles, emphasizing the need for ethical data governance when deploying AI in Islamic banking (Hasnat et al., 2025), and blockchain-AI integration for halal asset verification (Sunmola et al., 2025). Comparative analyses between Muslim-majority and Western FinTech markets (Baeshen, 2023) reveal that cultural and regulatory frameworks significantly influence adoption rates and trust dynamics. These studies collectively indicate that AI not only optimizes operational efficiency but also shapes behavioral constructs such as perceived usefulness, trust, and social influence – core variables adopted in this chapter's modeling framework.

Despite the increasing attention given to business models by research and practice in recent years, the literature has not yet reached a consensus on the precise definition of a business model (Javanmardi et al., 2024). A thorough literature review suggests there are several key theories applied in information systems research of business applications including the information system success model (ISSM) and its extended models by DeLone and McLean (D&M) (Wu et al., 2024), Technology Acceptance Model (TAM) (Adamu, 2024), Technology-Organization-Environment (TOE) (Gao et al., 2023), Theory of Reasoned Action (TRA) (Hossain & Biswas, 2024), and Diffusion of Innovation (DOI) (Adawiyah et al., 2024).

D&M mainly focuses on system quality, information quality (system) use, user satisfaction, and individual and organizational impact, which makes it unsuitable for this research. Similarly, TOE and DOI emphasize individual characteristics and the organization's internal and external characteristics as drivers for organizational innovativeness (Adawiyah et al., 2024). Likewise, TRA explains consumer online behavior, it is mainly used to explore an individual's psychological perceptions. Whereas TAM is employed at the individual level (Adawiyah et al., 2024) and is all about accepting technology into the organization (Adamu, 2024), which makes it the right fit for this research for evaluating customers' expectations.

Besides the above models that are not suitable for this research, research suggests that the Unified Theory of Acceptance and Use of Technology (UTAUT) is also one of the most used theories for developing a theoretical framework to be utilized at the individual level (Adawiyah et al., 2024), which consists performance requirement, social influence, efforts expected, and facilitating condition to adopt the technology (Adamu, 2024).

This study aims to understand the applications of AI algorithms in determining the use behavior of crowdfunding platforms in FinTech, with the help of a survey research method. Data are collected from Shariah-compliant P2B Financing Platforms in Bahrain. This chapter directly contributes to the volume's thematic pillars of innovation, inclusion, and ethical finance. Innovation is represented through the integration of AI-based predictive modeling into behavioral finance analysis; inclusion is reflected in the chapter's focus on improving access to alternative finance for MSMEs; and ethical finance is reinforced through adherence to Shariah principles of fairness, transparency, and risk sharing. By linking data-driven insights with Islamic ethical imperatives, this study bridges computational analytics and faith-based finance, offering a multidimensional perspective for scholars, policymakers, and practitioners.

While the existing literature provides strong conceptual grounding, empirical clarity on behavioral determinants within Islamic crowdfunding remains limited. The next section therefore describes the methodological approach adopted to operationalize these constructs and apply AI-driven predictive analysis.

2. RESEARCH METHODOLOGY

This research develops a model for understanding customers' expectations, combining TAM and UTAUT. The latest literature suggests nine different features and constructs including Cost (CO), Brand Image (BRI), Speed (SP), Customer Relationship Management (CRM), Perceived Ease of Use (PEOU), Perceived Usefulness (PU), Social Influence (SI), Behavioral Intention to Use (BIU), and Actual Use Behavior (AUB) to be used to analyze the conceptual framework for the micro, small, and medium enterprises (MSMEs) in their adoption and actual use behavior of crowdfunding platforms. All these constructs and their investigation questionnaire are presented in Table I. Taking all these parameters into consideration, this model highlights how the use of Shariah-compliant financing-based crowdfunding platforms, can support socially and economically reliable practices among MSMEs in Bahrain. The questionnaire is conducted for each construct based on whether the participant strongly disagrees, disagrees, neutral, agrees, or strongly agrees.

Table 1. The important features and the corresponding constructs.

No.	Question	Construct
CO1	It requires additional financial investment (e.g. marketing campaign or training the resources).	Cost (CO)
CO2	It can give my business good value for the money.	
CO3	I could get low financing rates.	
CO4	I could get lower cost of financing (including the financing rate, platform fees, transaction fees etc.).	
CO5	The Platform's efficiency of services can minimize my cost.	
BRI1	That I am familiar with its brand.	Brand Image (BRI)
BRI2	Based on its brand values.	
BRI3	If it has a good reputation.	
BRI4	If it provides good financial products.	
BRI5	Based on the Platform's brand origin (i.e. nationality of the Platform)	
SP1	If it takes less time for onboarding into the Platform.	Speed (SP)
SP2	If it can provide me with speedy access to funds.	
SP3	Based on the speed of raising financing from investors.	
SP4	If my business performance can influence the speed of fundraising.	
SP5	If it saves time more than traditional banks.	

continued on following page

Table 1. Continued

No.	Question	Construct
CRM1	I can track my fundraising progress.	Customer Relationship Management (CRM)
CRM2	I can receive prompt responses to my requests by email, phone call, or other quick means of communication.	
CRM3	I can get a good customer service.	
CRM4	The Platform provides me with personal attention to meet my business needs.	
CRM5	The Platform can quickly resolve problems I encounter.	
PEU1	I could easily learn using the Platform for fund raising.	Perceived Ease of Use (PEU)
PEU2	I could understand the Platform's process of the fund raising.	
PEU3	I could have smooth interaction with the Platform.	
PEU4	I could use it without an expert help.	
PEU5	It does not require a lot of mental effort.	
PU1	If it is useful for my business.	Perceived Usefulness (PU)
PU2	If it provides unbanked MSMEs with access to funds.	
PU3	To provide my business with its financial needs.	
PU4	To improve my business performance through accessing funds.	
PU5	To increase my business productivity through accessing funds.	
SI1	I was persuaded by my friends.	Social Influence (SI)
SI2	It was referred to me by important professional people who think that I should use the Platform to access funds.	
SI3	Important people to me would assist me in using the Platform.	
SI4	Using such Platform to access funds is a status of symbol in the market.	
SI5	I was advised by existing users (MSMES).	
BIU1	I believe using a Shariah Compliant financing-based crowdfunding platform is a wise idea.	Behavioural Intention to Use (BIU)
BIU2	I would like to gain more information on Shariah Compliant financing-based crowdfunding platforms.	
BIU3	I am willing to provide the information needed to start fund raising on a Shariah Compliant financing-based crowdfunding platform.	
BIU4	I am intending to use a Shariah Compliant financing-based crowdfunding platform's financial products once its available in Bahrain.	
BIU5	I will adopt a Shariah Compliant financing-based crowdfunding platform when it is popular in the market.	
AUB1	Recommend a Shariah Compliant financing-based crowdfunding platform to others	Actual Use Behaviour (AUB)
AUB2	Use a Shariah Compliant financing-based crowdfunding platform to access financing.	
AUB3	Make a Shariah Compliant financing-based crowdfunding platform as my main source of fund.	
AUB4	Use a Shariah Compliant financing-based crowdfunding platform to get other financial products such as factoring.	
AUB5	Use the Platform more than once.	

Online Survey

The results and discussion of this chapter synthesizes the analytical outcomes, linking the statistical and algorithmic results to the core behavioral and managerial arguments of the chapter. This narrative structure helps connect technical findings to broader theoretical and practical implications. The survey for this study has targeted MSMEs that are based in Bahrain and eligible to use a Shariah-compliant financing-based crowdfunding platform according to Central Bank of Bahrain regulation. The regulation indicates that for businesses eligible to use such a platform, their capital shall not exceed BHD 250,000- equivalent to USD 663,062.50 (Central Bank of Bahrain, 2017).

The survey questions were formed based on adapting existing questions in the literature, and then the questions were allocated to each relevant construct of the conceptual framework. Moreover, the survey has been divided into two parts. First, the demographics part covers four general questions about the businesses. Second, it focused on research constructs where each variable had five questions. The total number of questions was 49, all required to be answered. It is worth noting that a question in the demographic section about the capital of the business has been conditional, where if the answer indicates that the industry has more than BHD 250,000 capital, it terminates the survey and discards the response.

The survey has been conducted online and distributed via email as approved by the ethics approval. A simple random sampling method was followed, where the survey was distributed to the database of five MSME-related associations in Bahrain. Apart from the above online survey, this chapter also details the AI techniques were utilized to establish the results from the survey data.

Artificial Intelligence Procedures

AI methods are standard techniques in many fields like engineering, finance, etc. (Oates et al., 2022). AI methods simulate human intelligence to perform a seemingly intricate task by a computer system (Shafiabady et al., 2023; Curth et al., 2024). The decision tree (DT) method reaches findings according to previous decisions (Mienye & Jere, 2024). In the process, values are allocated to these findings and used to decide actions that can be done later (Santoso et al., 2024; Wu et al., 2023).

Extremely randomized trees classifier (extra trees classifier or ET) accumulates outcomes from several sources with a decor-related nature (Föge et al., 2024). The findings are grouped in a forest setting to produce the final classification outcome (Soltaninejad et al., 2017). The algorithm has multiple random decision trees without changing the generated samples. The k-nearest neighbors (KNN) method is a highly accurate algorithm that groups data based on closeness in a supervised manner (Qu & Pei, 2024). The prediction is conducted locally, while the calculation is carried out upon evolution (Everitt et al., 2011).

Logistic regression (LR) utilizes a group of data originating from independent variables to compute the probability of a status or a situation. Based on Berry's book (Berry, 1997) and Harrell's work (Steyerberg, 2016), a logistic regression classifier is divided into binomial, which gives binary outcomes, and multinomial, which produces non-binary results. For a set of data x, the classification function of the LR method is (Hou et al., 2023; James et al., 2013).

$$p(x) = \frac{1}{1 + e^{-\frac{x-\mu}{s}}} \quad (1)$$

where μ is a location parameter and s is a scale parameter.

The random forest (RF) method relies on random aspects to establish multiple trees as a forest of an uncorrelated nature (Hastie et al., 2009). The prediction of the forest is more precise than every single tree. The algorithm takes the average of samples to enhance the prediction further (Curth et al., 2024).

According to Piryonesi's paper (Piryonesi & El-Diraby, 2020), the method conducts prediction. $\hat{y}$ for a new point x' via utilizing training points (x_i,y_i), for n training times (James et al., 2013). The method performs the prediction by considering the neighborhood of the point at each training (Zhu et al., 2015). A weight function weights the training points W_j for tree j. Let m be the number of trees in the set. Upon averaging the predictions of a set of m trees, the prediction is given by (Painsky & Rosset, 2017).

$$\hat{y} = \frac{1}{\mathrm{m}}\sum_{j=1}^{m}\sum_{\mathrm{i=1}}^{\mathrm{n}} W_j(x_i, \acute{x})y_i = \sum_{i=1}^{n}\left(\frac{1}{\mathrm{m}}\sum_{\mathrm{j=1}}^{\mathrm{m}} W_j(x_i, \acute{x})\right)y_i \quad (2)$$

The support vector machines (SVM) method is a supervised linear learning algorithm that classifies data. SVM classifies data by mapping the points to a multi-dimensional space (Nie et al., 2024). Afterwards, a hyperplane border is created between the categories to conduct the classification. Assume there is a data set of n points (x1,y1) to (xn,yn). Let w be the normal vector to the data hyperplane. Based on Hastie's book (Hastie et al., 2009), the optimization problem of the classification is formulated into a depreciation of the following expression

$$minimize\ \beta\|\mathbf{w}\|^2 + \left[\frac{1}{n}\sum_{i=1}^{n}\max\left(0, 1 - y_i\left(\mathbf{w}^{\mathrm{T}}\mathbf{x}_i - b\right)\right)\right]$$

, (3)

where the parameter b determines the offset of the hyperplane and β determines the margin size of the hyperplane (Wan et al., 2024; Zaidi et al., 2023).

Extreme Gradient Boosting (XGBoost) classifier is an application of the gradient-boosted trees algorithm (Song et al., 2020; Bhandari et al., 2023). According to Seiffert's paper (Seiffert et al., 2010), the paradigm utilizes scalable decision trees to estimate a value precisely via consolidating predictions of base versions.

All the above AI computational techniques, including DT, ET, KNN, LR, RF, SVM, and XGBoost, are programmed to run for the responses from the survey with the MSMEs in this study. These computational techniques are used to evaluate the degree of importance of the tenets on "Actual Use Behaviour" of Shariah-compliant financing-based crowdfunding platforms.

Sample Characteristics

The responses received from the MSMEs based in Bahrain have been 161, of which 160 was the sample size needed for the final survey. All 161 responses were from MSMEs based in Bahrain with capital less than BHD 250,000 due to demographic question number four, where the question asked the MSMEs to indicate whether their capital is less than BHD 250,000. Table II presents demographic characteristics.

Based on the sample characteristics, the MSMEs that have responded to the survey are from different business activity categories. The survey has provided 20 different categories of businesses, yet most of the respondents mentioned others (28%). This has been followed by the top three categories, which are accommodation and food service activities (16.1%), information and communication (11.2%), arts, entertainment, sports, and recreation (8.7%). These platforms are not for dedicated business categories. Therefore, having respondents from various business categories has given a better indication of the overall MSMEs landscape in Bahrain.

Table 2. MSMEs Demographics Characteristic

Characteristic	Number of respondents	Percentage (%)
Business Activity Category		
Agriculture, animal production, and fishing	2	1.2%
Mining and quarrying	1	0.6%
Manufacturing	2	1.2%
Electricity, gas, steam, and air conditioning supply	2	1.2%
Water supply; sewerage, waste management, and remediation act	2	1.2%

continued on following page

Table 2. Continued

Characteristic	Number of respondents	Percentage (%)
Construction	4	2.5%
Sale/Trading Activities: repair of motor vehicles and motors	6	3.7%
Transportation and storage	4	2.5%
Accommodation and food service activities	26	16.1%
Information and communication	18	11.2%
Financial and insurance activities	8	5%
Real estate activities	2	1.2%
Professional, scientific, and technical activities	3	1.9%
Administrative and support service activities	1	0.6%
Education	12	7.5%
Human health and social work activities	6	3.7%
Arts, entertainment, sports, and recreation	14	18.7%
Personal service activities; Repair Activities	2	1.2%
Public administration	1	0.6%
Others	45	28%
Number of years in business		
0-5 years	86	53.4%
5-10 years	49	30.4%
More than 10 years	26	16.1%
What is your business size?		
Micro Enterprise/Business	66	41%
Small Enterprise/Business	68	42.2%
Medium Enterprise/Business	27	16.8%
Is your capital between BHD 1 to 250,000?		
Yes	161	100%
No	0	0%

Main Measurement Construct and AI Computational Techniques

The five indicators of the "Actual Use Behaviour" construct comprise the following:

- AUB1 – Recommend others to the Shariah Platform
- AUB2 – Use Platform to Access Shariah Financing

- AUB3 – Use Platform as Main Shariah Financing
- AUB4 – Use the Platform for other Shariah Products
- AUB5 – Use the Platform more than once.

In this study, we use AI computational techniques, namely decision tree, extra tree classification, KNN classification, logistic regression, random forest classification, SVM classification, and XGBoost classification, to evaluate the essential features of the "Actual use Behavior (AUB)".

3. RESULTS AND DISCUSSION

The indicator AUB1 ("Recommend others to the Shariah Platform," an indicator of the "Actual Use Behavior" (AUB) construct) is presented as an illustration of how the AI computational techniques were operationalized in this study. This section includes a discussion of the outputs from the various AI computational techniques with specific reference to being run against each indicator of independent constructs. It presents the finite aspects of each computational technique concerning their AI method and their respective importance.

We carried out thorough AI computational methods for each of the indicators of AUB1 to AUB5 in correspondence to the other independent and mediating indicators. The following section will provide the complete results of all the AI computations for AUB1, including "Importance of Features" using "Decision Tree Classifier" (Fig. 1), "Extra Tree Classification" (Fig. 2), "KNN Classification" (Fig. 3), "Logistic Regression" (Fig. 4), "Random Forest Classification" (Fig. 5), "SVM Classification" (Fig. 6), and "XGBoost Classification" (Fig. 7).

Although all the above AI computational methods were used for all the indicators (AUB1 to AUB5), to avoid duplication of explanations and maintain the brevity of the paper, this results section will only provide discussions in context for AUB1 ("Recommend others to the Shariah Platform" an indicator of the "Actual Use Behavior" (AUB) construct). Table III provides a summary of the test accuracies for each variable compared to the AUB1 variable and feature values of the AI as mentioned above methods.

Results of Complete AI Tests for AUB1 – "Recommend Others to Shariah Platform"

Fig. 1 shows results for the importance of features generated via the Decision Tree method. Notice that the BIU2 feature corresponds to the highest importance value around unity. On the other hand, the rest of the features have much lower importance values. For instance, several features, such as BRI3 and SI1, have surprisingly zero importance values. In other words, the standard deviation tends to be low with the decision tree algorithm.

Figure 1. The features versus the importance using the decision tree method.

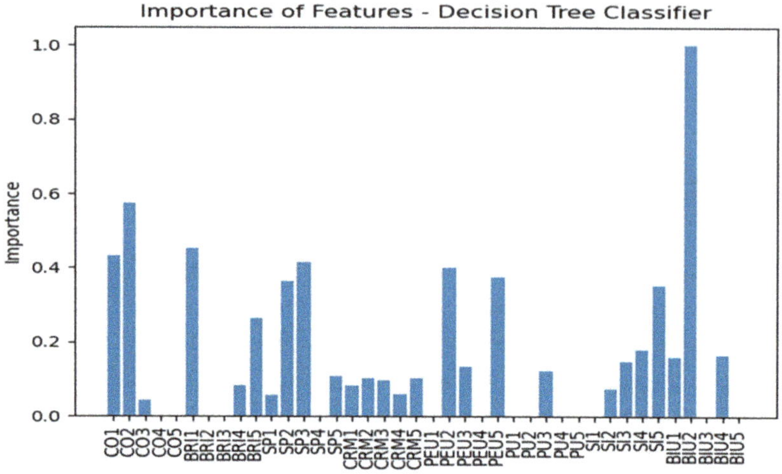

Fig. 2 displays the importance of features produced by the Extra Tree algorithm. Unlike the case with Fig. 1, the PEU3 feature is associated with the highest importance value. Whereas the importance values of the other features are lower but with less gap as compared with Fig. 1. There are few features with zero importance, such as SI4, but much fewer than the scenario in Fig. 1. Hence, the standard deviation in Fig. 2 is still low but higher than its counterpart in Fig. 1.

Figure 2. The features versus the importance of using the extra tree method.

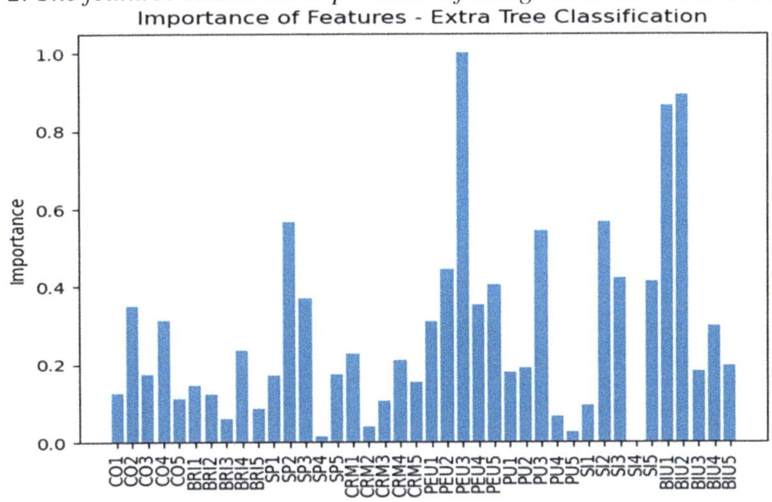

Fig. 3 depicts the importance of features when utilizing the KNN technique. Fig. 3 shows comparable values for the importance of features, unlike the cases in Figs. 1 and 2. This signals that the standard deviation is higher than those of Figs. 1 and 2. Nonetheless, SP5 and BUI1 features are accompanied by the highest importance values.

Figure 3. The features versus the importance using the KNN paradigm.

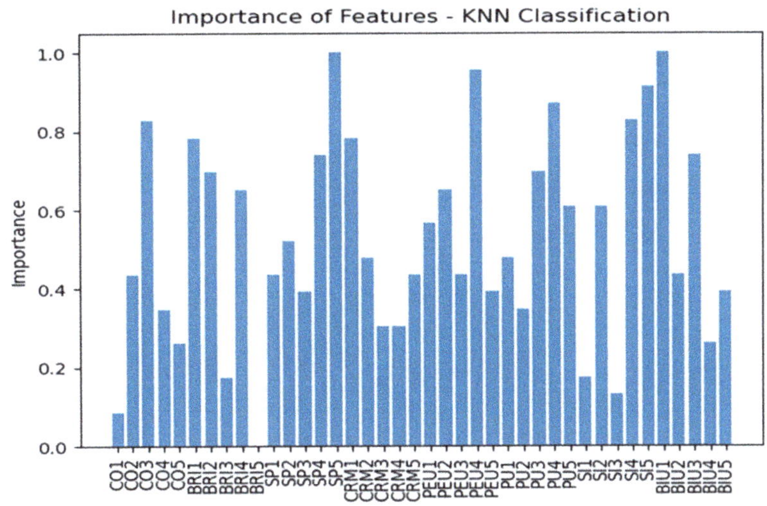

Fig. 4 shows essential outcomes for the features under study using the Logistic Regression algorithm. We notice that the importance of the PU1 feature is higher than the rest.

Figure 4. The features versus the importance using the logistic regression method.

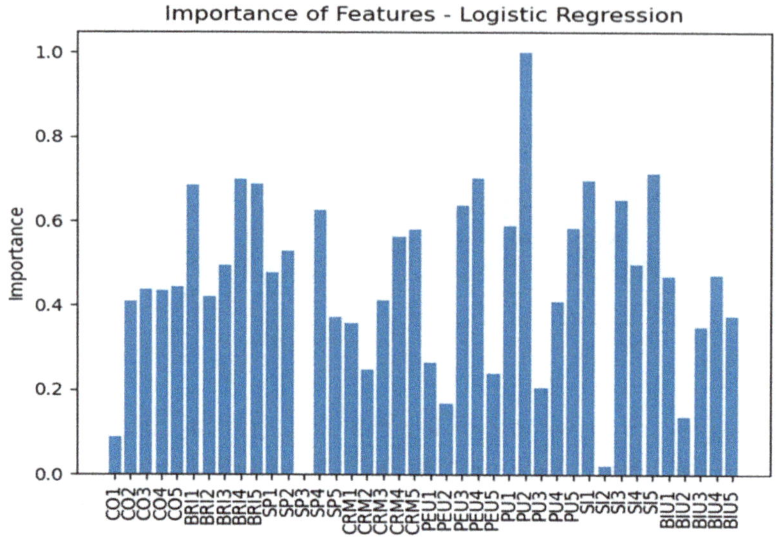

Fig. 5 displays the importance of features for the Random Forest Classifier. The BIU2 feature is the most important, followed by BIU1 and PEU3. This means that both random forest and decision tree algorithms resulted in the same feature with the highest importance, BIU2. However, both cases show different standard deviation trends, which are higher in Fig. 5.

Figure 5. The features versus the importance using the random forest method.

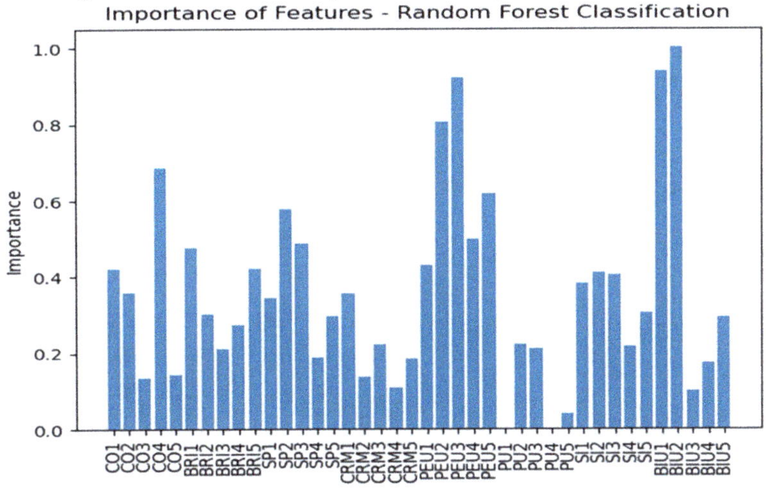

Fig. 6 depicts the importance of features when using the SVM algorithm. The CO4 feature is associated with the highest importance value.

Figure 6. The features versus the importance using the SVM method.

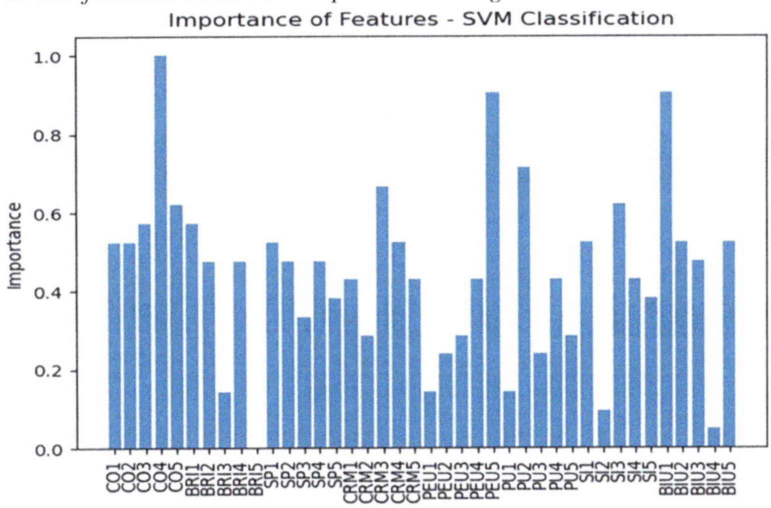

Fig. 7 depicts the importance of features via the XGBoost classifier. The highest importance value distinguishes the PEU1 variable.

Figure 7. The features versus the importance using the XGBoost algorithm.

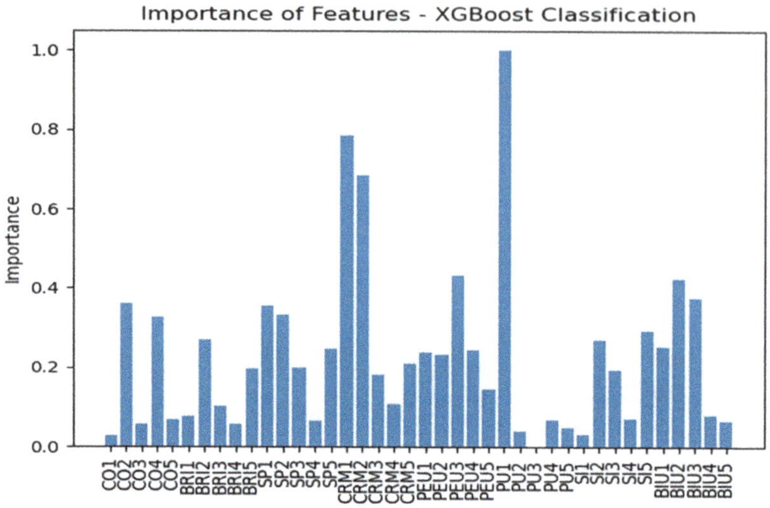

All these AI methods are explicitly programmed to simulate human intelligence by performing intricate computerized tasks for each of the indicators of the overall "Actual Use Behavior" (AUB) construct (explained in the Research Methodology section of the paper). A thorough analysis of the simulation results suggests that the RF algorithm is associated with the highest accuracy of 65.92, followed by both decision tree and KNN methods, each with an accuracy of 60.38. This is because the RF method randomly creates numerous trees and produces an outcome based on averaging all samples. Table III present presents the AI's test accuracies and feature values as mentioned for all the aforementioned methods.

Table 3. Test accuracy and feature value of the AI methods under AUB1.

XGB	SVM	RF	LR	KNN	ET	DT	Method
56.60	58.49	65.92	49.06	62.26	62.26	60.38	**Accuracy**
0.02878	0.52381	0.42103	0.08985	0.08696	0.12644	0.43135	**CO1**
0.36221	0.52381	0.35795	0.40917	0.43478	0.35119	0.57536	**CO2**
0.05843	0.57143	0.13312	0.43900	0.82609	0.17469	0.04455	**CO3**
0.32610	1.00000	0.68572	0.43401	0.34783	0.31386	0.00000	**CO4**
0.06736	0.61905	0.14121	0.44429	0.26087	0.11098	0.00000	**CO5**
0.07763	0.57143	0.47418	0.68521	0.78261	0.14432	0.45135	**BRI1**
0.26967	0.47619	0.30044	0.42223	0.69565	0.12315	0.00000	**BRI 2**
0.10331	0.14286	0.21106	0.49483	0.17391	0.06093	0.00000	**BRI 3**

continued on following page

Table 3. Continued

XGB	SVM	RF	LR	KNN	ET	DT	Method
0.05602	0.47619	0.27386	0.69875	0.65217	0.23642	0.08206	**BRI 4**
0.19648	0.00000	0.42170	0.68727	0.00000	0.08557	0.26597	**BRI 5**
0.35639	0.52381	0.34539	0.47910	0.43478	0.17212	0.05847	**SP1**
0.33258	0.47619	0.57817	0.53033	0.52174	0.56703	0.36374	**SP2**
0.19831	0.33333	0.48653	0.00000	0.39130	0.36901	0.41442	**SP3**
0.06642	0.47619	0.18755	0.62445	0.73913	0.01486	0.00000	**SP4**
0.24735	0.47619	0.29630	0.37414	1.00000	0.17486	0.10771	**SP5**
0.78406	0.42857	0.35444	0.35829	0.78261	0.22910	0.08206	**CRM1**
0.68580	0.28571	0.13807	0.24906	0.47826	0.03975	0.10258	**CRM2**
0.18329	0.66667	0.22169	0.41170	0.30435	0.10479	0.09848	**CRM3**
0.10727	0.52381	0.10815	0.56416	0.30435	0.21080	0.06155	**CRM4**
0.21173	0.42857	0.18444	0.58123	0.43478	0.15454	0.10258	**CRM5**
0.24028	0.14286	0.43015	0.26592	0.56522	0.31007	0.00000	**PEU1**
0.23347	0.23810	0.80462	0.16797	0.65217	0.44405	0.40014	**PEU2**
0.43234	0.28571	0.92175	0.63720	0.43478	1.00000	0.13400	**PEU3**
0.24462	0.42857	0.49775	0.70100	0.95652	0.35335	0.00000	**PEU4**
0.14466	0.90476	0.61577	0.23997	0.39130	0.40268	0.37471	**PEU5**
1.00000	0.14286	0.00062	0.58829	0.47826	0.18002	0.00000	**PU1**
0.03948	0.71429	0.22317	1.00000	0.34783	0.19134	0.00000	**PU2**
0.00000	0.23810	0.21028	0.20385	0.69565	0.54207	0.12299	**PU3**
0.06764	0.42857	0.00000	0.40913	0.86957	0.06544	0.00000	**PU4**
0.04929	0.28571	0.03927	0.58247	0.60870	0.02618	0.00000	**PU5**
0.03175	0.52381	0.38111	0.69611	0.17391	0.09342	0.00000	**SI1**
0.27173	0.09524	0.40980	0.02001	0.60870	0.56617	0.07327	**SI2**
0.19517	0.61905	0.40526	0.65106	0.13043	0.42095	0.14771	**SI3**
0.07207	0.42857	0.21738	0.49678	0.82609	0.00000	0.18025	**SI4**
0.29350	0.38095	0.30567	0.71314	0.91304	0.41230	0.35212	**SI5**
0.25247	0.90476	0.93748	0.46864	1.00000	0.86420	0.15879	**BIU1**
0.42332	0.52381	1.00000	0.13818	0.43478	0.89192	1.00000	**BIU2**
0.37432	0.47619	0.210077	0.35063	0.73913	0.18360	0.00000	**BIU3**
0.07944	0.04762	0.17414	0.47141	0.26087	0.29750	0.16413	**BIU4**
0.06626	0.52381	0.29444	0.37644	0.39130	0.19680	0.00000	**BIU5**

Hence, the methods show different importance patterns, including different identities for the feature with the highest importance. In other words, the behaviors of the algorithms resulted in inconsistent outcomes, albeit some similarity between

XGBoost and logistic regression, on the one hand, and between decision tree and random forest, on the other hand.

Beyond comparative accuracy, the relative strengths of ensemble models such as Random Forest and XGBoost suggest that multidimensional user data – including trust and ease-of-use indicators—carry substantial predictive value. This has direct implications for platform design, where adaptive interfaces could be developed to highlight features most relevant to distinct user segments.

4. DISCUSSIONS ON THE AUB CONSTRUCT'S FIVE INDICATORS (AUB1 TO AUB5)

AUB1 – Recommend Others to Shariah Platform

Table 4. Top five performing input indicators for AUB1 – "Recommend others to the Shariah Platform"

Method	Feature	Indicator Details	Importance Value
AUB1 Random Forest 65.92	BIU2	I would like to gain more information on Shariah Compliant financing-based crowdfunding platforms.	1
	BIU1	I believe using a Shariah-compliant financing-based crowdfunding platform is a wise idea.	0.93748
	PEU3	I could have smooth interaction with the Platform.	0.92175
	PEU2	I could understand the Platform's process of the fund raising.	0.80462
	CO4	I could get lower cost of financing (including the financing rate, platform fees, transaction fees etc.).	0.68572

The top five performing input indicators for AUB1 have been depicted in Table III. The Random Forest algorithm has the highest accuracy (65.92) for AUB1, and all discussions below will use its computational outputs. The main contributor for the AUB1 is (BIU2) - which is about wanting to gain new information (1), followed by (BIU1) – using the Platform as a wise idea (0.93748). The third and fourth contributors are from (PEU3) – smooth interaction with the Platform (0.92175) and (PEU2) – understand the platform process (0.80462). Finally, the fifth contributor was (CO4) – which could get a lower cost of financing (0.68572).

The "Behavioral intention to use" (BIU) seems to be the overarching construct concerning its contribution to AUB1 (i.e., recommend the use) compared to all the input constructs of the overall model. AI has indicated that the "Behavioral intention to use" is more important than the "Perceived ease of use" for recommending the actual use (AUB1). It is often assumed that lower costs would be the most essential factor. Interestingly, AI-simulated human intelligence does not seem to suggest the case. Lower cost was the least important of all the five top-performing input indicators for AUB1.

AUB2 – Use Platform to Access Shariah Financing

Table 5. Top five performing input indicators for AUB2 – "Use Platform to Access Shariah Financing"

Method		Indicator Details	Importance Value
AUB2 Extra Tree 75.47	PU1	If it is useful for my business.	1
	PEU3	I could have smooth interaction with the Platform.	0.78034
	SP2	If it can provide me with speedy access to funds.	0.67789
	SI2	It was referred to me by important professional people who think that I should use the Platform to access funds.	0.58268
	PEU1	I could easily learn using the Platform for fund raising.	0.50528

Table V demonstrates the top five performing input indicators for AUB2. The Extra Tree algorithm has the highest accuracy (75.47) for AUB2. The main contributor for AUB2 is (PU1) – which relates to perceptions of use for the respondents' business (1) and is followed by (PEU3) – expectations around how easily (smooth) the respondent interacts with the Platform (0.78034). The third and fourth contributors are (SP2) – the provision of rapid access to funds (0.67789), and (SI2) – an expert recommendation by external individuals who likely possess the requisite skills to offer the same view (0.58268). Finally, the fifth contributor was (PEU1) – the ease at which the Platform could be learned to achieve its fundraising objective (0.50528).

The PEU appears to drive more of the notable indicators than any of the other categories. To this end, the ease of use seems to be a noteworthy factor driving the selection of platforms for funding purposes. However, overall utility (PU1) ultimately drives AUB2, with the ability to access funds quickly and external expert recommendations influencing actual use from an AUB2 perspective. To this end, the Extra Tree algorithm appears to capture the perceived utility, ease, speed, and expert recommendation factors driving these funding platforms' actual use.

These findings not only validate established behavioral constructs but also inform segmentation strategies, enabling managers to tailor educational and marketing initiatives toward user groups with lower predicted adoption probabilities.

AUB3 – Use Platform as Main Shariah financing

Table 6. Top five performing input indicators for AUB3 – "Use Platform as Main Shariah Financing"

Method	Feature	Indicator Details	Importance Value
AUB3 KNN 58.49	CO1	It requires additional financial investment (e.g. marketing campaign or training the resources).	1
	PU2	If it provides unbanked MSMEs with access to funds.	0.73585
	BIU5	I will adopt a Shariah Compliant financing-based crowdfunding platform when it is popular in the market.	0.71698
	SI1	I was persuaded by my friends.	0.69811
	CRM2	I can receive prompt responses to my requests by email, phone call, or other quick means of communication.	0.67925

Table VI shows the top five performing input indicators for AUB3. The KNN algorithm (58.49) has the highest accuracy for AUB3. The main contributor for AUB3 is CO1, which requires additional financial investment delivered through marketing campaigns or training resources. This was followed by PU2, the ability to provide unbanked MSMEs access to funding. BIU5 was the next most significant contributor, being the willingness of an entity to provide the Shariah-based compliant financing-based Crowdfunding Platform and SI1, the extent to which decision-makers are influenced by others (friends). The least contributing factor was CRM2, receiving prompt responses to email requests – a signal of customer service and satisfaction.

AUB4 – Use the Platform for other Shariah Products

Table 7. Top five performing input indicators for AUB4 – "Use the Platform for other Shariah Products"

Method	Feature	Indicator Details	Importance Value
AUB4 KNN 62.26	CO1	It requires additional financial investment (e.g. marketing campaign or training the resources).	1
	PU2	If it provides unbanked MSMEs with access to funds.	0.91667
	PU1	If it is useful for my business.	0.80556
	PEU5	It does not require a lot of mental effort.	0.77778
	PEU4	To improve my business performance through accessing funds.	0.75000

The five top-performing input indicators for AUB4 are shown in Table VII. The KNN algorithm similarly had the highest accuracy for AUB4. The most significant contributor was CO1, the requirement for additional financial investment through marketing and training, closely followed by PU2, which provides fund access to unbanked MSMEs. The next most important was PU1, the perception of utility in the offering for one's business, closely followed by PEU5, which states that the Platform is easy to use and does not require much mental effort. The least contributing factor, but still somewhat consequential at 0.7500, is PEU4, which is the desire to improve business performance by accessing funds.

AUB5 – Use the Platform more than once

Table 8. Top five performing input indicators for AUB5 – "Use the platform more than once"

Method	Feature	Indicator Details	Importance Value
AUB5 KNN 56.60	SP4	If my business performance can influence the speed of fundraising.	1
	CO1	It requires additional financial investment (e.g. marketing campaign or training the resources).	0.76923
	CRM5	The Platform can quickly resolve problems I encounter.	0.69231
	PEU1	I could easily learn using the Platform for fund raising.	0. 69231
	PEU2	I could understand the Platform's process of the fund raising.	0. 65385

Table VIII shows the top five performing input indicators for AUB5. The KNN algorithm has the highest accuracy (56.60) for AUB5. The main contributor for AUB5 is (SP4), 'business performance can influence the speed of fundraising (1), followed by (CO1), 'requires additional financial investment' (0.76923). (CRM5) – 'platform can quickly resolve problems' and (PEU1) 'easily learn using the platform for fundraising' had similar importance values (0.69231). Finally, the fifth contributor was (PEU2) – 'understand the platform process' (0.65385).

The PEU appears to be a more notable indicator than any of the other categories (i.e., having 4th and 5th place as importance value weights). To this end, the perceived ease of use appears to be a noteworthy factor driving for using the Platform more than once. However, overall utility (SP4) ultimately drives AUB5, with the business performance influencing the speed of fundraising and the actual use of the Platform more than once. To this end, the KNN algorithm appears to capture the catalytic use of the Platform by the MSMEs.

Table 9. Best algorithm input indicator for all Dependent Indicators AUB1 to AUB5 of Construct AUB

Method (Accuracy Score)	Total Indicators	Best Indicator	Indicator Details
AUB1 Recommend other to Shariah Platform Random Forest (65.92)	40	BIU2	I would like to gain more information on Shariah Compliant financing-based crowdfunding platforms.
AUB2 Use Platform to Access Shariah Financing Extra Tree (75.47)	40	PU1	If it is useful for my business.
AUB3 Use Platform as Main Shariah Financing KNN (58.49)	40	CO1	It requires additional financial investment (e.g. marketing campaign or training the resources).
AUB4 Use Platform for Other Shariah Products KNN (62.26)	40	CO1	It requires additional financial investment (e.g. marketing campaign or training the resources).
AUB5 Use the Platform more than Once KNN (56.60)	40	SP4	If my business performance can influence the speed of fundraising.

Random Forrest, Extra Tree, and KNN provided the best algorithms for AUB1 to AUB5 indicators from the various AI methods, namely decision tree, extra tree classification (ET), KNN classification, logistic regression, random forest (RF) classification, SVM classification, and XGBoost classification in evaluating the importance features. Table VIII summarizes the best-performing algorithms for all the constructs (AUB1 To AUB5) and their corresponding top feature selected in the context of AI computations.

As is evident from Table IX, each indicator of the primary AUB construct is computationally cross-tested with AI, along with forty other indicators, to identify the best indicator from the independent and mediating indicators of the whole dataset. The following section will culminate with implications of each best indicator from the dataset for each dependent construct's indicator (AUB1 to AUB5).

5. IMPLICATIONS & RECOMMENDATIONS OF THE AI COMPUTATIONAL FINDINGS

Recommend Shariah Platform (AUB1)

As for recommending others to the Shariah Platform (AUB1) as part of the primary dependent construct, "Actual Use Behavior" (AUB), the construct of Behavioral Intention to Use (BIU) stood out from all the other independent and mediating constructs. Random Forest technique, with the highest AI computational accuracy from all the intense AI rigor has indicated that the MSMEs would like to gain more information on Shariah-compliant financing-based crowdfunding platforms before recommending others to use the Shariah-compliant platforms. Since the MSMEs need to acquire more details on crowdfunding-based platforms, the Shariah-compliant platforms would need to promote the plethora of their services in various social media channels more extensively to enable and foster the recommendation of using Shariah-compliant crowdfunding platforms. Promoting these platforms will not only support financial inclusion of MSMEs by encouraging responsible investment and fostering long-term economic resilience within the community.

Access Shariah Platform Alongside Others (AUB2)

As another indicator of the main AUB construct in the context of accessing the Shariah platform alongside other avenues, the Perceived Usefulness (PU) construct's indicator as being beneficial for business (PU1) was the best indicator from all the other thirty-nine indicators in the dataset. The Extra Tree technique produced the highest AI computational accuracy of all the other seven AI techniques for the MSMEs to experience the usefulness of the Platform to use it alongside other platforms in being the best indicator. Shariah-compliant platforms must highlight the usefulness of their respective platforms. It is recommended that the Shariah-compliant platforms identify potential MSMEs and communicate with them directly about how the platforms would benefit their business. Emphasizing the usefulness of such platforms will support business growth in practices by enabling MSMEs to make informed, responsible financial decisions. Moreover, such encouragement to MSMEs would direct them to utilize the Sharia-compliant platforms favorably alongside other avenues.

Shariah Platform used as the Main platform (AUB3)

Some of the MSMEs used the Shariah platform as their primary avenue of transacting fundraising. The KNN AI computational technique identified the Cost Factor (CO) construct ahead of the other independent and mediating constructs in ascertaining the best indicator for having the Shariah platform as their pivotal financing platform. On the same token, it was essential to have additional financial investment in areas of marketing and training for them to ensure that the Shariah platform be used as their main base in transacting businesses, which was evidenced by (CO1) being the best indicator when AI tested against thirty-nine other indicators of the dataset. The Shariah-compliant platforms would need to provide introductory offers to MSMEs by aiding with resources for training and marketing. Such strategies would stimulate the MSMEs to use niche Shariah-compliant platforms as their leading Platform of choice for crowdfunding purposes. By supporting MSMEs with sustainable financial practices through training and marketing investments, Shariah-compliant platforms can help reduce the impact associated with less efficient financing methods.

Use the Platform for other Shariah products (AUB4)

For the MSMEs using their Platform for other Shariah products, the KNN technique stood out again, identifying the best indicator out of the seven AI computational techniques with the highest accuracy. It was interesting to note that the Cost construct and the same indicator as for AUB3 had been identified as the best indicator. It has been evidenced by indicator "CO1" as the best indicator when AI computational tests were carried out with all thirty-nine indicators of the dataset. The need for additional financial investment in marketing and training by the MSMEs echoed the findings for using other Shariah platforms. As a final note, it must be reiterated that when the MSMEs need to employ the Platform for other non-financial Shariah products, they would need additional investments in marketing and training. By the MSMEs investing in marketing and training, they could reap economies of scale and tradeoffs from their existing Shariah-compliant crowdfunding platforms. By incorporating sustainable practices into the marketing and training efforts, MSMEs can ensure that their use of Shariah-compliant platforms not only supports their financial growth.

Use the Platform more than once (AUB5)

The Speed Factor (SP) construct was crucial for MSMEs to use the Shariah-compliant platform for their financing overtures repeatedly. The KNN AI computational technique identified the Speed Factor (SP) construct ahead of the other independent and mediating constructs in ascertaining the best indicator for repeated use of the Shariah platform. These MSMEs also postulated that their business performance was influenced repeatedly by the speed of fundraising for the usage of the Platform, and this was evidenced by the indicator SP4, which was identified as the best indicator. Again, this was also tested against the dataset's other thirty-nine independent and mediating indicators. The Shariah-compliant platforms are recommended to monitor and encourage the MSMEs with their business performances. This motivation and guidance would encourage the MSMEs to use their specific Shariah-compliant funding platforms continuously. Moreover, ensuring that the Platform aligns and supports reliable speed and efficiency of fundraising can reduce resource consumption, making the Platform a more sustainable choice for MSMEs.

6. EMERGING DIRECTIONS IN ISLAMIC FINTECH

Recent advances in financial technology are reshaping the contours of Islamic finance, particularly through the integration of artificial intelligence, blockchain, and sustainability-oriented design. Among these, Ethical AI has emerged as a key framework linking automation with Islamic ethical principles (Hasnat et al., 2025). Ethical AI emphasizes justice (adl), trust (amanah), and accountability – values aligned with Maqasid al-Shariah (Mustaffha, 2024). In Shariah-compliant crowdfunding, the use of explainable AI (XAI) models can enhance transparency by showing users and regulators why specific campaigns are recommended or prioritized (Baeshen, 2023). Such interpretability helps prevent algorithmic bias, reduces speculative elements (gharar), and reinforces trust in the fairness and Shariah compliance of platform operations (Mustaffha, 2024). Embedding these moral safeguards into AI-driven systems ensures that technological efficiency does not compromise the ethical integrity of Islamic finance.

At the same time, two complementary directions – Islamic Decentralized Finance (DeFi) and Social, and Governance (ESG) integration – are extending the reach of ethical finance (Kadir et al., 2023). Blockchain-enabled DeFi platforms are facilitating peer-to-peer halal financing, tokenized sukuk offerings, and transparent smart contracts that align with Islamic values of equity and disclosure (Sunmola et al., 2025). AI-driven analytics can strengthen these efforts by monitoring the sustainability performance of crowdfunding projects and automatically flagging compliance or ethical risks. Together, these developments signal a transition toward an AI-enhanced, sustainability-driven Islamic FinTech ecosystem – one that combines innovation with accountability, thereby strengthening the role of Islamic finance as a credible and future-ready component of the global digital economy (Mustaffha, 2024).

7. ETHICS, GOVERNANCE, AND REGULATORY PERSPECTIVES

As Islamic FinTech evolves, ensuring ethical alignment and sound governance becomes imperative. Regulatory authorities across Muslim-majority countries – such as the Central Bank of Bahrain, Bank Negara Malaysia, and the Dubai Financial Services Authority – are experimenting with FinTech sandboxes that balance innovation with compliance (Central Bank of Bahrain, 2017). These frameworks aim to safeguard consumer trust, maintain Shariah authenticity, and mitigate algorithmic risks.

AI-enables systems introduce both opportunities and challenges to Islamic financial regulation. While AI can enhance compliance monitoring through automated screening of Shariah rules and anomaly detection in transactions, opaque algorithms may raise concerns about fairness and accountability (Park et al., 2024). Embedding explainable AI (XAI) techniques allows regulators and Shariah boards to audit decision pathways, thereby ensuring transparency consistent with Islamic jurisprudenc (Hasnat et al., 2025).

Governance mechanisms should also extend to data ethics. Privacy protection, consent management, and avoidance of data exploitation are not only technical necessities but moral imperatives rooted in the Islamic principles of amanah (trust) and adl (justice) (Kadir et al., 2023). A collaborative governance model, linking data scientists, Islamic scholars, and policymakers, can provide multi-layered oversight (Kadir et al., 2023). In doing so, AI-enabled Islamic FinTech can mature into a responsibly regulated sector that advances both innovation and ethical integrity.

8. INTERPRETIVE AND MANAGERIAL INSIGHTS

While the algorithmic evaluations presented above underscore the comparative predictive strength of models such as Random Forest, XGBoost, and Extra Trees, a purely technical interpretation risks overlooking the human and managerial dimensions embedded in user adoption patterns (Central Bank of Bahrain, 2017). The analytical outcomes reveal that constructs such as Perceived Usefulness (PU), Effort Expectancy (EE), and Trust (TR) consistently emerged as dominant predictors across models. This implies that the determinants of Actual Use Behavior (AUB) are not merely technological but deeply socio-cognitive, emphasizing users' sense of confidence, ethical assurance, and perceived fairness of the platform (Park et al., 2024).

From a behavioral standpoint, the significance of trust and facilitating conditions points to a collective perception of institutional reliability, especially relevant in Shariah-compliant financial ecosystems where faith-based trust supplements conventional user confidence (Jhaveri et al., 2019). AI-driven insights thus provide a way to quantify and visualize latent behavioral constructs that have historically been difficult to measure. The higher predictive weight of trust-related features across models suggests that ensuring Shariah transparency, displaying certification badges, and enabling clear communication of ethical compliance can tangibly enhance adoption.

From a managerial perspective, the results call for a shift from viewing AI tools as end-user predictors to positioning them as decision-support instruments for platform managers, investors, and regulators. The ensemble learning models can serve as behavioral dashboards, allowing managers to continuously monitor the factors influencing engagement, repeat usage, and campaign success (Hasnat et al., 2025). For example, if model outputs indicate declining feature importance for Perceived Ease of Use (PEOU), this could signal the need to simplify interface design or streamline registration processes. Similarly, sustained importance of Social Influence (SI) highlights the marketing opportunity to leverage community-based endorsements or peer-sharing features on the platform.

In practice, these interpretive insights support the development of adaptive FinTech ecosystems, platforms that dynamically adjust their user experience and marketing strategies based on behavioral analytics (Sunmola et al., 2025). By linking machine learning predictions to user personas (e.g., first-time investors, returning contributors, or project initiators), platform managers can tailor educational content and digital literacy programs that foster inclusive participation. AI interpretability tools such as SHAP (SHapley Additive exPlanations) can further help stakeholders understand why specific factors drive user behavior (Baeshen, 2023), enhancing transparency and reducing resistance to algorithmic systems.

At a policy level, these findings highlight how AI can serve as a governance instrument rather than simply an operational technology. Regulators in Islamic finance can adopt similar predictive models to identify usage gaps among SMEs, assess compliance risks, and monitor ethical integrity indicators within crowdfunding transactions (Mustaffha, 2024). This form of predictive policy design ensures that innovation and inclusion, core themes of this volume are balanced with accountability and fairness. Tthe integration of algorithmic precision with managerial and ethical interpretability represents a pivotal step in evolving Shariah-compliant crowdfunding from a niche digital product into a scalable financial infrastructure (Kadir et al., 2023). These insights reinforce that AI is not only a computational tool but also a strategic enabler of trust, inclusion, and adaptive governance within Islamic digital finance.

9. CONCLUSION

The study employed advanced AI algorithms to analyze the use behavior of Shariah-compliant crowdfunding platforms by MSMEs in Bahrain, with a focus on understanding user behavior and optimizing platform performance. Seven AI techniques, including RF, ET, and KNN, were applied to evaluate the key features influencing actual use behavior. RF emerged as the most accurate and consistent method across various indicators, particularly for recommending the platform to others. ET proved effective in identifying perceived usefulness, which is critical for encouraging users to adopt the platform alongside other financing options. KNN also demonstrated its strength in understanding repeated use behavior, which is vital for ensuring long-term engagement with the platform. These findings highlight the significant role of AI in enhancing the functionality and appeal of crowdfunding platforms, ultimately enabling MSMEs to access resources more efficiently and promote financial inclusivity. By incorporating these insights, Shariah-compliant crowdfunding platforms can optimize their services to meet the specific needs of users, thereby fostering growth and supporting socially responsible financial practices. This chapter links computational findings with managerial, ethical, and policy perspectives, the chapter offers a coherent narrative that reinforces the broader themes of innovation, inclusion, and ethical finance central to this volume.

Despite its valuable insights, this research is subject to several limitations. The study is restricted to MSMEs in Bahrain and focuses exclusively on Shariah-compliant crowdfunding platforms, limiting the generalizability of its findings to broader regional or global contexts. Expanding future studies to include a more diverse range of MSMEs across different regions, or incorporating non-Shariah-compliant platforms, could provide comparative insights and a more holistic understanding of platform behavior. The findings of this study emphasize the importance of aligning platform services with user needs, particularly in areas like cost, speed, and accessibility, to encourage consistent use and support financial inclusion. By addressing these factors and building on the insights provided, Shariah-compliant platforms have the potential to play a transformative role in advancing sustainable development, empowering MSMEs, and fostering a more inclusive financial ecosystem.

STATEMENT OF DECLARATIONS

No funding was received to conduct this study. The authors have no relevant financial or non-financial interests to disclose.

REFERENCES

Abidin, A. Z., Kurniawan, M. R., & Pratama, K. P. M. P. (2025). The role of Islamic financial markets to support sustainable development goals in Indonesia. In *Islamic financial markets and institutions: Challenges, financial stability, and inclusivity* (pp. 251–273). Springer Nature Singapore. DOI: 10.1007/978-981-96-8650-6_12

Adamu, A. Y. (2024). Digitalization of higher education in Ethiopia. *Journal of Comparative and International Higher Education, 16*(2), 13–24. DOI: 10.32674/jcihe.v16i2.5978

Adawiyah, S. R., Purwandari, B., Eitiveni, I., & Purwaningsih, E. H. (2024). The influence of AI and AR technology in personalized recommendations on customer usage intention: A case study of cosmetic products on Shopee. *Applied Sciences (Basel, Switzerland), 14*(13), 5786. Advance online publication. DOI: 10.3390/app14135786

Baeshen, L. (2023). *Financial inclusion in Islamic vs. non-Islamic countries, FinTech and bank competition* [Doctoral dissertation, University of Essex]. https://repository.essex.ac.uk/36519/

Berry, M. J. A. (1997). *Data mining techniques for marketing, sales and customer support*. Wiley.

Bhandari, B., Park, G., & Shafiabady, N. (2023). Implementation of transformer-based deep learning architecture for the development of surface roughness classifier using sound and cutting force signals. *Neural Computing & Applications, 35*(18), 13275–13292. Advance online publication. DOI: 10.1007/s00521-023-08425-z

Central Bank of Bahrain. (2017). *Shari'a-compliant financing-based crowdfunding directives*. Central Bank of Bahrain.

Cicchiello, A. F., Gallo, S., & Monferrà, S. (2022). Mapping crowdfunding in cultural and creative industries: A conceptual and empirical overview. *European Management Review, 19*(1), 22–37. DOI: 10.1111/emre.12510

Cumming, D., Meoli, M., Rossi, A., & Vismara, S. (2024). ESG and crowdfunding platforms. *Journal of Business Venturing, 39*(1), 106362. Advance online publication. DOI: 10.1016/j.jbusvent.2023.106362

Curth, A., Jeffares, A., & van der Schaar, M. (2024). A u-turn on double descent: Rethinking parameter counting in statistical learning. *Advances in Neural Information Processing Systems*, 36.

Curth, A., Jeffares, A., & van der Schaar, M. (2024). Why do random forests work? Understanding tree ensembles as self-regularizing adaptive smoothers. *arXiv*. https://arxiv.org/abs/2402.01502

Din, F. U., & Anwer, S. (2013). ERP success and logistical performance indicators: A critical view. *International Journal of Computer Science Issues*, *10*(6), 223–229.

Everitt, B. S., Landau, S., Leese, M., & Stahl, D. (2011). *Cluster analysis* (5th ed.). Wiley. DOI: 10.1002/9780470977811

Föge, N., Pauly, M., Schmid, L., & Ditzhaus, M. (2024). From naive trees to Random Forests: A general approach for proofing consistency of tree-based methods. *arXiv*. https://arxiv.org/abs/2404.06850

Gao, J., Siddik, A. B., Khawar Abbas, S., Hamayun, M., Masukujjaman, M., & Alam, S. S. (2023). Impact of e-commerce and digital marketing adoption on the financial and sustainability performance of MSMEs during the COVID-19 pandemic: An empirical study. *Sustainability (Basel)*, *15*(2), 1594. Advance online publication. DOI: 10.3390/su15021594

Hasnat, M. A., Hasan, K. K., & Khandakar, H. (2025). Intelligent machines and organizational knowledge transformation in Bangladesh's Islamic banking sector: Navigating innovation and Shariah compliance. *Journal of Integrated Islamic Finance and Socio-Economic Systems*, *1*, 11–28. DOI: 10.65638/2978-8196.2025.01.02

Hastie, T., Tibshirani, R., & Friedman, J. (2009). *The elements of statistical learning: Data mining, inference, and prediction* (2nd ed.). Springer. DOI: 10.1007/978-0-387-84858-7

Hossain, M. E., & Biswas, S. (2024). Technology acceptance model for understanding consumer's behavioral intention to use artificial intelligence based online shopping platforms in Bangladesh. *SN Business & Economics*, *4*(12), 153. Advance online publication. DOI: 10.1007/s43546-024-00754-y

Hou, R., Ye, X., Zaki, H. B. O., & Omar, N. A. B. (2023). Marketing decision support system based on data mining technology. *Applied Sciences (Basel, Switzerland)*, *13*(7), 4315. Advance online publication. DOI: 10.3390/app13074315

James, G., Witten, D., Hastie, T., & Tibshirani, R. (2013). *An introduction to statistical learning*. Springer. DOI: 10.1007/978-1-4614-7138-7

Javanmardi, E., Maresova, P., Xie, N., & Mierzwiak, R. (2024). Exploring business models for managing uncertainty in healthcare, medical devices, and biotechnology industries. *Heliyon*, *10*(4), e25962. Advance online publication. DOI: 10.1016/j.heliyon.2024.e25962 PMID: 38370194

Jhaveri, S., Khedkar, I., Kantharia, Y., & Jaswal, S. (2019). Success prediction using Random Forest, Catboost, XGboost and Adaboost for kickstarter campaigns. In *2019 3rd international conference on computing methodologies and communication (ICCMC)* (pp. 1170–1173). IEEE.

Kadir, S., Rah, A. R., & Yusuf, N. I. A. (2023). Getting to know non-fungible tokens (NFT) and decentralized finance (DeFi) in the era of Society 5.0. *International Journal of Islamic Finance*, *1*(2), 149–162. DOI: 10.14421/ijif.v1i2.2020

Mienye, I. D., & Jere, N. (2024). A survey of decision trees: Concepts, algorithms, and applications. *IEEE Access : Practical Innovations, Open Solutions*, *12*, 86716–86727. Advance online publication. DOI: 10.1109/ACCESS.2024.3416838

Mustaffha, N. (2024). Financial justice and sustainable development: Reviving Maqasid Al-Shariah for a changing world. *Progress in Islamic Banking and Finance*, *1*(1), 30–41.

Najib, F., Nawawi, Z. M., & Tambunan, K. (2025). Digital payment, support, and ethics drive micro and small business income. *Academia Open*, *10*(1), 10–21070. DOI: 10.21070/acopen.10.2025.11091

Nie, F., Hao, Z., & Wang, R. (2024). Multi-class support vector machine with maximizing minimum margin. *Proceedings of the AAAI Conference on Artificial Intelligence*, *38*(13), 14466–14473. DOI: 10.1609/aaai.v38i13.29361

Oates, J., Shafiabady, N., Ambagtsheer, R., Beilby, J., Seiboth, C., & Dent, E. (2022). Evolving hybrid partial genetic algorithm classification model for cost-effective frailty screening: Investigative study. *JMIR Aging*, *5*(4), e38464. Advance online publication. DOI: 10.2196/38464 PMID: 36206042

Painsky, A., & Rosset, S. (2017). Cross-validated variable selection in tree-based methods improves predictive performance. *IEEE Transactions on Pattern Analysis and Machine Intelligence*, *39*(11), 2142–2153. DOI: 10.1109/TPAMI.2016.2636831 PMID: 28114007

Park, J., Na, H. J., & Kim, H. (2024). Development of a success prediction model for crowdfunding based on machine learning reflecting ESG information. *IEEE Access : Practical Innovations, Open Solutions*, *12*, 197275–197289. Advance online publication. DOI: 10.1109/ACCESS.2024.3519219

Piryonesi, S. M., & El-Diraby, T. E. (2020). Role of data analytics in infrastructure asset management: Overcoming data size and quality problems. *Journal of Transportation Engineering. Part B, Pavements*, *146*(2), 04020022. Advance online publication. DOI: 10.1061/JPEODX.0000175

Qu, L., & Pei, Y. (2024). A comprehensive review on discriminant analysis for addressing challenges of class-level limitations, small sample size, and robustness. *Processes (Basel, Switzerland), 12*(7), 1382. Advance online publication. DOI: 10.3390/pr12071382

Rejeb, A., Rejeb, K., Appolloni, A., & Treiblmaier, H. (2023). Navigating the crowdfunding landscape: A study of knowledge trajectories based on main path analysis. *European Journal of Innovation Management, 26*(7), 415–448. DOI: 10.1108/EJIM-03-2023-0201

Santoso, H. A., Fandhi Safsalta, B., Febrianto, N., Wilujeng Saraswati, G., & Haw, S.-C. (2024). Comparative analysis of convolutional neural network and DenseNet121 transfer learning in agriculture focusing on crop leaf disease identification. *Applied Computing and Informatics*. Advance online publication. DOI: 10.1108/ACI-03-2024-0132

Seiffert, C., Khoshgoftaar, T. M., Van Hulse, J., & Napolitano, A. (2010). RUSBoost: A hybrid approach to alleviating class imbalance. *IEEE Transactions on Systems, Man, and Cybernetics. Part A, Systems and Humans, 40*(1), 185–197. DOI: 10.1109/TSMCA.2009.2029559

Shafiabady, N., Hadjinicolaou, N., Ud Din, F., Bhandari, B., Wu, R. M. X., & Vakilian, J. (2023). Using artificial intelligence (AI) to predict organizational agility. *PLoS One, 18*(5), e0283066. Advance online publication. DOI: 10.1371/journal.pone.0283066 PMID: 37163532

Sharma, S. K., Ilavarasan, P. V., & Karanasios, S. (2023). Small businesses and FinTech: A systematic review and future directions. *Electronic Commerce Research*. Advance online publication. DOI: 10.1007/s10660-023-09705-5

Soltaninejad, M., Yang, G., Lambrou, T., Allinson, N., Jones, T. L., Barrick, T. R., Howe, F. A., & Ye, X. (2017). Automated brain tumour detection and segmentation using superpixel-based extremely randomized trees in FLAIR MRI. *International Journal of Computer Assisted Radiology and Surgery, 12*(2), 183–203. DOI: 10.1007/s11548-016-1483-3 PMID: 27651330

Song, L. L., Wang, S. H., & Yang, C. (2020). Application research of improved XGBoost in imbalanced data processing. *Computer Science, 47*(6), 98–103.

Stefanelli, V., Ferilli, G. B., & Boscia, V. (2022). Exploring the lending business crowdfunding to support SMEs' financing decisions. *Journal of Innovation & Knowledge, 7*(4), 100278. Advance online publication. DOI: 10.1016/j.jik.2022.100278

Steyerberg, E. W. (2016). *Regression modeling strategies: With applications to linear models, logistic and ordinal regression, and survival analysis* (2nd ed.). Springer.

Sunmola, F., Baryannis, G., Tan, A., Co, K., & Papadakis, E. (2025). Holistic framework for blockchain-based halal compliance in supply chains enabled by artificial intelligence. *Systems, 13*(1), 21. DOI: 10.3390/systems13010021

Ud Din, F., Henskens, F., Paul, D., & Wallis, M. (2019). Agent-oriented smart factory (AOSF): An MAS based framework for SMEs under Industry 4.0. In Jezic, G., Chen-Burger, Y. H., Howlett, R., Jain, L., Vlacic, L., & Šperka, R. (Eds.), *Agents and multi-agent systems: Technologies and applications 2018* (pp. 45–57). Springer., DOI: 10.1007/978-3-319-92031-3_5

Wan, H. P., Gan, J. R., Zhu, Y. K., & Meng, Z. (2024). SS-MASVM: An advanced technique for assessing failure probability of high-dimensional complex systems using the multi-class adaptive support vector machine. *Computer Methods in Applied Mechanics and Engineering, 418*, 116568. Advance online publication. DOI: 10.1016/j.cma.2023.116568

Wu, R. M. X., Shafiabady, N., Gide, E., & Dianati, S. (2024). E-commerce success research in the age of digital transformation for post-COVID-19: From qualitative models to a quantitative model. *Technological Forecasting and Social Change*. Advance online publication.

Wu, R. M. X., Wang, Y., Shafiabady, N., Zhang, H., Yan, W., Gou, J., Shi, Y., Liu, B., Gide, E., Kang, C., Zhang, Z., Shen, B., Li, X., Fan, J., He, X., Soar, J., Zhao, H., Sun, L., Huo, W., & Wang, Y. (2023). Using multi-focus group method as an effective tool for eliciting business system requirements: Verified by a case study. *PLoS One, 18*(3), e0281603. Advance online publication. DOI: 10.1371/journal.pone.0281603 PMID: 36897871

Zaidi, S., Shafiabady, N., & Beilby, J. (2023). Identifying presence of cybersickness symptoms using AI based predictive learning algorithms. *Virtual Reality (Waltham Cross), 27*(4), 3613–3620. Advance online publication. DOI: 10.1007/s10055-023-00813-z

Zhu, R., Zeng, D., & Kosorok, M. R. (2015). Reinforcement learning trees. *Journal of the American Statistical Association, 110*(512), 1770–1784. DOI: 10.1080/01621459.2015.1036994 PMID: 26903687

Chapter 7
AI-Driven Volatility Prediction in GCC Financial Markets:
A CNN-LSTM-Attention Approach

Zakia Zouaghia
http://orcid.org/0000-0002-3102-6559
SMART Lab, ISG Tunis, University of Tunis, Tunisia

Zahra Kodia
http://orcid.org/0000-0002-1872-9364
SMART Lab, ISG Tunis, University of Tunis, Tunisia

Lamjed Ben Said
SMART Lab, ISG Tunis, University of Tunis, Tunisia

ABSTRACT

This chapter explores the potential of advanced deep learning for financial forecasting in emerging economies. It develops a hybrid AI framework combining CNN, LSTM, and an attention mechanism to predict stock market volatility in the GCC, focusing on the Saudi Tadawul All Share Index (TASI). Using real-time data from TASI, Brent crude, VIX, S&P 500, and gold, the model forecasts short-term (1-day) and medium-term (5-day) volatility. CNN extracts features, LSTM captures temporal dependencies, and attention highlights critical time steps. Experiments show superior performance over ARIMA, SVR, and Persistence, with MAE of 0.0171 (1-day) and 0.0186 (5-day), improving 81–83%. The model is robust to shocks, adapts to GCC markets, and supports risk management and investment decisions. Ethical considerations include transparency, interpretability, and data reliability.

DOI: 10.4018/979-8-2600-1603-9.ch007

INTRODUCTION

Over the past decade, global financial markets have undergone profound transformations driven by disruptive events (Zouaghia et al., 2025a). The COVID-19 pandemic, geopolitical tensions, recurring financial crises, and major policy shifts have ushered in an era of heightened uncertainty and volatility (Zouaghia et al., 2024a). Pandemic-induced lockdowns caused one of the steepest market contractions in modern history, while subsequent inflationary pressures and supply chain disruptions continued to test economic resilience (World Bank, 2023). Meanwhile, conflicts in Eastern Europe and the Middle East further destabilized commodity prices and investor confidence, underscoring the interconnectedness and fragility of global financial systems (Borio, 2024).

Within this context, the Gulf Cooperation Council (GCC) economies—Saudi Arabia, the UAE, Qatar, Kuwait, Oman, and Bahrain, occupy a distinctive position. Historically dependent on hydrocarbon revenues, they remain highly exposed to fluctuations in global energy prices and regional geopolitics (Boubaker et al., 2022). Diversification programs such as Saudi Vision 2030 (Al-Roubaie, 2025) and the UAE's Centennial 2071 (Litsas, 2023) aim to build more resilient economies, yet GCC markets remain sensitive to external shocks. The Saudi Tadawul All Share Index (TASI), the region's largest exchange, reflects this volatility, often reacting sharply to changes in oil prices, U.S. monetary policy, and geopolitical developments (Alqahtani et al., 2019).

Such volatility intensifies during global crises, when uncertainty fuels speculative behavior and rapid capital reallocations. For investors, this increases risk and portfolio instability; for policymakers, it complicates efforts to preserve financial stability. Consequently, accurate and timely volatility prediction has become a strategic priority for investors, regulators, and decision-makers (Behera et al., 2024). Reliable forecasts support informed asset allocation, sound policy interventions, and effective risk management in markets shaped by global uncertainty.

However, volatility forecasting remains challenging—particularly in emerging markets like the GCC (Aljughaiman et al., 2025). Traditional econometric models such as ARIMA and GARCH (Engle, 1982; Bollerslev, 1986) are limited by linear assumptions and struggle to capture the nonlinear, non-stationary, and high-dimensional nature of financial data (Islam et al., 2025). Their accuracy often deteriorates during turbulent periods, precisely when robust predictions are most needed (Boudri & El Bouhadi, 2024).

In contrast, Artificial Intelligence (AI) and Machine Learning (ML) have emerged as transformative tools for financial forecasting. These methods handle vast heterogeneous datasets, uncover complex nonlinear relationships, and adapt dynamically to market changes (Olubusola et al., 2024). Deep learning models, including

Convolutional Neural Networks (CNNs), Recurrent Neural Networks (RNNs), and Long Short-Term Memory (LSTM) networks, have shown strong performance in modeling sequential and temporal data (Zouaghia et al., 2023, 2025b; Jlifi et al., 2024). Recent advances such as attention mechanisms further enhance interpretability and predictive power by focusing on the most relevant features driving volatility (Dehimi & Tolba, 2024).

Despite this progress, few studies have applied AI-driven forecasting to GCC financial markets. Existing research largely centers on developed economies, where market structures and data transparency differ markedly (Zouaghia et al., 2024; Ampountolas, 2023). The GCC presents unique challenges, dependence on oil prices, evolving regulations, concentrated sectors, and geopolitical exposure (Fasanya, 2021), that demand tailored AI frameworks capable of integrating multiple data sources and learning from complex, often noisy, signals.

Research Objectives

In response to these challenges, this study aims to develop a hybrid deep learning model that combines the strengths of Convolutional Neural Networks (CNN), Long Short-Term Memory (LSTM) networks, and an attention mechanism to forecast stock market volatility in GCC financial markets, with a focus on the Saudi Tadawul All Share Index (TASI). Specifically, the objectives of this research are:

- To design and implement a CNN-LSTM-Attention model that captures non-linear temporal dependencies in GCC stock market data.
- To evaluate the model's predictive performance using multi-source datasets encompassing both local and global indicators (e.g., oil prices, VIX, gold, and S&P 500).
- To compare its forecasting accuracy and robustness against traditional econometric and machine learning models, including ARIMA, SVR, and Persistence models.
- To provide practical insights for investors, portfolio managers, and policy-makers in managing volatility and systemic risk under global uncertainty.
- To contribute to the advancement of AI applications in financial markets by demonstrating how deep learning techniques can be effectively adapted to region-specific contexts.

Contributions to Financial Science and Practice

This research contributes to both the theoretical and practical dimensions of financial science. From an academic perspective, it fills a clear gap in the literature by offering one of the first comprehensive applications of an integrated CNN-LSTM-Attention model to GCC stock market volatility forecasting. The study advances understanding of how AI architectures can capture the nonlinear interdependencies between oil prices, global uncertainty indices, and regional market behavior.

From a practical perspective, the findings offer valuable implications for decision-makers in GCC financial markets. Accurate volatility forecasts can serve as early warning signals for regulators, supporting macroprudential oversight and financial stability. Investors and portfolio managers can use the model's insights to enhance hedging strategies, optimize portfolio allocation, and mitigate exposure to external shocks. Furthermore, the study supports the development of AI technologies within the GCC financial sector, encouraging the adoption of data-driven frameworks that enhance transparency, efficiency, and resilience.

Paper Organization

The remainder of this chapter is structured as follows: Section 2 reviews the relevant literature on AI-based volatility forecasting and its applications in emerging markets. Section 3 provides the theoretical background of the study. Section 4 introduces the theoretical foundation for AI-driven volatility prediction in GCC markets. Section 5 presents a case study applying the CNN-LSTM-Attention model to predict volatility in GCC financial markets, including a detailed description of data sources and methodological framework. Section 6 reports empirical results and comparative analyses. Section 7 discusses the proposed framework. Section 8 outlines the practical recommendations. Section 9 outlines directions for future research, and Section 10 concludes the chapter by summarizing key findings and their broader implications.

BACKGROUND

Volatility is a key measure of financial market uncertainty and investor sentiment, reflecting the rate and magnitude of price fluctuations. It serves as a central input in portfolio optimization, risk management, and derivative pricing. In emerging, energy-dependent economies like those of the Gulf Cooperation Council (GCC), volatility reflects not only internal market behavior but also global macroeconomic and geopolitical dynamics.

GCC financial markets operate within a distinctive economic structure, strongly linking oil prices, fiscal revenues, and capital flows. While diversification efforts such as Saudi Vision 2030 and UAE Centennial 2071 are reshaping the region, hydrocarbon dependency remains a major determinant of market performance.

Consequently, global oil price volatility often translates into instability in regional equity indices, such as the Saudi Tadawul All Share Index (TASI).

Traditionally, volatility forecasting has relied on econometric approaches assuming linearity and stationarity, including ARCH and GARCH models. While these frameworks help understand conditional variance dynamics, they struggle in non-linear, regime-shifting, and high-dimensional environments. The growing influence of exogenous variables—energy prices, global indices, and policy shocks, further exposes the limits of conventional models.

Advances in artificial intelligence and deep learning offer new avenues for modeling volatility through data-driven feature discovery. Architectures like CNNs, RNNs, LSTMs, and attention mechanisms learn non-linear dependencies directly from data, extracting latent structures from noisy signals and capturing local and global coupling effects typical of GCC markets.

Within this context, this chapter frames GCC volatility forecasting at the intersection of economic transformation, market complexity, and methodological innovation, establishing a foundation for exploring hybrid AI architectures that integrate CNN, LSTM, and attention mechanisms for enhanced predictive modeling in dynamic emerging financial systems.

LITERATURE REVIEW

Ghysels et al., (2006) In their paper, the authors examine volatility persistence and show how mixed-frequency regressions (MIDAS) and lag-structure models exploit returns sampled at different frequencies to improve volatility forecasts. Their work demonstrates that daily realized-power and range-based measures can outperform simpler persistence or single-frequency models, and that long lag structures (one to two months) are often sufficient to capture the persistence of volatility. The paper therefore provides a rigorous benchmark for persistence-type approaches and highlights how careful choice of regressors and sampling frequency materially affects forecast performance.

Rubio et al. (2023) The authors evaluate ARIMA (often combined with GARCH and wavelet preprocessing) for volatility forecasting, showing ARIMA-based pipelines remain competitive for capturing medium-term dynamics, particularly after appropriate denoising or decomposition of the series. They emphasize ARIMA's interpretability and low computational cost, but also note ARIMA's limitations during abrupt regime changes and extreme events, motivating hybrid approaches that combine ARIMA with volatility-specific models or machine learning layers in practice.

Zeng et al. (2023) This recent study demonstrates combining CNN layers for local pattern extraction with Transformer (attention) blocks to capture long-range dependencies in financial time series. Their experiments show CNNs can quickly learn short-term motifs (volatility bursts, local trends) which, once encoded, allow attention mechanisms to model global context and long-term relationships more effectively than recurrent models alone. The work supports hybrid CNN + attention architectures as a state-of-the-art pathway for feature extraction plus global sequence modeling in finance.

Zouaghia et al. (2025) The authors proposed the SMAPF-HNNA framework, which integrates CNNs as a primary component for feature extraction in financial time series analysis. In their approach, CNN layers effectively capture local temporal and spatial patterns within stock market data, allowing subsequent neural modules such as recurrent and multilayer perceptron networks to focus on higher-level dependencies. The study demonstrates that CNNs can serve as powerful front-end processors, transforming noisy, high-frequency financial inputs into structured feature representations that enhance the overall predictive capacity of hybrid AI models.

Fischer & Krauss (2018) Fischer and Krauss apply LSTM networks to predict directional movements of S&P 500 constituents and show that LSTMs can capture temporal patterns that improve out-of-sample directional accuracy versus standard benchmarks. They provide practical guidance on input construction, network architecture, and evaluation in a large-scale equity setting, illustrating LSTM's strength at modeling sequential dependencies in noisy financial data and its utility as a building block for ensemble trading systems.

Joshi et al. (2025) In their research, the authors present a hybrid model in which Convolutional Neural Networks (CNNs) are leveraged as the front-end module to automatically extract spatial and local temporal features from raw stock market data, which are then input into an LSTM network to capture longer-term dependencies. Their architecture is designed to combine CNN's pattern-recognition strengths (identifying short-term motifs and smoothing noise) with LSTM's capacity for sequential modeling in dynamic market environments. This approach exemplifies how CNNs can function as an effective feature encoder for financial time series, producing richer representations that enhance the performance of downstream sequence models.

Qiu et al. (2020) combining LSTM with an attention layer contribute to improve interpretability and forecast accuracy for multiple major indices. They apply wavelet denoising before feeding sequences into an LSTM+attention architecture, finding that the attention module helps the model selectively focus on critical time steps (for example, volatility spikes or regime changes). Empirical comparisons show the attention-augmented model outperforms plain LSTM and GRU variants on several forecasting horizons, supporting attention's role in enhancing both performance and explainability.

Chen and Zhang Zili (2019) Chen and Zhang introduce attention into LSTM architectures to forecast the dynamic implied-volatility surface used in option pricing. Their model demonstrates that attention helps the network select influential maturities and strikes across time, improving surface forecasts and enabling trading strategies with superior Sharpe ratios. The study is an early, influential example of attention mechanisms applied directly to volatility modeling, showing concrete economic value for risk management and derivatives pricing.

Al-Najjar et al., (2022) In this research work, the authors conducted an empirical analysis examining the dual effects of COVID-19 indicators and the 2020 oil-price collapse on the Saudi Exchange (Tadawul). Their findings reveal that fluctuations in oil prices were the predominant driver of TASI movements during the pandemic period, as the collapse in oil demand and production cuts led to sharp declines in investor confidence and trading volume. This underscores the structural sensitivity of the Saudi market to commodity price shocks.

Boukhatem and Alhazmi (2024) demonstrated that oil prices exert a significantly stronger influence on the TASI compared to other macroeconomic and pandemic-related variables. Their results emphasize that the principal transmission channel of global shocks to Saudi equity markets operates through energy price volatility rather than direct pandemic or policy effects. This highlights the extent to which the Saudi market's performance remains intertwined with global oil market dynamics.

Hussain and Rehman (2023) documents volatility connectedness between global oil and equity indices and the major GCC stock markets. Their study documented strong volatility spillovers and contagion effects across the region, showing that external shocks, whether financial, geopolitical, or commodity-based, rapidly transmit into GCC markets, amplifying systemic risk.

THEORETICAL FRAMEWORK FOR AI-DRIVEN VOLATILITY PREDICTION IN GCC MARKETS

Theoretical Foundations of Financial Volatility Modeling

Efficient Market Hypothesis and Its Limitations

The Efficient Market Hypothesis (EMH), developed by Fama (1970), posits that asset prices fully reflect all available information, making it impossible to consistently achieve abnormal returns through prediction. However, the GCC financial markets exhibit characteristics that challenge the strict form of EMH. The region's heavy dependence on oil prices, concentrated ownership structures, and evolving regulatory frameworks create market inefficiencies that can be exploited through advanced predictive modeling. Our CNN-LSTM-Attention approach acknowledges these market imperfections and leverages them to develop superior volatility forecasting capabilities.

ARCH/GARCH Family of Models

The theoretical groundwork for volatility modeling was established by Engle's (1982) Autoregressive Conditional Heteroskedasticity (ARCH) model and its generalization by Bollerslev (1986) as GARCH. These models recognize that volatility clusters in time-periods, high volatility tends to be followed by high volatility, and low by low. While traditional GARCH models provide a solid statistical foundation, they suffer from limitations in capturing complex non-linear patterns and long-range dependencies present in GCC markets, particularly during oil price shocks and geopolitical events(Aslam et al., 2022; Alharbi, 2023).

Deep Learning Theoretical Framework

Neural Network Approximation Theory

The theoretical justification for using deep learning models stems from the Universal Approximation Theorem, which states that a neural network with a single hidden layer containing a finite number of neurons can approximate any continuous function on compact subsets of R^N. Our multi-layer CNN-LSTM-Attention architecture extends this theoretical foundation by combining multiple approximation capabilities:

- **CNN Component**: Leverages convolutional operations to extract local temporal patterns and spatial features from financial time series
- **LSTM Component**: Incorporates memory cells and gating mechanisms to capture long-term dependencies
- **Attention Mechanism**: Implements content-based addressing to dynamically weight important time steps

Temporal Dependency Modeling Theory

The The Long Short-Term Memory (LSTM) architecture, originally introduced by Hochreiter and Schmidhuber (1997), provides a robust theoretical framework for modeling long-range temporal dependencies in sequential data. LSTMs achieve this by employing a sophisticated gating mechanism that regulates the flow of information through the network, allowing it to retain relevant information over extended periods while mitigating the problem of vanishing or exploding gradients commonly observed in traditional recurrent neural networks (RNNs).

The key components of the LSTM architecture can be mathematically expressed as follows:

- **Input Gate:**

$$i_t = \sigma\left(W_i * [h_{\{t-1\}}, x_t] + b_i\right)$$

- **Forget Gate:**

$$f_t = \sigma\left(W_f * [h_{\{t-1\}}, x_t] + b_f\right)$$

- **Output Gate:**

$$o_t = \sigma\left(W_o * [h_{\{t-1\}}, x_t] + b_o\right)$$

- **Cell State Update:**

$$C_t = f_t \circ C_{\{t-1\}} + i_t \circ \tanh\left(W_C * [h_{\{t-1\}}, x_t] + b_C\right)$$

- **Hidden State:**

$$h_t = o_t \circ \tanh\left(C_t\right)$$

In this formulation:

- x_t is the input at time step t.
- $h_{\{t-1\}}$ is the previous hidden state.
- $C_{\{t-1\}}$ is the previous cell state.
- σ denotes the sigmoid activation function.
- $\circ$ represents element-wise multiplication.
- W_i, W_f, W_o, W_C are weight matrices, and b_i, b_f, b_o, b_C are bias vectors, all learned during training.

This gating structure enables the LSTM network to selectively retain and update information across long temporal sequences. This capability is particularly valuable for modeling volatility patterns in GCC financial markets, which are influenced by quarterly oil production cycles, seasonal variations, and long-term economic factors. By preserving critical information over extended periods, LSTMs can effectively capture complex temporal dependencies and delayed effects, thereby enhancing the predictive accuracy of volatility forecasting models.

Attention Mechanism Theoretical Framework

Information Bottleneck Theory

The attention mechanism in our model is theoretically grounded in the Information Bottleneck (IB) principle (Li et al., 2025), which seeks to learn a compressed representation of the input that retains maximal information about the output while discarding irrelevant details. In the context of time-series modeling, this allows the model to focus selectively on the most informative temporal segments, thereby improving predictive performance and interpretability.

Formally, the attention mechanism computes a set of weights $\boldsymbol{\alpha}_t$ for each time step $\boldsymbol{t}$ as follows:

Score Computation:

$$e_t = v^T * \tanh\left(W * h_t + b\right)$$

Attention Weights:

$$\alpha_t = \frac{\exp\left(e_t\right)}{\Sigma_{\{j=1\}}^{\{T\}\exp}\left(e_j\right)}$$

Here, h_t represents the hidden state at time step $\boldsymbol{t}$, W and v are learnable weight matrices, and b is a bias vector. The resulting context vector c is computed as a weighted sum of the hidden states:

$$c = \Sigma_{\{t=1\}_t^{\{T\}\alpha}} * h_t$$

This context vector effectively summarizes the input sequence by emphasizing the most informative time steps, allowing the model to allocate computational resources efficiently. By leveraging the IB principle, the attention mechanism not only enhances prediction accuracy but also improves interpretability, as it highlights which periods have the greatest impact on the target output.

Behavioral Finance Integration

The attention mechanism aligns with theoretical concepts from behavioral finance, particularly the limited attention hypothesis proposed by Sims (2003). Investors in GCC markets, like elsewhere, have bounded rationality and processing capacity. Our model's attention mechanism mimics this selective focus, concentrating on periods of market stress, significant oil price movements, or geopolitical events that disproportionately impact volatility.

Financial Economics of GCC Markets

Petrodollar Recycling Theory

The theoretical framework incorporates the petrodollar recycling mechanism, where oil revenues flow into GCC financial markets, creating unique volatility dynamics. Our model captures these flows through features derived from Brent oil prices and their relationship with GCC equity market volatility, providing a computational implementation of the theoretical relationship formalized by Arouri et al. (2011).

Islamic Finance Principles

GCC markets operate within Sharia-compliant frameworks, introducing theoretical considerations distinct from conventional markets. The prohibition of excessive uncertainty (gharar) and speculation (maysir) creates different volatility characteristics that our model accommodates through specialized feature engineering and regime detection.

Integration Framework: Bridging Theory and Practice

Multi-Theoretical Synthesis

Our CNN-LSTM-Attention framework represents a theoretical synthesis that integrates:

- **Statistical Theory**: Through volatility clustering and persistence modeling
- **Financial Economics**: Via GCC-specific market microstructure considerations
- **Computational Theory**: Through deep learning architectures and optimization
- **Behavioral Finance**: By mimicking investor attention and reaction patterns

Theoretical Validation Framework

The model's theoretical soundness is validated through multiple lenses:

1. **Economic Significance**: Parameter stability and interpretability
2. **Statistical Robustness**: Out-of-sample performance and residual analysis
3. **Computational Efficiency**: Training convergence and generalization capability
4. **Market Realism**: Alignment with GCC market characteristics and constraints

This comprehensive theoretical framework provides the foundation for our empirical investigation and justifies the superior performance of the CNN-LSTM-Attention approach over traditional statistical models in capturing the complex, multi-scale volatility dynamics of GCC financial markets.

CASE STUDY: AI-DRIVEN VOLATILITY PREDICTION IN GCC FINANCIAL MARKETS USING A CNN-LSTM-ATTENTION APPROACH

Building Building on the preceding theoretical and empirical insights, this case study applies the proposed CNN-LSTM-Attention hybrid model to predict market volatility in the Gulf Cooperation Council (GCC) region, focusing on the Saudi Tadawul All Share Index (TASI). Given their dependence on hydrocarbons and sensitivity to global economic and geopolitical shocks, GCC markets provide a challenging yet insightful setting for testing AI-based financial forecasting. This study demonstrates how advanced deep learning architectures can effectively capture complex temporal and cross-market dynamics, enhancing predictive accuracy and interpretability over traditional econometric models.

The proposed framework combines CNNs for feature extraction, LSTM networks for sequential learning, and an attention mechanism to emphasize key time steps influencing volatility. This multi-layered design enables the model to uncover nonlinear relationships among key inputs, TASI, Brent crude oil prices, the CBOE Volatility Index (VIX), the S&P 500, and gold prices, that collectively shape GCC market behavior. The goal is to deliver accurate short-term (1-day) and medium-term (5-day) volatility forecasts while analyzing the impact of external factors on regional financial stability.

The case study follows a transparent and reproducible structure: it outlines data sources, preprocessing steps, and experimental setup; details the hybrid architecture; and presents comparative results against benchmarks such as Persistence, ARIMA, and Support Vector Regression (SVR). The discussion highlights both quantitative outcomes and qualitative insights, including interpretability, robustness to shocks, and implications for investors and policymakers. Ultimately, this study bridges theoretical AI advancements with practical financial applications, demonstrating the transformative potential of intelligent forecasting systems in emerging markets.

Data Collection and Feature Engineering

To develop and evaluate the proposed CNN-LSTM-Attention model, a comprehensive dataset was built using real-time financial data from Yahoo Finance and other verified sources. The sample period, spanning January 2020 to October 2025, encompasses major global disruptions, such as the COVID-19 pandemic, geopolitical tensions, and post-crisis recoveries, alongside key economic developments in the Gulf Cooperation Council (GCC) region. This diverse timeframe offers an ideal foundation for training and testing models designed to predict volatility under varying market conditions.

The Saudi Tadawul All Share Index (TASI) serves as the target variable, representing market performance and investor sentiment in the region's largest and most liquid exchange. To capture broader macro-financial influences, several external indicators were included as inputs: Brent crude oil futures (reflecting oil dependency), the CBOE Volatility Index (VIX) (global risk sentiment), the S&P 500 Index (global equity trends), gold futures (safe-haven asset), and regional indices such as the Qatar Exchange (QE) and Abu Dhabi Securities Exchange (ADX). Together, these variables create a multidimensional feature space that captures both local and international forces shaping GCC market volatility.

Feature Engineering and Preprocessing

To enhance predictive capability, several engineered features were designed to capture different dimensions of market behavior: volatility clustering, momentum effects, and market regime shifts. Specifically:

- **Volatility Measures:**

Rolling-window volatility indicators were computed using 5-day and 20-day log-return standard deviations to represent short-term and medium-term market fluctuations. These measures capture persistence and clustering patterns typical of emerging markets.

- **Momentum Indicators:**

Price change ratios over 1-day, 5-day, and 10-day horizons were calculated to quantify short-term trends and reversals in market momentum. These indicators help the model identify directional signals associated with speculative behavior and investor overreaction.

- **Market Regime Features:**

Exogenous variables such as VIX levels, Brent oil returns, S&P 500 returns, and gold returns were included to represent different market regimes—ranging from risk-on to risk-off conditions. This helps the model contextualize TASI's movements within broader global sentiment.

- **Technical Indicators:**

A 14-day Relative Strength Index (RSI) was computed to capture overbought or oversold market conditions, a commonly used signal in quantitative trading and technical analysis.

Mathematical Formulation of Features

The construction of input features for the CNN–LSTM–Attention model relies on transformations of raw financial price series into quantitative indicators that capture market dynamics, momentum, and volatility. Let P_t denote the adjusted closing price of the Saudi Tadawul All Share Index (TASI) at time t.

Logarithmic Returns

The daily log return measures the proportional change in price and is computed as:

$$\mathbf{r} = \mathbf{ln(P / P)}$$

This transformation stabilizes variance and converts multiplicative changes into additive ones.

Rolling Volatility

Volatility reflects the standard deviation of log returns over a rolling window of *n* days. For a window of 5 or 20 days, the realized volatility is given by:

$$\boldsymbol{\sigma}^{\mathbf{n}} = \sqrt{252} \times \sqrt{(\,(1/\mathbf{n}) \times \boldsymbol{\Sigma}\,(\mathbf{r} - \bar{\mathbf{r}})^2\,)}$$

where the factor $\sqrt{252}$ annualizes the volatility (assuming 252 trading days per year).

Two measures are used:

- **5-day volatility:** $\sigma^{(5)}$
- **20-day volatility:** $\sigma^{(20)}$

These capture short- and medium-term fluctuations in the TASI.

Momentum Indicators

Momentum quantifies recent price movements over different horizons. The *k*-day momentum is defined as:

$$\mathbf{M} = (\mathbf{P} - \mathbf{P})/\mathbf{P}$$

for $k = 1, 5$, and 10 days.

Market Regime Features

Market-regime indicators integrate global and regional conditions that influence GCC volatility. They are expressed as:

$$VIX\ level : VIX$$

$$VIX\ \boldsymbol{change} : (VIX - VIX)/VIX$$

$$\boldsymbol{Brent\ oil\ returns} : \boldsymbol{ln}(\boldsymbol{Brent} / \boldsymbol{Brent})$$

$$S\ \&\ P\ 500\ returns : ln(SP / SP)$$

$$\boldsymbol{Gold\ returns} : \boldsymbol{ln}(\boldsymbol{Gold} / \boldsymbol{Gold})^{**}$$

These features reflect global risk sentiment, energy market movements, and macro-financial linkages.

Relative Strength Index (RSI)

The 14-day Relative Strength Index measures price momentum and overbought/oversold conditions, defined as:

$$\boldsymbol{RSI} = 100 - [100/(1 + \boldsymbol{RS})]$$

Where

$RS = (Average\ Gain\ over\ 14\ days) / (Average\ Loss\ over\ 14\ days)$

Gains and losses are computed as positive and negative changes in consecutive daily prices:

$\boldsymbol{Gain} = \boldsymbol{max}(\boldsymbol{P} - \boldsymbol{P} , 0)$

$\boldsymbol{Loss} = \boldsymbol{max}(\boldsymbol{P} - \boldsymbol{P} , 0)$

Target Variables

The prediction targets correspond to 1-day-ahead and 5-day-ahead volatilities, obtained by shifting the 5-day rolling volatility series:

$Target\ d = \sigma$

$Target\ d = \sigma$

Feature Alignment and Data Imputation

All time series were synchronized to a common daily frequency to ensure temporal consistency. Missing observations were handled using a hybrid imputation strategy that combined forward-fill methods for short gaps and interpolated estimates for longer missing periods, ensuring continuity without introducing artificial trends. Each feature was subsequently standardized through z-score normalization to mitigate scale discrepancies and improve neural network convergence during training.

This structured feature engineering process not only enriches the dataset with economically meaningful signals but also enhances the robustness and generalizability of the proposed CNN-LSTM-Attention model, enabling it to learn both short-term fluctuations and long-term dependencies across local and global financial indicators.

Final Feature Vector

For each observation date t, the final feature vector $\mathbf{X}$ is composed of:

$X = [\boldsymbol{r}, \boldsymbol{\sigma}, \boldsymbol{\sigma}^2, \boldsymbol{M}^1, \boldsymbol{M}, \boldsymbol{M}^1, VIX, \boldsymbol{\Delta} VIX, \boldsymbol{Brent}, \boldsymbol{SP}500, \boldsymbol{Gold}, \boldsymbol{RSI}]$

This vector serves as the input to the CNN–LSTM–Attention model for forecasting short- and medium-term volatility in the GCC markets.

Model Architecture

The proposed The proposed CNN-LSTM-Attention framework is designed to predict short-term (1-day) and medium-term (5-day) volatility in Gulf Cooperation Council (GCC) financial markets. It combines convolutional, recurrent, and attention mechanisms to capture both spatial and temporal dependencies in financial time series.

- **Convolutional Layers:**

Two 1D CNN layers (64 and 32 filters) extract local spatial-temporal features such as abrupt price changes and micro-volatility clusters. Max-pooling follows each layer to reduce dimensionality and overfitting while retaining key patterns.

- **LSTM Layer:**

A 128-unit LSTM captures long-term temporal dependencies, enabling the model to learn delayed market reactions and persistent volatility regimes characteristic of GCC markets.

- **Attention Mechanism:**

An attention layer atop the LSTM output assigns dynamic weights to the most influential time steps, enhancing interpretability and emphasizing critical volatility events.

- **Dense Layers:**

Attention-weighted features pass through three dense layers (256, 128, and 64 neurons) with dropout rates of 0.4, 0.3, and 0.2 to ensure hierarchical feature learning and prevent overfitting.

- **Output Layers:**

Dual output branches generate 1-day and 5-day volatility forecasts, each producing a single scalar value for its respective horizon.

The model uses the *Huber loss function*, balancing Mean Squared Error (MSE) and Mean Absolute Error (MAE) to maintain robustness against outliers. Optimization is handled by the *Adam optimizer* with a learning rate of 0.001.

Training incorporates *early stopping* and *adaptive learning rate reduction* based on validation loss, ensuring efficient convergence and stable performance under volatile market conditions. Figure 1 summarizes the architecture of the proposed approach.

Benchmark Models

To evaluate the predictive performance of the proposed CNN-LSTM-Attention model, three benchmark models are employed, representing increasingly sophisticated forecasting approaches: statistical, naïve, and machine learning-based.

- **Persistence Model:**

This baseline assumes that future volatility equals the most recent observed value (volatility at *t+1* = volatility at *t*). Despite its simplicity, it often performs competitively in stable markets and serves as a lower bound for assessing the added value of advanced AI models.

- **ARIMA Model:**

The AutoRegressive Integrated Moving Average (ARIMA) model captures linear temporal dependencies through autoregressive and moving-average components. While effective for mean-reverting structures, it struggles with the nonlinearities and regime shifts typical of volatile, emerging markets such as those in the GCC.

- **Support Vector Regression (SVR) Model:**

SVR based on Support Vector Machine principles, models nonlinear relationships using a radial basis function (RBF) kernel. It minimizes prediction error within a tolerance margin while preserving generalization capability (Ampountolas, 2024). Although widely used in financial forecasting, its accuracy depends heavily on kernel and parameter tuning.

Together, these benchmarks, Persistence, ARIMA, and SVR—form a robust comparative framework that spans naïve, statistical, and traditional machine-learning paradigms, enabling an objective evaluation of the CNN-LSTM-Attention model's predictive advantage in forecasting GCC market volatility.

Investment and Risk Decisions Process

The proposed framework translates CNN-LSTM-Attention volatility forecasts into actionable, data-driven investment strategies, linking predictive analytics directly to portfolio management decisions. It operates across short-term tactical actions and medium-term strategic allocation, integrating adaptive, quantitative rules to enhance financial decision-making.

Short-Term (1-Day) Tactical Decisions

1-day volatility forecasts guide immediate trading and risk-control measures. Elevated predicted volatility triggers defensive actions, including:

- Dynamic position sizing to reduce exposure;
- Stop-loss recalibration to limit downside risk;
- Intraday hedging with futures or options.

During low-volatility periods, the system supports selective advantage or position expansion. Decisions are based on quantitative thresholds: forecasts above the 75th percentile prompt defensive positioning, while below the 25th percentile encourage opportunity-driven allocations, ensuring responsiveness to shifting market regimes without discretionary bias.

Medium-Term (5-Day) Strategic Portfolio Management

5-day forecasts inform strategic portfolio optimization via a mean-variance framework, adjusting asset weights and sector allocations dynamically:

- High-predicted volatility shifts exposure toward defensive sectors (utilities, telecom, and consumer staples).
- Low-volatility periods favor cyclical sectors (technology, finance, energy).

Brent oil sensitivity is incorporated through attention weights, enabling allocations across GCC markets that reflect oil-driven volatility spillovers and regional risk asymmetries.

Adaptive Feedback and Risk Governance

A closed-loop feedback mechanism continuously evaluates trading and allocation outcomes, comparing realized returns, volatility, and Sharpe ratios against benchmarks. This feedback refines model parameters and decision thresholds, creating a self-learning, adaptive system.

The attention mechanism enhances interpretability, revealing which temporal patterns and external indicators (e.g., oil prices, VIX, global indices) drive forecasts.

This transparency supports institutional trust, accountability, and compliance with emerging AI governance standards.

In sum, this framework operationalizes AI-driven volatility forecasts into a multi-horizon, adaptive decision-support system, combining short-term agility with medium-term strategic foresight. It enhances resilience, optimizes returns, and embeds transparency and region-specific intelligence into GCC investment workflows.

Figure 1. Architecture of the Proposed Approach

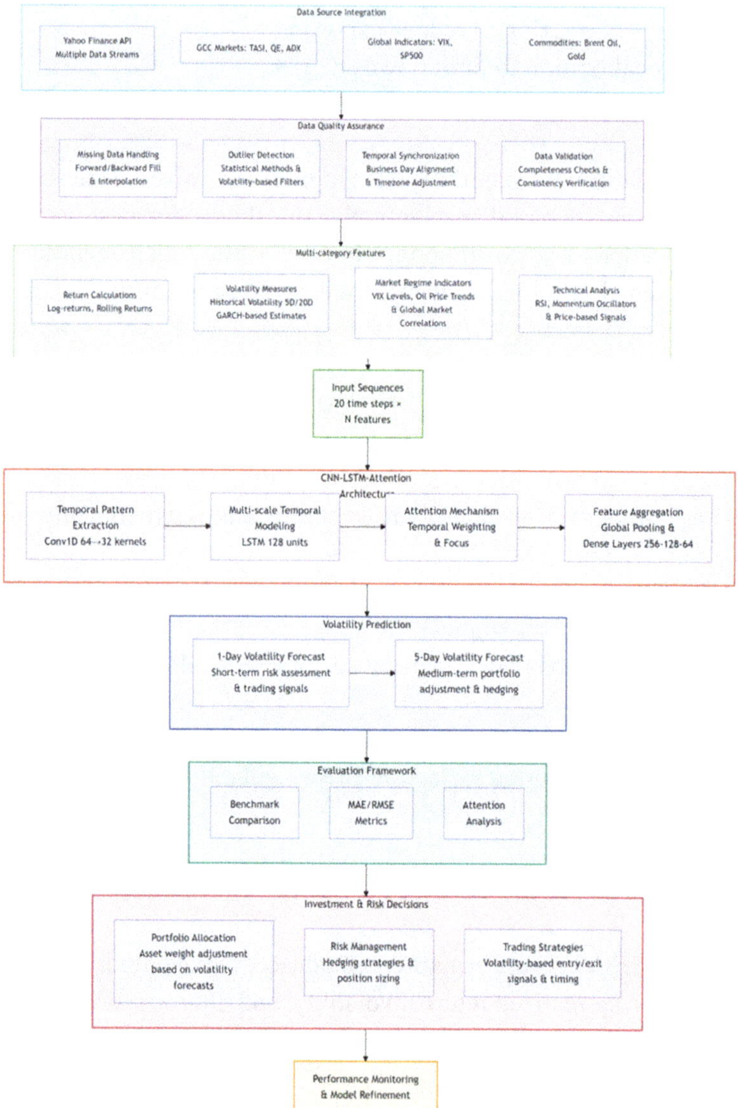

EMPIRICAL RESULTS AND COMPARATIVE ANALYSIS

Experiments Environment

This section describes the computational and software setup used to conduct the experiments. It outlines both the hardware infrastructure supporting the computations and the software stack employed for model development, training, and evaluation.

Computational Infrastructure

The experimental framework was implemented using the hardware and computational infrastructure as shown in Table 1.

Table 1. Hardware and Computational Infrastructure

Component	Specification
Processor	Multi-core CPU architecture
Memory	32 GB RAM
Storage	Solid-State Drive (SSD)
Acceleration	TensorFlow (CPU-optimized)

This setup enables consistent computational performance, ensuring reproducibility and scalability across experimental sessions.

Software Stack

The software environment integrates modern data analysis, statistical modeling, and machine learning frameworks, all implemented in Python. This combination allows for efficient data handling, model training, and performance visualization. Table 2 shows the applied packages in our experiments.

Table 2. Software Stack and Dependencies

Category	Package	Purpose
Core Data Processing	numpy	Numerical computations and array operations
	pandas	Data manipulation, transformation, and analysis
Machine Learning Frameworks	tensorflow	Implementation of deep learning architectures
	scikit-learn	Machine learning utilities for preprocessing and evaluation

continued on following page

Table 2. Continued

Category	Package	Purpose
Statistical Modeling	statsmodels	Time series analysis and ARIMA implementation
Data Visualization	matplotlib	Plotting model performance and financial trends
	seaborn	Enhanced statistical visualizations
Financial Data Acquisition	yfinance	Real-time market data retrieval from Yahoo Finance

This comprehensive software stack ensures stable, reproducible experiments and seamless integration of data preprocessing, model training, and result visualization.

Model Training and Performance

The CNN-LSTM-Attention architecture was trained on time series sequences consisting of 20 historical time steps, enabling the model to learn short-term and intermediate temporal dependencies within the volatility dynamics of the GCC financial markets. The dataset was divided into 80% for training and 20% for testing, ensuring an unbiased evaluation of predictive performance.

Model Evaluation Metrics

The performance of the model was evaluated using three standard statistical measures: Mean Absolute Error (MAE), Mean Squared Error (MSE), and Root Mean Squared Error (RMSE). These metrics quantify the deviation between the predicted volatility values (ŷ) and the observed actual values (y) across N test samples.

1. Mean Absolute Error (MAE)

$$MAE = (1 / N) \times \Sigma |y - \hat{y}|$$

MAE measures the average magnitude of forecast errors, providing an intuitive sense of how close predictions are to actual values without exaggerating large deviations.

2. Mean Squared Error (MSE)

$$MSE = (1 / N) \times \Sigma (y - \hat{y})^2$$

MSE penalizes larger errors more severely and is useful for capturing the presence of large deviations in predicted volatility.

3. Root Mean Squared Error (RMSE)

$$RMSE = \sqrt{[(1 / N) \times \Sigma (y - \hat{y})^2]}$$

RMSE expresses the model's error in the same unit as the target variable, allowing for direct interpretability of forecasting accuracy.

Empirical Results and Comparative Analysis

The CNN-LSTM-Attention model demonstrated superior performance, on the test dataset, it achieved the following evaluation results as illustrated in Table 3:

Table 3. Performance Analysis of the CNN-LSTM-Attention Model

Forecast Horizon	MAE	MSE	RMSE
1-Day Volatility	0.0171	0.000459	0.0214
5-Day Volatility	0.0186	0.000534	0.0231

These results indicate that the model effectively captures the nonlinear and temporal dependencies inherent in GCC market volatility with high precision. The MAE values, both below 0.019, demonstrate the model's strong forecasting stability and reliability across short-term (1-day) and medium-term (5-day) horizons.

The relatively low MSE and RMSE values confirm the model's capacity to generalize effectively across unseen data while maintaining sensitivity to volatility shifts triggered by exogenous market factors such as oil price fluctuations or global index movements. The attention layer's adaptive weighting further enhances interpretability by indicating which temporal patterns most contributed to forecast accuracy, providing transparency for financial decision-makers.

Overall, the training outcomes and evaluation metrics collectively demonstrate that the CNN-LSTM-Attention model delivers a robust, interpretable, and high-performing volatility forecasting framework, well-suited to the dynamic conditions of GCC financial markets.

Benchmarking of the Results

The comparative evaluation highlights the superiority of the proposed CNN-LSTM-Attention model over traditional and machine learning benchmarks in predicting both short-term (1-day) and medium-term (5-day) volatility within the GCC financial markets. All performance metrics reported in this section are based on rigorous out-of-sample testing, where the model was trained on data from 2020-2023 and evaluated on completely unseen data from 2024-2025. This temporal split ensures that the results reflect true generalization capability to previously unencountered market conditions, validating the model's practical applicability.

Table 4 presents the detailed performance metrics (MAE, MSE, and RMSE) across all models on the test set, revealing substantial performance gaps that warrant a deeper analysis of the underlying causes.

Table 4. Model Performance Comparison (Test Set)

Model	MAE (1-Day)	MSE (1-Day)	RMSE (1-Day)	MAE (5-Day)	MSE (5-Day)	RMSE (5-Day)
Persistence	0.0529	0.010811	0.1040	0.0759	0.017722	0.1331
ARIMA	0.1028	0.033015	0.1817	0.1009	0.030344	0.1742
SVR	0.2355	0.055561	0.2357	0.2355	0.055561	0.2357
CNN-LSTM-Attention	**0.0171**	**0.000459**	**0.0214**	**0.0186**	**0.000534**	**0.0231**

It is clearly shown that the CNN-LSTM-Attention architecture demonstrates superior predictive capability, achieving an 83.4% reduction in MAE compared to ARIMA for 1-day forecasts and an 81.6% reduction for 5-day forecasts. The substantial drop in both MSE and RMSE further confirms that the proposed model not only reduces the average magnitude of errors but also effectively controls large deviations, which is critical in financial forecasting where outlier events can cause sudden market swings.

Figures 2 and 3 illustrate the comparative performance of different models in forecasting 1-day and 5-day GCC market volatility. Each figure presents the error metrics, MAE, MSE, and RMSE, for all considered models, highlighting the superior predictive accuracy of the CNN-LSTM-Attention architecture relative to traditional statistical and machine learning benchmarks

Figure 2. Comparison of 1-Day Volatility Prediction Metrics across Models (MAE, MSE, RMSE)

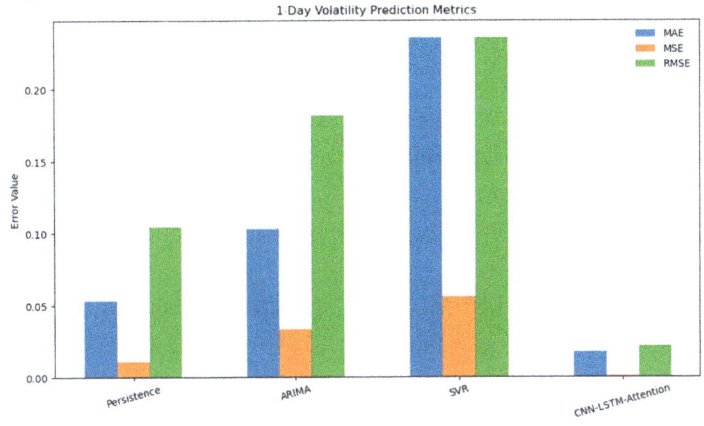

Figure 3. Comparison of 5-Day Volatility Prediction Metrics across Models (MAE, MSE, RMSE)

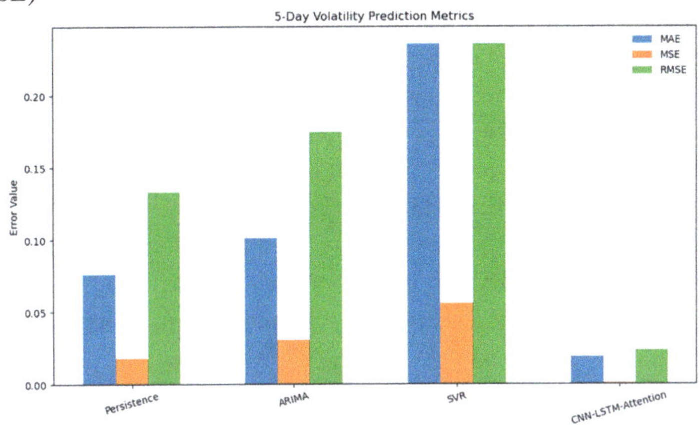

Persistence Model - Strengths and Limitations

Strengths: The persistence model performs reasonably during stable market periods, with MAE values of 0.0529 (1-day) and 0.0759 (5-day), reflecting its assumption that future volatility resembles recent volatility. Its simplicity provides a useful baseline and captures mean-reverting behavior typical of calm GCC markets.

Weaknesses: Its performance deteriorates sharply in volatile periods; MAE is 200% higher than the CNN-LSTM-Attention model, due to:

- Inability to anticipate volatility spikes from OPEC decisions, geopolitical events, or sudden oil price changes.
- Failure to adapt to regime shifts.
- Ignoring forward-looking indicators from VIX, gold, or the S&P 500.

AI Advantage: The CNN-LSTM-Attention model addresses these gaps via LSTM components capturing temporal patterns and the attention mechanism detecting transitions between stable and volatile regimes, enabling proactive forecasting.

ARIMA Model - Linear Strengths, Nonlinear Limitations

Strengths: ARIMA captures gradual, autocorrelated volatility changes (MAE: 0.1028) in normal market conditions.

Weaknesses: Its linear framework fails under non-linear GCC market dynamics:

- Threshold effects and asymmetric oil price responses.
- Regime-dependent correlations and inability to integrate exogenous factors (geopolitics, global volatility, commodity shocks).
- Sensitivity to structural breaks from OPEC policies, regional events, and global economic shifts (MSE: 0.033015, 70× higher than CNN-LSTM-Attention).

AI Advantage: CNN-LSTM-Attention overcomes these through CNN layers detecting non-linear interactions, multi-source integration (oil, indices, and volatility), structural-break robustness, and adaptive regime switching.

SVR Model - Nonlinear Potential, Practical Shortcomings

Strengths: SVR theoretically captures non-linear relationships using kernels.

Weaknesses: In practice (MAE: 0.2355, 14× worse than our model), SVR struggles with:

- Temporal dependencies and path-dependent behavior.
- Reliance on manual feature engineering.
- High computational cost without commensurate performance gains.

Interpretability and AI Superiority

The CNN-LSTM-Attention model excels in GCC volatility forecasting by:

1. Capturing oil-equity nonlinear relationships.
2. Adapting to geopolitical shocks.
3. Integrating global market spillovers.
4. Automatically adjusting to changing regimes.

Its multi-source learning, long-term memory, and attention-based interpretability provide a transparent, adaptive, and robust solution for navigating the GCC's complex volatility dynamics, addressing the fundamental limitations of traditional approaches.

Feature Importance and Attention Analysis

Understanding which factors drive market volatility is crucial for informed investment and risk management decisions, particularly in the GCC context where oil dependency, geopolitical sensitivity, and global market interconnections create complex dynamics. Feature importance and attention analysis provide decision-makers with actionable insights by highlighting the most influential variables and temporal patterns affecting regional financial stability.

CNN Feature Importance Analysis

Figure 4. CNN-Extracted Feature Importance and Temporal Dynamics in Volatility Prediction

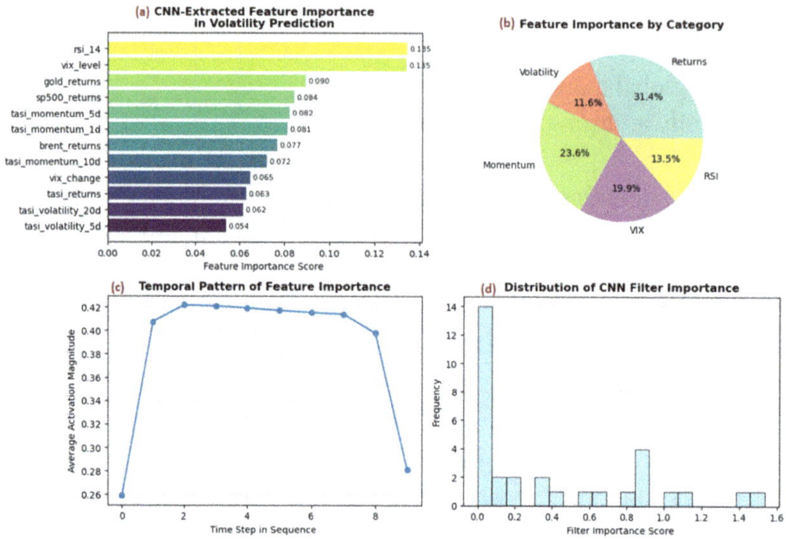

The CNN-LSTM-Attention model provides a data-driven perspective on the key drivers of volatility in GCC markets by automatically learning and weighting feature importance through its convolutional layers.

Figure 4.a shows individual feature importance scores, with RSI-14 (0.135) emerging as the most influential predictor, highlighting overbought and oversold conditions as early signals of volatility shifts. VIX (0.135) reflects global risk spill-overs into regional markets. Commodity-related variables, including gold returns (0.090) and Brent oil returns (0.077), underscore GCC economies' dependence on commodities, while S&P 500 returns (0.084) reveal interconnectedness with global equity markets. Local market behavior is captured by TASI momentum indicators across 1-day (0.072), 5-day (0.082), and 10-day (0.065) horizons, providing complementary short-, medium-, and long-term predictive signals.

Figure 4.b aggregates these features into thematic categories: returns-based features dominate with 31.4%, followed by momentum (23.6%), global risk sentiment (19.9%), technical indicators (13.5%), and historical volatility (11.6%), reflecting the multi-dimensional drivers of GCC volatility.

Temporal patterns in feature importance are shown in *Figure 4.c*, where compressed CNN time steps (0–9) reveal a rapid increase from 0.26 to 0.425 at step 2, a plateau through steps 2–6 (≈0.41-0.425), and a gradual decline to 0.28 at step

9. This non-monotonic profile indicates that the model emphasizes intermediate periods containing critical regime-dependent structures while still incorporating recent information. *Figure 4.d* examines CNN filter importance, revealing a right-skewed distribution: most filters contribute moderately, but a few dominate predictive power, reflecting filter specialization in detecting distinct volatility patterns and market regimes.

Methodologically, the CNN-LSTM-Attention model provides a systematic, automated quantification of feature importance, reducing reliance on subjective judgment. Practically, it suggests that portfolio managers monitor RSI and VIX, risk officers focus on recent 5-10 day data, and policymakers consider commodity linkages for stability monitoring. Theoretically, results confirm that GCC volatility arises from interacting technical indicators, global spillovers, and commodity dependencies. Overall, this analysis demonstrates that the model not only achieves superior predictive accuracy but also generates economically interpretable insights, bridging advanced AI techniques with financial theory.

Attention Mechanism Analysis

Figure 5. Temporal Attention Distributions Across Sample Sequences

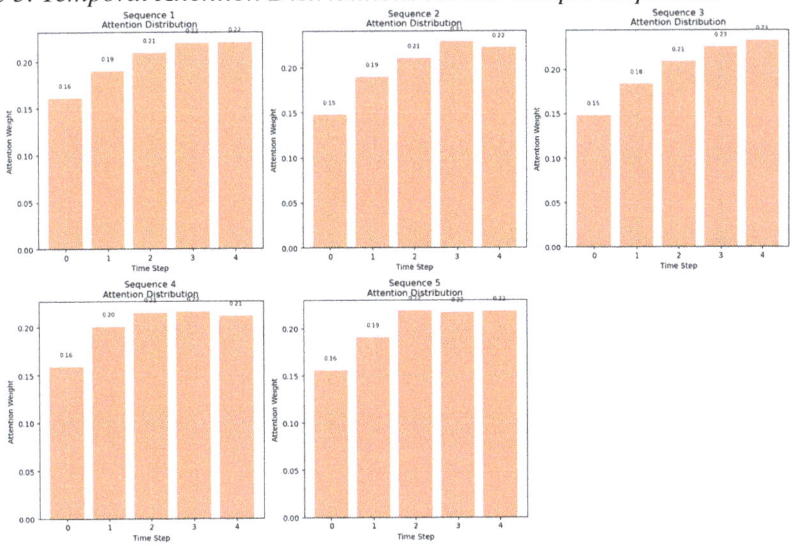

The attention mechanism analysis reveals sophisticated temporal pattern recognition capabilities in the CNN-LSTM-Attention model, demonstrating how the architecture dynamically allocates computational resources across different time steps within the input sequence. As illustrated across the five sample sequences in

Figure 5, the model exhibits varying attention distributions that adapt to different market conditions and volatility regimes.

The varying attention patterns collectively (from sequence 1 to sequence 5) demonstrate the model's adaptive intelligence in responding to different market regimes: recent-biased attention during turbulent periods prioritizes immediate developments, distributed attention in stable conditions captures multi-horizon factors, and historical-focused attention during consolidation phases identifies mean-reversion patterns or cyclical components. The attention mechanism thus provides the model with dynamic temporal flexibility, enabling it to weight historical information according to current market context rather than relying on fixed temporal dependencies, significantly enhancing its predictive capability for GCC market volatility across diverse market conditions.

Comprehensive Market Regime Analysis

To evaluate the model sensivity analysis against against extreme market Scenarions, an automated regime identification system was implemented to categorize market conditions based on rolling volatility thresholds, creating three distinct testing environments:

- **High Volatility Regime**: Periods exceeding volatility threshold of 0.5283
- **Low Volatility Regime**: Periods below volatility threshold of 0.4229
- **Normal Volatility Regime**: Intermediate volatility conditions (0.4229 - 0.5283)

The regime-specific performance analysis yielded critical insights into model behavior across market conditions as depicted in Table 5.

Table 5. Market Regime Performance Analysis

Market Regime	Volatility Threshold	1-Day MAE	Performance Change
High Volatility	> 0.5283	0.0186	-7.1%
Low Volatility	< 0.4229	0.0158	+8.6%
Normal Volatility	0.4229 - 0.5283	0.0171	(baseline)

It is clearly shown that the model exhibits regime-sensitive predictive behavior, achieving its best performance during low-volatility periods with a 1-Day MAE of 0.0158, reflecting an 8.6% improvement relative to the baseline (normal volatility in this studied case). In contrast, predictive accuracy moderately declines during high-volatility conditions (MAE = 0.0186, −7.1%), indicating sensitivity to abrupt market fluctuations. Nevertheless, the baseline MAE of 0.0171 under normal volatility conditions demonstrates stable and reliable forecasting capability across regimes. This adaptive performance pattern is particularly relevant for GCC markets, where rapid shifts between volatility regimes, driven by oil price movements and geopolitical dynamics, are frequent and consequential.

Leveraging Model-Derived Feature Importance for Evidence-Based Investment and Policy Decisions

The The CNN-LSTM-Attention model not only delivers accurate volatility forecasts but also generates actionable insights through feature importance analysis, enabling evidence-based decisions for investors, portfolio managers, and policy-makers in GCC markets. By quantifying the influence of individual indicators and broader feature categories, the model reveals key volatility drivers and informs both tactical and strategic actions.

For investment and portfolio management, top predictors include RSI (0.135), VIX (0.135), gold returns (0.090), S&P 500 returns (0.084), and TASI 5-day momentum (0.082). Aggregated categories show returns-based features dominate (31.4%), followed by momentum patterns (23.6%), global risk sentiment (19.9%), technical indicators (13.5%), and historical volatility (11.6%). Integrating individual and category importance allows multi-dimensional strategies balancing short-term responsiveness with medium-term trend anticipation.

From a policy perspective, these insights support financial stability by helping regulators anticipate stress periods, design macroprudential measures, and guide fiscal and sovereign risk planning linked to commodity returns. Temporal attention analysis further highlights critical periods, enabling prioritization of key variables and horizons. Overall, the model bridges deep learning outputs with actionable investment and policy strategies, enhancing risk management and regional financial stability.

DISCUSSION

The Methodological Innovation and Model Performance

The CNN-LSTM-Attention framework represents a major methodological advancement in volatility forecasting, integrating three complementary deep learning components to overcome the limitations of conventional models. The CNN component automatically extracts localized temporal patterns, volatility clusters, and cross-asset interactions from multivariate financial inputs, eliminating the need for manual feature engineering and capturing nonlinear relationships that linear models cannot detect. The LSTM network captures long-term dependencies, contextualizing current market conditions within historical regimes, such as prolonged oil price declines or extended recovery periods. The attention mechanism introduces context-aware weighting, emphasizing critical periods and filtering noise, effectively focusing the model on economically significant events.

Empirical results demonstrate the framework's superior performance. The LSTM component maintains long-term temporal modeling, capturing multi-quarter oil trends and geopolitical influences where ARIMA and similar models struggle. CNN layers detect complex nonlinear patterns, including volatility spillovers and asymmetric responses to shocks, particularly relevant in oil-dependent GCC markets. The attention mechanism enables dynamic regime adaptation, shifting focus from technical indicators during stable periods to external shocks during crises. Integration of a Huber loss function further enhances robustness against extreme outliers, while attention provides interpretability, addressing a common limitation of deep learning approaches.

Economic and Practical Implications

Reliable volatility forecasts are crucial in GCC economies, heavily dependent on hydrocarbon revenues. Equity market volatility serves as a leading indicator of fiscal pressures, investor sentiment, and liquidity conditions. The CNN-LSTM-Attention model achieves an 83.4% reduction in one-day forecast MAE and an 81.6% reduction in five-day MAE compared to ARIMA, providing tangible benefits for investors, policymakers, and financial institutions.

For Investors and Financial Institutions:

- Enhanced risk management and dynamic Value-at-Risk calculations.
- Optimized portfolio allocation and tactical adjustments during high-volatility periods.
- Regime-sensitive asset allocation and sector rotation, particularly in energy-concentrated portfolios.

For Policymakers and Regulators:

- Early-warning indicators for systemic risk.
- Informed fiscal and monetary interventions, including interest rate calibration and targeted liquidity injections.
- Dynamic management of sovereign wealth funds and debt issuance to mitigate exposure to volatile periods.

By quantifying both individual feature importance (e.g., RSI, VIX, gold returns, S&P 500 returns, TASI momentum) and broader categories (returns-based, momentum, global risk sentiment, technical indicators, historical volatility), the model informs evidence-based tactical and strategic decisions, enhancing financial stability in GCC markets.

Crisis Resilience, Adaptive Response, and Interpretability

A key strength of the CNN-LSTM-Attention architecture lies in its adaptive learning during crises. CNN layers detect emergent localized volatility patterns, LSTM networks contextualize these within long-term sequences, and attention dynamically prioritizes critical features. This synergistic interaction ensures reliable forecasts under extreme conditions, where traditional models often fail.

The attention mechanism simultaneously enhances predictive accuracy and interpretability, bridging complex forecasting with actionable insights. Historical periods and market indicators driving predictions are highlighted, while dominant predictors such as RSI and VIX (both 13.5%) and commodity returns are quantified. Portfolio managers can leverage attention patterns as early-warning indicators for rebalancing, and regulators gain audit trails to support macroprudential policy. The framework demonstrates robust accuracy during stress episodes (MAE: 0.0171-0.0197), reinforcing its value in crisis preparedness and decision-making.

Theoretical Contributions

The CNN-LSTM-Attention framework advances volatility modeling by unifying spatial feature extraction, temporal dependency learning, and adaptive attention within a single architecture. Unlike linear models such as ARIMA or Persistence, it captures nonlinear interactions, structural breaks, and exogenous effects characteristic of oil-dependent, geopolitically sensitive economies.

By modeling volatility as an emergent property of interconnected financial and macroeconomic signals, the framework bridges empirical prediction and theoretical understanding, transforming forecasting from a purely statistical task into a dynamic systems analysis. This approach enriches both methodological and theoretical foundations in financial econometrics, offering a robust blueprint for AI-driven volatility modeling in emerging and commodity-dependent markets.

PRACTICAL RECOMMENDATIONS AND FUTURE DIRECTIONS

The findings underscore the effectiveness of AI-driven volatility forecasting while highlighting the need for context-specific strategies to integrate such models sustainably into the GCC financial ecosystem.

Integration of AI Forecasting into Financial Decision Systems

To maximize the utility of the CNN-LSTM-Attention model, financial institutions should embed AI-driven forecasts into portfolio management, trading, and risk oversight. Automated decision-support dashboards can translate predictions into actionable indicators, while dynamic asset allocation algorithms can adjust exposures based on forecasted volatility, improving responsiveness to oil price shocks and global market spillovers. Hybrid human–AI workflows ensure that automated recommendations are validated by domain experts before execution.

Enhancing Data Infrastructure and Interoperability

The success of deep learning models relies on high-quality, granular, and consistent data. GCC regulators and exchanges should develop integrated platforms combining equity, commodity, and macroeconomic datasets. Cross-border data sharing among GCC states can enhance analytics capabilities, while real-time pipelines and quality assurance systems are essential for maintaining model accuracy, especially in volatile periods.

Model Governance and Risk Control

Institutions adopting AI tools must implement robust governance frameworks, including periodic Backtesting, stress testing, and scenario analysis. Model risk committees should oversee calibration, retraining, and bias detection, with thorough documentation of data sources, feature engineering, and decision rules to ensure auditability and regulatory compliance.

Capacity Building and Human Capital Development

Effective AI adoption requires technical, analytical, and financial expertise. GCC institutions should invest in training programs on machine learning, explainable AI (XAI), and data ethics, and foster partnerships between universities, AI labs, and financial authorities to accelerate knowledge transfer. AI literacy programs for policymakers will support evidence-based supervision of AI-driven tools.

Regulatory and Ethical Standardization

A harmonized AI governance framework is critical across GCC markets. Regional authorities should establish standards for model validation, transparency, and accountability, while ethical AI certification programs can assess fairness, interpretability, and privacy compliance. Regulatory sandboxes can provide controlled environments for testing AI forecasting systems before large-scale deployment.

Research and Technological Advancements

Future research should explore multimodal learning that integrates textual data (news, social media sentiment) with quantitative indicators, enhancing responsiveness during geopolitical crises. Transfer learning can adapt models trained on mature markets to the GCC context, while XAI and causal inference techniques improve interpretability. Energy-efficient model architectures can reduce computational costs and support sustainability goals.

Strategic Vision for GCC Market Transformation

Institutionalizing AI in financial risk management and market surveillance can enhance resilience, transparency, and investor confidence. Coordinated action among regulators, financial institutions, and technology developers is critical to translating predictive capabilities into long-term financial stability and innovation-led growth.

Research Limitations

Despite its predictive gains, the CNN-LSTM-Attention framework has limitations. Model performance depends on the quality and scope of input data; additional sources such as high-frequency data, alternative financial indicators, or social media sentiment could further improve robustness. Sensitivity to hyperparameters and architecture variations has not been exhaustively evaluated, and Backtesting across diverse historical volatility regimes would provide more insight into practical applicability. Cross-market and transfer learning applications remain underexplored, and extending the framework could help determine generalizability across different markets.

Future-Oriented Research Insights

Future studies could integrate alternative and unstructured data sources to enhance responsiveness to real-time market signals. Transfer-learning approaches can adapt models from developed markets to the GCC, leveraging structural similarities while capturing regional specifics. Multi-modal learning frameworks combining textual, numerical, and technical data, alongside explainable AI techniques, can further improve forecast robustness and interpretability, supporting informed decision-making for investors, regulators, and policymakers.

CONCLUSION

This chapter introduced and validated a robust CNN-LSTM-Attention hybrid framework designed for volatility forecasting in GCC financial markets, demonstrating substantial improvements over traditional statistical models. Empirical results show that the proposed architecture achieves remarkable accuracy, reducing MAE by 83.4% for 1-day and 81.6% for 5-day forecasts compared to ARIMA, with similar gains over Persistence and SVR benchmarks. These findings highlight the model's transformative potential for financial decision-making in oil-dependent economies.

The core innovation lies in integrating three complementary deep learning components: CNNs for extracting localized temporal patterns and feature interactions, LSTMs for capturing long-range dependencies and sequential market dynamics, and attention mechanisms for interpretable, dynamically weighted temporal focus. This design addresses the unique challenges of GCC markets, including sensitivity to oil prices, exposure to external shocks, and complex non-linear volatility patterns that conventional models fail to capture.

Beyond technical achievements, the study contributes to both theory and practice. Theoretically, it demonstrates how hybrid deep learning architectures can model intricate volatility dynamics in commodity-dependent emerging markets. Practically, it offers financial institutions, regulators, and investors a transparent tool to enhance risk management, portfolio optimization, and policy formulation, maintaining robust performance during high-volatility periods.

The attention mechanism enhances interpretability, allowing stakeholders to understand not only what the model predicts but also why. By identifying the historical periods and indicators most influencing forecasts, the framework provides actionable insights that support informed investment decisions and regulatory compliance. Successful application in GCC markets suggests potential for similar commodity-exporting economies and emerging markets, offering a blueprint for region-specific AI solutions that navigate the interplay between global commodity cycles, geopolitical developments, and domestic market dynamics.

Future research could extend the framework by incorporating real-time sentiment analysis, alternative data sources such as satellite imagery, cross-market volatility spillover modeling, or federated learning for collaborative, privacy-preserving model training. As AI reshapes global finance, the CNN-LSTM-Attention framework represents a strategic step toward intelligent, interpretable, and adaptive financial systems. Its success in the GCC emphasizes the value of specialized AI solutions that reflect regional economic structures, advancing financial machine learning while enhancing risk management and supporting market development and economic diversification in similar contexts worldwide.

REFERENCES

Al-Najjar, D. (2022). Impact of the twin pandemics: COVID-19 and oil crash on Saudi exchange index. *PLoS One*, *17*(5), e0268733. DOI: 10.1371/journal.pone.0268733 PMID: 35594304

Al-Roubaie, A. S. (2025). Impact of emerging technologies on economic diversification: the case of Saudi Arabia. Journal of Business and Socio-economic Development, 1-15. DOI: 10.1108/JBSED-12-2024-0130

Alharbi, F. R. (2023). Gulf Cooperation Council Countries' Electricity Sector Forecasting: Consumption Growth Issue and Renewable Energy Penetration Progress Challenges (Doctoral dissertation, Lancaster University (United Kingdom)).

Aljughaiman, A. A., Tabash, M. I., Issa, S. S., & Almulhim, A. A. (2025). Shock transmission from global financial stress, bitcoin sentiment indices, US and euro financial market uncertainty toward the GCC stock volatility. *Cogent Business & Management*, *12*(1), 2514811. DOI: 10.1080/23311975.2025.2514811

Alqahtani, A., Klein, T., & Khalid, A. (2019). The impact of oil price uncertainty on GCC stock markets. *Resources Policy*, *64*, 101526. DOI: 10.1016/j.resourpol.2019.101526

Ampountolas, A. (2023). Comparative analysis of machine learning, hybrid, and deep learning forecasting models: Evidence from European financial markets and bitcoins. *Forecasting*, *5*(2), 472–486. DOI: 10.3390/forecast5020026

Ampountolas, A. (2024). Enhancing forecasting accuracy in commodity and financial markets: Insights from garch and svr models. *International Journal of Financial Studies*, *12*(3), 59. DOI: 10.3390/ijfs12030059

Arouri, J., Lahiani, R., & Nguyen, A. (2011). Oil price shocks and stock markets in the U.S. and 13 European countries. *Energy Economics*, *30*(5), 2587–2608.

Aslam, F., Ferreira, P., Ali, H., & José, A. E. (2022). Application of multifractal analysis in estimating the reaction of energy markets to geopolitical acts and threats. *Sustainability (Basel)*, *14*(10), 5828. DOI: 10.3390/su14105828

Behera, I., Nanda, P., Mitra, S., & Kumari, S. (2024). *Machine Learning Approaches for Forecasting Financial Market Volatility. Machine Learning Approaches in Financial Analytics*. Springer. DOI: 10.1007/978-3-031-61037-0_20

Bollerslev, T. (1986). Generalized autoregressive conditional heteroskedasticity. *Journal of Econometrics*, *31*(3), 307–327. DOI: 10.1016/0304-4076(86)90063-1

Borio, C. (2024). *Macro-financial challenges in the post-COVID world.* Monetary Policy Responses to the Post-Pandemic Inflation.

Boubaker, H., Saidane, B., & Ben Saad Zorgati, M. (2022). Modelling the dynamics of stock market in the gulf cooperation council countries: Evidence on persistence to shocks. *Financial Innovation*, *8*(1), 46. DOI: 10.1186/s40854-022-00348-3

Boudri, I., & El Bouhadi, A. (2024). Modeling and Forecasting Historical Volatility Using Econometric and Deep Learning Approaches: Evidence from the Moroccan and Bahraini Stock Markets. *Journal of Risk and Financial Management*, *17*(7), 300. DOI: 10.3390/jrfm17070300

Boukhatem, J., & Alhazmi, A. M. (2024). COVID-19 pandemic, oil prices and Saudi stock market: Empirical evidence from ARDL modeling and Bayer–Hanck cointegration approach. *Future Business Journal*, *10*(1), 58. DOI: 10.1186/s43093-024-00338-0

Chen, S., & Zhang, Z. (2019). Forecasting implied volatility smile surface via deep learning and attention mechanism. arXiv preprint arXiv:1912.11059

Dehimi, N. E. H., & Tolba, Z. (2024, April). Attention mechanisms in deep learning: Towards explainable artificial intelligence. In 2024 6th International Conference on Pattern Analysis and Intelligent Systems (PAIS) (pp. 1-7). IEEE. DOI: 10.1109/PAIS62114.2024.10541203

Engle, R. F. (1982). Autoregressive conditional heteroscedasticity with estimates of the variance of United Kingdom inflation. *Econometrica*, *50*(4), 987–1007. DOI: 10.2307/1912773

Fama, E. F. (1970). Efficient capital markets: A review of theory and empirical work. *The Journal of Finance*, *25*(2), 383–417. DOI: 10.2307/2325486

Fasanya, I. O., Oyewole, O. J., Adekoya, O. B., & Badaru, F. O. (2021). Oil price and stock market behaviour in GCC countries: Do asymmetries and structural breaks matter? *Energy Strategy Reviews*, *36*, 100682. DOI: 10.1016/j.esr.2021.100682

Fischer, T., & Krauss, C. (2018). Deep learning with long short-term memory networks for financial market predictions. *European Journal of Operational Research*, *270*(2), 654–669. DOI: 10.1016/j.ejor.2017.11.054

Ghysels, E., Santa-Clara, P., & Valkanov, R. (2006). Predicting volatility: Getting the most out of return data sampled at different frequencies. *Journal of Econometrics*, *131*(1-2), 59–95. DOI: 10.1016/j.jeconom.2005.01.004

Hochreiter, S., & Schmidhuber, J. (1997). Long short-term memory. *Neural Computation*, *9*(8), 1735–1780. DOI: 10.1162/neco.1997.9.8.1735 PMID: 9377276

Hussain, M., & Rehman, R. U. (2023). Volatility connectedness of GCC stock markets: How global oil price volatility drives volatility spillover in GCC stock markets? *Environmental Science and Pollution Research International*, *30*(6), 14212–14222. DOI: 10.1007/s11356-022-23114-5 PMID: 36138292

Islam, M. S., Ahmed, F., Islam, M. M., Rehman, A. U., & Alam, M. F. (2025). The impact of oil price shocks on oil and gas production amidst geopolitical risk in OPEC: Insights from method of moments quantile regression. *Journal of the Knowledge Economy*, *16*(2), 9776–9805. DOI: 10.1007/s13132-024-02296-y

Jlifi, B., Medini, M., & Duvallet, C. (2024). A guided genetic algorithm-based ensemble voting of polynomial regression and LSTM (GGA-PolReg-LSTM) for congestion prediction using IoT and air quality data in sustainable cities. *The Journal of Supercomputing*, *80*(13), 18797–18837. DOI: 10.1007/s11227-024-06186-7

Joshi, S., Mahanthi, B. L., Pokkuluri, K. S., Ninawe, S. S., & Sahu, R. (2025). Integrating LSTM and CNN for Stock Market Prediction: A Dynamic Machine Learning Approach. *Journal of Artificial Intelligence and Technology*, *5*, 168–179. DOI: 10.37965/jait.2025.0652

Li, Y., Chen, L., Dong, W., Gong, S., Kang, Z., Wei, B., . . . Wang, N. (2025). Information bottleneck-guided heterogeneous graph learning for interpretable neurodevelopmental disorder diagnosis. arXiv preprint arXiv:2502.20769.

Litsas, S. N. (2023). Internal and External Challenges for the Years to Come. In Smart Instead of Small in International Relations Theory: The Case of the United Arab Emirates (pp. 145-192). Cham: Springer Nature Switzerland. DOI: 10.1007/978-3-031-44637-5_7

Olubusola, O., Mhlongo, N. Z., Daraojimba, D. O., Ajayi-Nifise, A. O., & Falaiye, T. (2024). Machine learning in financial forecasting: A US review: Exploring the advancements, challenges, and implications of AI-driven predictions in financial markets. *World Journal of Advanced Research and Reviews*, *21*(2), 1969–1984. DOI: 10.30574/wjarr.2024.21.2.0444

Qiu, J., Wang, B., & Zhou, C. (2020). Forecasting stock prices with long-short term memory neural network based on attention mechanism. *PLoS One*, *15*(1), e0227222. DOI: 10.1371/journal.pone.0227222 PMID: 31899770

Rubio, L., Palacio Pinedo, A., Mejía Castaño, A., & Ramos, F. (2023). Forecasting volatility by using wavelet transform, ARIMA and GARCH models. *Eurasian Economic Review, 13*(3), 803–830. DOI: 10.1007/s40822-023-00243-x

Sims, C. A. (2003). Implications of rational inattention. *Journal of Monetary Economics, 50*(3), 665–690. DOI: 10.1016/S0304-3932(03)00029-1

World Bank. (2023). *Global economic prospects: Enduring challenges.* World Bank Publications.

Zeng, Z., Kaur, R., Siddagangappa, S., Rahimi, S., Balch, T., & Veloso, M. (2023). Financial time series forecasting using cnn and transformer. arXiv preprint arXiv:2304.04912

Zouaghia, Z., Aouina, Z. K., & Said, L. B. (2023, October). Hybrid machine learning model for predicting NASDAQ composite index. In *2023 International Symposium on Networks, Computers and Communications (ISNCC)* (pp. 1-6). IEEE. DOI: 10.1109/ISNCC58260.2023.10323903

Zouaghia, Z., Kodia, Z., & Ben Said, L. (2024a). A novel AutoCNN model for stock market index prediction. *Journal of Telecommunications and the Digital Economy, 12*(1), 612–636. DOI: 10.18080/jtde.v12n1.843

Zouaghia, Z., Kodia, Z., & Ben Said, L. (2024b). Predicting the stock market prices using a machine learning-based framework during crisis periods. *Multimedia Tools and Applications, 84*(24), 28873–28907. DOI: 10.1007/s11042-024-20270-3

Zouaghia, Z., Kodia, Z., & Ben Said, L. (2025a). A novel approach for dynamic portfolio management integrating K-means clustering, mean-variance optimization, and reinforcement learning: Z. Zouaghia et al. Knowledge and Information Systems, 1-73. DOI: 10.1007/s10115-025-02475-6

Zouaghia, Z., Kodia, Z., & Ben Said, L. (2025b). Smapf-hnna: A novel Stock Market Analysis and Prediction Framework using Hybrid Neural Network Architectures Across Major US Indices. *International Journal of Data Science and Analytics, 20*(6), 5775–5811. DOI: 10.1007/s41060-025-00811-1

Chapter 8

Harnessing AI for Citizen Financial Literacy to Strengthen Oman's Stock Market

Zeeshan Asim
http://orcid.org/0000-0002-2156-5006
University of Buraimi, Oman

ABSTRACT

Oman's path to growth may rely on turning data into cash and providing awareness related to financial literacy people about money. Globally, stock exchanges get about 40% of earnings from data, while the Arab world only sees 6%, so Oman sits in a tricky spot. Lack of know-how in commercializing data and shifting rules appears to slow things down. Yet advanced analytics, smart partners and emergence of AI (Artificial intelligence) could boost investment, even double it. At the same time, citizens need better financial literacy; without its savings stay idle instead of becoming investments. This study highlights the potential barriers that lead to higher market participation. Therefore, blending stronger AI perspective with inclusive individual investor financial literacy might firm up Omani stock market. It could also diversify the economy and put the country on a regional leadership track. The challenge is real, but the opportunity feels within reach.

1. INTRODUCTION

Both developed and developing countries are swept up in the centrifugal force of the financial markets, but that does not mean they are all equally endowed or

DOI: 10.4018/979-8-2600-1603-9.ch008

equally fortunate when it comes to these market structures (Özveren, 2025). The established financial market structures of the developed capitalist countries do a much better job of channelling necessary investment funds to the sectors of the economy where they are most needed than do the relatively shallow, unstable, and predatory financial market structures of many of the so-called developing countries (Qadeer & Sarfraz, 2025). For that reason, and because of the otherwise abysmal investment climate, the citizens of countries with underdeveloped financial markets have many more reasons to be unhappy than the citizens of countries with developed financial markets. For sure, the developments within the financial market have induced a partial shift of emphasis (Qadeer & Sarfraz, 2025). There is no doubt that things have improved a good deal in the personal finance domain over the last half-century for the citizens of both developed and developing countries (Nogueira et al., 2025a). But still, in an overall area assessment, the level of personal finance knowledge among the citizens of many countries with otherwise relatively good financial market structures falls well short of what it should be. However, as to Lusardi (2019) points out, even if programs like Money Smart reach the people who most need financial literacy and teach them the necessary skills, those individuals still must labor under the oppressive conditions that make their financial lives so fragile. To effectively address financial inequality, we must also address the underlying problems that keep people in financial trouble.

A substantial body of research has shown that individuals with higher financial literacy achieve superior economic outcomes, particularly in their understanding of the capital market real time decision making (Ansari et al., 2023; Antwi et al., 2024; Reddy et al., 2024).

Understanding personal finance is likely to help people comprehend the market's volatility. The 'finance' in personal finance means so much more than just money. Covering the daily necessary habits of life-spending, and budgeting, yields the bigger moves like saving and investing. Covering these kinds of 'know-hows' leads to 'better money decisions' (Nogueira et al., 2025b).

I believe 'better money decisions' yield 'better money outcomes'. If they do, we could unpack outcomes related to individuals spotting scams and committing fewer financial frauds. However, we have no idea whether 'better outcomes' in relation to spotting scams or committing fewer financial frauds hold up. And we have even less idea about why they might hold up(Koskelainen et al., 2023).

Across many countries, AI-based money knowledge appears to raise savings, improve debt handling, and guide smarter investing; therefore, people's finance habits seem healthier overall (Katnic et al., 2024; Tyrell Curry, 2025). Various habits may maybe foster personal and social economic stability therefore boosting general resilience (Liu et al., 2025). It seems that a person's level of money knowledge influences how they decide on money matters. When that knowledge is low, people appear less willing to buy stocks. So, they're ending up joining the market less often generally (Parsai & Chandok, 2025). Although many families are careful with their spending, they are sometimes caught off guard by unexpected demands for cash that seem to come out of nowhere (Parsai & Chandok, 2025; Wang, 2025). These were the typical encounters with money that many Middle Eastern families used to have, partly because they relied on financial strategies that kept them far below any formal economy (Lyons & Kass-Hanna, 2018). However, during the past two years, when even the most straightforward jobs seemed to disappear, the Middle East's cash economy may have started its own "softer slump" (Glenda, 2024)

2. BACKGROUND

In Oman maybe, learning about budgeting and saving boost the market, therefore it seems a simple money-skill can raise the stock scene. The country runs on oil and tourism; therefore, maybe simple education could steer investors toward wiser choice. According Mirzaei & Buer (2022) Markets opened, rules switched, and social security got tighter now—so it feels tighter all around. Moreover, people now need watch their own money more. Save harder, plan smarter . (Michailidis et al., 2025; S. Razavi, 2022). Even though many scholars point out that money-savvy skills matter for stock market entry, Oman's participation stays barely a whisper (Lakoni et al., 2023). Therefore, the work shows up 2023. Only 10.5 out of 21 for Omanis on the financial literacy test, so they're below the OECD average. Their attitude and behavior scores? They pretty much match the OECD average (Mirzaei & Buer, 2022). AI tools can't fix the fact that Oman and other Gulf nations still missing basic finance skill (Menberu, 2024). There's a gap everywhere, therefore big roadblocks show up whenever we try to snag every benefit that financial inclusion could bring (Janzen, 2021) . Oman's stock market participation stays low; basically, they don't have solid intel. Access keeps growing, users engage more; therefore, the amount of info and clear data just skyrockets big (Janzen, 2021). Therefore, this wave has got investors everywhere pouring massive cash into trying to cash in on that data's value. Leading stock exchanges worldwide have opened new ways to bring in cash; therefore, some of them earn roughly forty percent of their total revenue just from data services (Janzen, 2021).

This enormous revenue opportunity remains largely unrealized in the Arab world, where stock exchanges and financial services earn only an average of 6 percent of their income from clearly understandable information and digital services—compared to more developed markets (Janzen, 2021). Oman's stock market is small, reaching only $22 billion at the end of 2022 (which is 19.4 percent of GDP), and it has lagged regional and emerging market peers for much of the time (Kroen, 2024). Oman has a market capitalization that is only 20 percent of what neighbours like Saudi Arabia have (Alharbi, 2024; Hakimi et al., 2025; Somaia Salem, 2025). Conversely, the higher that financial literacy is in Oman, the more that economic growth can be retained—not just this year but in the future (Mirzaei & Buer, 2022).

3. GLOBAL TREND SHAPING STOCK MARKET DYNAMICS

The customized digital platforms that investors use to access comprehensive data are no longer provided only by the big brokerage firms (Janzen, 2021; Koskelainen et al., 2023). Investors now find such platforms available from a wider array of providers—from investment advisors such as lead to completely independent firms (Qayoom & Chisti, 2025; Supawat & Arnat, 2023). Consequently, the exchanges are no longer just dealing with their traditional stockbrokers (Colgate & Lang, 2001).

The investors themselves have evolved from being passive to being more engaged and active—a change with dividends in terms of likelihood to tip (Klitkou et al., 2022). If the stock exchanges were to shrink in terms of the amount of information they provide, there would be no more play for the different kinds of equity instruments. Consumers are showing an ever-growing interest in being able to see and imitate the trades of important figures in the investment world (Johri et al., 2023). This practice, often called social trading, seems to be gaining ground. It is even more interesting to think about what might be driving it. To what extent and why are people moving toward seeing and imitating not only the trades of their friends but also those of famous investors? (Dorf Leitner & Streckenbach, 2022).

Forecasting future shifts in stock prices on a global scale is an undertaking that many have tried but few have succeeded in mastering (Saberironaghi et al., 2025). This is no doubt because the task is seen as the most arduously difficult Golden Goose of the financial realm, given the non-linear price movement and high volatility of the financial market data that make up the collective wisdom of the market (Saberironaghi et al., 2025). Yet, for the public's sake, for the welfare of ordinary lives, the issue of informing the naive investor from the pernicious wolf of Wall Street must be addressed at all costs (Agarwal et al., 2025). And yes, these pernicious wolves, who profit off lost naive investors, do employ exactly the kinds of tools we've been discussing—digital platforms and advanced AI algorithms such as *Transformers & LLM, GNN, causal ML & uplifting modelling* (Onyenahazi & Antwi, 2024; Pazouki et al., 2025).

Today's global investment scene is very much affected by the digital world. And, in an increasingly interconnected and digital global marketplace, the need for digital literacy has emerged as one of the foremost prerequisites for the acceptance of the types of technologies that are now transforming our lives (Subedi & Bhandari,

2024). If investors are to make intelligent decisions about which stocks to buy, they absolutely must understand these technologies (Subedi & Bhandari, 2024). And we're not just talking about the domestic stock markets; investors also need this knowledge when making decisions in international markets. Knowledge is essential because our era offers no guarantees (Islam et al., 2024; Shahzad et al., 2024). What AI stocks might represent as a prospect today could be seen in hindsight as yet another technological bust 10 or 20 years from now—or much sooner, given the current accelerated pace of technological development. If nothing else, the promise of AI ought to make investors pay more attention to the types of technologies in which they're choosing to invest and the underlying business models that are supposed to drive those technologies.

4. ADOPTION OF AI TECHNOLOGIES AND ITS IMPACT ON INDIVIDUAL AND INSTITUTIONAL INVESTMENT BEHAVIOR

Investors worldwide feel a huge change in how they choose and act. Therefore, decisions look different, all because AI now shows up. What does that mean? Researchers now realize that this massive force has already begun to crush the entire investment arena in a juggernaut-like way (Machucho & Ortiz, 2025; Pattnaik et al., 2024). From strategies to analysis to performance, all seen worldwide, AI seems to shift everything; therefore, even the finance world, where we just count numbers in our heads fast, well, expertly, gets altered, doesn't it? New AI inventions give the finance sector a huge lift; not just because we keep grabbing and analysing mountains of data. Because it's basically built as a business tool at its core, therefore the reason feels clearer (Chua et al., 2023). Is AI simply a brain boost for our company; it pushes the business smarter and oddly nudges us to put money in better spots (Chua et al., 2023). that's when it happened. Now, with smart computer tools we've plowed through massive oceans of data, catching winning investment ideas fast—so fast a human brain can barely keep up (Onyenahazi & Antwi, 2024). Link from AI to money plan is a straight path of simple code tools that push bigger abilities; that's called quantitative analysis. Clever quant-handling systems, also service algorithms, can easily outdo any human financial advisor. Therefore, Hossain & Siddiqua (2024) point out a surprising trend many missed; and it really sticks with me. Research finds that for portfolio diversification more isn't always better, therefore maybe fewer choices work. Shafiee et al (2023) note investors who see the value of a mixed portfolio often build one that outperforms typical risk-return; therefore, it ends up a better fit. Investors with low financial literacy, so they don't have the skill to put together a portfolio that balances risk and return. Cupák et al (2022) note that people with low financial know-how often keep their holdings cramped; that means more risk you can't dodge.

5. INVESTMENT BEHAVIOR: A ROLE OF AI ACROSS ARAB STOCK EXCHANGES

The Arab world is an incredibly diverse region, with capital markets that reflect the unique economic and regulatory conditions of each market (Ochi et al., 2025). The countries of the Arab world comprise a vast spectrum of economic development—from very poor to relatively rich—that affects both the quantity and the sort of financial instruments available to investors (Bourveau et al., 2025). The domestically and internationally oriented investors who participate in the region's capital markets run the gamut from high-net-worth individuals and family offices to large institutional investors (Hammad Naeem et al., 2023). With investor types and risk appetites that span the spectrum, the Arab capital markets are far from monolithic, both in terms of the regulatory structure of individual markets and the sort of financial products (and the presentations thereof) that these markets offer.

Those were decades during which the region enjoyed a remarkable wave of privatization (Akang, 2024). They were decades during which the establishment of sovereign wealth funds added a fresh layer of depth—if not sophistication—to our conversation about the Arab region's "vibrant" capital markets (Alhajri & Alshebli, 2023).

Executives overseeing Arab stock markets view them as being in a rudimentary, early stage but projecting strong growth (Adel, 2024). The regional exchanges are hardly comparable in quality to the mature global stock exchanges (H. Razavi & Habibnia, 2024). Some progress has been made in recent years, as the Arab stock markets have become better integrated in terms of structure and operation with the global financial system (H. Razavi & Habibnia, 2024). However, the lack of liquidity is a defining problem for many of the regional exchanges, which seems largely a function of low investor confidence (Alshareef, 2025). Despite these drawbacks, significant opportunities for investment are available on the Arab stock markets (Alshareef, 2025). Investment technology is transforming the Arab stock markets despite their many deficiencies. The two prime ingredients are artificial intelligence and digital transformation. Both these phenomena are being put to use in the major Arab stock markets. An initiative in artificial intelligence aimed at financial technology was established by the government of Bahrain (Abdulla et al., 2020).

6. ADOPTION OF AI TO STRENGTHEN OMAN'S STOCK MARKET

Oman offers a valuable context for studying individual financial literacy even emergence of AI. As a frontier economy, the Sultanate of Oman is actively modernizing its economic structure through strategic reforms (Mirzaei & Buer, 2022; Uddin, 2020). Since 2020, under new leadership and in response to the 2021 oil-price shock, Oman has accelerated the modernization of its state institutions and the diversification of its economy (Due-Gundersen & Owtram, 2022). The introduction of new institutions, including digital mechanism for taxation measures, AI enables stock market and social insurance schemes is both necessary and forthcoming (Torm & Oehme, 2024). If financial reforms in Oman are not aligned with the population's level of financial literacy, they may prove ineffective or ultimately fail (Khan et al., 2024; Mirzaei & Buer, 2022). Although financial literacy has been widely researched in developed countries and major emerging economies, empirical evidence on the financial literacy levels of Omanis and populations in neighbouring Gulf Cooperation Council (GCC) countries remains limited (Song et al., 2025). The data's applicability to Oman is questionable because of the insufficient reflection of the nation's unique socioeconomic and cultural makeup in the relevant literature (Lusardi, 2019). While we have some data on financial literacy from the new industrialized countries, comprehensive and reliable data that would allow us to understand the frontier markets like Oman and other countries in the Middle East are simply not available (Rehman & Mia, 2024). In this vacuum of data, we aren't able to ascertain with any certainty the levels of financial literacy among the Omani population.

Nonetheless, we understand that financial literacy is a key factor in individuals' abilities to handle their finances capably (Rehman & Mia, 2024). Achieving long-term, financially secure outcomes is heavily reliant on knowing how to invest and how not to invest. The big unknown for me, and a possible potential breakthrough for Oman's people, is: How well do adults in Oman grasp these critical life matters? This question is the mother's milk of my research (Rehman & Mia, 2024). It allows me to understand something vital about Omanis' behavior in the way they use emerging technologies (like AI) in their financial decision-making processes (Alshubiri & Hammami, 2025). The comprehension gained from this research is then, of course, fed back into the way I understand the basic tenets of wise investing—tenant one being there's a lot that isn't known about the adults in Oman themselves (Rehman & Mia, 2024).

As part of its broader transformative agenda, Oman aims to accelerate digitalization, leverage AI across the financial sector especially enabling financial literacy among Omani citizen, and enhance domestic capacities in innovation and creativity (Mirzaei & Buer, 2022). However, the effectiveness of financial literacy interventions may vary across economies due to differences in financial systems and institutional contexts. Furthermore, variations in financial literacy levels across developing and emerging economies may be influenced by cultural differences (Mirzaei & Buer, 2022). Furthermore, disparities in financial literacy across economies may be shaped by cultural factors, the degree of financial inclusion, and individual attitudes and behaviors.

In general, Financial literacy levels vary significantly according to individuals' education, age, income, and gender (Mulia Pratama, 2021). A few other factors potentially influence the individuals' financial literacy. For example, financial education programmes show a positive effect on financial behavior (Lusardi & Mitchell, 2009; Mireku et al., 2023). Currently, no comprehensive model support AI to which financial literacy, combined with other behavioural characteristics, enhances an individual's likelihood of strengthen stock market development in country specific setting. This study aims to develop a model examining the holistic role of artificial intelligence in enhancing financial literacy and shaping behavioral tendencies to strengthen stock market development within a country-specific context.

6.1 Financial Literacy

Studying financial literacy shows us that the changing economic world requires an in-depth grasp of basic financial concepts.(Darwish, 2025). The principles serve as a cornerstone for making timely and effective financial decisions in an economy that is rapidly evolving under the influence of artificial intelligence.(Lakshmi, 2024).

These necessities make it very clear to a person what they should do to enjoy the life of their dreams with no major financial problems (Lakshmi, 2024). Many individuals attempt to manage their personal finances without the basic education and access to tools that would enable them to do so effectively (Lang et al., 2024). As a consequence, they are left with the most rudimentary financial tools that make even the most basic kind of personal finance all but impossible (Czech et al., 2024). The first problem that these folks have when it comes to personal finance is that they save way too little, if anything at all. The second problem is that their budgeting and cash flow management is virtually nonexistent or just plain awful (Hilbert et al., 2022). When these individuals manage to do the basic kinds of things that are absolutely essential to rendering a personal and household finance situation at least somewhat manageable, they avoid thinking seriously about investing (Czech et al., 2024). Our behavior is shaped by economic cycles, technological change, and the generational differences that always influence our actions. And low financial literacy makes us more likely to fall for financial scams and frauds (Wei et al., 2021)..

In summary, financial literacy enhances not only the ability of individuals to invest but also their capacity to protect themselves from would-be con artists. Both the good decisions and the bad decisions that individuals make about money are heavily influenced by fintech (Du & Chen, 2023). Because fintech companies are spreading across thc financial decision-making landscape like little Gremlins, a consortium of scholars and practitioners have gotten together to understand just what this all adds up to, particularly from the perspective of financial socialization (Mallikarjuna Paramesha et al., 2024). That is, how are all these emerging technologies helping individuals make better financial decisions? And how are they potentially endangering us without our knowledge (Mallikarjuna Paramesha et al., 2024)

It is common knowledge that machine learning is the most potent artificial intelligence technique. In contrast to traditional analytical methods, it informs decision-making with a clearer analysis of available data and recognition of the patterns hidden within that data.(Mohamed, 2025). AI's influence in finance is slowly but surely becoming a reality, and it has the potential to touch nearly every aspect of a financial institution's operations—from front-office decision-making (risk management, credit assessment, and investment strategies) to customer service (chatbots) and back-office operations (compliance, data processing, and anomaly detection) particularly for individuals with limited financial literacy shaping behavioral tendencies to strengthen stock market (Haosen Xu et al., 2024; Sarioguz & Miser, 2024). This study identifies the potential technological factors that drive financial literacy (Rehman & Mia, 2024).

Innovation in the global financial sector increasingly derives from the application of artificial intelligence (AI) (Del Sarto & Ozili, 2025). This technology has become an essential engine for engine driving the development of digital financial solutions (Naeem et al., 2025). AI may, in fact, confer an almost equalizing power across the population, since it seems to offer "something even more fundamental: equal access to financial services" (Naeem et al., 2025).

A substantial body of research those includes Rehman & Mia (2024), Yu & Xiao (2025), Yang (2023), (Mahaney, 2024) Mahaney (2024), Lakshmi (2024), Imjai et al (2025) highlighted, the significance of integrating technological elements such as AI into financial literacy. Artificial intelligence's part in digital financial literacy deals with the procurement of understanding, knowledge, skill, and competence on the part of users—customer, client, and consumer—of digitally delivered financial products and services (Choung et al., 2023).

Hesami (2025), Chhillar et al (2025), Akanfe et al (2025), Al-Afeef & Alsmadi (2025) Suggested that digital financial literacy with AI entails educating individuals in the use of digital financial tools and applications to improve their comprehension of financial concepts and decision-making (Ahmad et al., 2025; M. R. Hossain et al., 2024). This involves utilizing digital tools and platforms that drives AI based Financial Literacy—such as AI Chatbots & Coaches, Generative AI (LLMs), AI Gamification, Financial Health Scoring (Bernatska et al., 2025; Lakshmi, 2024).

6.2 Financial Behavior

Money-related actions of individuals form the basis for financial behavior. It investigates the ways in which individuals are influenced by factors of psychology, even those decisions they make that might be better off if they were made by someone or something else in a seemingly optimal way (Almansour et al., 2023). Financial receptivity is the name given to the condition where individuals' living expenses are in a relationship with their income levels (Rahman et al., 2021).

Bringing artificial intelligence into financial behavior research has propelled us into a new realm of offers and transformative progress. useful tools and strategies to help us make better decisions and assess risk more accurately.(Gupta & Sajjan, 2025; Masood, 2024). In this context this study identifying the potential technological factors that help individual shaping behavioral tendencies to strengthen stock market. A substantial body of research those includes Goswami et al.(2024), Gupta & Sajjan (2025), Vyas(2025), (Najem et al., 2025) Suggested that AI can shaping Financial behavioral tendencies entails educating individuals to get proactive approach to invest in stock market. Aditya & Azmansyah (2021) four significant factors that are essential for financial behavior for individuals: budgeting, Money saving and shopping pattern, saving & investments and insurance and Payment of obligations

Advanced artificial intelligence systems, including LLMs and anomaly detection algorithms, vigorously estimates financial behaviors, forecast fiscal trends, and create tailored recommendations to promote responsible financial management (Bayakhmetova et al., 2025; Devan et al., 2023; Hesami, 2025). According to Jain & Kulkarni (2023) the use of artificial intelligence in budgeting can significantly improve resource allocation processes by enhancing efficiency, accuracy, and strategic decision-making (Marotta & Au, 2022).

For some time, the only use for personal finance apps seemed to be as tools for monitoring, recording, and just barely keeping oneself within the boundaries of a budget (Marzuki, 2024). These rudimentary applications lacked any semblance of true intelligence or personalization, offering no analysis beyond being able to tell us how much money we had or hadn't made (and they couldn't even do that very well) (Kobi, 2024). In terms of user experience, we were expected to interact with them in a sort of "garbage in, garbage out" way; if we put in just the right amount of our information and kept it tidy, maybe they would give us back something (beyond their standard reports) that we could understand as either an intelligent recommendation or some sort of useful nudge toward the path of financial righteousness (Hesami, 2025).

In the same way, prior to delving into the precise function that artificial intelligence serves in consumer saving and spending, it's necessary to comprehend the various cultural dimensions that mold the impact of decisions about money across the globe (Karami Nasrabad Sofla, 2024). This is an influence that's felt in all societies and must be acknowledged if AI's effects on saving and spending behaviors are to be rationally interpreted (Nayeem, 2012).

Culturally conditioned is the widespread sense of the worth of money, commodities, and goods. When we consider what makes a possession valuable, we are swayed by historical, social, and economic forces reaching into our lives in subtle and not-so-subtle ways (Alijoyo et al., 2025). If anything works across our cultures as a marketing strategy, it is an AI-powered marketing strategy; and the reason for this—at least in part—is because strategies that work "across" cultures tend to be those that most effectively resonate within specific ones (Alijoyo et al., 2025).

These applications mark and monitor in real-time the inflowing and outflowing of one's various income streams and obligation-bound debts (Hesami, 2025). Payments can be optimized with the help of artificial intelligence. This emerging technology uses algorithms to generate personalized recommendations for paying off debt. Among the strategies recommended are the familiar avalanche and snowball methods. (Onabowale, 2025).

6.3 AI Enabled Stock Market

A financial marketplace exists where shares of publicly traded firms are transacted. When one talks of the stock market, one usually means the equity market, where the buying and selling of equity securities occur (Nnakee et al., 2025). The ups and downs of the stock market represent a significant and necessary problem for not just investors and traders but also for researchers to study and understand (Ananth et al., 2025). The global stock market is rapidly evolving, and artificial intelligence is, simultaneously and in concert with other technologies, transforming the landscape. When it comes to reshaping investment decision-making and financial market analysis, the global stock market is no exception (Ibrahim et al., 2024; Medina Gonzalez, 2025). The equity market is a financial market in which shares of publicly held companies are issued and traded, either through exchanges or over-the-counter markets (Anvari & Fooladi, 2025). The platform enables the efficient and transparent exchange of corporate shares and securities between buyers and sellers. (Zhang & Sok, 2025). The stock market works according to the basic rule of supply and demand (Struckell et al., 2022). When demand is greater than supply, a stock's price goes up; when supply is greater than demand, a stock's price goes down. A stock's price can be affected by a variety of things, including but not limited to the performance of our economy, the performance of the corporation that issued the stock, and the performance of the stock in relation to how well other stocks are doing. (Korsah et al., 2024). Today's stock markets see transactions take place at a rapid pace. This is due to our powerful electronic trading and algorithmic systems (Lawrence Damilare Oyeniyi et al., 2024). Electronic trading has vastly speeded up the transactions themselves, but even more, it has made it very efficient for the buyer and seller to execute trades—far more efficient than they could do in the past when everything was manual. (Lawrence Damilare Oyeniyi et al., 2024).

Stock price changes are vitally important in financial markets, and that's why we pay so much attention to their predictions. We want to know how they will change in order to make investments based on something more than just random decision-making (Bao et al., 2025). And when we talk about predictions today, we must also talk about artificial intelligence, because it (and especially its subfield of deep learning) occupies such a pivotal place in the transformation of the models used to make them (Bao et al., 2025). In today's market, we want model performance, and we want it to be efficient (Rezaei et al., 2025).

For much of history, forecasting the movements of the stock market was done predominantly by people. These individuals used their experience and judgment, which is to say, their biases, to make predictions. On the other hand, when artificial intelligence, large-scale rapid data analysis, and human expertise are combined, the stock market predictions gained from that combination are much more reliable and accurate.

Bellaly et al., (2025), Lin & Lobo Marques (2024), Dakalbab et al., (2024), Azzi & Ajaka, (2025) Suggested that the integration of artificial intelligence has led to the continuous emergence of AI-driven models that utilize diverse data sources to forecast future stock market trends. This involves potential digital tools that drivers stock market such as: AI powered market explainer, personalized stock learning assistant, AI driver trades simulated trading platform, Behavior Bais Detection, AI powered portfolio (Naz & Kashif, 2025), (S et al., 2021), (Leela Sri Kalyan Gowtham Yaramolu, 2025), (Wang, 2023)

7. DISCUSSION

Our goal is to build a model that looks at the role of AI in raising financial knowhow, thereby nudging people's choices to push a country stock market forward. Therefore, model could help GCC states, Oman, in particular. This study highlights the influence of financial literacy on investment behavior to stock market involvement through comprehensive use of AI. From user perspective traditional financial literacy required complex pathways to understand the potential knowledge on stock market participation. Our finding illustrates technological intervention at financial literacy allows us to drive investment behavior which enables individuals to participate more effectively in stock market activity.

The study says AI driven money lessons will really shake up stock market understanding, therefore you get know how, skill, confidence to use digital finance tools safely and then you can make better choices, could it change everything. On the other hand, the AI rush into money-study research shook things up, broke old habits and handed us fresh ways to pick moves and see risk, therefore the whole field feels brand new. Did you know that after learning about money you tend to pick smarter investments, you spread your cash over many things, therefore the chance of a big loss goes down. With some money smarts investors can pick right choices, they're able think ahead and avoid risky bets; that's what solid cash knowledge does. What if an AI app looks at your bank numbers, then instantly gives you budgeting ideas, savings tips, debt-pay-off steps and even investment plans. Thus, it's advice seems hand-picked for you. This research says clarity and openness matter a lot — AI is now steering the global stock market, a transformational force that's reshaping how we choose investments and how analysts examine finance.

Our finding suggests that financial literacy with AI entails educating individuals in the use of digital financial tools and applications to improve their comprehension of financial concepts and decision-making such as digital tools and platforms that drive AI based Financial Literacy—such as AI Chatbots & Coaches, Generative AI (LLMs), AI Gamification, Financial Health Scoring. Similarly, by utilizing such AI based financial literacy impact on financial behavior which required technological navigation to develop the investment habits such as budgeting, Money saving and shopping pattern, saving & investments and insurance and Payment of obligations. Based on these factors overall impact of stock market participation will improve.

We've combined everything; meanwhile AI based finance lessons let each individual boost stock market sense easily. Therefore, previous research mainly stuck with old ways making people aware of how the stock market matters. They've pretty much stretched our view, so the picture looks far wider now.

Now AI's role isn't just about the single user; it actually stretches across the whole finance world; therefore, it shapes every bank and market. What we learn that AI tweaks money smarts, and with Oman as a stand-in other Gulf states get a taste of the same picture. Four claims it makes, based on what the literature says; moreover, a few groundbreaking ideas that showed up in this research. AI's shift how we teach, therefore financial smarts up to levels never seen before.

Financial smarts are required; still don't ensure a stock market that functions well, it's the next idea we consider. If you know how money works, then check your spending way is improving and staying solid. Four Because the world faces big risks and also real chances, the stock market can be good only if it's backing projects sustainably, handing risk assessment to AI inside a clear, open system, and ensuring that AI works under an honest framework.

8. CONCLUSION

The present state of financial literacy exists in-depth for all kinds of factors. It affects the development of the stock market, and when we sum it up, it gives us the picture of financial literacy in the world. Our study integrates various components of financial literacy—first by going through the available literature, then by adding a layer of technological Digital Artificial Intelligence (AI) tools to the mix, and finally by asking whether AI is going to make us all more financially literate, by what means, and with what potential effectiveness. To enrich our story, we also ask how much of an impact AI could possibly have on us soon, as it seems to have almost an infinite amount of new life and power as a new digital tool in this past decade, as well as a view in reaching the foreseeable future. We give you some stock characters and then a clearer narrative by clearly integrating a few variables along the way.

REFERENCES

Abdulla, Y., Ebrahim, R., & Kumaraswamy, S. (2020). Artificial Intelligence in Banking sector: Evidence from Bahrain. *2020 International Conference on Data Analytics for Business and Industry: Way Towards a Sustainable Economy (ICDABI)*, 1–6. DOI: 10.1109/ICDABI51230.2020.9325600

Adel, N. (2024). The impact of digital literacy and technology adoption on financial inclusion in Africa, Asia, and Latin America. *Heliyon*, *10*(24), e40951. DOI: 10.1016/j.heliyon.2024.e40951

Aditya, D. & Azmansyah. (2021). Pengaruh Financial Knowledge, Financial Attitude, dan Income terhadap Financial Behavior pada Usaha Mikro kecil dan Menengah di Kecamatan Marpoyan Damai Pekanbaru. *Jurnal Ekonomi KIAT, 32*(2). DOI: 10.25299/kiat.2021.vol32(2).8564

Agarwal, A., Rao, N. V. M., & Nogueira, M. C. (2025). Financially Savvy or Swayed by Biases? The Impact of Financial Literacy on Investment Decisions: A Study on Indian Retail Investors. *Journal of Risk and Financial Management*, *18*(6), 322. DOI: 10.3390/jrfm18060322

Ahmad, F., Boumaiza, A., Sanfilippo, A., & Al-Fagih, L. (2025). A Detailed Comprehensive Role of Digital Technologies in Green Finance Initiative for Net-Zero Energy Transition. *Advanced Energy and Sustainability Research*, *2500066*(10), 2500066. Advance online publication. DOI: 10.1002/aesr.202500066

Akanfe, O., Bhatt, P., & Lawong, D. A. (2025). Technology Advancements Shaping the Financial Inclusion Landscape: Present Interventions, Emergence of Artificial Intelligence and Future Directions. *Information Systems Frontiers*, *27*(5), 2189–2212. Advance online publication. DOI: 10.1007/s10796-025-10597-z

Akang, A. U. (2024). Regulatory Compliance and Access to Finance: Implications for Business Growth in Developing Economies. *Sciental Journal of Education Humanities and Social Sciences*, *1*(2), 8–23. DOI: 10.62536/sjehss.2023.v1.i2.pp8-23

Al-Afeef, M. A., & Alsmadi, A. A. (2025). Digital empowerment: Unraveling the impact of digital literacy on financial mastery. *Discover Sustainability*, *6*(1), 311. DOI: 10.1007/s43621-025-01137-5

Alhajri, T. M., & Alshebli, A. (2023). The Development of the Stock Exchanges in Saudi Arabia, Kuwait and Qatar from a Legal Perspective. *Journal of Law and Sustainable Development*, *11*(12), e2379. DOI: 10.55908/sdgs.v11i12.2379

Alharbi, F. (2024). The Impact of ESG Reforms on Economic Growth in GCC Countries: The Role of Financial Development. *Sustainability (Basel), 16*(24), 11067. DOI: 10.3390/su162411067

Alijoyo, F. A., Aziz, T. S. A., Omer, N., Yusuf, N., Kumar, M. D., Ramesh, A. V. N., Ulmas, Z., & Baker El-Ebiary, Y. A. (2025). Personalized marketing: Leveraging AI for culturally aware segmentation and targeting. *Alexandria Engineering Journal, 119*, 8–21. DOI: 10.1016/j.aej.2025.01.074

Almansour, B. Y., Elkrghli, S., & Almansour, A. Y. (2023). Behavioral finance factors and investment decisions: A mediating role of risk perception. *Cogent Economics & Finance, 11*(2), 2239032. DOI: 10.1080/23322039.2023.2239032

Alshareef, M. N. (2025). Artificial Intelligence-Enhanced Environmental, Social, and Governance Disclosure Quality and Financial Performance Nexus in Saudi Listed Companies Under Vision 2030. *Sustainability (Basel), 17*(16), 7421. DOI: 10.3390/su17167421

Alshubiri, F., & Hammami, S. (2025). Is digitalisation in the economy a source of innovative performance? *Digital Policy. Regulation & Governance*. Advance online publication. DOI: 10.1108/DPRG-03-2025-0059

Ansari, Y., Albarrak, M. S., Sherfudeen, N., & Aman, A. (2023). Examining the relationship between financial literacy and demographic factors and the overconfidence of Saudi investors. *Finance Research Letters, 52*, 103582. DOI: 10.1016/j.frl.2022.103582

Antwi, P. K. A., Addai, B., Duah, E., & Kubi, M. T. (2024). *The impact of financial literacy on financial well-being: A systematic literature review*. In Review. DOI: 10.21203/rs.3.rs-5187088/v2

Bayakhmetova, A., Rudenko, L., Krylova, L., Suleimenova, B., Niyazbekova, S., & Nurpeisova, A. (2025). Artificial Intelligence in Financial Behavior: Bibliometric Ideas and New Opportunities. *Journal of Risk and Financial Management, 18*(3), 159. DOI: 10.3390/jrfm18030159

Bernatska, N., Dzhumelia, E., Kochan, O., & Salamon, I. (2025). Digital Economy and Smart Financial Management: Using AI Tools for Financial Literacy. In Hu, Z., Zhang, Q., He, M., & Yanovsky, F. (Eds.), *Advances in Transdisciplinary Engineering*. IOS Press. DOI: 10.3233/ATDE250123

Bourveau, T., Gao, X., Li, R., & Zhou, F. S. (2025). Comply-or-explain regulation and investor protection. *Journal of Accounting and Economics, 79*(2–3), 101765. DOI: 10.1016/j.jacceco.2025.101765

Chhillar, N., Sharma, K., & Arora, S. (2025). Exploring the role of digital financial literacy and personal financial behavior in shaping financial stress and well-being in the digital age. *Acta Psychologica*, *259*, 105308. DOI: 10.1016/j.actpsy.2025.105308

Choung, Y., Chatterjee, S., & Pak, T.-Y. (2023). Digital financial literacy and financial well-being. *Finance Research Letters*, *58*, 104438. DOI: 10.1016/j.frl.2023.104438

Chua, A. Y. K., Pal, A., & Banerjee, S. (2023). AI-enabled investment advice: Will users buy it? *Computers in Human Behavior*, *138*, 107481. DOI: 10.1016/j.chb.2022.107481

Colgate, M., & Lang, B. (2001). Switching barriers in consumer markets: An investigation of the financial services industry. *Journal of Consumer Marketing*, *18*(4), 332–347. DOI: 10.1108/07363760110393001

Cupák, A., Fessler, P., Hsu, J. W., & Paradowski, P. R. (2022). Investor confidence and high financial literacy jointly shape investments in risky assets. *Economic Modelling*, *116*, 106033. DOI: 10.1016/j.econmod.2022.106033

Czech, K., Ochnio, L., Wielechowski, M., & Zabolotnyy, S. (2024). Financial Literacy: Identification of the Challenges, Needs, and Difficulties among Adults Living in Rural Areas. *Agriculture*, *14*(10), 1705. DOI: 10.3390/agriculture14101705

Darwish, F. S. M. (2025). Financial literacy and investment decision: An empirical study from the Palestine Stock Exchange. *Frontiers in Behavioral Economics*, *4*, 1444022. DOI: 10.3389/frbhe.2025.1444022

Del Sarto, N., & Ozili, P. K. (2025). FinTech and financial inclusion in emerging markets: A bibliometric analysis and future research agenda. *International Journal of Emerging Markets*, *20*(13), 270–290. DOI: 10.1108/IJOEM-08-2024-1428

Devan, M., Tillu, R., & Shanmugam, L. (2023). Personalized Financial Recommendations: Real-Time AI-ML Analytics in Wealth Management. *Journal of Knowledge Learning and Science Technology ISSN: 2959-6386 (Online)*, *2*(3), 547–559. DOI: 10.60087/jklst.vol2.n3.p559

Du, W., & Chen, M. (2023). Too much or less? The effect of financial literacy on resident fraud victimization. *Computers in Human Behavior*, *148*, 107914. DOI: 10.1016/j.chb.2023.107914

Due-Gundersen, N., & Owtram, F. (2022). The Foundation, Development and Future of the Omani Rentier State: From the Dhofar War to Vision 2040. *Arabian Humanities*, *16*. Advance online publication. DOI: 10.4000/cy.8328

Glenda, M. (2024). Financial literacy and its role in promoting sustainable investment. *World Journal of Advanced Research and Reviews, 24*(1), 212–232. DOI: 10.30574/wjarr.2024.24.1.2986

Goswami, V., Joshi, V. K., & Sharma, G. (2024). Unveiling the Investment Behaviour of Gen Y and Z: A Study on Artificial Intelligence Stocks Awareness and Decision-Making. In A. Tripathi, S. Birla, M. Soni, J. Sahariya, & M. Sharma, *multidisciplinary approaches for sustainable development* (1st ed., pp. 321–327). CRC Press. DOI: 10.1201/9781003543633-52

Gupta, S., & Sajjan, S. (2025). The Impact of Artificial Intelligence on Financial Decision Making and Risk Management. In P. Mittal & P. K. Gupta (Eds.), *Integrating Management Principles with Business Analytics Concepts and Applications* (pp. 14–28). QTanalytics India. DOI: 10.48001/978-81-980647-9-0-2

Hakimi, A., Saidi, H., & Adili, L. (2025). Achieving a More Inclusive Financial System: What Does the MENA Region Need? A Sensitivity Analysis for GCC and Non-GCC Countries. *Economies (Basel), 13*(7), 190. DOI: 10.3390/economies13070190

Hammad Naeem, M., Subhan, M., Alam, M. S., Al-Faryan, M. A. S., & Yameen, M. (2023). Examining the role of financial innovation on economic growth: Fresh empirical evidence from developing and developed countries. *Cogent Economics & Finance, 11*(1), 2170000. DOI: 10.1080/23322039.2023.2170000

Hesami, S. (2025). Navigating the AI-driven transformation of personal finance: Opportunities, challenges, and ethical imperatives. *Strategy and Leadership*. Advance online publication. DOI: 10.1108/SL-02-2025-0019

Hilbert, L. P., Noordewier, M. K., & Van Dijk, W. W. (2022). Financial scarcity increases discounting of gains and losses: Experimental evidence from a household task. *Journal of Economic Psychology, 92*, 102546. DOI: 10.1016/j.joep.2022.102546

Hossain, M. R., Rao, A., Sharma, G. D., Dev, D., & Kharbanda, A. (2024). Empowering energy transition: Green innovation, digital finance, and the path to sustainable prosperity through green finance initiatives. *Energy Economics, 136*, 107736. DOI: 10.1016/j.eneco.2024.107736

Hossain, T., & Siddiqua, P. (2024). Exploring the influence of behavioral aspects on stock investment decision-making: A study on Bangladeshi individual investors. *PSU Research Review, 8*(2), 467–483. DOI: 10.1108/PRR-10-2021-0054

Imjai, N., Yordudom, T., Yaacob, Z., Saad, N. H. M., & Aujirapongpan, S. (2025). Impact of AI literacy and adaptability on financial analyst skills among prospective Thai accountants: The role of critical thinking. *Technological Forecasting and Social Change*, *210*, 123889. DOI: 10.1016/j.techfore.2024.123889

Islam, K. U., Bhat, S. A., Lone, U. M., Darzi, M. A., & Malik, I. A. (2024). Financial risk propensity and investment decisions: An empirical analysis using behavioural biases. *IIMB Management Review*, *36*(3), 213–229. DOI: 10.1016/j.iimb.2024.06.004

Jain, V., & Kulkarni, P. A. (2023). Integrating AI Techniques for Enhanced Financial Forecasting and Budgeting Strategies. *International Journal of Economics and Management Studies*, *10*(09), 9–15. DOI: 10.14445/23939125/IJEMS-V10I9P102

Janzen, M. (2021). *Data Monetization in Capital Markets* (pp. 1–27). Arab-Exchange.org. https://arab-exchanges.org/upload/9271websiteData%20Monetization%20En.pdf

Johri, A., Wasiq, M., Kaur, H., & Asif, M. (2023). Assessment of users' adoption behaviour for stock market investment through online applications. *Heliyon*, *9*(9), e19524. DOI: 10.1016/j.heliyon.2023.e19524

Karami Nasrabad Sofla, K. (2024). Investigating the Role of Artificial Intelligence in Predicting Consumer Preferences (A Little Study in the Tehran Market). *International Journal of Applied Research in Management. Economics and Accounting*, *1*(4), 27–40. DOI: 10.63053/ijmea.28

Katnic, I., Katnic, M., Orlandic, M., Radunovic, M., & Mugosa, I. (2024). Understanding the Role of Financial Literacy in Enhancing Economic Stability and Resilience in Montenegro: A Data-Driven Approach. *Sustainability (Basel)*, *16*(24), 11065. DOI: 10.3390/su162411065

Khan, M. S., Azad, I., Moosa, S., & Javed, M. Y. (2024). Do we really need financial literacy to access the behavioral dynamics of generation Z? A case of Oman. *Heliyon*, *10*(13), e32739. DOI: 10.1016/j.heliyon.2024.e32739

Klitkou, A., Bolwig, S., Huber, A., Ingeborgrud, L., Pluciński, P., Rohracher, H., Schartinger, D., Thiene, M., & Żuk, P. (2022). The interconnected dynamics of social practices and their implications for transformative change: A review. *Sustainable Production and Consumption*, *31*, 603–614. DOI: 10.1016/j.spc.2022.03.027

Kobi, J. (2024). Developing Dashboard Analytics and Visualization Tools for Effective Performance Management and Continuous Process Improvement. *International Journal of Innovative Science and Research Technology (IJISRT)*, 1697–1709. DOI: 10.38124/ijisrt/IJISRT24MAY1147

Koskelainen, T., Kalmi, P., Scornavacca, E., & Vartiainen, T. (2023). Financial literacy in the digital age—A research agenda. *The Journal of Consumer Affairs, 57*(1), 507–528. DOI: 10.1111/joca.12510

Kroen, T. (2024). *A Financial Sector for the Economy of the Future: Oman* (No. 9798400278778; pp. 1–16). IMF. https://www.imf.org/en/Publications/selected-issues-papers/Issues/2024/06/12/A-Financial-Sector-for-the-Economy-of-the-Future-Oman-550249

Lakoni, I., Nurazi, R., Aziza, N., & Novitasari, N. (2023). Relationship of financial literacy to stock market participation. *Journal of Economics and Business Letters, 3*(6). Advance online publication. DOI: 10.55942/jebl.v3i6.270

Lakshmi, Y. (2024). The Impact Of Artificial Intelligence On Financial Literacy. *ShodhKosh: Journal of Visual and Performing Arts, 5*(5). Advance online publication. DOI: 10.29121/shodhkosh.v5.i5.2024.1606

Lang, N. D., Tran, H. M., Nguyen, G. T., & Vo, D. H. (2024). An Untapped Instrument in the Fight Against Poverty: The Impacts of Financial Literacy on Poverty Worldwide. *Social Indicators Research, 174*(2), 657–695. DOI: 10.1007/s11205-024-03404-w

Liu, X., Zhou, C., Li, Y., & Fang, F. (2025). How economic stability shapes social relationship expenditures: Moderating effects of health and education. *International Review of Economics & Finance, 99*, 104041. DOI: 10.1016/j.iref.2025.104041

Lusardi, A. (2019). Financial literacy and the need for financial education: Evidence and implications. *Swiss Journal of Economics and Statistics, 155*(1), 1. DOI: 10.1186/s41937-019-0027-5

Lusardi, A., & Mitchell, O. (2009). *How Ordinary Consumers Make Complex Economic Decisions: Financial Literacy and Retirement Readiness* (No. w15350; p. w15350). National Bureau of Economic Research. DOI: 10.3386/w15350

Lyons, A., & Kass-Hanna, J. (2018). Financial Inclusion, Financial Literacy and Economically Vulnerable Populations in the Middle East and North Africa. SSRN *Electronic Journal*. DOI: 10.2139/ssrn.3189563

Machucho, R., & Ortiz, D. (2025). The Impacts of Artificial Intelligence on Business Innovation: A Comprehensive Review of Applications, Organizational Challenges, and Ethical Considerations. *Systems, 13*(4), 264. DOI: 10.3390/systems13040264

Mahaney, J. (2024). *Artificial Intelligence: Shaping the Future of Financial Literacy. SSRN*. DOI: 10.2139/ssrn.4866396

Marotta, G., & Au, C.-D. (2022). Budgeting in the Age of Artificial Intelligence – New Approaches, Old Challenges? *International Journal of Artificial Intelligence and Machine Learning*, *2*(2), 1–11. DOI: 10.51483/IJAIML.2.2.2022.1-11

Marzuki, N. A. A. B. (2024). *The Influence of Technology in Personal Finance Management*. DOI: 10.13140/RG.2.2.16119.02727

Masood, F. (2024). Impact of Artificial Intelligence on Financial Markets. *International Journal of Emerging Multidisciplinaries: Social Science*, *3*(1), 8. DOI: 10.54938/ijemdss.2024.03.1.359

Menberu, A. W. (2024). Technology-mediated financial education in developing countries: A systematic literature review. *Cogent Business & Management*, *11*(1), 2294879. DOI: 10.1080/23311975.2023.2294879

Michailidis, M., Zafeiriou, E., Kantartzis, A., Galatsidas, S., & Arabatzis, G. (2025). Governance, Energy Policy, and Sustainable Development: Renewable Energy Infrastructure Transition in Developing MENA Countries. *Energies*, *18*(11), 2759. DOI: 10.3390/en18112759

Mireku, K., Appiah, F., & Agana, J. A. (2023). Is there a link between financial literacy and financial behaviour? *Cogent Economics & Finance*, *11*(1), 2188712. DOI: 10.1080/23322039.2023.2188712

Mirzaei, M., & Buer, T. (2022). First results on financial literacy in Oman. *Managerial Finance*, *48*(9/10), 1413–1429. DOI: 10.1108/MF-09-2021-0456

Mohamed, N. (2025). Artificial intelligence and machine learning in cybersecurity: A deep dive into state-of-the-art techniques and future paradigms. *Knowledge and Information Systems*, *67*(8), 6969–7055. DOI: 10.1007/s10115-025-02429-y

Mulia Pratama, I. (2021). Effects of Age, Gender and Education Level on Financial Literacy Level (Study of Vocational School Teachers in Padang City). *Economica*, *9*(1), 143–150. DOI: 10.22202/economica.2020.v9.i2.4606

Naeem, M. A., Arfaoui, N., & Yarovaya, L. (2025). The contagion effect of artificial intelligence across innovative industries: From blockchain and metaverse to cleantech and beyond. *Technological Forecasting and Social Change*, *210*, 123822. DOI: 10.1016/j.techfore.2024.123822

Najem, R., Bahnasse, A., Fakhouri Amr, M., & Talea, M. (2025). Advanced AI and big data techniques in E-finance: A comprehensive survey. *Discover Artificial Intelligence*, *5*(1), 102. DOI: 10.1007/s44163-025-00365-y

Nayeem, T. (2012). Cultural Influences on Consumer Behaviour. *International Journal of Business and Management, 7*(21), 78. DOI: 10.5539/ijbm.v7n21p78

Nogueira, M. C., Almeida, L., & Tavares, F. O. (2025a). Financial Literacy, Financial Knowledge, and Financial Behaviors in OECD Countries. *Journal of Risk and Financial Management, 18*(3), 167. DOI: 10.3390/jrfm18030167

Nogueira, M. C., Almeida, L., & Tavares, F. O. (2025b). Financial Literacy, Financial Knowledge, and Financial Behaviors in OECD Countries. *Journal of Risk and Financial Management, 18*(3), 167. DOI: 10.3390/jrfm18030167

Ochi, A., Nouaili, M., Saidi, Y., Haouas, A., & Saidi, A. (2025). Foreign Direct Investment and Economic Growth in Arab Countries: Do Institutions, Financial Development, and Knowledge Economy Matter? *Journal of the Knowledge Economy, 17*(2), 5145–5179. Advance online publication. DOI: 10.1007/s13132-025-02794-7

Onabowale, O. (2025). AI and Real-Time Financial Decision Support. *International Journal of Research Publication and Reviews, 6*(6), 329–350. DOI: 10.55248/gengpi.6.0625.2260

Onyenahazi, O. B., & Antwi, B. O. (2024). The Role of Artificial Intelligence in Investment Decision-Making: Opportunities and Risks for Financial Institutions. *International Journal of Research Publication and Reviews, 5*(10), 70–85. DOI: 10.55248/gengpi.5.1024.2701

Özveren, E. (2025). The Role of the State in the Big Picture of Economic Development: Mainstream-versus-Heterodox Approaches and Historical Evidence. *The Forum for Social Economics*, 1–32. DOI: 10.1080/07360932.2025.2507583

Paramesha, M., Rane, N. L., & Rane, J. (2024). *Big Data Analytics, Artificial Intelligence, Machine Learning, Internet of Things, and Blockchain for Enhanced Business Intelligence*. DOI: 10.2139/ssrn.4855856

Parsai, P., & Chandok, A. K. (2025). The Role of Financial Literacy in Investment Decision-Making: A Review. *International Journal of Innovations in Science Engineering And Management*, 296–301. DOI: 10.69968/ijisem.2025v4i1296-301

Pattnaik, D., Ray, S., & Raman, R. (2024). Applications of artificial intelligence and machine learning in the financial services industry: A bibliometric review. *Heliyon, 10*(1), e23492. DOI: 10.1016/j.heliyon.2023.e23492

Pazouki, S., Jamshidi, M., Jalali, M., & Tafreshi, A. (2025). Artificial Intelligence and Digital Technologies in Finance: A Comprehensive Review. *Journal of Economics. Finance and Accounting Studies, 7*(2), 54–69. DOI: 10.32996/jefas.2025.7.2.5

Qadeer, H., & Sarfraz, M. (2025). Capital Structure Choices: The Role of Financial Development and Institutional Quality. *The Critical Review of Social Sciences Studies*, *3*(1), 2347–2363. DOI: 10.59075/j2sr6063

Qayoom, I., & Chisti, K. (2025). "Earnings transparency: A systematic review, integrated framework and future perspectives." *Journal of Financial Reporting and Accounting*. DOI: 10.1108/JFRA-11-2024-0815

Rahman, M., Isa, C. R., Masud, M. M., Sarker, M., & Chowdhury, N. T. (2021). The role of financial behaviour, financial literacy, and financial stress in explaining the financial well-being of B40 group in Malaysia. *Future Business Journal*, *7*(1), 52. DOI: 10.1186/s43093-021-00099-0

Razavi, H., & Habibnia, A. (2024). The Rise of AI in Middle Eastern Fintech With the Case Studies From the UAE and Turkey. In Taherdoost, H., Le, N., Madanchian, M., & Farhaoui, Y. (Eds.), (pp. 259–297). Advances in Finance, Accounting, and Economics. IGI Global. DOI: 10.4018/979-8-3693-1561-3.ch010

Razavi, S. (2022). Making the Right to Social Security a Reality for All Workers. *The Indian Journal of Labour Economics : The Quarterly Journal of the Indian Society of Labour Economics*, *65*(2), 269–294. DOI: 10.1007/s41027-022-00378-6

Reddy, K., Wallace, D., & Wellalage, N. H. (2024). The impact of financial literacy on financial inclusion. *Australian Journal of Management, 03128962241270809*. Advance online publication. DOI: 10.1177/03128962241270809

Rehman, K., & Mia, M. A. (2024). Determinants of financial literacy: A systematic review and future research directions. *Future Business Journal*, *10*(1), 75. DOI: 10.1186/s43093-024-00365-x

Saberironaghi, M., Ren, J., & Saberironaghi, A. (2025). Stock Market Prediction Using Machine Learning and Deep Learning Techniques: A Review. *AppliedMath*, *5*(3), 76. DOI: 10.3390/appliedmath5030076

Salem, S. (2025). *The Role of Financial Technology and Financial Literacy in Achieving Sustainable Development with The Mediating Effect of Financial Inclusion*. DOI: 10.13140/RG.2.2.15168.65284

Sarioguz, O., & Miser, E. (2024). Integrating AI in financial risk management: Evaluating the effects of machine learning algorithms on predictive accuracy and regulatory compliance. *International Journal of Science and Research Archive*, *13*(2), 789–811. DOI: 10.30574/ijsra.2024.13.2.2206

Shahzad, M. A., Jianguo, D., Jan, N., & Rasool, Y. (2024). Perceived Behavioral Factors and Individual Investor Stock Market Investment Decision: Multigroup Analysis and Major Stock Markets Perspectives. *SAGE Open*, *14*(2), 21582440241256210. DOI: 10.1177/21582440241256210

Song, X., Qin, X., Wang, W., & Man Li, R. Y. (2025). Financial inclusion, technologies, and worldwide economic development: A spatial Durbin model approach. *The Journal of Financial Data Science*, *11*, 100155. DOI: 10.1016/j.jfds.2025.100155

Subedi, D. P., & Bhandari, D. R. (2024). Assessing the Role of Digital Literacy in Investment Decisions among Graduate Business Students in Nepal: The Mediating Effects of Peer Group Influence. *Multi-Disciplinary Explorations: The Kasthamandap College Journal*, *2*(2), 47–62. DOI: 10.3126/mdekcj.v2i2.74174

Supawat, L., & Arnat, L. (2023). Market Reaction to Corporate Releases and News Articles: Evidence from Thailand's Stock Market. *International Journal of Financial Studies*, *11*(3), 111. DOI: 10.3390/ijfs11030111

Torm, N., & Oehme, M. (2024). Social protection and formalization in low- and middle-income countries: A scoping review of the literature. *World Development*, *181*, 106662. DOI: 10.1016/j.worlddev.2024.106662

Tyrell Curry, J. (2025). Modeling the dynamic interplay between financial literacy, resilience, and emotional well-being across diverse demographics. *Cogent Economics & Finance*, *13*(1), 2544177. DOI: 10.1080/23322039.2025.2544177

Uddin, M. A. (2020). Impact of Financial Literacy on Individual Saving: A Study in the Omani Context. SSRN *Electronic Journal*. DOI: 10.2139/ssrn.4012631

Vyas, A. (2025). *Revolutionizing Risk: The Role of Artificial Intelligence in Financial Risk Management, Forecasting, and Global Implementation. SSRN*. DOI: 10.2139/ssrn.5224657

Wang, J. (2025). The Impact of Unexpected Events and Household Financial Fragility. *Emerging Markets Finance & Trade*, 1–23. DOI: 10.1080/1540496X.2025.2535706

Wei, L., Peng, M., & Wu, W. (2021). Financial literacy and fraud detection—Evidence from China. *International Review of Economics & Finance*, *76*, 478–494. DOI: 10.1016/j.iref.2021.06.017

Xu, H., Niu, K., Lu, T., & Li, S. (2024). Leveraging artificial intelligence for enhanced risk management in financial services: Current applications and future prospects. *Engineering Science & Technology Journal*, *5*(8), 2402–2426. DOI: 10.51594/estj.v5i8.1363

Yang, J., Wu, Y., & Huang, B. (2023). Digital finance and financial literacy: Evidence from Chinese households. *Journal of Banking & Finance, 156*, 107005. DOI: 10.1016/j.jbankfin.2023.107005

Yu, T., & Xiao, J. (2025). *Applying Generative AI in Financial Literacy Research: A Demonstration. SSRN*. DOI: 10.2139/ssrn.5291736

Compilation of References

Abdulla, Y., Ebrahim, R., & Kumaraswamy, S. (2020). Artificial Intelligence in Banking sector: Evidence from Bahrain. *2020 International Conference on Data Analytics for Business and Industry: Way Towards a Sustainable Economy (ICDABI)*, 1–6. DOI: 10.1109/ICDABI51230.2020.9325600

Abidin, A. Z., Kurniawan, M. R., & Pratama, K. P. M. P. (2025). The role of Islamic financial markets to support sustainable development goals in Indonesia. In *Islamic financial markets and institutions: Challenges, financial stability, and inclusivity* (pp. 251–273). Springer Nature Singapore. DOI: 10.1007/978-981-96-8650-6_12

ACFE. 2004, Association of Certified Fraud Examiners. (2004). What Is Fraud? Retrieved Dec. 2, 2020, from https://www.acfe.com/fraud-101.aspx

ACFE. 2020. Association of Certified Fraud Examiners. (2020). Report to the Nations. Retrieved Dec. 5,2020, from https://acfepublic.s3-us-west-2.amazonaws.com/2020-Report-to-the

Adamu, A. Y. (2024). Digitalization of higher education in Ethiopia. *Journal of Comparative and International Higher Education*, *16*(2), 13–24. DOI: 10.32674/jcihe.v16i2.5978

Adawiyah, S. R., Purwandari, B., Eitiveni, I., & Purwaningsih, E. H. (2024). The influence of AI and AR technology in personalized recommendations on customer usage intention: A case study of cosmetic products on Shopee. *Applied Sciences (Basel, Switzerland)*, *14*(13), 5786. Advance online publication. DOI: 10.3390/app14135786

Adel, N. (2024). The impact of digital literacy and technology adoption on financial inclusion in Africa, Asia, and Latin America. *Heliyon*, *10*(24), e40951. DOI: 10.1016/j.heliyon.2024.e40951

Adhikari, P.Jnr. (2024). Artificial Intelligence in fraud detection: Revolutionizing financial security. *International Journal of Science and Research Archive, 13*(1), 1457–1472. DOI: 10.30574/ijsra.2024.13.1.1860

Aditya, D. & Azmansyah. (2021). Pengaruh Financial Knowledge, Financial Attitude, dan Income terhadap Financial Behavior pada Usaha Mikro kecil dan Menengah di Kecamatan Marpoyan Damai Pekanbaru. *Jurnal Ekonomi KIAT, 32*(2). DOI: 10.25299/kiat.2021.vol32(2).8564

Agarwal, A., Rao, N. V. M., & Nogueira, M. C. (2025). Financially Savvy or Swayed by Biases? The Impact of Financial Literacy on Investment Decisions: A Study on Indian Retail Investors. *Journal of Risk and Financial Management, 18*(6), 322. DOI: 10.3390/jrfm18060322

Ahmad, F., Boumaiza, A., Sanfilippo, A., & Al-Fagih, L. (2025). A Detailed Comprehensive Role of Digital Technologies in Green Finance Initiative for Net-Zero Energy Transition. *Advanced Energy and Sustainability Research, 2500066*(10), 2500066. Advance online publication. DOI: 10.1002/aesr.202500066

Akanfe, O., Bhatt, P., & Lawong, D. A. (2025). Technology Advancements Shaping the Financial Inclusion Landscape: Present Interventions, Emergence of Artificial Intelligence and Future Directions. *Information Systems Frontiers, 27*(5), 2189–2212. Advance online publication. DOI: 10.1007/s10796-025-10597-z

Akang, A. U. (2024). Regulatory Compliance and Access to Finance: Implications for Business Growth in Developing Economies. *Sciental Journal of Education Humanities and Social Sciences, 1*(2), 8–23. DOI: 10.62536/sjehss.2023.v1.i2.pp8-23

Al-Afeef, M. A., & Alsmadi, A. A. (2025). Digital empowerment: Unraveling the impact of digital literacy on financial mastery. *Discover Sustainability, 6*(1), 311. DOI: 10.1007/s43621-025-01137-5

Al-Araj, R., Haddad, H., Shehadeh, M., Hasan, E., & Nawaiseh, M. (2022). The effect of artificial intelligence on service quality and customer satisfaction in Jordanian banking sector. *WSEAS Transactions on Business and Economics, 19*, 1929–1947. DOI: 10.37394/23207.2022.19.173

Alfadhel, K. A. (2017). The GCC human rights declaration: An instrumentation of cultural relativism. *arab law quarterly, 31*(1), 89-98.

Alhajri, T. M., & Alshebli, A. (2023). The Development of the Stock Exchanges in Saudi Arabia, Kuwait and Qatar from a Legal Perspective. *Journal of Law and Sustainable Development, 11*(12), e2379. DOI: 10.55908/sdgs.v11i12.2379

Alharbi, F. R. (2023). Gulf Cooperation Council Countries' Electricity Sector Forecasting: Consumption Growth Issue and Renewable Energy Penetration Progress Challenges (Doctoral dissertation, Lancaster University (United Kingdom)).

Alharbi, F. (2024). The Impact of ESG Reforms on Economic Growth in GCC Countries: The Role of Financial Development. *Sustainability (Basel), 16*(24), 11067. DOI: 10.3390/su162411067

Ali, A., Elshafie, H., Eisa, T. A. E., Al-Dhaqm, A., Othman, S. H., Elhassan, T., Nasser, M., Saif, A., & Abd Razak, S. (2022). Financial Fraud Detection Based on Machine Learning: A Systematic Literature Review. *Applied Sciences (Basel, Switzerland), 12*(19), 9637. DOI: 10.3390/app12199637

Alijoyo, F. A., Aziz, T. S. A., Omer, N., Yusuf, N., Kumar, M. D., Ramesh, A. V. N., Ulmas, Z., & Baker El-Ebiary, Y. A. (2025). Personalized marketing: Leveraging AI for culturally aware segmentation and targeting. *Alexandria Engineering Journal, 119*, 8–21. DOI: 10.1016/j.aej.2025.01.074

Aljawareen, A. F. (2017). Innovation in the GCC countries: An economic analysis. *Journal of Economics, 5*(4), 51–62.

Aljughaiman, A. A., Tabash, M. I., Issa, S. S., & Almulhim, A. A. (2025). Shock transmission from global financial stress, bitcoin sentiment indices, US and euro financial market uncertainty toward the GCC stock volatility. *Cogent Business & Management, 12*(1), 2514811. DOI: 10.1080/23311975.2025.2514811

Almansour, B. Y., Elkrghli, S., & Almansour, A. Y. (2023). Behavioral finance factors and investment decisions: A mediating role of risk perception. *Cogent Economics & Finance, 11*(2), 2239032. DOI: 10.1080/23322039.2023.2239032

Al-Najjar, D. (2022). Impact of the twin pandemics: COVID-19 and oil crash on Saudi exchange index. *PLoS One, 17*(5), e0268733. DOI: 10.1371/journal.pone.0268733 PMID: 35594304

Alqahtani, A., Klein, T., & Khalid, A. (2019). The impact of oil price uncertainty on GCC stock markets. *Resources Policy, 64*, 101526. DOI: 10.1016/j.resourpol.2019.101526

Al-Roubaie, A. S. (2025). Impact of emerging technologies on economic diversification: the case of Saudi Arabia. Journal of Business and Socio-economic Development, 1-15. DOI: 10.1108/JBSED-12-2024-0130

Alshareef, M. N. (2025). Artificial Intelligence-Enhanced Environmental, Social, and Governance Disclosure Quality and Financial Performance Nexus in Saudi Listed Companies Under Vision 2030. *Sustainability (Basel), 17*(16), 7421. DOI: 10.3390/su17167421

Alshubiri, F., & Hammami, S. (2025). Is digitalisation in the economy a source of innovative performance? *Digital Policy. Regulation & Governance*. Advance online publication. DOI: 10.1108/DPRG-03-2025-0059

Alsubaei, F. S. (2025). Smart deep learning model for enhanced IoT intrusion detection. *Scientific Reports, 15*(1), 20577. DOI: 10.1038/s41598-025-06363-5 PMID: 40596059

Ampountolas, A. (2023). Comparative analysis of machine learning, hybrid, and deep learning forecasting models: Evidence from European financial markets and bitcoins. *Forecasting, 5*(2), 472–486. DOI: 10.3390/forecast5020026

Ampountolas, A. (2024). Enhancing forecasting accuracy in commodity and financial markets: Insights from garch and svr models. *International Journal of Financial Studies, 12*(3), 59. DOI: 10.3390/ijfs12030059

Angwin, J., Larson, J., Kirchner, L., & Mattu, S. (2017, April 5). Minority Neighborhoods Pay Higher Car Insurance Premiums Than White Areas With the Same Risk. *ProPublica*. Retrieved from www.propublica.org/article/minority-neighborhoods-higher-car-insurance-premiums-white-areas-same-risk. Accessed September 5, 2025.

ANI. (2024, Dec 8). Banks to use AI & machine learning to safeguard customers from financial frauds. The Economic Times. https://economictimes.indiatimes.com/tech/artificial-intelligence/banks-to-use-ai-machine-learning-to-safeguard-customers-from-financial-frauds/articleshow/116093347.cms?from=mdr

Ansari, Y., Albarrak, M. S., Sherfudeen, N., & Aman, A. (2023). Examining the relationship between financial literacy and demographic factors and the overconfidence of Saudi investors. *Finance Research Letters, 52*, 103582. DOI: 10.1016/j.frl.2022.103582

Antwi, P. K. A., Addai, B., Duah, E., & Kubi, M. T. (2024). *The impact of financial literacy on financial well-being: A systematic literature review*. In Review. DOI: 10.21203/rs.3.rs-5187088/v2

Aros Hernandez, L., Bustamante Molano, L. X., & Gutierrez-Portela, F.. (2024). Financial fraud detection through the application of machine learning techniques: A literature review. *Humanities & Social Sciences Communications, 11*(1), 1130. DOI: 10.1057/s41599-024-03606-0

Arouri, J., Lahiani, R., & Nguyen, A. (2011). Oil price shocks and stock markets in the U.S. and 13 European countries. *Energy Economics*, *30*(5), 2587–2608.

Aslam, F., Ferreira, P., Ali, H., & José, A. E. (2022). Application of multifractal analysis in estimating the reaction of energy markets to geopolitical acts and threats. *Sustainability (Basel)*, *14*(10), 5828. DOI: 10.3390/su14105828

Aslam, F., Hunjra, A. I., Ftiti, Z., Louhichi, W., & Shams, T. (2022). Insurance fraud detection: Evidence from artificial intelligence and machine learning. *Research in International Business and Finance*, *62*, 101744. DOI: 10.1016/j.ribaf.2022.101744

Baeshen, L. (2023). *Financial inclusion in Islamic vs. non-Islamic countries, FinTech and bank competition* [Doctoral dissertation, University of Essex]. https://repository.essex.ac.uk/36519/

Bansal, U., Bharatwal, S., Bagiyam, D. S., & Kismawadi, E. R. (2024). Fraud detection in the era of AI: Harnessing technology for a safer digital economy. In *AI-driven decentralized finance and the future of finance* (pp. 143–164).

Bao, Y., Ke, B., Li, B., Yu, Y. J., & Zhang, J. (2020). Detecting accounting fraud in publicly traded U.S. firms using a machine learning approach. *Journal of Accounting Research*, *58*(1), 199–235. DOI: 10.1111/1475-679X.12292

Barocas, S., & Selbst, A. D. (2016). Big data's disparate impact. *California Law Review*, *104*, 671.

Bartlett, R., Morse, A., Stanton, R., & Wallace, N. (2022). Consumer-lending discrimination in the FinTech Era. *Journal of Financial Economics*, *143*(1), 30–56. DOI: 10.1016/j.jfineco.2021.05.047

Basel Committee on Banking Supervision. (2024). *Core Principles for Effective Banking Supervision*. Retrieved from https://www.bis.org/bcbs/publ/d573.pdf. Accessed September 1, 2025.

Bayakhmetova, A., Rudenko, L., Krylova, L., Suleimenova, B., Niyazbekova, S., & Nurpeisova, A. (2025). Artificial Intelligence in Financial Behavior: Bibliometric Ideas and New Opportunities. *Journal of Risk and Financial Management*, *18*(3), 159. DOI: 10.3390/jrfm18030159

Behera, I., Nanda, P., Mitra, S., & Kumari, S. (2024). *Machine Learning Approaches for Forecasting Financial Market Volatility. Machine Learning Approaches in Financial Analytics*. Springer. DOI: 10.1007/978-3-031-61037-0_20

Bellamy, R. K., Dey, K., Hind, M., Hoffman, S. C., Houde, S., Kannan, K., Lohia, P., Martino, J., Mehta, S., Mojsilović, A., Nagar, S., Ramamurthy, K. N., Richards, J., Saha, D., Sattigeri, P., Singh, M., Varshney, K. R., & Zhang, Y. (2019). AI Fairness 360: An extensible toolkit for detecting and mitigating algorithmic bias. *IBM Journal of Research and Development*, *63*(4/5), 4–1. DOI: 10.1147/JRD.2019.2942287

Bello, H., Iyelolu, T., & Idemudia, C. (2024). Implementing machine learning algorithms to detect and prevent financial fraud in real-time. Computer Science &amp. *IT Research Journal*, *5*(7), 1539–1564. DOI: 10.51594/csitrj.v5i7.1274

Beneish, M. D. (1999). The detection of earnings manipulation. *Financial Analysts Journal*, *55*(5), 24–36. DOI: 10.2469/faj.v55.n5.2296

Bernardy, J., & Spiwack, A. (2021). Artefact for _Evaluating linear functions to symmetric monoidal categories_ [Dataset]. In *Artifact Digital Object Group*. DOI: 10.1145/3462282

Bernatska, N., Dzhumelia, E., Kochan, O., & Salamon, I. (2025). Digital Economy and Smart Financial Management: Using AI Tools for Financial Literacy. In Hu, Z., Zhang, Q., He, M., & Yanovsky, F. (Eds.), *Advances in Transdisciplinary Engineering*. IOS Press. DOI: 10.3233/ATDE250123

Berry, M. J. A. (1997). *Data mining techniques for marketing, sales and customer support*. Wiley.

Bhandari, B., Park, G., & Shafiabady, N. (2023). Implementation of transformer-based deep learning architecture for the development of surface roughness classifier using sound and cutting force signals. *Neural Computing & Applications*, *35*(18), 13275–13292. Advance online publication. DOI: 10.1007/s00521-023-08425-z

Bollerslev, T. (1986). Generalized autoregressive conditional heteroskedasticity. *Journal of Econometrics*, *31*(3), 307–327. DOI: 10.1016/0304-4076(86)90063-1

Bolton, R. J., & Hand, D. J. (2001). Unsupervised profiling methods for fraud detection. Credit Scoring and Credit Control Conference VII. Edinburgh, UK.

Borio, C. (2024). *Macro-financial challenges in the post-COVID world*. Monetary Policy Responses to the Post-Pandemic Inflation.

Boubaker, H., Saidane, B., & Ben Saad Zorgati, M. (2022). Modelling the dynamics of stock market in the gulf cooperation council countries: Evidence on persistence to shocks. *Financial Innovation*, *8*(1), 46. DOI: 10.1186/s40854-022-00348-3

Boudri, I., & El Bouhadi, A. (2024). Modeling and Forecasting Historical Volatility Using Econometric and Deep Learning Approaches: Evidence from the Moroccan and Bahraini Stock Markets. *Journal of Risk and Financial Management*, *17*(7), 300. DOI: 10.3390/jrfm17070300

Boukhatem, J., & Alhazmi, A. M. (2024). COVID-19 pandemic, oil prices and Saudi stock market: Empirical evidence from ARDL modeling and Bayer–Hanck cointegration approach. *Future Business Journal*, *10*(1), 58. DOI: 10.1186/s43093-024-00338-0

Bourveau, T., Gao, X., Li, R., & Zhou, F. S. (2025). Comply-or-explain regulation and investor protection. *Journal of Accounting and Economics*, *79*(2–3), 101765. DOI: 10.1016/j.jacceco.2025.101765

Brey, P., & Dainow, B. (2024). Ethics by design for artificial intelligence. *AI and Ethics*, *4*(4), 1265–1277. DOI: 10.1007/s43681-023-00330-4

Butt, J. S. (2024). From bureaucracy to black box: Revolutionizing natural justice and due process in administrative law. *Acta Universitatis Danubius. Administratio*, *16*(1), 7–47.

Camilleri, M. A. (2023). Artificial intelligence governance: Ethical considerations and implications for social responsibility. *Expert Systems: International Journal of Knowledge Engineering and Neural Networks*, *41*(7), e13406. Advance online publication. DOI: 10.1111/exsy.13406

Cecchini, M., Aytug, H., Koehler, G. J., & Pathak, P. (2010). Detecting management fraud in public companies. *Management Science*, *56*(7), 1146–1160. DOI: 10.1287/mnsc.1100.1174

Çela, E., Vajjhala, N. R., & Aslani, B. (2025). Artificial intelligence in legal systems. In *Chapman and Hall/CRC eBooks*. DOI: 10.1201/9781003541899

Central Bank of Bahrain. (2017). *Shari'a-compliant financing-based crowdfunding directives*. Central Bank of Bahrain.

Cepec, J., & Grajzl, P. (2021). Creditors, Plan Confirmations, and Bankruptcy Reorganizations: Lessons from Slovenia. *European Business Organization Law Review*, *22*(3), 559–589. DOI: 10.1007/s40804-021-00221-3

Cervellati, E. M., Stella, G. P., & Angelini, N. (2024). *Behavioral finance and wealth management: Market anomalies, investors' behavior and the role of financial advisors*. Virtus Interpress. DOI: 10.22495/bfwm

Chatila, R., Firth-Butterfield, K., & Havens, J. C. (2018). Ethically aligned design: A vision for prioritizing human well-being with autonomous and intelligent systems version 2.

Chen, S., & Zhang, Z. (2019). Forecasting implied volatility smile surface via deep learning and attention mechanism. arXiv preprint arXiv:1912.11059

Chen, Z. Z., Ma, J., Zhang, X., Hao, N., Yan, A., Nourbakhsh, A., Yang, X., McAuley, J., Petzold, L., & Wang, W. Y. (2024, May 2). *A survey on large language models for critical societal domains: finance, healthcare, and law*. arXiv.org. https://arxiv.org/abs/2405.01769

Chen, B., Wu, Z., & Zhao, R. (2023). From fiction to fact: The growing role of generative AI in business and finance. *Journal of Chinese Economic and Business Studies, 21*(4), 471–496. DOI: 10.1080/14765284.2023.2245279

Cheng, L., & Gong, X. (2024). *Appraising regulatory Framework towards Artificial General Intelligence (AGI) under Digital Humanism.* Deleted Journal., DOI: 10.1515/ijdlg-2024-0015

Chen, X., Cho, Y. H., Dou, Y., & Lev, B. (2022). Predicting future earnings changes using machine learning and detailed financial data. *Journal of Accounting Research, 60*(2), 467–515. DOI: 10.1111/1475-679X.12429

Chhillar, N., Sharma, K., & Arora, S. (2025). Exploring the role of digital financial literacy and personal financial behavior in shaping financial stress and well-being in the digital age. *Acta Psychologica, 259*, 105308. DOI: 10.1016/j.actpsy.2025.105308

Choi, D., & Lee, K. (2018). An artificial intelligence approach to financial fraud detection under IoT environ-ment: A survey and implementation. *Security and Communication Networks, 2018*(1), 5483472. Advance online publication. DOI: 10.1155/2018/5483472

Choung, Y., Chatterjee, S., & Pak, T.-Y. (2023). Digital financial literacy and financial well-being. *Finance Research Letters, 58*, 104438. DOI: 10.1016/j.frl.2023.104438

Chua, A. Y. K., Pal, A., & Banerjee, S. (2023). AI-enabled investment advice: Will users buy it? *Computers in Human Behavior, 138*, 107481. DOI: 10.1016/j.chb.2022.107481

Chung, T. K., Gueldner, P. H., Aloziem, O. U., Liang, N. L., & Vorp, D. A. (2024). An artificial intelligence based abdominal aortic aneurysm prognosis classifier to predict patient outcomes. *Scientific Reports, 14*(1), 3390. DOI: 10.1038/s41598-024-53459-5 PMID: 38336915

Cicchiello, A. F., Gallo, S., & Monferrà, S. (2022). Mapping crowdfunding in cultural and creative industries: A conceptual and empirical overview. *European Management Review, 19*(1), 22–37. DOI: 10.1111/emre.12510

Colgate, M., & Lang, B. (2001). Switching barriers in consumer markets: An investigation of the financial services industry. *Journal of Consumer Marketing, 18*(4), 332–347. DOI: 10.1108/07363760110393001

Cumming, D., Meoli, M., Rossi, A., & Vismara, S. (2024). ESG and crowdfunding platforms. *Journal of Business Venturing, 39*(1), 106362. Advance online publication. DOI: 10.1016/j.jbusvent.2023.106362

Cupák, A., Fessler, P., Hsu, J. W., & Paradowski, P. R. (2022). Investor confidence and high financial literacy jointly shape investments in risky assets. *Economic Modelling, 116*, 106033. DOI: 10.1016/j.econmod.2022.106033

Curth, A., Jeffares, A., & van der Schaar, M. (2024). A u-turn on double descent: Rethinking parameter counting in statistical learning. *Advances in Neural Information Processing Systems*, 36.

Curth, A., Jeffares, A., & van der Schaar, M. (2024). Why do random forests work? Understanding tree ensembles as self-regularizing adaptive smoothers. *arXiv*. https://arxiv.org/abs/2402.01502

Czech, K., Ochnio, L., Wielechowski, M., & Zabolotnyy, S. (2024). Financial Literacy: Identification of the Challenges, Needs, and Difficulties among Adults Living in Rural Areas. *Agriculture, 14*(10), 1705. DOI: 10.3390/agriculture14101705

Dahiya, V. K., Dahiya, R., Dev, R., Sharma, A., Sharma, A., Kiran, P. B. N., Yadav, P. S., & Yadav, S. (2024). Exploring the role of artificial intelligence in predictive analytics for financial markets. In *Proceedings of the 2024 International Conference on Computing, Sciences and Communications (ICCSC 2024)*. DOI: 10.1109/ICCSC62048.2024.10830442

Darwish, F. S. M. (2025). Financial literacy and investment decision: An empirical study from the Palestine Stock Exchange. *Frontiers in Behavioral Economics, 4*, 1444022. DOI: 10.3389/frbhe.2025.1444022

De Almcida, P. G. R., Santos, C. D. D., & Farias, J. S. (2021). Artificial Intelligence Regulation: A framework for governance. *Ethics and Information Technology, 23*(3), 505–525. DOI: 10.1007/s10676-021-09593-z

De Carvalho, P. S. (2022). Retaining Influence in Post-Brexit International Financial Regulation: Lessons from the UK's FinTech Framework. *Journal of Financial Regulation, 8*(1), 104–131. DOI: 10.1093/jfr/fjac004

Dechow, P. M., Ge, W., Larson, C. R., & Sloan, R. G. (2011). Predicting material accounting misstatements. *Contemporary Accounting Research, 28*(1), 17–82. DOI: 10.1111/j.1911-3846.2010.01041.x

Dehimi, N. E. H., & Tolba, Z. (2024, April). Attention mechanisms in deep learning: Towards explainable artificial intelligence. In 2024 6th International Conference on Pattern Analysis and Intelligent Systems (PAIS) (pp. 1-7). IEEE. DOI: 10.1109/PAIS62114.2024.10541203

Del Sarto, N., & Ozili, P. K. (2025). FinTech and financial inclusion in emerging markets: A bibliometric analysis and future research agenda. *International Journal of Emerging Markets, 20*(13), 270–290. DOI: 10.1108/IJOEM-08-2024-1428

Deliema, M., Shadel, D., & Pak, K. (2019). Profiling Victims of Investment Fraud: Mindsets and Risky Behaviors. *The Journal of Consumer Research, 46*(5), 904–914. DOI: 10.1093/jcr/ucz020

Devan, M., Tillu, R., & Shanmugam, L. (2023). Personalized Financial Recommendations: Real-Time AI-ML Analytics in Wealth Management. *Journal of Knowledge Learning and Science Technology ISSN: 2959-6386 (Online), 2*(3), 547–559. DOI: 10.60087/jklst.vol2.n3.p559

Dichev, A., Zarkova, S., & Angelov, P. (2025). Machine learning as a tool for assessment and management of fraud risk in banking transactions. *Journal of Risk and Financial Management, 18*(3), 130. DOI: 10.3390/jrfm18030130

Din, F. U., & Anwer, S. (2013). ERP success and logistical performance indicators: A critical view. *International Journal of Computer Science Issues, 10*(6), 223–229.

Dramé-Maigné, S., Laurent, M., Castillo, L., & Ganem, H. (2021). Centralized, Distributed, and Everything in between. *ACM Computing Surveys, 54*(7), 1–34. DOI: 10.1145/3465170

Drew, J. M. (2020, April 22). A study of cybercrime victimisation and prevention: Exploring the use of online crime prevention behaviours and strategies. *Journal of Criminological Research, Policy and Practice, 6*(1), 17–33. DOI: 10.1108/JCRPP-12-2019-0070

Dudík, M., Chen, W., Barocas, S., Inchiosa, M., Lewins, N., Oprescu, M., Qiao, J., Sameki, M., Schlener, M., Tuo, J., & Wallach, H. (2020). Assessing and mitigating unfairness in credit models with the fairlearn toolkit. *White paper. URL:* https:// tinyurl. com/2x37jece

Due-Gundersen, N., & Owtram, F. (2022). The Foundation, Development and Future of the Omani Rentier State: From the Dhofar War to Vision 2040. *Arabian Humanities, 16*. Advance online publication. DOI: 10.4000/cy.8328

Du, W., & Chen, M. (2023). Too much or less? The effect of financial literacy on resident fraud victimization. *Computers in Human Behavior, 148*, 107914. DOI: 10.1016/j.chb.2023.107914

Dwork, C., Hardt, M., Pitassi, T., Reingold, O., & Zemel, R. (2012, January). Fairness through awareness. In *Proceedings of the 3rd innovations in theoretical computer science conference* (pp. 214-226). DOI: 10.1145/2090236.2090255

Engle, R. F. (1982). Autoregressive conditional heteroscedasticity with estimates of the variance of United Kingdom inflation. *Econometrica, 50*(4), 987–1007. DOI: 10.2307/1912773

European Parliament. (2025 Feb. 19). "EU AI Act: First Regulation on Artificial Intelligence." *European Parliament*. Retrieved from www.europarl.europa.eu/topics/en/article/20230601STO93804/eu-ai-act-first-regulation-on-artificial-intelligence

Everitt, B. S., Landau, S., Leese, M., & Stahl, D. (2011). *Cluster analysis* (5th ed.). Wiley. DOI: 10.1002/9780470977811

Faisal, S. M., Khan, W., & Ishrat, M. (2025). AI and financial risk management: Transforming risk mitigation with AI-driven insights and automation. In *Artificial intelligence for financial risk management and analysis* (pp. 281–305).

Fama, E. F. (1970). Efficient capital markets: A review of theory and empirical work. *The Journal of Finance, 25*(2), 383–417. DOI: 10.2307/2325486

Fasanya, I. O., Oyewole, O. J., Adekoya, O. B., & Badaru, F. O. (2021). Oil price and stock market behaviour in GCC countries: Do asymmetries and structural breaks matter? *Energy Strategy Reviews, 36*, 100682. DOI: 10.1016/j.esr.2021.100682

Fischer, T., & Krauss, C. (2018). Deep learning with long short-term memory networks for financial market predictions. *European Journal of Operational Research, 270*(2), 654–669. DOI: 10.1016/j.ejor.2017.11.054

Fligstein, N., & Roehrkasse, A. F. (2016). The Causes of Fraud in the Financial Crisis of 2007 to 2009. *American Sociological Review, 81*(4), 617–643. DOI: 10.1177/0003122416645594

Föge, N., Pauly, M., Schmid, L., & Ditzhaus, M. (2024). From naive trees to Random Forests: A general approach for proofing consistency of tree-based methods. *arXiv*. https://arxiv.org/abs/2404.06850

Foorthuis, R. (2021). On the nature and types of anomalies: A review of deviations in data. *International Journal of Data Science and Analytics*, *12*(4), 297–331. DOI: 10.1007/s41060-021-00265-1 PMID: 34368422

Freeda, A. R., Anju, A., Kanthavel, R., Dhaya, R., & Vijay, F. (2024). Integrating AI-Driven technologies into service marketing. In *Advances in marketing, customer relationship management, and e-services book series* (pp. 375–394). DOI: 10.4018/979-8-3693-7122-0.ch018

Friedler, S. A., Scheidegger, C., Venkatasubramanian, S., Choudhary, S., Hamilton, E. P., & Roth, D. (2019, January). A comparative study of fairness-enhancing interventions in machine learning. In *Proceedings of the conference on fairness, accountability, and transparency* (pp. 329-338). DOI: 10.1145/3287560.3287589

FTC. 2024, Federal trade commission, retrieved on 15th september 2025 from https://www.ftc.gov/news-events/news/press-releases/2025/03/new-ftc-data-show-big-jump-reported-losses-fraud-125-billion-2024

Gao, J., Siddik, A. B., Khawar Abbas, S., Hamayun, M., Masukujjaman, M., & Alam, S. S. (2023). Impact of e-commerce and digital marketing adoption on the financial and sustainability performance of MSMEs during the COVID-19 pandemic: An empirical study. *Sustainability (Basel)*, *15*(2), 1594. Advance online publication. DOI: 10.3390/su15021594

Gebru, T., Morgenstern, J., Vecchione, B., Vaughan, J. W., Wallach, H., Iii, H. D., & Crawford, K. (2021). Datasheets for datasets. *Communications of the ACM*, *64*(12), 86–92. DOI: 10.1145/3458723

Ghysels, E., Santa-Clara, P., & Valkanov, R. (2006). Predicting volatility: Getting the most out of return data sampled at different frequencies. *Journal of Econometrics*, *131*(1-2), 59–95. DOI: 10.1016/j.jeconom.2005.01.004

Giumelli, F., & Onderco, M. (2021). States, firms, and security: How private actors implement sanctions, lessons learned from the Netherlands. *European Journal of International Security*, *6*(2), 190–209. DOI: 10.1017/eis.2020.21

Glenda, M. (2024). Financial literacy and its role in promoting sustainable investment. *World Journal of Advanced Research and Reviews*, *24*(1), 212–232. DOI: 10.30574/wjarr.2024.24.1.2986

Goel, M., Tomar, P. K., Vinjamuri, L. P., Reddy, G. S., Al-Taee, M., & Alazzam, M. B. (2023). Using AI for predictive analytics in financial management. In *Proceedings of the 2023 3rd International Conference on Advance Computing and Innovative Technologies in Engineering (ICACITE 2023)* (pp. 963–967). DOI: 10.1109/ICACITE57410.2023.10182711

Goodman, B., & Flaxman, S. (2017). European Union regulations on algorithmic decision-making and a "right to explanation". *AI Magazine*, *38*(3), 50–57. DOI: 10.1609/aimag.v38i3.2741

Goswami, V., Joshi, V. K., & Sharma, G. (2024). Unveiling the Investment Behaviour of Gen Y and Z: A Study on Artificial Intelligence Stocks Awareness and Decision-Making. In A. Tripathi, S. Birla, M. Soni, J. Sahariya, & M. Sharma, *multidisciplinary approaches for sustainable development* (1st ed., pp. 321–327). CRC Press. DOI: 10.1201/9781003543633-52

Gottschalk, P. (2010). Categories of financial crime. *Journal of Financial Crime*, *17*(4), 441–458. DOI: 10.1108/13590791011082797

Gupta, S., & Sajjan, S. (2025). The Impact of Artificial Intelligence on Financial Decision Making and Risk Management. In P. Mittal & P. K. Gupta (Eds.), *Integrating Management Principles with Business Analytics Concepts and Applications* (pp. 14–28). QTanalytics India. DOI: 10.48001/978-81-980647-9-0-2

Gupta, P. (2023). Leveraging machine learning and artificial intelligence for fraud prevention. *SSRG International Journal of Computer Science and Engineering*, *10*(5), 47–52. DOI: 10.14445/23488387/IJCSE-V10I5P107

Gupta, R., & Singh Gill, N. (2012). A data mining framework for prevention and detection of financial statement fraud. *International Journal of Computer Applications*, *50*(8), 7–14. DOI: 10.5120/7789-0889

Hajek, P., & Henriques, R. (2017). Mining corporate annual reports for intelligent detection of financial statement fraud – A comparative study of machine learning methods. *Knowledge-Based Systems*, *128*, 139–152. DOI: 10.1016/j.knosys.2017.05.001

Hakimi, A., Saidi, H., & Adili, L. (2025). Achieving a More Inclusive Financial System: What Does the MENA Region Need? A Sensitivity Analysis for GCC and Non-GCC Countries. *Economies (Basel)*, *13*(7), 190. DOI: 10.3390/economies13070190

Hammad Naeem, M., Subhan, M., Alam, M. S., Al-Faryan, M. A. S., & Yameen, M. (2023). Examining the role of financial innovation on economic growth: Fresh empirical evidence from developing and developed countries. *Cogent Economics & Finance*, *11*(1), 2170000. DOI: 10.1080/23322039.2023.2170000

Han, J., Huang, Y., Liu, S., & Towey, K. (2020). Artificial intelligence for anti-money laundering: A review and extension. *Digital Finance*, *2*(3-4), 211–239. DOI: 10.1007/s42521-020-00023-1

Hardt, M., Price, E., & Srebro, N. (2016). Equality of opportunity in supervised learning. *Advances in Neural Information Processing Systems*, •••, 29.

Hasnat, M. A., Hasan, K. K., & Khandakar, H. (2025). Intelligent machines and organizational knowledge transformation in Bangladesh's Islamic banking sector: Navigating innovation and Shariah compliance. *Journal of Integrated Islamic Finance and Socio-Economic Systems*, *1*, 11–28. DOI: 10.65638/2978-8196.2025.01.02

Hastie, T., Tibshirani, R., & Friedman, J. (2009). *The elements of statistical learning: Data mining, inference, and prediction* (2nd ed.). Springer. DOI: 10.1007/978-0-387-84858-7

He, G. (2015). The effect of CEO inside debt holdings on financial reporting quality. *Review of Accounting Studies*, *20*(1), 501–536. DOI: 10.1007/s11142-014-9305-8

He, G., Li, Z., & Shen, D. (2022). The role of earnings management in equity valuation. In Lee, C., & Lee, A. (Eds.), *Encyclopedia of Finance* (pp. 2061–2094). Springer Nature. DOI: 10.1007/978-3-030-91231-4_90

Hesami, S. (2025). Navigating the AI-driven transformation of personal finance: Opportunities, challenges, and ethical imperatives. *Strategy and Leadership*. Advance online publication. DOI: 10.1108/SL-02-2025-0019

Hilbert, L. P., Noordewier, M. K., & Van Dijk, W. W. (2022). Financial scarcity increases discounting of gains and losses: Experimental evidence from a household task. *Journal of Economic Psychology*, *92*, 102546. DOI: 10.1016/j.joep.2022.102546

Hochreiter, S., & Schmidhuber, J. (1997). Long short-term memory. *Neural Computation*, *9*(8), 1735–1780. DOI: 10.1162/neco.1997.9.8.1735 PMID: 9377276

Hong, J., Zhu, Z., Yu, S., Wang, Z., Dodge, H. H., & Zhou, J. (2021, August). Federated adversarial debiasing for fair and transferable representations. In *Proceedings of the 27th ACM SIGKDD Conference on Knowledge Discovery & Data Mining* (pp. 617-627). DOI: 10.1145/3447548.3467281

Hossain, M. E., & Biswas, S. (2024). Technology acceptance model for understanding consumer's behavioral intention to use artificial intelligence based online shopping platforms in Bangladesh. *SN Business & Economics*, *4*(12), 153. Advance online publication. DOI: 10.1007/s43546-024-00754-y

Hossain, M. R., Rao, A., Sharma, G. D., Dev, D., & Kharbanda, A. (2024). Empowering energy transition: Green innovation, digital finance, and the path to sustainable prosperity through green finance initiatives. *Energy Economics*, *136*, 107736. DOI: 10.1016/j.eneco.2024.107736

Hossain, T., & Siddiqua, P. (2024). Exploring the influence of behavioral aspects on stock investment decision-making: A study on Bangladeshi individual investors. *PSU Research Review*, *8*(2), 467–483. DOI: 10.1108/PRR-10-2021-0054

Hou, R., Ye, X., Zaki, H. B. O., & Omar, N. A. B. (2023). Marketing decision support system based on data mining technology. *Applied Sciences (Basel, Switzerland)*, *13*(7), 4315. Advance online publication. DOI: 10.3390/app13074315

How, M., Cheah, S., Khor, A., & Chan, Y. (2020). Artificial intelligence-enhanced predictive insights for advancing financial inclusion: A human-centric AI-thinking approach. *Big Data and Cognitive Computing*, *4*(2), 8. DOI: 10.3390/bdcc4020008

Hussain, M., & Rehman, R. U. (2023). Volatility connectedness of GCC stock markets: How global oil price volatility drives volatility spillover in GCC stock markets? *Environmental Science and Pollution Research International*, *30*(6), 14212–14222. DOI: 10.1007/s11356-022-23114-5 PMID: 36138292

Ibrahim, A., Almasria, N. A., Alhatabat, Z. A., Ershaid, D. J. A., & Aldboush, H. H. (2024). Transforming financial services with artificial intelligence and machine learning. In *Advances in finance, accounting, and economics book series* (pp. 129–148). DOI: 10.4018/979-8-3693-8507-4.ch008

Imjai, N., Yordudom, T., Yaacob, Z., Saad, N. H. M., & Aujirapongpan, S. (2025). Impact of AI literacy and adaptability on financial analyst skills among prospective Thai accountants: The role of critical thinking. *Technological Forecasting and Social Change*, *210*, 123889. DOI: 10.1016/j.techfore.2024.123889

Ishrat, M., Khan, W., & Faisal, S. M. (2025). AI and risk forecasting: Leveraging AI for environmental, social, and governance compliance. In *Artificial intelligence for financial risk management and analysis* (pp. 307–334).

Islam, K. U., Bhat, S. A., Lone, U. M., Darzi, M. A., & Malik, I. A. (2024). Financial risk propensity and investment decisions: An empirical analysis using behavioural biases. *IIMB Management Review*, *36*(3), 213–229. DOI: 10.1016/j.iimb.2024.06.004

Islam, M. S., Ahmed, F., Islam, M. M., Rehman, A. U., & Alam, M. F. (2025). The impact of oil price shocks on oil and gas production amidst geopolitical risk in OPEC: Insights from method of moments quantile regression. *Journal of the Knowledge Economy*, *16*(2), 9776–9805. DOI: 10.1007/s13132-024-02296-y

Islam, S., Rezaul Karim, A. N. M., & Haque, M. M. (2024). A rule-based machine learning model for financial fraud detection. [IJECE]. *International Journal of Electrical and Computer Engineering*, *14*(1), 759. DOI: 10.11591/ijece.v14i1.pp759-771

Ismaeil, M. K. A. (2024). Harnessing AI for next-generation financial fraud detection: A data-driven revolution. *Journal of Ecohumanism*, *3*(7), 811–821. DOI: 10.62754/joe.v3i7.4248

Jain, V., & Kulkarni, P. A. (2023). Integrating AI Techniques for Enhanced Financial Forecasting and Budgeting Strategies. *International Journal of Economics and Management Studies*, *10*(09), 9–15. DOI: 10.14445/23939125/IJEMS-V10I9P102

James, G., Witten, D., Hastie, T., & Tibshirani, R. (2013). *An introduction to statistical learning*. Springer. DOI: 10.1007/978-1-4614-7138-7

Jannah, N., Bahri, M. I., Kismawadi, E. R., & Handriana, T. (2024). The effect of green brand image and green satisfaction on green brand equity mediated green trust outpatient's. *Quality - Access to Success*, *25*(198), 381–390. DOI: 10.47750/QAS/25.198.40

Janzen, M. (2021). *Data Monetization in Capital Markets* (pp. 1–27). Arab-Exchange.org. https://arab-exchanges.org/upload/9271websiteData%20Monetization%20En.pdf

Javanmardi, E., Maresova, P., Xie, N., & Mierzwiak, R. (2024). Exploring business models for managing uncertainty in healthcare, medical devices, and biotechnology industries. *Heliyon*, *10*(4), e25962. Advance online publication. DOI: 10.1016/j.heliyon.2024.e25962 PMID: 38370194

Jhaveri, S., Khedkar, I., Kantharia, Y., & Jaswal, S. (2019). Success prediction using Random Forest, Catboost, XGboost and Adaboost for kickstarter campaigns. In *2019 3rd international conference on computing methodologies and communication (ICCMC)* (pp. 1170–1173). IEEE.

Jlifi, B., Medini, M., & Duvallet, C. (2024). A guided genetic algorithm-based ensemble voting of polynomial regression and LSTM (GGA-PolReg-LSTM) for congestion prediction using IoT and air quality data in sustainable cities. *The Journal of Supercomputing*, *80*(13), 18797–18837. DOI: 10.1007/s11227-024-06186-7

Johri, A., Wasiq, M., Kaur, H., & Asif, M. (2023). Assessment of users' adoption behaviour for stock market investment through online applications. *Heliyon*, *9*(9), e19524. DOI: 10.1016/j.heliyon.2023.e19524

Joshi, S., Mahanthi, B. L., Pokkuluri, K. S., Ninawe, S. S., & Sahu, R. (2025). Integrating LSTM and CNN for Stock Market Prediction: A Dynamic Machine Learning Approach. *Journal of Artificial Intelligence and Technology*, *5*, 168–179. DOI: 10.37965/jait.2025.0652

Kadir, S., Rah, A. R., & Yusuf, N. I. A. (2023). Getting to know non-fungible tokens (NFT) and decentralized finance (DeFi) in the era of Society 5.0. *International Journal of Islamic Finance*, *1*(2), 149–162. DOI: 10.14421/ijif.v1i2.2020

Kallus, N., & Zhou, A. (2018, July). Residual unfairness in fair machine learning from prejudiced data. In *International Conference on Machine Learning* (pp. 2439-2448). PMLR.

Karami Nasrabad Sofla, K. (2024). Investigating the Role of Artificial Intelligence in Predicting Consumer Preferences (A Little Study in the Tehran Market). *International Journal of Applied Research in Management. Economics and Accounting*, *1*(4), 27–40. DOI: 10.63053/ijmea.28

Kashefi, P., Kashefi, Y., & Mirsaraei, A. G. (2024). *Shaping the future of AI: balancing innovation and ethics in global regulation.* Uniform Law Review., DOI: 10.1093/ulr/unae040

Katamaneni, M., Agrawal, P., Veera, S., Sahoo, A. K., Sidhu, K. S., & Hasan, M. F. (2024). AI-based risk management in financial services. In *Proceedings of the 2024 2nd International Conference on Computational and Characterization Techniques in Engineering and Sciences (IC3TES 2024).*

Kataria, A. N., Zaveri, T. H., Adhyaru, D. M., & Sharma, A. K. (2013). A survey of automated biometric authentication techniques. 1–6. DOI: 10.1109/NUiCONE.2013.6780190

Katnic, I., Katnic, M., Orlandic, M., Radunovic, M., & Mugosa, I. (2024). Understanding the Role of Financial Literacy in Enhancing Economic Stability and Resilience in Montenegro: A Data-Driven Approach. *Sustainability (Basel)*, *16*(24), 11065. DOI: 10.3390/su162411065

Kayani, U., & Hasan, F. (2024). Unveiling Cryptocurrency impact on financial markets and traditional banking Systems: Lessons for sustainable blockchain and interdisciplinary Collaborations. *Journal of Risk and Financial Management*, *17*(2), 58. DOI: 10.3390/jrfm17020058

Kernel Methods in Computational Biology. (2004). Massachusetts Institute Of Technology. DOI: 10.7551/mitpress/4057.001.0001

Khan, W., Ishrat, M., & Faisal, S. M. (2025). AI-powered risk assessment: Innovations, challenges, and future prospects. In *Artificial intelligence for financial risk management and analysis* (pp. 59–91).

Khan, M. S., Azad, I., Moosa, S., & Javed, M. Y. (2024). Do we really need financial literacy to access the behavioral dynamics of generation Z? A case of Oman. *Heliyon, 10*(13), e32739. DOI: 10.1016/j.heliyon.2024.e32739

Khemakhem, S., Said, F., & Boujelbène, Y. (2018). Credit risk assessment for unbalanced datasets based on data mining, artificial neural network and support vector machines. *Journal of Modelling in Management, 13*(4), 932–951. DOI: 10.1108/JM2-01-2017-0002

Kismawadi, E. R. (2024). Sustainable Islamic financial inclusion: The ethical challenges of generative AI in product and service development. In *Exploring the ethical implications of generative AI* (pp. 237–258).

Kismawadi, E. R., Irfan, M., Al Muddatstsir, U. D., & Abdulkarim, F. M. (2023). Fintech innovations: Risk mitigation strategies in Islamic finance. In *Fintech applications in Islamic finance: AI, machine learning, and blockchain techniques* (pp. 35–58).

Kleinberg, J., Ludwig, J., Mullainathan, S., & Rambachan, A. (2018, May). Algorithmic fairness. In *Aea papers and proceedings* (Vol. 108, pp. 22-27). 2014 Broadway, Suite 305, Nashville, TN 37203: American Economic Association. DOI: 10.1257/pandp.20181018

Kleinberg, J., Mullainathan, S., & Raghavan, M. (2016). Inherent trade-offs in the fair determination of risk scores. *arXiv preprint arXiv:1609.05807.*

Klitkou, A., Bolwig, S., Huber, A., Ingeborgrud, L., Pluciński, P., Rohracher, H., Schartinger, D., Thiene, M., & Żuk, P. (2022). The interconnected dynamics of social practices and their implications for transformative change: A review. *Sustainable Production and Consumption, 31*, 603–614. DOI: 10.1016/j.spc.2022.03.027

Kobi, J. (2024). Developing Dashboard Analytics and Visualization Tools for Effective Performance Management and Continuous Process Improvement. *International Journal of Innovative Science and Research Technology (IJISRT)*, 1697–1709. DOI: 10.38124/ijisrt/IJISRT24MAY1147

Kordzadeh, N., & Ghasemaghaei, M. (2022). Algorithmic bias: Review, synthesis, and future research directions. *European Journal of Information Systems*, *31*(3), 388–409. DOI: 10.1080/0960085X.2021.1927212

Koskelainen, T., Kalmi, P., Scornavacca, E., & Vartiainen, T. (2023). Financial literacy in the digital age—A research agenda. *The Journal of Consumer Affairs*, *57*(1), 507–528. DOI: 10.1111/joca.12510

Kou, Y., Lu, C.-T., Sirwongwattana, S., & Huang, Y.-P. (2004). Survey of Fraud Detection

Kour, M., & Schutte, D. P. (2025a). Artificial intelligence and accounting. In *Routledge eBooks*. DOI: 10.4324/9781003571643

Kroen, T. (2024). *A Financial Sector for the Economy of the Future: Oman* (No. 9798400278778; pp. 1–16). IMF. https://www.imf.org/en/Publications/selected-issues-papers/Issues/2024/06/12/A-Financial-Sector-for-the-Economy-of-the-Future-Oman-550249

Krupa, J., & Minutti-Meza, M. (2022). Regression and machine learning methods to predict discrete outcomes in accounting research. *Journal of Financial Reporting*, *7*(2), 131–178. DOI: 10.2308/JFR-2021-010

Kurshan, E., & Shen, H. (2020). Graph Computing for Financial Crime and Fraud Detection: Trends, Challenges and Outlook. *International Journal of Semantic Computing*, *14*(04), 565–589. DOI: 10.1142/S1793351X20300022

Lakoni, I., Nurazi, R., Aziza, N., & Novitasari, N. (2023). Relationship of financial literacy to stock market participation. *Journal of Economics and Business Letters*, *3*(6). Advance online publication. DOI: 10.55942/jebl.v3i6.270

Lakshmi, Y. (2024). The Impact Of Artificial Intelligence On Financial Literacy. *ShodhKosh: Journal of Visual and Performing Arts*, *5*(5). Advance online publication. DOI: 10.29121/shodhkosh.v5.i5.2024.1606

Lalchand, S., Srinivas, V., Maggiore, B., & Henderson, J. (2024, May 29). Generative AI is expected to magnify the risk of deepfakes and other fraud in banking. Financial Services. https://www.deloitte.com/us/en/insights/industry/financial-services/deepfake-banking-fraud-risk-on-the-rise.html

Lang, N. D., Tran, H. M., Nguyen, G. T., & Vo, D. H. (2024). An Untapped Instrument in the Fight Against Poverty: The Impacts of Financial Literacy on Poverty Worldwide. *Social Indicators Research*, *174*(2), 657–695. DOI: 10.1007/s11205-024-03404-w

Li, Y., Chen, L., Dong, W., Gong, S., Kang, Z., Wei, B., . . . Wang, N. (2025). Information bottleneck-guided heterogeneous graph learning for interpretable neurodevelopmental disorder diagnosis. arXiv preprint arXiv:2502.20769.

Litsas, S. N. (2023). Internal and External Challenges for the Years to Come. In Smart Instead of Small in International Relations Theory: The Case of the United Arab Emirates (pp. 145-192). Cham: Springer Nature Switzerland. DOI: 10.1007/978-3-031-44637-5_7

Liu, X., Zhou, C., Li, Y., & Fang, F. (2025). How economic stability shapes social relationship expenditures: Moderating effects of health and education. *International Review of Economics & Finance*, *99*, 104041. DOI: 10.1016/j.iref.2025.104041

Loukas, O., & Chung, H. R. (2023). Demographic parity: Mitigating biases in real-world data. *arXiv preprint arXiv:2309.17347.*

Lusardi, A., & Mitchell, O. (2009). *How Ordinary Consumers Make Complex Economic Decisions: Financial Literacy and Retirement Readiness* (No. w15350; p. w15350). National Bureau of Economic Research. DOI: 10.3386/w15350

Lusardi, A. (2019). Financial literacy and the need for financial education: Evidence and implications. *Swiss Journal of Economics and Statistics*, *155*(1), 1. DOI: 10.1186/s41937-019-0027-5

Lyons, A., & Kass-Hanna, J. (2018). Financial Inclusion, Financial Literacy and Economically Vulnerable Populations in the Middle East and North Africa. SSRN *Electronic Journal*. DOI: 10.2139/ssrn.3189563

Machucho, R., & Ortiz, D. (2025). The Impacts of Artificial Intelligence on Business Innovation: A Comprehensive Review of Applications, Organizational Challenges, and Ethical Considerations. *Systems*, *13*(4), 264. DOI: 10.3390/systems13040264

Mahaney, J. (2024). *Artificial Intelligence: Shaping the Future of Financial Literacy. SSRN*. DOI: 10.2139/ssrn.4866396

Marotta, G., & Au, C.-D. (2022). Budgeting in the Age of Artificial Intelligence – New Approaches, Old Challenges? *International Journal of Artificial Intelligence and Machine Learning*, *2*(2), 1–11. DOI: 10.51483/IJAIML.2.2.2022.1-11

Marzuki, N. A. A. B. (2024). *The Influence of Technology in Personal Finance Management*. DOI: 10.13140/RG.2.2.16119.02727

Masood, F. (2024). Impact of Artificial Intelligence on Financial Markets. *International Journal of Emerging Multidisciplinaries: Social Science*, *3*(1), 8. DOI: 10.54938/ijemdss.2024.03.1.359

Meenakshi, A., & Jayakani, S. (2025). Exploring the impact of artificial intelligence on financial risk prediction and management. In *AIP Conference Proceedings* (Vol. 3306). DOI: 10.1063/5.0276529

Mehrabi, N., Morstatter, F., Saxena, N., Lerman, K., & Galstyan, A. (2021). A survey on bias and fairness in machine learning. *ACM Computing Surveys*, *54*(6), 1–35. DOI: 10.1145/3457607

Memish, Z. A., Altuwaijri, M. M., Almoeen, A. H., & Enani, S. M. (2021). The Saudi Data & Artificial Intelligence Authority (SDAIA) vision: Leading the kingdom's journey toward global leadership. *Journal of Epidemiology and Global Health*, *11*(2), 140–142. DOI: 10.2991/jegh.k.210405.001 PMID: 33876596

Menberu, A. W. (2024). Technology-mediated financial education in developing countries: A systematic literature review. *Cogent Business & Management*, *11*(1), 2294879. DOI: 10.1080/23311975.2023.2294879

Miao, Z. (2024). Financial Fraud Detection and Prevention. *Journal of Organizational and End User Computing*, *36*(1), 1–27. DOI: 10.4018/JOEUC.354411

Michailidis, M., Zafeiriou, E., Kantartzis, A., Galatsidas, S., & Arabatzis, G. (2025). Governance, Energy Policy, and Sustainable Development: Renewable Energy Infrastructure Transition in Developing MENA Countries. *Energies*, *18*(11), 2759. DOI: 10.3390/en18112759

Mienye, I. D., & Jere, N. (2024). A survey of decision trees: Concepts, algorithms, and applications. *IEEE Access : Practical Innovations, Open Solutions*, *12*, 86716–86727. Advance online publication. DOI: 10.1109/ACCESS.2024.3416838

Mienye, I. D., & Jere, N. (2024). Deep Learning for Credit Card Fraud Detection: A Review of Algorithms, Challenges, and Solutions. *IEEE Access : Practical Innovations, Open Solutions*, *12*, 96893–96910. DOI: 10.1109/ACCESS.2024.3426955

Minkkinen, M., Zimmer, M. P., & Mäntymäki, M. (2022). Co-Shaping an ecosystem for responsible AI: Five types of expectation work in response to a technological frame. *Information Systems Frontiers*, *25*(1), 103–121. DOI: 10.1007/s10796-022-10269-2

Mircku, K., Appiah, F., & Agana, J. A. (2023). Is there a link between financial literacy and financial behaviour? *Cogent Economics & Finance*, *11*(1), 2188712. DOI: 10.1080/23322039.2023.2188712

Mirzaei, M., & Buer, T. (2022). First results on financial literacy in Oman. *Managerial Finance*, *48*(9/10), 1413–1429. DOI: 10.1108/MF-09-2021-0456

Mitchell, M., Wu, S., Zaldivar, A., Barnes, P., Vasserman, L., Hutchinson, B., Spitzer, E., Raji, I. D., & Gebru, T. (2019, January). Model cards for model reporting. In *Proceedings of the conference on fairness, accountability, and transparency* (pp. 220-229). DOI: 10.1145/3287560.3287596

Mohamed, N. (2025). Artificial intelligence and machine learning in cybersecurity: A deep dive into state-of-the-art techniques and future paradigms. *Knowledge and Information Systems*, *67*(8), 6969–7055. DOI: 10.1007/s10115-025-02429-y

Mohammad, N., Khatoon, R., Sharmin, S., Imran, M. A. U., & Prabha, M. (2024). Combating banking fraud with it: integrating machine learning and data analytics. *The American Journal of Management and Economics Innovations*, *6*(7), 39–56. DOI: 10.37547/tajmei/Volume06Issue07-04

Monamo, P., Marivate, V., & Twala, B. (2016). Unsupervised learning for robust Bitcoin fraud detection. 129–134. DOI: 10.1109/ISSA.2016.7802939

Morán Dávila, R. C., Castillo Sáenz, R. A., Vargas Murillo, A. R., García Huamantumba, E., Velarde Dávila, L., Pasquel Cajas, R. F., García Huamantumba, C. F., & Guanilo Paredes, C. E. (2023). Application of Machine Learning Models in Fraud Detection in Financial Transactions. *Data and Metadata*, *2*, 109. DOI: 10.56294/dm2023109

Mor, S., Aneja, R., Madan, S., & Gupta, S. (2022). Artificial intelligence and loan default: The case of commercial banks in India. *Strategic Change*, *31*(6), 571–580. DOI: 10.1002/jsc.2529

Mougan, C., State, L., Ferrara, A., Ruggieri, S., & Staab, S. (2023). Beyond demographic parity: Redefining equal treatment. *arXiv preprint arXiv:2303.08040.*

Mujahid, M., Kına, E. R. O. L., Rustam, F., Villar, M. G., Alvarado, E. S., De La Torre Diez, I., & Ashraf, I. (2024). Data oversampling and imbalanced datasets: An investigation of performance for machine learning and feature engineering. *Journal of Big Data*, *11*(1), 87. DOI: 10.1186/s40537-024-00943-4

Mukherjee, M., & Khushi, M. (2021). SMOTE-ENC: A novel SMOTE-based method to generate synthetic data for nominal and continuous features. *Applied System Innovation*, *4*(1), 18. DOI: 10.3390/asi4010018

Mulia Pratama, I. (2021). Effects of Age, Gender and Education Level on Financial Literacy Level (Study of Vocational School Teachers in Padang City). *Economica*, *9*(1), 143–150. DOI: 10.22202/economica.2020.v9.i2.4606

Mustaffha, N. (2024). Financial justice and sustainable development: Reviving Maqasid Al-Shariah for a changing world. *Progress in Islamic Banking and Finance, 1*(1), 30–41.

Mytnyk, B., Tkachyk, O., Shakhovska, N., Fedushko, S., & Syerov, Y. (2023). Application of artificial intelligence for fraudulent banking operations recognition. *Big Data and Cognitive Computing*, *7*(2), 93. DOI: 10.3390/bdcc7020093

Naeem, M. A., Arfaoui, N., & Yarovaya, L. (2025). The contagion effect of artificial intelligence across innovative industries: From blockchain and metaverse to cleantech and beyond. *Technological Forecasting and Social Change*, *210*, 123822. DOI: 10.1016/j.techfore.2024.123822

Najem, R., Bahnasse, A., Fakhouri Amr, M., & Talea, M. (2025). Advanced AI and big data techniques in E-finance: A comprehensive survey. *Discover Artificial Intelligence*, *5*(1), 102. DOI: 10.1007/s44163-025-00365-y

Najib, F., Nawawi, Z. M., & Tambunan, K. (2025). Digital payment, support, and ethics drive micro and small business income. *Academia Open*, *10*(1), 10–21070. DOI: 10.21070/acopen.10.2025.11091

Nayeem, T. (2012). Cultural Influences on Consumer Behaviour. *International Journal of Business and Management*, *7*(21), 78. DOI: 10.5539/ijbm.v7n21p78

Nie, F., Hao, Z., & Wang, R. (2024). Multi-class support vector machine with maximizing minimum margin. *Proceedings of the AAAI Conference on Artificial Intelligence*, *38*(13), 14466–14473. DOI: 10.1609/aaai.v38i13.29361

Nogueira, M. C., Almeida, L., & Tavares, F. O. (2025a). Financial Literacy, Financial Knowledge, and Financial Behaviors in OECD Countries. *Journal of Risk and Financial Management*, *18*(3), 167. DOI: 10.3390/jrfm18030167

Noviandy, T. R., Idroes, G. M., Maulana, A., Hardi, I., Ringga, E. S., & Idroes, R. (2023). Credit Card Fraud Detection for Contemporary Financial Management Using XGBoost-Driven Machine Learning and Data Augmentation Techniques. *Indatu Journal of Management and Accounting*, *1*(1), 29–35. DOI: 10.60084/ijma.v1i1.78

Nuti, A. (2019). *Injustice and the reproduction of history: Structural inequalities, gender and redress*. Cambridge University Press. DOI: 10.1017/9781108325592

O'neil, C. (2017). *Weapons of math destruction: How big data increases inequality and threatens democracy*. Crown.

Oates, J., Shafiabady, N., Ambagtsheer, R., Beilby, J., Seiboth, C., & Dent, E. (2022). Evolving hybrid partial genetic algorithm classification model for cost-effective frailty screening: Investigative study. *JMIR Aging*, *5*(4), e38464. Advance online publication. DOI: 10.2196/38464 PMID: 36206042

Obeng, S., Iyelolu, T., Akinsulire, A., & Idemudia, C. (2024). Utilizing machine learning algorithms to prevent financial fraud and ensure transaction security. *World Journal of Advanced Research and Reviews*, *23*(1), 1972–1980. DOI: 10.30574/wjarr.2024.23.1.2185

Ochi, A., Nouaili, M., Saidi, Y., Haouas, A., & Saidi, A. (2025). Foreign Direct Investment and Economic Growth in Arab Countries: Do Institutions, Financial Development, and Knowledge Economy Matter? *Journal of the Knowledge Economy*, *17*(2), 5145–5179. Advance online publication. DOI: 10.1007/s13132-025-02794-7

Odeyemi, O., Soyombo, O., Nwankwo, E., & Mhlongo, N. (2024). Reviewing the role of AI in fraud detection and prevention in financial services. *International Journal of Science and Research Archive*, *11*(1), 2101–2110. DOI: 10.30574/ijsra.2024.11.1.0279

Olasiuk, H., Kumar, S., Singh, S., Nagpal, G., & Ganushchak, T. (2023). Exploring the thematic clusters of artificial intelligence applications in supply chains using topic modelling and text mining: A machine learning insight. In *Proceedings of the 4th IEEE International Conference on Smart Technologies in Computing, Electrical and Electronics (ICSTCEE 2023)*. DOI: 10.1109/ICSTCEE60504.2023.10584847

Olubusola, O., Mhlongo, N. Z., Daraojimba, D. O., Ajayi-Nifise, A. O., & Falaiye, T. (2024). Machine learning in financial forecasting: A US review: Exploring the advancements, challenges, and implications of AI-driven predictions in financial markets. *World Journal of Advanced Research and Reviews*, *21*(2), 1969–1984. DOI: 10.30574/wjarr.2024.21.2.0444

Onabowale, O. (2025). AI and Real-Time Financial Decision Support. *International Journal of Research Publication and Reviews*, *6*(6), 329–350. DOI: 10.55248/gengpi.6.0625.2260

Onyenahazi, O. B., & Antwi, B. O. (2024). The Role of Artificial Intelligence in Investment Decision-Making: Opportunities and Risks for Financial Institutions. *International Journal of Research Publication and Reviews*, *5*(10), 70–85. DOI: 10.55248/gengpi.5.1024.2701

Özveren, E. (2025). The Role of the State in the Big Picture of Economic Development: Mainstream-versus-Heterodox Approaches and Historical Evidence. *The Forum for Social Economics*, 1–32. DOI: 10.1080/07360932.2025.2507583

Padmavathy, M. (2024). Behavioral Finance and Stock Market Anomalies: Exploring Psychological Factors Influencing Investment Decisions. Shanlax International Journal of Management, 11(iS1-Jan), 191–197. DOI: 10.34293/management.v11iiS1-Jan.7164

Painsky, A., & Rosset, S. (2017). Cross-validated variable selection in tree-based methods improves predictive performance. *IEEE Transactions on Pattern Analysis and Machine Intelligence*, *39*(11), 2142–2153. DOI: 10.1109/TPAMI.2016.2636831 PMID: 28114007

Palakurti, N.Naga Ramesh Palakurti. (2023). Emerging Trends in Financial Fraud Detection: Machine Learning and Big Data Analytics in Risk Management. International Journal of Advanced Research in Science. *Tongxin Jishu*, , 625–635. DOI: 10.48175/IJARSCT-13555D

Palepu, K., & Healy, P. M. (2003). The Fall of Enron. *The Journal of Economic Perspectives*, *17*(2), 3–26. DOI: 10.1257/089533003765888403

Pang, G., Shen, C., Cao, L., & Hengel, A. V. D. (2021). Deep Learning for Anomaly Detection. *ACM Computing Surveys*, *54*(2), 1–38. DOI: 10.1145/3439950

Paramesha, M., Rane, N. L., & Rane, J. (2024). *Big Data Analytics, Artificial Intelligence, Machine Learning, Internet of Things, and Blockchain for Enhanced Business Intelligence*. DOI: 10.2139/ssrn.4855856

Pardhey, N., & Yuni, D. N. (2023). Legal efficiency of Secure Transactions Framework in India. In *Advances in finance, accounting, and economics book series* (pp. 171–182). DOI: 10.4018/979-8-3693-1038-0.ch011

Park, J., Na, H. J., & Kim, H. (2024). Development of a success prediction model for crowdfunding based on machine learning reflecting ESG information. *IEEE Access : Practical Innovations, Open Solutions*, *12*, 197275–197289. Advance online publication. DOI: 10.1109/ACCESS.2024.3519219

Parsai, P., & Chandok, A. K. (2025). The Role of Financial Literacy in Investment Decision-Making: A Review. *International Journal of Innovations in Science Engineering And Management*, 296–301. DOI: 10.69968/ijisem.2025v4i1296-301

Pattnaik, D., Ray, S., & Raman, R. (2024). Applications of artificial intelligence and machine learning in the financial services industry: A bibliometric review. *Heliyon*, *10*(1), e23492. DOI: 10.1016/j.heliyon.2023.e23492

Pazouki, S., Jamshidi, M., Jalali, M., & Tafreshi, A. (2025). Artificial Intelligence and Digital Technologies in Finance: A Comprehensive Review. *Journal of Economics. Finance and Accounting Studies*, *7*(2), 54–69. DOI: 10.32996/jefas.2025.7.2.5

Pereira, C. M. (2020). Unregulated Algorithmic trading: Testing the boundaries of the European Union Algorithmic Trading regime. *Journal of Financial Regulation, 6*(2), 270–305. DOI: 10.1093/jfr/fjaa008

Piryonesi, S. M., & El-Diraby, T. E. (2020). Role of data analytics in infrastructure asset management: Overcoming data size and quality problems. *Journal of Transportation Engineering. Part B, Pavements, 146*(2), 04020022. Advance online publication. DOI: 10.1061/JPEODX.0000175

Podkolzina, Irina & Belousov, Anatoliy & Uzdenova, Fatima & Romanko, Lyudmila & Chernikova, Olga. (2021). Forms of Financial Fraud and Ways to Minimize Risks. . DOI: 10.1007/978-3-030-69415-9_241

Qadeer, H., & Sarfraz, M. (2025). Capital Structure Choices: The Role of Financial Development and Institutional Quality. *The Critical Review of Social Sciences Studies, 3*(1), 2347–2363. DOI: 10.59075/j2sr6063

Qayoom, I., & Chisti, K. (2025). "Earnings transparency: A systematic review, integrated framework and future perspectives." *Journal of Financial Reporting and Accounting*. DOI: 10.1108/JFRA-11-2024-0815

Qiu, J., Wang, B., & Zhou, C. (2020). Forecasting stock prices with long-short term memory neural network based on attention mechanism. *PLoS One, 15*(1), e0227222. DOI: 10.1371/journal.pone.0227222 PMID: 31899770

Qu, L., & Pei, Y. (2024). A comprehensive review on discriminant analysis for addressing challenges of class-level limitations, small sample size, and robustness. *Processes (Basel, Switzerland), 12*(7), 1382. Advance online publication. DOI: 10.3390/pr12071382

Rahman, M., Isa, C. R., Masud, M. M., Sarker, M., & Chowdhury, N. T. (2021). The role of financial behaviour, financial literacy, and financial stress in explaining the financial well-being of B40 group in Malaysia. *Future Business Journal, 7*(1), 52. DOI: 10.1186/s43093-021-00099-0

Raschka, S. (2018). Model evaluation, model selection, and algorithm selection in machine learning. *arXiv preprint*, available at: https://arxiv.org/abs/1811.12808 (accessed 19 December 2024).

Ratmono, D., Darsono, D., & Cahyonowati, N. (2020). Financial Statement Fraud Detection with Beneish M-Score and Dechow F-Score Model: An Empirical Analysis of Fraud Pentagon Theory in Indonesia. *International Journal of Financial Research, 11*(6), 154. DOI: 10.5430/ijfr.v11n6p154

Rawal, R., Sachdeva, P., & Singhvi, A. S. (2025). The Significance of Generative AI in Enhancing Fraud Detection and Prevention Within the Banking Industry. Generative Artificial Intelligence in Finance: Large Language Models, Interfaces, and Industry Use Cases to Transform Accounting and Finance Processes, 159-173. DOI: 10.1002/9781394271078.ch9

Razavi, H., & Habibnia, A. (2024). The Rise of AI in Middle Eastern Fintech With the Case Studies From the UAE and Turkey. In Taherdoost, H., Le, N., Madanchian, M., & Farhaoui, Y. (Eds.), (pp. 259–297). Advances in Finance, Accounting, and Economics. IGI Global. DOI: 10.4018/979-8-3693-1561-3.ch010

Razavi, S. (2022). Making the Right to Social Security a Reality for All Workers. *The Indian Journal of Labour Economics : The Quarterly Journal of the Indian Society of Labour Economics*, *65*(2), 269–294. DOI: 10.1007/s41027-022-00378-6

Reddy, K., Wallace, D., & Wellalage, N. H. (2024). The impact of financial literacy on financial inclusion. *Australian Journal of Management*, *03128962241270809*. Advance online publication. DOI: 10.1177/03128962241270809

Rehman, K., & Mia, M. A. (2024). Determinants of financial literacy: A systematic review and future research directions. *Future Business Journal*, *10*(1), 75. DOI: 10.1186/s43093-024-00365-x

Rej, M. (2024). Credit Card Fraud Statistics 2025, Retrieved Sept. 09, 2025 from https://merchantcostconsulting.com/lower-credit-card-processing-fees/credit-card-fraud-statistics/

Rejeb, A., Rejeb, K., Appolloni, A., & Treiblmaier, H. (2023). Navigating the crowdfunding landscape: A study of knowledge trajectories based on main path analysis. *European Journal of Innovation Management*, *26*(7), 415–448. DOI: 10.1108/EJIM-03-2023-0201

Ren, M., Zeng, W., Yang, B., & Urtasun, R. (2018, July). Learning to reweight examples for robust deep learning. In *International conference on machine learning* (pp. 4334-4343). PMLR.

Reurink, A. (2018). Financial fraud: a literature review. *Journal of Economic Surveys*, *32*(5), 1292–1325. DOI: 10.1111/joes.12294

Rezaee, Z. (2005). Causes, consequences, and deterence of financial statement fraud. *Critical Perspectives on Accounting*, *16*(3), 277–298. DOI: 10.1016/S1045-2354(03)00072-8

Richardson, S. A., Wysocki, P. D., & Tuna, A. I. (2010). Accounting Anomalies and Fundamental Analysis: A Review of Recent Research Advances. SSRN Electronic Journal. DOI: 10.2139/ssrn.1762124

Ridho Kismawadi, E., Irfan, M., & Shah, S. M. A. R. (2023). Revolutionizing Islamic finance: Artificial intelligence's role in the future of industry. In *The impact of AI innovation on financial sectors in the era of industry 5.0* (pp. 184–207).

Ridzuan, N. N., Masri, M., Anshari, M., Fitriyani, N. L., & Syafrudin, M. (2024). AI in the Financial Sector: The Line between Innovation, Regulation and Ethical Responsibility. *Information (Basel), 15*(8), 432. DOI: 10.3390/info15080432

Robles, P., & Mallinson, D. J. (2025). Advancing AI governance with a unified theoretical framework: A systematic review. *Perspectives on Public Management and Governance, 8*(4), 213–227. Advance online publication. DOI: 10.1093/ppmgov/gvaf013

Roush, T. (2024, Oct. 23). *Apple and Goldman Sachs Fined over $89 Million for Misleading Apple Card Customers. Forbes.* Retrieved from www.forbes.com/sites/tylerroush/2024/10/23/apple-and-goldman-sachs-fined-over-89-million-for-misleading-apple-card-customers/. Accessed August 22, 2025.

Rubio, L., Palacio Pinedo, A., Mejía Castaño, A., & Ramos, F. (2023). Forecasting volatility by using wavelet transform, ARIMA and GARCH models. *Eurasian Economic Review, 13*(3), 803–830. DOI: 10.1007/s40822-023-00243-x

Saberironaghi, M., Ren, J., & Saberironaghi, A. (2025). Stock Market Prediction Using Machine Learning and Deep Learning Techniques: A Review. *AppliedMath, 5*(3), 76. DOI: 10.3390/appliedmath5030076

Sadaiyandi, J., Arumugam, P., Sangaiah, A. K., & Zhang, C. (2023). Stratified sampling-based deep learning approach to increase prediction accuracy of unbalanced dataset. *Electronics (Basel), 12*(21), 4423. DOI: 10.3390/electronics12214423

Sahin, Y., & Duman, E. (2011). Detecting credit card fraud by ANN and logistic regression. 315–319. DOI: 10.1109/INISTA.2011.5946108

Sailusha, R., Ramesh, R., Rao, G. R., & Gnaneswar, V. (2020). Credit Card Fraud Detection Using. *Machine Learning*, , 1264–1270. DOI: 10.1109/ICICCS48265.2020.9121114

Saleh, M. M. A., Aladwan, M., Alsinglawi, O., & Almari, M. O. S. (2021). Predicting Fraudulent Financial Statements Using Fraud Detection Models. *Academy of Strategic Management Journal, 20*(3), 1–2.

Salem, S. (2025). *The Role of Financial Technology and Financial Literacy in Achieving Sustainable Development with The Mediating Effect of Financial Inclusion*. DOI: 10.13140/RG.2.2.15168.65284

Sanad, Z., & Al-Sartawi, A. (2021). *Financial Statements Fraud and Data Mining: A Review*. Springer., DOI: 10.1007/978-3-030-77246-8_38

Santoso, H. A., Fandhi Safsalta, B., Febrianto, N., Wilujeng Saraswati, G., & Haw, S.-C. (2024). Comparative analysis of convolutional neural network and DenseNet121 transfer learning in agriculture focusing on crop leaf disease identification. *Applied Computing and Informatics*. Advance online publication. DOI: 10.1108/ACI-03-2024-0132

Sarioguz, O., & Miser, E. (2024). Integrating AI in financial risk management: Evaluating the effects of machine learning algorithms on predictive accuracy and regulatory compliance. *International Journal of Science and Research Archive*, *13*(2), 789–811. DOI: 10.30574/ijsra.2024.13.2.2206

Scaria, A. G., Subramanian, V., George, N. K., & Sengupta, N. (2024, October). Algorithms and recidivism: A multi-disciplinary systematic review. In *Proceedings of the AAAI/ACM Conference on AI, Ethics, and Society* (Vol. 7, pp. 1292-1305). DOI: 10.1609/aies.v7i1.31724

Seiffert, C., Khoshgoftaar, T. M., Van Hulse, J., & Napolitano, A. (2010). RUSBoost: A hybrid approach to alleviating class imbalance. *IEEE Transactions on Systems, Man, and Cybernetics. Part A, Systems and Humans*, *40*(1), 185–197. DOI: 10.1109/TSMCA.2009.2029559

Shafiabady, N., Hadjinicolaou, N., Ud Din, F., Bhandari, B., Wu, R. M. X., & Vakilian, J. (2023). Using artificial intelligence (AI) to predict organizational agility. *PLoS One*, *18*(5), e0283066. Advance online publication. DOI: 10.1371/journal.pone.0283066 PMID: 37163532

Shahzad, M. A., Jianguo, D., Jan, N., & Rasool, Y. (2024). Perceived Behavioral Factors and Individual Investor Stock Market Investment Decision: Multigroup Analysis and Major Stock Markets Perspectives. *SAGE Open*, *14*(2), 21582440241256210. DOI: 10.1177/21582440241256210

Shalaby, A. (2024). Digital Sustainable Growth Model (DSGM): achieving synergy between economy and technology to mitigate AGI risks and address global debt challenges. *Journal of Economy and Technology*. DOI: 10.1016/j.ject.2024.08.003

Sharma, N., Beniwal, S., & Garg, P. (2022). ANT Colony based Optimization model for QOS-Based task scheduling in cloud computing environment. SSRN *Electronic Journal*. DOI: 10.2139/ssrn.4237751

Sharma, S. K., Ilavarasan, P. V., & Karanasios, S. (2023). Small businesses and FinTech: A systematic review and future directions. *Electronic Commerce Research*. Advance online publication. DOI: 10.1007/s10660-023-09705-5

Shkodinsky, S., Syrovatskaya, V., & Khokhoeva, Z. (2024). The role of artificial intelligence in forecasting and managing technical risks. *Reliability: Theory and Applications, 19*(Special Issue 6), 210–216. DOI: 10.24412/1932-2321-2024-681-210-216

Sims, C. A. (2003). Implications of rational inattention. *Journal of Monetary Economics, 50*(3), 665–690. DOI: 10.1016/S0304-3932(03)00029-1

Singh, B., Kaunert, C., & Kaushik, T. K. (2024). Unscrambling financial fraud with AI and machine learning in E-Commerce transactions. In *Advances in finance, accounting, and economics book series* (pp. 253–271). DOI: 10.4018/979-8-3693-4382-1.ch013

Singh, V. K. (2022). Regulatory and legal framework for promoting green digital Finance. In *Economics, law, and institutions in Asia Pacific* (pp. 3–27). DOI: 10.1007/978-981-19-2662-4_1

Sizan, M. M. H., Akter, J., Islam, D. A., Ridoy, M. H., Sartaz, M. S., Roy, A., Tannier, N. R., Jobaer, M. A. A., & Chouksey, A. (2025). Advanced Machine Learning Approaches for Credit Card Fraud Detection in the USA: A Comprehensive Analysis. *Journal of Ecohumanism, 4*(2). Advance online publication. DOI: 10.62754/joe.v4i2.6377

Soltaninejad, M., Yang, G., Lambrou, T., Allinson, N., Jones, T. L., Barrick, T. R., Howe, F. A., & Ye, X. (2017). Automated brain tumour detection and segmentation using superpixel-based extremely randomized trees in FLAIR MRI. *International Journal of Computer Assisted Radiology and Surgery, 12*(2), 183–203. DOI: 10.1007/s11548-016-1483-3 PMID: 27651330

Song, L. L., Wang, S. H., & Yang, C. (2020). Application research of improved XGBoost in imbalanced data processing. *Computer Science, 47*(6), 98–103.

Song, X., Qin, X., Wang, W., & Man Li, R. Y. (2025). Financial inclusion, technologies, and worldwide economic development: A spatial Durbin model approach. *The Journal of Financial Data Science, 11*, 100155. DOI: 10.1016/j.jfds.2025.100155

Stefanelli, V., Ferilli, G. B., & Boscia, V. (2022). Exploring the lending business crowdfunding to support SMEs' financing decisions. *Journal of Innovation & Knowledge, 7*(4), 100278. Advance online publication. DOI: 10.1016/j.jik.2022.100278

Steyerberg, E. W. (2016). *Regression modeling strategies: With applications to linear models, logistic and ordinal regression, and survival analysis* (2nd ed.). Springer.

Subedi, D. P., & Bhandari, D. R. (2024). Assessing the Role of Digital Literacy in Investment Decisions among Graduate Business Students in Nepal: The Mediating Effects of Peer Group Influence. *Multi-Disciplinary Explorations: The Kasthamandap College Journal, 2*(2), 47–62. DOI: 10.3126/mdekcj.v2i2.74174

Sunmola, F., Baryannis, G., Tan, A., Co, K., & Papadakis, E. (2025). Holistic framework for blockchain-based halal compliance in supply chains enabled by artificial intelligence. *Systems, 13*(1), 21. DOI: 10.3390/systems13010021

Supawat, L., & Arnat, L. (2023). Market Reaction to Corporate Releases and News Articles: Evidence from Thailand's Stock Market. *International Journal of Financial Studies, 11*(3), 111. DOI: 10.3390/ijfs11030111

Taherdoost, H. (2023). Deep learning and neural networks: Decision-making implications. *Symmetry, 15*(9), 1723. DOI: 10.3390/sym15091723

Tanaka, T., & Shimoda, M. (2023). Pre-and post-processing techniques for reinforcement-learning-based routing and spectrum assignment in elastic optical networks. *Journal of Optical Communications and Networking, 15*(12), 1019–1029. DOI: 10.1364/JOCN.503599

Tarjo, , & Herawati, N.Tarjo and Herawati. (2015). Application of Beneish M-score models and data mining to detect financial fraud. *Procedia: Social and Behavioral Sciences, 211*, 924–930. DOI: 10.1016/j.sbspro.2015.11.122

The Alan Turing Institute. (2023). Data Protection, AI, and Fairness. Retrieved from www.turing.ac.uk/data-protection-ai-and-fairness. Accessed September 1, 2025.

Torm, N., & Oehme, M. (2024). Social protection and formalization in low- and middle-income countries: A scoping review of the literature. *World Development, 181*, 106662. DOI: 10.1016/j.worlddev.2024.106662

Tyrell Curry, J. (2025). Modeling the dynamic interplay between financial literacy, resilience, and emotional well-being across diverse demographics. *Cogent Economics & Finance, 13*(1), 2544177. DOI: 10.1080/23322039.2025.2544177

Ud Din, F., Henskens, F., Paul, D., & Wallis, M. (2019). Agent-oriented smart factory (AOSF): An MAS based framework for SMEs under Industry 4.0. In Jezic, G., Chen-Burger, Y. H., Howlett, R., Jain, L., Vlacic, L., & Šperka, R. (Eds.), *Agents and multi-agent systems: Technologies and applications 2018* (pp. 45–57). Springer., DOI: 10.1007/978-3-319-92031-3_5

Uddin, M. A. (2020). Impact of Financial Literacy on Individual Saving: A Study in the Omani Context. SSRN *Electronic Journal*. DOI: 10.2139/ssrn.4012631

Umeaduma, C. M. G. (2024). Behavioral biases influencing individual investment decisions within volatile financial markets and economic cycles. *Int J Eng Technol Res Manag*, *8*(03), 191.

Vettriselvan, R., Velmurugan, P. R., Regins, J. C., Maheswari, S. U., & Joyce, R. (2025). Best practices, ethical challenges, and regulatory frameworks for AI integration in banking. In *Advances in computational intelligence and robotics book series* (pp. 377–410). https://doi.org/DOI: 10.4018/979-8-3693-9356-7.ch015

Vuković, D. B., Dekpo-Adza, S., & Matović, S. (2025). AI integration in financial services: A systematic review of trends and regulatory challenges. *Humanities & Social Sciences Communications*, *12*(1), 562. Advance online publication. DOI: 10.1057/s41599-025-04850-8

Vyas, A. (2025). *Revolutionizing Risk: The Role of Artificial Intelligence in Financial Risk Management, Forecasting, and Global Implementation. SSRN*. DOI: 10.2139/ssrn.5224657

Wamsley, L. (2024, Oct. 23). *Apple and Goldman Sachs Ordered to Pay $89 Million over Apple Card Failures. NPR*. Retrieved from www.npr.org/2024/10/23/g-s1-29566/apple-goldman-sachs-fine-apple-card-cfpb. Accessed August 28, 2025

Wang, J. (2025). The Impact of Unexpected Events and Household Financial Fragility. *Emerging Markets Finance & Trade*, 1–23. DOI: 10.1080/1540496X.2025.2535706

Wan, H. P., Gan, J. R., Zhu, Y. K., & Meng, Z. (2024). SS-MASVM: An advanced technique for assessing failure probability of high-dimensional complex systems using the multi-class adaptive support vector machine. *Computer Methods in Applied Mechanics and Engineering*, *418*, 116568. Advance online publication. DOI: 10.1016/j.cma.2023.116568

Wei, L., Peng, M., & Wu, W. (2021). Financial literacy and fraud detection—Evidence from China. *International Review of Economics & Finance*, *76*, 478–494. DOI: 10.1016/j.iref.2021.06.017

World Bank. (2023). *Global economic prospects: Enduring challenges*. World Bank Publications.

Wu, R. M. X., Shafiabady, N., Gide, E., & Dianati, S. (2024). E-commerce success research in the age of digital transformation for post-COVID-19: From qualitative models to a quantitative model. *Technological Forecasting and Social Change*. Advance online publication.

Wu, R. M. X., Wang, Y., Shafiabady, N., Zhang, H., Yan, W., Gou, J., Shi, Y., Liu, B., Gide, E., Kang, C., Zhang, Z., Shen, B., Li, X., Fan, J., He, X., Soar, J., Zhao, H., Sun, L., Huo, W., & Wang, Y. (2023). Using multi-focus group method as an effective tool for eliciting business system requirements: Verified by a case study. *PLoS One*, *18*(3), e0281603. Advance online publication. DOI: 10.1371/journal.pone.0281603 PMID: 36897871

Wyrobek, J. (2020). Application of machine learning models and artificial intelligence to analyze annual financial statements to identify companies with unfair corporate culture. *Procedia Computer Science*, *176*, 3037–3046. DOI: 10.1016/j.procs.2020.09.335

Xinying Chen, V., & Hooker, J. N. (2023). A guide to formulating fairness in an optimization model. *Annals of Operations Research*, *326*(1), 581–619. DOI: 10.1007/s10479-023-05264-y PMID: 37361073

Xu, H., Niu, K., Lu, T., & Li, S. (2024). Leveraging artificial intelligence for enhanced risk management in financial services: Current applications and future prospects. *Engineering Science & Technology Journal*, *5*(8), 2402–2426. DOI: 10.51594/estj.v5i8.1363

Yadav, S., & Shukla, S. (2016). Analysis of k-fold cross-validation over hold-out validation on colossal datasets for quality classification. *2016 IEEE 6th International Conference on Advanced Computing (IACC)*, 78-83.

Yang, J., Wu, Y., & Huang, B. (2023). Digital finance and financial literacy: Evidence from Chinese households. *Journal of Banking & Finance*, *156*, 107005. DOI: 10.1016/j.jbankfin.2023.107005

Yousefimehr, B., Ghatee, M., Seifi, M. A., Fazli, J., Tavakoli, S., Rafei, Z., Ghaffari, S., Nikahd, A., Gandomani, M. R., Orouji, A., & Kashani, R. M. (2025). Data Balancing Strategies: A Survey of Resampling and Augmentation Methods. *arXiv preprint arXiv:2505.13518*.

Yu, T., & Xiao, J. (2025). *Applying Generative AI in Financial Literacy Research: A Demonstration. SSRN*. DOI: 10.2139/ssrn.5291736

Zaidi, S., Shafiabady, N., & Beilby, J. (2023). Identifying presence of cybersickness symptoms using AI based predictive learning algorithms. *Virtual Reality (Waltham Cross)*, *27*(4), 3613–3620. Advance online publication. DOI: 10.1007/s10055-023-00813-z

Zeng, Z., Kaur, R., Siddagangappa, S., Rahimi, S., Balch, T., & Veloso, M. (2023). Financial time series forecasting using cnn and transformer. arXiv preprint arXiv:2304.04912

Zetzsche, D. A., Arner, D. W., & Buckley, R. P. (2020). Decentralized finance. *Journal of Financial Regulation*, *6*(2), 172–203. DOI: 10.1093/jfr/fjaa010

Zhang, C. A., Jiang, L., Cho, S., & Vasarhelyi, M. A. (2025). Predicting material misstatements using machine learning. *The Accounting Review*, *100*(6), 225–262. DOI: 10.2308/TAR-2024-0035

Zhu, R., Zeng, D., & Kosorok, M. R. (2015). Reinforcement learning trees. *Journal of the American Statistical Association*, *110*(512), 1770–1784. DOI: 10.1080/01621459.2015.1036994 PMID: 26903687

Žliobaitė, I. (2017). Measuring discrimination in algorithmic decision making. *Data Mining and Knowledge Discovery*, *31*(4), 1060–1089. DOI: 10.1007/s10618-017-0506-1

Zouaghia, Z., Kodia, Z., & Ben Said, L. (2025a). A novel approach for dynamic portfolio management integrating K-means clustering, mean-variance optimization, and reinforcement learning: Z. Zouaghia et al. Knowledge and Information Systems, 1-73. DOI: 10.1007/s10115-025-02475-6

Zouaghia, Z., Aouina, Z. K., & Said, L. B. (2023, October). Hybrid machine learning model for predicting NASDAQ composite index. In *2023 International Symposium on Networks, Computers and Communications (ISNCC)* (pp. 1-6). IEEE. DOI: 10.1109/ISNCC58260.2023.10323903

Zouaghia, Z., Kodia, Z., & Ben Said, L. (2024a). A novel AutoCNN model for stock market index prediction. *Journal of Telecommunications and the Digital Economy*, *12*(1), 612–636. DOI: 10.18080/jtde.v12n1.843

Zouaghia, Z., Kodia, Z., & Ben Said, L. (2024b). Predicting the stock market prices using a machine learning-based framework during crisis periods. *Multimedia Tools and Applications*, *84*(24), 28873–28907. DOI: 10.1007/s11042-024-20270-3

Zouaghia, Z., Kodia, Z., & Ben Said, L. (2025b). Smapf-hnna: A novel Stock Market Analysis and Prediction Framework using Hybrid Neural Network Architectures Across Major US Indices. *International Journal of Data Science and Analytics*, *20*(6), 5775–5811. DOI: 10.1007/s41060-025-00811-1

About the Contributors

Afef Amdouni is an Assistant Professor of Finance in the Department of Finance, College of Business Administration, Taibah University, Medina, Saudi Arabia. Her research interests focus on financial markets, artificial intelligence applications in finance, behavioral finance, and financial risk modeling. Prior to joining Taibah University, she was affiliated with the Faculty of Economic Sciences and Management at the University of Tunis El Manar, Tunisia. Dr. Amdouni earned her Ph.D. in Finance from the same institution, where she also completed her Master's and Bachelor's degrees. She is actively engaged in academic publishing and peer review activities and has held leadership roles in coordinating editorial initiatives related to interdisciplinary research at the intersection of finance and artificial intelligence.

***

Muntadher Ali received the M.Sc. degree (Hons.) in wireless communications from the University of New Haven, West Haven, CT, USA, in 2016, and the Ph.D. degree from the Wireless Networking Group (WiNG), School of Electrical and Information Engineering, The University of Sydney, Sydney, NSW, Australia, under the supervision of Prof. A. Jamalipour and Dr. Y. Zeng. He is a member of the Institution of Engineers Australia. He has been identified by the Australian government under the Global Distinguished Talent Program. He worked as a Telecom Planning and Resilience Intern with the New York City (NYC) Department of Information Technology and Telecommunication (DoITT). His research interests include UAV communication, resource allocation, and optimization. He was a recipient of the University of Sydney International Scholarship (USydIS). Currently, he is an ICT Senior Lecturer with the National Academy of Professional Studies (NAPS).

Yue Chen earned a postgraduate degree from Durham University, and with a research focus covering risk and financial management, empirical economics, as well as the intersection of emerging technologies with accounting and finance, Yue Chen has delivered academic presentations at a series of prestigious international conferences, including The 1st International Conference on Risk and Financial Management: Big Data, Artificial Intelligence, and Machine Learning in Finance (in which the best oral presentation award was conferred), the 2025 International Conference on Empirical Economics, and the 2025 Hanyang Accounting Research Symposium themed "Recent Technologies in Accounting and Finance". This academic trajectory not only reflects Yue Chen's solid educational foundation from Durham University but also demonstrates active engagement with cutting-edge discussions in the fields of finance, economics, and accounting, fostering the exchange of insights with global peers at influential academic forums.

Guanming He is a professor at Durham University, currently serving as the International Coordinator (Champion) and Library Representative for the department and the business school. Guanming's research appears in a variety of prestigious international journals (FT 50/ABS 4-3 ranked) and has been featured in numerous mainstream media and press releases. He serves as the ac hoc reviewer for a wide range of internationally reputable accounting, finance, management, and economics journals (FT 50/ABS 4-3 ranked) and books (by Cengage/Pearson/SAGE). Thus far, he has performed hundreds of paper reviews as fairly and objectively as possible for various top-tier and second-tier international journals, and received multiple reviewer awards. He presented his papers at the American Accounting Association annual meeting in 2009, 2010, 2012-2016, as well as at other major accounting conferences including AAA Financial Accounting and Reporting Section mid-year meeting. His papers also went for presentations at a host of major economics and finance conferences, including the American Economic Association annual meeting, Society of Government Economist conference, European meeting of the Econometric Society, China International Conference in Finance (CICF), SAFE Market Microstructure conference, Money, Macro, & Finance conference, Financial Risks International forum, and International Behavioral Finance conference, among others. He earned best paper awards at the UK Academy for Information Systems 2025 annual conference, 3rd Australian Financial Market & Corporate Governance conference, 5th Research Symposium on Finance and Economics (RSFE), 7th Indonesian Finance Association International Conference, and 24th & 26th International Business Research conference, obtained a top paper award at the 28th annual Global Finance conference as well as a Best-in-Track paper award at the 35th annual meeting of the Academy of Finance, and was nominated as a finalist for the best conference paper award of European Financial Management Association. In addition, he received the best oral presentation award at the inaugural International Conference on Risk and Financial Management: Big Data, Artificial Intelligence, and Machine Learning in Finance. In recognition of his teaching, he was honored with excellent teaching awards in the Nanyang Technological University and University of Warwick, respectively. At the Durham University, he attained a number of teaching evaluation scores of 90%+ for his module teaching and received the faculty awards for research contribution to pedagogy, research mentorship, cross-disciplinarity, and internationalisation. He has served as Director of the Accounting PhD Program, and as the Business School representative on the university's research degree committee, from 2019 to 2023.

Mohammad Irfan is a Professor at the School of Business and Commerce, Chandigarh University, Lucknow (Unnao), India, with over eighteen years of teaching and research experience. He has published more than 126 Scopus-indexed research papers, accumulating 898+ citations with an H-index of 16. He has authored 14 books with leading international publishers, including Springer and IGI Global, and is recognized among the World's Top 2% Scientists. His research expertise covers Security Analysis and Portfolio Management, Artificial Intelligence, Machine Learning, Blockchain, Cryptocurrency, Financial Engineering, FinTech, Green Finance, and Alternative Finance. He earned his Ph.D. from the Central University of Haryana and holds an MBA in Finance, an M.Com in Accounts and Law, and an MA in Economics. A UGC-JRF/SRF/NET qualifier in Management and Commerce, he also holds professional certifications from NSE (NCFM) and BSE.

Early Kismawadi, S.E.I, MA is a lecturer at the Department of Islamic Banking, Faculty of Islamic Economics and Business IAIN Langsa, Aceh, Indonesia, he has been a lecturer since 2013, he has completed a doctoral program in 2018 majoring in Sharia economics at the State Islamic University of North Sumatra. He was appointed head of the Islamic economics Law study program (2023) Islamic banking study program (2020) and Islamic financial management study program (2019) at Langsa State Islamic Institute (IAIN Langsa), Aceh, Indonesia. His research interests include financial economics, applied econometrics, Islamic economics, banking, and finance. He has published articles in national and international journals. In addition, he is also a reviewer of several reputable international journals such as Finance Research Lctters, Financial Innovation, Cogent Business &; Management, Journal of Islamic Accounting and Business Research. He has also presented his papers at various local and international seminars. Dr. Early Ridho Kismawadi, S.E.I, MA, can be contacted at kismawadi@iainlangsa.ac.id.

Zahra Kodia is an Associate professor at University of Tunis. She received the B.Sc. degree in Business Computing from the Institut Supérieur de Gestion, University of Tunis (ISG-Tunis), Tunisia, in 2006. the M.Sc. and Ph.D. degrees in Computer Science from Ecole Nationale des Sciences de l'Informatique (ENSI), University of Mannouba, in 2008 and 2014, respectively. She is a member of the scientific laboratory of the SMART Lab (Strategies for Modelling and ARtificial inTelligence Laboratory). She is an associate professor in computer science in since September 2024 in ISG-Tunis, University of Tunis. Since 2009, she has been conducting research on improving decision-making in complex systems such as stock markets, business processes, and recommender systems.

Sandhya Rai is an accomplished academician, researcher, and institutional leader with over two decades of experience in higher education, research, consulting, and executive training. She currently serves as Program Chair – BBA at the School of Management, Bennett University, Greater Noida. Prior to this, she held senior leadership positions, including Dean and Controller of Examinations at IILM Graduate School of Management, where she played a pivotal role in academic administration, strategic curriculum development, accreditation processes, and institutional governance. Dr. Rai holds dual postgraduate degrees in Mathematics and Management, as well as a Doctorate (Ph.D.) in Management. A distinguished researcher and thought leader, Dr. Rai has authored nine books and has an extensive portfolio of research publications in reputed national and international journals. She is an active member of academic boards, advisory committees, and professional associations, contributing to policy development, curriculum enhancement, and industry-academia collaboration. A dedicated educator and mentor, Dr. Rai is committed to pedagogical innovation, experiential learning, and the professional development of students and executives. Through her leadership, research, and academic initiatives, she continues to shape the landscape of management education, fostering critical thinking, data-driven decision-making, and entrepreneurial leadership in the next generation of business professionals

Lamjed Saïd is a full professor in Computer Science and Head of the SMART Lab. He received the B.Sc. degree in Business Comput ing from the Institut Supérieur de Gestion, University of Tunis (ISG Tunis), Tunisia, in 1998, the M.Sc. and Ph.D. degrees in Computer Sci ence from the University of Paris VI, Paris, France, in 1999 and 2003, respectively, and the Habilitation degree from the University of Tunis in 2011. He was a Research Fellow with France Telecom, Research and Development Department, Paris, for three years. From 2014 to 2020, he was the Dean of the ISG-Tunis where he is currently a Full Pro fessor in Computer Science, University of Tunis, Tunis, Tunisia, and the Head of the SMART Lab (Strategies for Modelling and ARtificial inTelligence Laboratory). He published over 300 research papers in ref ereed international journals, conference proceedings, and book series. His current research interests include multiagent simulation, multicrite ria decision-making, evolutionary computation, supply chain manage ment, and behavioral economics. Dr. Ben Said is a Reviewer for several artificial intelligence journals and conferences, and he is responsible of several national and international projects.

Niusha Shafiabady is an internationally recognised expert in the field of Computational Intelligence with many years of professional experience in both academia and industry. She is the Head of Discipline of Information Technology-Peter Faber Business School at Australian Catholic University, North Sydney Campus, Australia. She is the Director of Women in AI for Social Good Lab. She is the inventor of a computational optimisation algorithm and has developed Ai-Labz which is a simple Computational Intelligence predictive analysis tool. She has published many research articles in high-ranking journals, supervised many HDR candidates and is the recipient of several awards and credentials. She is a Fellow of the Higher Education Academy of the United Kingdom. Her key areas of expertise are design and development of smart algorithms for data analysis and interpretation, prediction of different phenomena, clustering and classification of unorganised data and creating smart decision-making systems for different applications. The highlight of her work is blending academic knowledge and research findings into industrial applications and creating a bridge between academia and industry. She has developed expert decision-making systems for variety of applications using Artificial Intelligence in solving real-world problems. Her ultimate vision is to utilise her expertise in Computational and Artificial Intelligence for enhancing human life.

Taiwo Shotunde is a finance and strategy professional with expertise spanning business strategy deployment, emerging technologies, technology governance, risk management, and regulatory compliance. Taiwo has worked with organizations such as KPMG, the United Nations Development Programme (UNDP), and the Oxford Creative Destruction Lab. An MBA graduate and Dean's List awardee from the University of Oxford. Her work bridges finance, innovation, and governance and has contributed to high-impact initiatives across smart technologies and sustainable finance, bringing a structured, data-driven, and strategic lens to complex business challenges.

Sheetal Singh is a seasoned legal academic with over 15 years of experience in teaching, research, and academic administration. Currently serving as Assistant Professor at the School of Law, CHRIST (Deemed to be University), Delhi NCR Campus, she previously held senior faculty roles at Amity Law School, Noida, where she also founded the Amity Legal Aid Cell. She holds a Ph.D. in Law from Amity University and is UGC-NET qualified, with expertise spanning Family Law, Criminal Law, Constitutional Law, Property Law, and Human Rights. Dr. Singh has guided more than 150 LLB and LLM dissertations and supervises Ph.D. research on gender justice and victimology. Her scholarly contributions include chapters in edited volumes published by Thomson Reuters, CRC Press, Springer, and Cambridge Scholars Publishing, covering topics such as media law, reproductive rights, cybersecurity, and comparative constitutional analysis. She has presented papers at national and international conferences, delivered guest lectures, and organized seminars and workshops on legal education, gender sensitization, and human rights. Her administrative roles include serving as Head of Department, Program Coordinator, and member of various university committees such as IQAC, Moot Court, and Placement. Widely recognized for her commitment to legal education and interdisciplinary research, Dr. Singh continues to contribute meaningfully to academia and social justice initiatives.

Shashank Solanki is a distinguished legal researcher and corporate governance professional working at the intersection of law, technology, and environmental policy. Currently affiliated with Christ University, India, he brings a multidisciplinary lens to global governance, innovation, and ethical regulation. His research spans artificial intelligence regulation, cybersecurity, climate resilience, quantum computing ethics, and digital forensics, with a strong emphasis on the legal and policy implications of emerging technologies. Solanki has co-authored over 40 book chapters and journal articles, many of which are published or accepted in Scopus-indexed volumes by leading academic publishers such as IGI Global, Springer, Elsevier, Taylor & Francis, and Wiley. His scholarly contributions explore themes including AI-driven financial analytics, smart mining, healthcare cybersecurity, compact AI regulation, and sustainable infrastructure, reflecting his ability to synthesize complex legal frameworks with cutting-edge technological advancements. Professionally, he has interned with some of India's top law firms, including Shardul Amarchand Mangaldas & Co., Karanjawala & Co., and Singhania & Partners LLP, gaining hands-on experience in litigation, arbitration, tech policy, and commercial dispute resolution. He also served as in-house counsel at Shree Cement Ltd., handling contract review, environmental law, and litigation coordination. Notably, he collaborated with Hon'ble Mr. Justice Ashok Bhushan at the National Company Law Appellate Tribunal (NCLAT), contributing to judicial research and documentation in insolvency and corporate law. Solanki has presented at international conferences, including the NMIMS-Boston University School of Law Human Rights Conference, and participated in multiple moot court competitions, securing finalist and runner-up positions. His academic rigor is complemented by certifications in personal data protection, intellectual property litigation, and information technology (RS-CIT), along with a 7th-level certification in Abacus and Mental Arithmetic from UCMAS. Beyond academia, he has demonstrated leadership and social commitment as Convener of the Legal Aid and Awareness Society at Christ University, earning multiple Certificates of Appreciation from university bodies including the Student Welfare Office and Student Council, and is a decorated athlete, having won gold medals in district-level handball championships and intra-departmental volleyball competitions. With a deep commitment to academic excellence, policy dialogue, and social impact, Shashank Solanki continues to shape conversations around law and technology.

James Vakilian is an expert in Applied mathematics, Project management and Management systems. He has held several senior positions in reputable companies in both Energy and IT sectors for the past 25 years and has collaborated with various internationally recognized companies such as Samsung Heavy Industries (SHI), Eni, Statoil, Technip, Worley-Parsons, Lloyds; etc.; during which he managed several projects- collectively worth more than 1.6 Billion US Dollars. At the time being, he is a university lecturer and in addition provides consultancy and training services. His main interests are mathematical modeling, analysis and management of complex systems and has publishes number of articles in peered reviewed journals.

Robert Wu works in the School of Professional Practice and Leadership at the Faculty of Engineering and Information Technology, University of Technology Sydney. He is also an associate editor of the Electronic Journal of Business Research Methods (Australian Business Deans Council - ABDC journal). Dr. Wu holds a diploma in computer science, a bachelor's degree in economics, a master's program in computer science, a master's degree in e-commerce, and a Ph.D. in E-commerce. His research interests predominantly focus on digital transformation, e-commerce/e-Business, digital processing visualization, business intelligence (BI), business information systems (BIS), business analytics, Information systems, ICT higher education, and mobile Health (m-health). Dr. Wu is a pioneering researcher on digital transformation to drive the transition from traditional business to digital business or e-business. As a senior reviewer and special issue editor, he serves 12 SCImago Q1 and A*/A journals listed in the ABDC. A Q1 Elsevier journal awarded him "Outstanding Contribution in Reviewing" twice in 2016 and 2018. Dr. Wu is also an internationally renowned consulting expert on leading interdisciplinary and industry-engaged research projects. He has demonstrated exceptional leadership, expertise, and innovation throughout his career, particularly in industry-engaged international collaborations. Over the past decade, he has successfully spearheaded more than ten large-scale international projects in partnership with Fortune Global

500 companies, prestigious universities, and various governments and industry stakeholders. His track record demonstrates his dedication to fostering meaningful connections in the global academic and business communities.

Zakia Zouaghia is a faculty member at the Institut Supérieur d'Informatique (ISI) of the University of Tunis El Manar. She received her B.Sc., M.Sc., and Ph.D. degrees in Business Computing from the Institut Supérieur de Gestion, University of Tunis (ISG-Tunis), Tunisia, in 2007, 2021, and 2025, respectively. She is a member of the SMART Lab (Strategies for Modelling and ARtificial inTelligence Laboratory). Since 2020, her research has focused on improving decision-making in stock markets. She also serves as a reviewer for several international journals and conferences.

Index

H

I

L

M

P

R

S

V

www.ingramcontent.com/pod-product-compliance
Lightning Source LLC
LaVergne TN
LVHW081525300926
849161LV00006B/1299